Children's Rights and the Capability Approach

Children's Well-Being: Indicators and Research Series

Volume 8

This new series focuses on the subject of measurements and indicators of children's well being and their usage, within multiple domains and in diverse cultures. More specifically, the series seeks to present measures and data resources, analysis of data, exploration of theoretical issues, and information about the status of children, as well as the implementation of this information in policy and practice. By doing so it aims to explore how child indicators can be used to improve the development and the well being of children.

With an international perspective the series will provide a unique applied perspective, by bringing in a variety of analytical models, varied perspectives, and a variety of social policy regimes.

Children's Well-Being: Indicators and Research will be unique and exclusive in the field of measures and indicators of children's lives and will be a source of high quality, policy impact and rigorous scientific papers

For further volumes:
http://www.springer.com/series/8162

Daniel Stoecklin • Jean-Michel Bonvin
Editors

Children's Rights and the Capability Approach

Challenges and Prospects

Springer

Editors
Daniel Stoecklin
University Institute Kurt Bösch (IUKB)
Sion, Switzerland

Jean-Michel Bonvin
Univ. of Applied Sciences Western Switzerland
Lausanne, Switzerland

This book has benefited from the scientific meeting "Children's Rights and the Capability Approach" held in Sion, Switzerland, on 5–6 July 2012, with the support of the Swiss National Science Foundation.

ISSN 1879-5196 ISSN 1879-520X (electronic)
ISBN 978-94-017-9090-1 ISBN 978-94-017-9091-8 (eBook)
DOI 10.1007/978-94-017-9091-8
Springer Dordrecht Heidelberg New York London

Library of Congress Control Number: 2014944133

Printed on acid-free paper

Springer is part of Springer Science+Business Media (www.springer.com)

Foreword

This exceptional collection of papers is about the growing discourse on children's rights and the capability approach. My colleagues who contributed these fine chapters have done a splendid work in discussing various aspects in children's life by looking at them in a children's right or capability framework. In this short foreword I would like to add my personal thoughts on both frameworks and their contribution to our understanding of the "new" concept of children's well-being. Children's well-being is a desirable status in life referring to being happy and satisfied with one's own life. Well-being is also related to the fulfilment of desires, to the balance of pleasure and pain, and to children's living conditions and quality of life. Thus, well-being is related to individual preferences and opportunity structures. From a children's rights perspective that would mean that rights are implicitly creating opportunities for well-being, hence the freedom of choice becomes a crucial component of well-being. From a capability approach it is apparent that the same level of commodities and resources do not produce the same level of well-being for all individuals.

The sociology of childhood underscores two dimension or axes in the understanding of childhood and children that have their origin in the Greek philosophy that conceived the concepts of *being* (object or state) and *becoming* (change or development). These concepts refer to life as it is experienced in the present, and life as development towards adulthood.

Children's rights refer both to their rights in the present childhood and to their right to develop and "become" (realize their potentials) successful adults. We may view *being* as a state at a given point in time, and *becoming* as the unfolding of the life course along trajectories shaped by social structures and the agency of the actor. The sociology of childhood as well as modern advocacy of children's right have underlined children's right as citizens of the present, not only as beings underway to an adult positions. Yet, the two are interfolded in each other as for example, child labor may represent the theft of the child's present as well as of his or her future.

The relationship between being and becoming is in itself a part of children's well-being. The child who devotes endless hours every week for school work may lose out on leisure activities of play in childhood, but may gain in the future, and the child that invests little in the school work may enjoy the moment but weaken his or her future well-being. The status and position of children have to be understood within the framework of the present, as description, and within a framework of life course and development, as predictions. The *total well-being* will therefore consist of both the well-being of the present, and the predicted well-being of the future.

Thus, well-being is a process; the understanding of the well-being of children requires a model that encapsulates the dynamics of present, and the dynamic relationship between the present and the possible future. The capability approach dominates the understanding of human development, commodities and resources both when it is related to the differentiated sets or combinations of utilities available to different children and as they relate to what the children are able to achieve with their resources. The child must be able to trade his or her resources for other valuable resources in given contexts. The level of well-becoming a child can achieve depends on the structure of the environment and his or her strategies and goals. Within such a framework, freedom to act and choose becomes a central issue; as well as the set or combination of the resources, and the relationship between the resources and the environment.

Capabilities refer to interaction and relationships, not only individual resources. The concept of capabilities is especially relevant to children's well-being because their movement through the life course produces new contexts assigning new values to resources and commodities, and because socialization is understood not only as the evolving of capacities (as IQ or economic or cultural capital) but as the evolving of capabilities. The concept of capability is bridging development at a societal level and socialization and self-realization on the individual level. Children's well-being in a capabilities approach will therefore be based on subjective as well as objective components, and be anchored in a matrix of being and becoming, in the experiences of the moment as well as in the capacities for development. It seems we can define well-being, as a state, as a process and as a development.

That the capabilities framework and the children's rights approach influenced our understanding of children's well-being illustrates their significance. Thus, the new concept of children's well-being includes two axes. The first is about children life course, both as the cognitive and social dimension of development and as the relationship between the present and the future. The second is about experiences, freedom and rights. Freedom is not only related to the economic and political participation as such, but to children's development, competence and life course.

Well-being is a relationship, not just a status and it is not only a reflection of level of income or consumption. Values and references are likely to vary with cultural framework and historical period. The context defining values and well-being changes not only because of historical changes, but because the factors producing well-being at one age level do not necessarily do it at another level. An ideal environment for the four-years old may not be ideal for the young teenagers, and contexts may provide different conditions related to social groups and gender. At the core of all analysis of children's life and development is that there is a developmental relationship between today and tomorrow; the conditions of the present influence further development. This implies that factors of children's well-being have to be understood within a different framework than related to other age groups.

Both the capability approach and the children's rights framework provide such a tool to better understand children's well-being. Combining these two approaches and the discourse between them is a promising step forward in our understanding of children's well-being. This collection of papers takes us one step forward in this crucial route. It contributes to the growing discourse and to our better understanding of the relations between these two dominant contemporary approaches. But most important – it takes us a few steps closer for a better understanding of children's well-being.

Asher Ben-Arieh
Paul Baerwald School of Social Work and Social Welfare,
The Hebrew University of Jerusalem,
Jerusalem, Israel

Contents

List of Contributors

Sabine Andresen Institut für Sozialpädagogik und Erwachsenenbildung, Goethe-Universität Frankfurt, Frankfurt am Main, Germany

Claudio Baraldi Department of Studies on Language and Culture, University of Modena and Reggio Emilia, Modena, Italy

Mario Biggeri Department of Economics and Management, University of Florence, Florence, Italy

Jean-Michel Bonvin Ecole d'études sociales et pédagogiques (EESP), University of Applied Sciences Western Switzerland, Lausanne, Switzerland

Zoë Clark Fachbereich Erziehungswissenschaften, Institut für Sozialpädagogik und Erwachsenenbildung, Goethe-Universität, Frankfurt am Main, Germany

Stephan Dahmen École d'études sociale et pédagogiques, University of Applied Sciences Western Switzerland, Lausanne, Switzerland

Frédéric Darbellay University Institute Kurt Bösch, Sion, Switzerland

Katharina Gerarts World Vision Institute für Forschung und Innovation, Friedrichsdorf, Germany

Dominique Golay Haute école de travail social et de la santé, EESP, Lausanne, Switzerland

Karl Hanson Children's Rights Unit, University Institute Kurt Bösch, Sion, Switzerland

Vittorio Iervese Department of Studies on Language and Culture, University of Modena and Reggio Emilia, Modena, Italy

Ravi Karkara Partners and Youth Branch, United Nations Human Settlements Programme, New York, USA

Manfred Liebel Fachbereich Erziehungswissenschaft und Psychologie, Freie Universität Berlin, Berlin, Germany

Dominique Malatesta Haute école de travail social et de la santé, EESP, Lausanne, Switzerland

Michele Poretti University Institute Kurt Bösch, Sion, Switzerland

Didier Reynaert Faculty of Education, Health and Social Work, University College Ghent, Ghent, Belgium

Irene Rizzini Departamento de Serviço Social, Universidade Católica do Rio de Janeiro, Rio de Janeiro, RJ, Brazil

Pierrine Robin Laboratoire Interdisciplinaire de Recherche sur les Transformations des pratiques Educatives et des pratiques Sociales (LIRTES), Université de Paris-Est, Créteil, France

Rudi Roose Faculty of Psychology and Educational Sciences, Ghent University, Ghent, Belgium

Daniel Stoecklin Children's Rights Unit, University Institute Kurt Bösch, Sion, Switzerland

Danielle Strickland Doctorado en Desarollo Educativo, Universidad Pedagogica Nacional, Guadalajara, Mexico

Holger Ziegler Faculty of Pedagogy, Centre for Social Service Studies, Bielefeld University, Bielefeld, Germany

Chapter 1
Introduction

Jean-Michel Bonvin and Daniel Stoecklin

Children's rights have hardly been analysed in terms of the capability approach (CA), which was developed by Amartya Sen (1999) and Martha Nussbaum (2000), and many other scholars. This book is among the first attempts to bridge the two, and it appears after a few contributions to this endeavour (Biggeri et al. 2010, 2011; Dixon and Nussbaum 2012). First of all, we want to clearly establish how we see the relation between children's rights and the capability approach. Children's rights and the capability approach are not of the same nature: children's rights are a social reality and the capability approach is a perspective to reflect on it. According to Sen and also to Nussbaum, the capability approach is a way to operationalize formal freedoms (entitlements), and hence children's rights.

Therefore, the capability approach is used to inspire us on dimensions to look at when it comes to implementing formal rights as the ones contained in the UNCRC. It attracts our attention to the fact that there is a gap between children's formal liberties (rights) and their real freedom (capability). The question is then how individual and social conversion factors act as facilitators, or on the contrary as obstacles, to the transformation of formal entitlements into real capability. Dixon and Nussbaum emphasize that "rights are not fully secured unless the related capabilities are actually present: otherwise rights are mere words on the paper" (2012: 561). They insist that special kinds of policies, or more widely conversion factors, are needed to guarantee each and everyone's access to a list of capabilities considered as fundamental to the recognition of human dignity. In their perspective, children have specific relevance in this regard and there are reasons to provide them

J.-M. Bonvin (✉)
Ecole d'études sociales et pédagogiques (EESP), University of Applied Sciences Western Switzerland, Chemin des Abeilles 14, CH 1010 Lausanne, Switzerland
e-mail: jmbonvin@eesp.ch

D. Stoecklin
Children's Rights Unit, University Institute Kurt Bösch, P. O. Box 4176, CH 1950 Sion 4, Switzerland
e-mail: daniel.stoecklin@iukb.ch

D. Stoecklin and J.-M. Bonvin (eds.), *Children's Rights and the Capability Approach*, Children's Well-Being: Indicators and Research 8, DOI 10.1007/978-94-017-9091-8_1,

with special priority programmes, due to their vulnerability on the one hand and to the cost-effectiveness of measures designed for children on the other hand. In this book, we seek to further explore this perspective in two ways: first, to examine in detail what is specific about children; second, to identify more precisely the individual and social conversion (or conversely: obstruction) factors facilitating or impeding the transformation of rights into capabilities in the case of children. We thereby seek to make a significant step forward in the understanding of the link between children's rights and capabilities, as well as their effective implementation.

The contributors of this volume address the conditions allowing the transformation of specific children's rights into capabilities in settings as different as children's parliaments, organized leisure activities, contexts of vulnerability, children in care. They also tackle theoretical issues linked to children's agency and reflexivity, education, the life cycle perspective, child participation, evolving capabilities, and citizenship. The volume highlights important dimensions that have to be taken into account for the implementation of human rights and the development of peoples' capabilities. The focus on children's rights along a capability approach is an inspiring perspective that researchers and practitioners in the field of human rights should explore.

To gauge the importance of this new path, we invite readers, within the scope of this brief introduction, to first consider the capability approach and then the main perspectives regarding children's rights. We will then see how the field of children's rights can benefit from this approach and this will allow us to situate the contributions to this volume. This will bring us to identify the main challenges, and how the contributors see and tackle them. The prospects will become clearer when the reader arrives to the conclusion, so we will substantially dedicate our conclusion to the prospects of a capability approach to children's rights. We therefore consider that the book is not just a collection of papers that one might read in disorder. The order of the chapters, although it is not bound to a dissertation-like argument, is nevertheless arranged along a thread that helps situate the relevance of the capability approach as a new way of grasping children's rights. This journey begins now with an introduction on the capability approach.

1.1 The Capability Approach

The CA insists that the yardstick for assessing human development should be the real freedom people have to lead a life they have reason to value (Sen 1992, 1999; Nussbaum 2000). It thereby demarcates itself from strictly growth-based models insisting on GDP level as the main criterion for human development. Two key distinctions are at the core of the capability approach and its combined focus on opportunity freedom or well-being freedom on the one hand, process freedom or agency freedom on the other hand (Sen 1993, 2002).

First, resources or commodities are not equated with capabilities: as a matter of fact, an equal distribution of goods, services, cash or in-kind transfers, etc. does not necessary translate into an equal distribution of capabilities. The ability of people to convert the possession of such resources into capabilities or real freedoms to live a life they have reason to value, depends on individual and social factors, e.g. physical or mental abilities, etc. on the one hand, social norms, available policies, socio-economic opportunities, etc. on the other hand. Nussbaum calls these internal and external capabilities (Nussbaum 2000, 2011), while other proponents of the CA use the terms S-capabilities (skills) and O-capabilities (options) (Gasper 2003). Whatever the designation used, the focus is on the necessary presence of individual and social parameters that act as facilitators for the conversion of resources or commodities into capabilities. Hence, public action in favour of the development of capabilities should not stop with the provision of resources (such as the cash benefits paid by the welfare State), but also encompass these conversion factors. This calls for a situated public action, insofar as these conversion factors will not be the same for all categories of people. Therefore their identification, for each target group as well as in each and every country with its various socio-economic settings and cultural backgrounds, will require a specific task. With regard to this point, there is disagreement among the two main proponents of the CA: while Nussbaum insists that a list of essential capabilities should be drawn in order to orient the work to be accomplished at national or local level (she thus endorses "a partial theory of social justice"), Sen suggests that the identification of relevant capabilities and conversion factors should be entirely left to the initiative of local actors. This point of disagreement should, however, not occult the wide-ranging agreement about the relevance and importance of the issue of conversion factors and the necessity to go beyond so-called resourcist approaches that focus only on resources and neglect such factors.

Second, capabilities do not coincide with functionings, i.e. what people are and what they actually do. Indeed, two people displaying the same kind of functioning may well enjoy a very different level of capabilities. Therefore, what should be centre stage in the capability approach is not the peoples' actual functionings, but their real freedom to choose between valuable alternative functionings: in other words, opportunities (their quantity and quality) matter more than outcomes or facts. In such a perspective, public action is expected not to gear people towards precise behaviours or outcomes, e.g. in accordance with dominant social norms, but to empower them toward the autonomous choice of a life that is valuable in their eyes. All forms of paternalism, though benevolent they may be, are to be questioned in this framework that emphasizes people's autonomy in their choices.

Hence, the CA insists on both of these dimensions: people should be provided with real opportunities, which extends beyond resources and formal rights; they should be left autonomous in deciding about the way they want to use these opportunities and not be constrained toward compliance with specific norms or official directives.

With regard to the situation of children, the CA perspective raises many controversies: is process freedom, i.e. the second dimension outlined above, relevant for them? Should they not be provided with extensive opportunity freedom in the first stage, while process freedom would be granted only when they eventually become adults? In this debate, all extreme positions are of little use: indeed, children do not enjoy the same degree of agency as adults and therefore cannot be provided with the same measure of process freedom; all the same, they cannot be confined in the position of "becoming adults", thus having to expect this age before enjoying any degree of process freedom. Thus, the dichotomy between "no process freedom for children" and "full process freedom for children" does not help. An insightful contribution in this respect is that of Biggeri et al. (2011) and their concept of 'evolving capabilities'. During early childhood, external capabilities provided by caregivers or informal human relationships play a central role, but with the passing of time children get access to a more extensive set of internal capabilities, which significantly influences their situation. The concept of "feedback loops" is used to describe the dynamic process, whereby resources and external capabilities provided at T0 will impact on the internal capabilities enjoyed at T1 and will therefore require an adjusted action in favour of the development of the children's capabilities and some (increasing) space left for process freedom. Human development must then be conceived as a dynamic and complex process, where resources and individual and social conversion factors constantly interact with feedback loops reshaping the capability set of the child at every stage. Therefore, the most appropriate combination between opportunity and process freedom cannot follow on the divide between children and adults, but needs to take account of this dynamic process. This is also a major challenge for the effective implementation of children's rights, as will be presented in the next section of this introduction.

1.2 Children's Rights

The status of the child has considerably evolved with the adoption by the United Nations of the Convention on the Rights of the Child (UNCRC 1989). The State parties to the UNCRC recognize the child as a rights holder and must therefore grant him/her protection, provision of services and effective possibilities for participation. The latter are supposed to be favoured by rights contained in the UNCRC that are considered as "participation rights": the right to be heard (art. 12), the right to freedom of expression (art. 13), the right to freedom of thought, conscience and religion (art. 14), the right to freedom of association and peaceful assembly (art. 15), the right to privacy (art. 16), the right to have access to information (art. 17), and the right to participate freely in cultural life and the arts (art. 31).

The right to be heard is considered the masterpiece for child participation. The first paragraph of this article reads as follows:

> States Parties shall assure to the child who is capable of forming his or her own views the right to express those views freely in all matters affecting the child, the views of the child being given due weight in accordance with the age and maturity of the child. (UNCRC 1989, art. 12.1)

It is the masterpiece of participation rights, because, among these rights, art. 12 (the right to be heard) is also a general principle: this means that it is not only a substantial right but also a procedural guarantee in the implementation of other rights. As an example, let's take education: the right to education (art. 28) is to be implemented with regard to children's opinions (both as a group and as individuals) about education, and the authorities should provide a space where these opinions can be expressed (like for instance school councils). Art. 12 is therefore a general principle that is transversal to the implementation of other rights. It is one of the UNCRC's four general principles, the other ones being the principle of the best interests of the child (art. 3), the principle of non-discrimination (art. 2), and the principle of protecting the child's life, survival and development (art. 6).

With the principle of the consideration for the child's opinion (art. 12), we see that participation rights are closely linked to protection and provision rights. Several authors underline that protections and provisions can improve when children's participation is fostered. And this in turn only happens once children's agency is acknowledged (Freeman 2007: 18). This is the point where children's rights can be bridged with the debate about children's agency within the sociology of childhood, to which, in our view, the capability approach brings a great contribution because there is a very close connection between the implementation of this general principle and the understanding of children's agency. The relationship goes in both directions. Empirical observations of the extents and limits of children's influence over social structures in various fields and contexts inform us about the challenges of implementing the child's right to be heard. And, reversely, a thorough analysis of art. 12 UNCRC (Zermatten and Stoecklin 2009) reveals how much the different elements contained in it presuppose that children have, or should be allowed, a growing agency. Let us briefly examine these elements and how we can connect them with the debate on children's agency in the sociology of childhood.

First of all, art. 12.1 UNCRC is concerned with the child's "own" views, which actually raises the question of where agency is situated: is it located in the relationships social actors have among them, or does it already start with one's own reflexivity? The authors in this volume address this issue by situating the child's capability both in the relationships (notably Baraldi and Iervese, Liebel, Dahmen) and in the actor's reflexivity (notably Stoecklin and Bonvin, Robin), but there is no clear opposition. Rather, it can be suggested that the dialogues within individuals (inner-dialogue) and among them (social relations) are retroacting one on the other, and it would actually be misleading to end up in a "chicken-egg" debate over which one is determining the other.

Already on this first point, we can clearly show the necessity to make a distinction between the subject of rights and the social actor (Stoecklin 2014). Actually, the formation of "own views" that are expressed in a socially recognizable discourse is a culturally acquired competence. The social actor is acting in a pragmatic way which derives from experience (James 1910; Dewey 1910), allowing adjustment of thoughts, expressions, and lines of conduct, through interactions with others (Weber 1968). The child's competence of building views that would be socially considered as mature is in fact actualized through interactions. Actually, social interactions in specific contexts always shape the expression of "own views" and this is where the capability approach comes in: the evaluation of one's maturity is therefore bound to mutual adjustments, such as being able to recognize the points of views of others and being open to information (Sen 2009). Eventually, it is hard to think of an opinion that would be absolutely free of influences conveyed by the opinions of others. Participation is itself the process whereby children acquire the capacity to build their "own views", and therefore the implementation of art. 12 UNCRC should build on sociological observations around this complex issue.

Art. 12.1 UNCRC is also concerned with other elements that involve rather large sociological debates, namely on how views are expressed (freely), the range of matters on which these views are expressed (all matters affecting the child), the consideration that is given to these views (due weight given in accordance with the age and maturity of the child), and, most importantly, who is forming the views (the child who is capable of forming "own views"). There are two elements of this article that put some restrictions according to the capacity of the child. However, the criteria are implicit: the formulation "*the child who is capable of forming his or her own views*" leaves open the question of how we assess this capacity. The consideration given to these views "*in accordance with the age and maturity of the child*" also does not specify the criteria to evaluate maturity. While the CRC sets no age limit on participation rights, one clearly sees that implicit restrictions are left to the assessment of decision-makers. A challenge is therefore to make the criteria as transparent as possible, because they are all too often left to decision-makers' discretion. How "free" is the building of one's views at different ages and in different settings? As we know, expression and recognition are interdependent: a discourse can be recognized only if it is expressed in such a way that it can be socially shared. It is eventually the consideration for the child's reflexivity that is at stake. Processes allowing to take seriously into account what children express are of crucial importance. They are especially interesting to observe when it comes to children suffering from a stereotyped definition of their situation and consequent stigmatisation, like for instance "street children" (Aptekar and Stoecklin 2014).

The second paragraph of art. 12 is concerned with administrative measures that are needed to guarantee the right of the child to express one's views:

> For this purpose, the child shall in particular be provided the opportunity to be heard in any judicial and administrative proceedings affecting the child, either directly, or through a representative or an appropriate body, in a manner consistent with the procedural rules of national law. (UNCRC 1989, Art. 12.2)

This is the opportunity to be heard, which is a crucial component of the child's capability to express one's views, and this opportunity is linked to the procedural rules that frame judicial and administrative proceedings. It is important however to underline that "all matters affecting the child" are not to be reduced *stricto sensu* to matters that directly affect a particular child, but in a larger sense as more general issues that also affect children as a group. Therefore, the civil freedoms of children that are called "participation rights" (CRC art. 12–17 and 31), and of which art. 12 is the central pillar, involve more than formal proceedings. They encompass broader and informal social processes, not reducible to the formal administrative system. The difficulties with the transversal cooperations that are needed in the formal system, at national and local levels, to truly respect the child's right to be heard, cannot be divorced from the broader picture of what we might call the "culture of participation" that is more or less present and that evolves along very complex social dynamics.

Children's rights therefore are best studied from an interdisciplinary angle, whereby the sociology of childhood, developmental psychology, legal studies, peadagogic sciences, and other relevant disciplines, are mobilised to highlight specific and complementary dimensions of the worldwide challenges that appear when children are considered as holders of rights. Hence, what we might call the "sociology of children's rights" cannot really exist without engaging in a dialogue with other disciplines. This dialogue necessarily involves some common ground to build on, a paradigm that may transcend the epistemological, theoretical and methodological frontiers. Can we call the capability approach such a paradigm? This question can be best answered when scholars have sufficiently tried to integrate the CA in their own thematic and disciplinary fields and when they eventually see whether this approach helps the interdisciplinary dialogue that is necessary to fully embrace and comprehend the very huge and complex issue of children's rights.

Since we have applied the capability approach to assess the implementation of article 12 in the field of organized leisure (see Stoecklin and Bonvin in this volume), we found that the approach is particularly relevant to come closer to an operational definition of agency. This has led us to organize a scientific meeting in July 2012 in Sion, Switzerland, where we have invited colleagues to elaborate on children's rights from the perspective of the capability approach. Most of us start from and build on the sociology of childhood, and the debates within this field have inevitably given the flavour of this book. We therefore must briefly situate these debates as they help better situate the specific challenges in applying the capability approach in the field of children's rights.

As Hanson et al. (in this volume) underline, the children's rights movement, beginning with the twentieth century (Veerman 1992), preceded academic recognition that children have rights that has emerged only round the time of the adoption of the UNCRC in 1989. The first period of research was mainly dealing with philosophical arguments for and against children's rights, and on legal issues about the applicability of these rights. The "new paradigm in childhood studies", also called the "new social studies of childhood" claimed that "generation" should be added to other distinctive categories like class, gender and ethnicity (see notably James and Prout 1990; Qvortrup et al. 1994; James et al. 1998).

1.3 Features of the New Social Studies of Childhood

As Alanen summarizes, the sociology of childhood is built around "*the ways in which childhood is socially constructed and reconstructed in relation to time and place*" (Alanen 2011: 147). This underlines the historical and cultural variability of the definition of childhood, and therefore the task of social scientists is, according to Alanen (ibid.), to unveil the often "hidden" political definition of children that creates assumptions about children that become naturalized over the years.

The universality of childhood and the diversity of children's real lives are difficult to reconcile. Some authors (Allison James, personal communication; Hartas 2008) advise to use the plural form "childhoods" when speaking of the particularity and diversity of the experiences made by children, and the singular form "childhood" when speaking of children's life course position. Hence, "childhood" is only a social construct, or a "word" as Bourdieu said about "youth". But the opposition between lived "childhoods" and the socially constructed period of life one calls "childhood" is probably a false debate, as "childhood" has no existence as such if it is reduced to the only dimension of a time frame. What is actually referred to when people speak of "childhood" is an assemblage of core elements of dominant social representations which are historical constructs. It is a conjunction of diverse and equivocal images and projections of both adults and children regarding what *they* would see as a specific sphere (or realm) that in *their* views characterize children. The opposition between "childhood" as a universal stage in life course, and "childhoods" as a diversity of life experiences is therefore misleading. First of all because any experience is primarily subjective and the different ways in which children experience their worlds cannot be named "childhoods": this would mean that we conflate subjective experiences with objective things (childhoods). Subjective experiences can only become an intersubjective reality (an "object") if they are externalized in such ways that they can be recognized by others and aggregated as a concept, and this is possible only if the subjective experience is mediated by a social process. What is understood under the term "childhood" is the result of a mediation process through which individual perceptions and expressions are conceptualized.

Therefore there is no "childhood" if there is no mediation of particular subjectivities. We may say that "childhood" is an intersubjective construct. Therefore, the concept "childhoods" could only be valid if we mean by this the different intersubjective constructs, or different particular ways of defining "childhood". With a focus on the social construction of childhood, proponents of the "new sociology of childhood" have developed a critical view on children's rights. Claiming that diversity must be taken into account, some scholars held that the child portrayed implicitly by the UNCRC is a Eurocentric construction. The proto-adult conception of children, as becomings, was then heavily criticized and replaced by the consideration for children's being and their own views, which many authors illustrated in different fields, from child labour to street children and many other situations.

The emphasis on the social construction of childhood has brought up the necessity to observe their agency (James and Prout 1990; Archard 20004; Qvortrup et al. 1994; Corsaro 1997; Sirota 2006). But, as we have suggested (Stoecklin 2013), agency still seems to be mostly used as a slogan and it does not yet represent an operational concept constructed along an explicit theory of action. This has probably something to do with a reaction towards the former psychological dominance in childhood studies. Consequently, the "social turn" tends to situate the limitations of children's agency merely in the social structure and power relationships (Stoecklin 2013: 446). It forgets the other side of the coin that the CA identifies as the individual skills.

Therefore, by trying to identify the bi-directional links between social opportunities and individual skills, the CA has much to offer to the new sociology of childhood. It is relevant to consider children as "social actors who are not only shaped by their circumstances but also, and most importantly, help shape them" (James et al. 1998: 123). However, "few studies actually respond to the crucial question of how children of different ages and in different settings shape their environments" (Stoecklin 2013: 446). By criticizing "proto-adult" conceptions of children (Matthews 2003), by which only small forms of adult maturity are recognized in children, the new paradigm in childhood studies was certainly right. But the critique of developmental psychology probably went too far and, forgetting the personal evolutive competences and the fact that their limitations can result not only from social but also from individual parameters, the approach ironically became a new norm. A paradox is there. The critical position, to see children as *beings* and not *becomings*, fostered another normativity, which sometimes contemplates children's agency as attached to them (as much as to adults), as if this would give children more recognition. By contrast, the capability approach helps situate agency as a reality constructed in the relationships between individuals. When agency becomes a slogan, it is like a tree that hides the forest of children's capabilities. It seems rather difficult, if not impossible, to make a genuine non-normative critique, as critique in itself involves a value-oriented perspective. It would therefore be advisable to recognize the inevitably normative position from where one speaks or writes in order to circumscribe it to the best extent, which still seems to us the most appropriate way towards objectivity since Max Weber's (1968, 1992a, b) discussion of axiologic neutrality.

1.4 Beyond the Pitfalls of the New Social Studies of Childhood: A Capability Approach to Children's Rights

By contrast, the UNCRC and the CA assume their normative character and do not claim to be beyond normativity. Indeed, as underlined by Hanson et al. (in this volume), both the children's rights contained in the UNCRC and the capability approach are normative and prescriptive as they promote social arrangements and policies that are meant to enhance respect for people's dignity. Meanwhile, both approaches explicitly acknowledge their respective normativity. Nevertheless, their status is different. The UNCRC is a legally binding instrument, whereas the capability approach is a paradigmatic perspective. The latter can serve as a theoretical account of children's rights, as is claimed by Dixon and Nussbaum (2012). According to these authors, the CA is an emerging theory based on the idea of human dignity and it helps explain why it makes sense to recognize a range of rights for children, both in the UNCRC and in national constitutions, with due respect to children's welfare needs because of their vulnerability but also to their agency (Dixon and Nussbaum 2012: 552–553). It is because of human frailty, all the more so regarding children, that "the State has an obligation to ensure that all persons have access to a life worthy of human dignity" (Dixon and Nussbaum 2012: 549).

But what is dignity? The signatories of the Universal Declaration of Human Rights (UDHR) merely make a declaration of intention agreeing that "All human beings are born free and equal in dignity and rights. They are endowed with reason and conscience and should act towards one another in a spirit of brotherhood". The UNCRC in contrast is legally binding, and it also refers to the notion of dignity in its preamble: "Considering that, in accordance with the principles proclaimed in the Charter of the United Nations, recognition of the inherent dignity and of the equal and inalienable rights of all members of the human family is the foundation of freedom, justice and peace in the world (. . .)". Thus we can consider that the peculiar definitions of rights contained in the UNCRC are a specification of what "a life worthy of human dignity" could be. Dignity would therefore encompass general principles (including the right to life, survival and development, the right to non-discrimination, respect for the views of children, the requirement to give primary consideration to the child's best interests in all matters affecting them), civil rights and freedoms (including the right to a name and nationality; the right to freedom of expression, thought and association; the right to access to information; the right not to be subjected to torture), family environment and alternative care (including the right to live with and have contact with both parents; the right to be reunited with parents if separated from them; the right to the provision of appropriate alternative care where necessary), basic heath and welfare (including the rights of disabled children; the right to healthcare, social security, childcare services and an adequate standard of living), education, leisure and cultural activities (including the right to education; the right to play, leisure and participation in cultural life and the arts), and finally special protection measures (covering the rights of refugee children, those affected by armed conflicts, children in the juvenile justice system, children deprived of their liberty, and children suffering economic, sexual or other forms of exploitation).

But if all these "entitlements are held to be required by the notion of a life worthy of people's equal human dignity" (Dixon and Nussbaum, p. 567), then how should we consider consider Nussbaum's list of central human capabilities? It is debatable whether these ten capabilities (Life. Bodily health. Bodily integrity. Senses, imagination, and thought. Emotions. Practical reason. Affiliation. Other species. Play.

Control over one's environment) are to be seen as a parallel list of entitlements or as another sub-grouping of the ones already contained in the human rights treaties. Clark and Ziegler (in this volume) underline that Nussbaum's aim is not to impose a normative framework on individual conduct but rather to identify "general pre-requisites for various versions of leading a good life" that would need to be adapted to the diversity of contexts where people live. Andresen and Gerarts (in this volume) also stress that the capabilities included in Nussbaum's list can only develop if they are nurtured and, consequently that human dignity, equality and freedom (of choice) should be seen as guidelines towards the universal ethics of equal opportunities. The challenge here is how these dimensions of the "good life" are negotiated. Moreover how children can be included in this discussion.

The issue here is not to attempt at escaping or erasing any form of normativity in order to reach what should be interpreted as a kind of objective truth about the definition of children's rights or human dignity. Indeed, such an attempt would be doomed to failure, as normativity is an inherent part of such debates. Rather, what is pursued is a negotiation between the various possible normativities about these issues, in order to reach acceptable solutions for the concerned actors in every specific context, i.e. solutions that will allow them to lead a life they have reason to value. A key feature of normativity in this framework is its incompleteness: it does not claim to give a precise rule in all cases, on the contrary it constantly strives to leave enough space for negotiating rules and rights at situated level.

Therefore, looking at children's rights using a capability approach invites to situate normativity where it really stands. It is not because it speaks of the "good life" that the CA would be imposing dogmatic and therefore condemnable approach. The CA is a normative approach but its normativity stands at another level. It is situated in a position where one looks at individuals leading "the life one has reasons to value". The normativity included here therefore coincides with the valuation of differences and the respect for individual preferences.

Applying a capability approach to children's rights is a relevant way to consider children's rights as a construct involving both individual and social dimensions. We believe that the authors in this volume have made a substantial contribution to children's rights and/or the capability approach. In doing so, they bridge the analysis of the social construction of childhood, and more precisely the sociology of children's rights, with the considerations over children's agency that the capability approach can help better observe.

1.5 Children's Rights Approached in New Ways

Taking a capability approach to highlight children's rights opens new ways that are both interesting and challenging. Recent developments show a growing interest to integrate the capability approach (CA) in the field of the children's rights (CR) studies. Reciprocally, children's rights are a major issue for the development of the capability approach. Children's rights can be seen as formal resources or entitlements. Consequently, the gap between formal liberties (rights) and real freedom (capability) can be more precisely explained in terms of individual and social conversion factors.

The editors of this volume have organized a scientific meeting that took place on 5 and 6 July 2012, at Institut Universitaire Kurt Bösch (IUKB), in Sion, Switzerland, with the support of the Swiss National Science Foundation. Representatives of these two fields of studies converged with the aim to cross-fertilize their perspectives. The focal point of this starting dialogue lies in the identification of conditions allowing transform formal rights into real freedom or capabilities. The book presents the participants' contributions as well as supplementary invited papers and reflects the most important challenges and prospects that emerge from this dialogue. The volume highlights important issues that have to be taken into account for the implementation of human rights and the development of peoples' capabilities. The focus on children's capabilities along a rights-based approach is an inspiring perspective that researchers and practitioners in the field of human rights should deepen. The scientific meeting held in Sion was among the first attempts in this direction and the present volume is an invitation to continue and broaden this dialogue. A short overview of the contributions gives an idea of the wealth of dimensions involved in this debate.

Mario Biggeri and Ravi Karkara (Chap. 2) highlight relevant relationships and synergies between the capability approach (CA) and the human rights approach (HRA). This is especially interesting in the case of children. They try to see whether equity, participatory and life cycle perspectives allow to analyse and to translate these relationships into practice. They underline that both CA and HRA are opportunity-oriented approaches, which facilitates the combination of these two slightly different perspectives. While the HRA focuses on deprivations, the CA analyses the causes of the lack of freedom. Moreover, the authors underline the important policy implications that can stem from the positive synergies between children rights and the capability approach.

Claudio Baraldi and Vittorio Iervese (Chap. 3) explore how communication systems and interactions can facilitate children's agency. They focus on the processes and factors that convert children's ability into capabilities and functionings. They use Conversation Analysis and Social Systems Theory to highlight these processes and factors. Analysing data on interactions in educational settings, they show that these are produced in adult-children interactions and demonstrate how the facilitation of children's agency in the interaction can be a potential social conversion process. They show how different forms of facilitation promote opportunities for children's agency and hence children's rights to participate in decision making.

Manfred Liebel (Chap. 4) holds that a crucial point revolves around the conditions that are necessary for children to make use of their rights. While children are entitled to human rights regardless of their capacities, the concept of 'evolving capacities' is understood in different ways: some view the child's growing agency as a precondition for the use of rights while others see it as a result of a learning process. Liebel takes another position. He uses a contextualized concept of children's rights whereby the subjective capacities are connected with the social prerequisites that foster children as wilful rights holders. The author proposes the notion of "evolving capabilities" to refine the concept of capabilities that are diversely elaborated in the Capability Approach. He uses Brighouse's (2002) concept of "agency rights" to qualify all the subjective rights contained in the UNCRC, and not only the participation rights, as long as these rights are "re-conceptualized in such a way that they might become an entitlement or instrument in the hands of children". He discusses whether the Capability Approach can contribute to transform the rights contained in the UNCRC into "agency rights", that is to let children reach and influence these rights.

Sabine Andresen and Katharina Gerarts (Chap. 5) show how recent approaches in childhood studies proceed along a paradigmatic shift from adult well-becoming to child well-being. Children's rights can therefore be used to study children as autonomous actors situated in the here and now. The authors adopt a sociology of science perspective which allows them to look at childhood studies in terms of educational science. Focusing more systematically on the relation between well-being and well-becoming, they use the Capability Approach and its theory of the "good life" to analyse empirical data, namely children's own childrearing concepts, and children's concepts on freedom and the "good life". They see children's own views as an important perspective for the development of the Children's Rights Approach.

Dominique Golay and Dominique Malatesta (Chap. 6) observed children's councils in Switzerland. They raise fundamental questions regarding child participation when considering how these devices provide social recognition. The authors use three major theories of social justice, Sen's capability approach, Fraser's theory of social justice and Honneth's theory of recognition, in order to see whether children's councils can be valuable means to implement the right to freedom of expression (art. 13 UNCRC) and the right to be heard (art. 12 UNCRC). Basing on a qualitative research on children's citizenship in the city of Lausanne, they discuss the conditions of children empowerment. They identify two kinds of children councils according to the goals followed by the professionals. The city-oriented type of council involves children's participation and citizenship education directed towards formal procedures such as voting. The second type, which they identify as child-oriented, focuses on children's experiences and expectations. They finally compare how differently these two sets influence children's social recognition.

Daniel Stoecklin and Jean-Michel Bonvin (Chap. 7) explore new ways of conceptualizing children's citizenship and participation through the capability approach applied to children. On the basis of qualitative research conducted in Switzerland and in France in the field of organised leisure activities, they identify several conditions that allow converting the child's right to be heard (art. 12 UNCRC) into effective participation. They highlight four sets of factors: economical, political, organisational and personal. Along these dimensions, they identify two ideal-types, namely the bottom-up participation and the top-down participation, and underline the sequential aspect of participation as a process. Using an original tool, the "actor's system", they show why children's reflexivity is a major converting factor. This model is helpful in capturing and reflecting the recursivity of experience. The results contribute to the theoretical model used in the capability approach and to the sociology of action. They also enrich the theory of child participation.

Stephan Dahmen (Chap. 8) addresses the strong focus on children's agency that is found in the recent developments within the discussion on children's rights as well as in the new sociology of childhood. According to him, the view of the child as a social and political actor, as well as the rhetoric of *being*, can be considered a new "theoretical orthodoxy", stressing children's autonomy. Its side-effect is an overly optimistic view on children's agency, overlooking important inequalities. The author looks at the capability approach as more appropriate to situate these inequalities within the space of youth and childhood. He suggests that the capability approach provides a hyphen between prescriptive treaties (like the UNCRC) and descriptive-analytic approaches (like the sociology of childhood and youth). He analyses the differences in children's agency within the transitions from school to work and highlights the role of the State for their access to citizenship rights. He ends with considerations on how the capability approach might foster new venues of childhood and youth research.

Didier Reynaert and Rudi Roose (Chap. 9) ask how agency, while a fundamental notion in both the frameworks of children's rights and the capability approach, can be understood and supported in order to guarantee children's human dignity. They consider the historical and socio-cultural structuring of childhood and use the notion "youth moratorium" or the "institutionalised youth land" to situate children's agency within a "strong egalitarian individualism" based on the idea of personal responsibility. They suggest that the capability approach is a departure towards a more ambiguous position regarding children and that the framework of children's rights and the framework of the capability approach could gain from an understanding of children's agency that acknowledges interrelationship and solidarity.

Pierrine Robin (Chap. 10) shows how the child protection policy in France still regards children as objects to be protected rather than as subjects of rights. The French Child Protection Reform Law sets out a number of specific rights for children living in care, such as the right to take part in the assessment process. This corresponds to the new status of children in care since the adoption of the UNCRC. However, the author identifies a huge gap between the formal rights of the child and the opportunities for children to actually exercise them. Her empirical study shows that the context is marked by constrained and descending participation. She analyses the interdependences and complementarity of individual features and social opportunities in decision-making processes in care. She also concludes that participation can be approached as a non-linear, cumulative and retroactive process.

Zoë Clark and Holger Ziegler (Chap. 11) assess the role of the family and the State within the UNCRC. They focus on some children's rights in relation to parent's rights and duties, and show how the UNCRC has an (implicit) normativity as regards the family and how it consequently entails certain power relations within families. They critically address these normative foundations and refer to the capabilities approach and feminist considerations on social justice to show that the UNCRC favours a reduced approach to child welfare. They challenge the expectations towards the UNCRC as an instrument that would really favour child participation and children seen as agentic subjects of rights.

Karl Hanson, Michele Poretti and Frederic Darbellay (Chap. 12) discuss distinctions and overlaps between the normative ambitions of both children's rights and the capability approach. When situating recent developments and critical enquiries in children's rights studies, they look at links between rights, emancipation and interdisciplinarity. Building on discussions about child participation, they present the results of an interdisciplinary research project on priorities in international children's rights advocacy. Their intention is to explore how children's own conceptualisations of their rights are recognized. They use for this the notions of "living rights" and translations and analyse their material to further explore what these insights can tell about the capability approach. They find that since the 1990s the iconography of victimhood mobilized by child rights advocates has evolved, using 'the child victim of violence' to replace 'the street child' as the dominant icon on the international agenda (Poretti et al. 2014). They address tensions between normative and empirical realms and advocate for giving equal consideration to competing social practices as a way to provide equal access to the production of universality. It is in this way that they see children's rights studies and the capability approach as mutually enriching.

Irene Rizzini and Danielle Strickland (Chap. 13) depict the progress in the field of children's and adolescents' rights in Brazil and Mexico, the most rapidly developing nations in Latin America. Although both nations are committed to human rights ideals, there are many obstacles that impinge on the full enforcement of laws and treaties. The authors suggest that the strategies developed in Brazil to promote youth participation, specifically the Children's Rights Councils, should inspire Mexico to increase their involvement in the efforts to promote their own rights. The gap between the legal framework for children's rights in Mexico and the concrete actions to make rights truly respected remains rather wide, especially regarding street children.

Stoecklin and Bonvin's conclusion finally identify the main prospects raised by these contributions. They especially focus on three main issues: individual and social conversion factors, participation and agency, and finally the vulnerable and competent child.

References

Alanen, L. (2011). Critical childhood studies? *Childhood, 18*(2), 147–150.

Aptekar, L., & Stoecklin, D. (2014). *Street children and homeless youth: A cross-cultural perspective*. Dordrecht: Springer.

Archard, D. (2004). *Children, rights and childhood*. London: Routledge.

Biggeri, M., Ballet, J., & Comim, F. (2010). The capability approach and research on children: Capability approach and children' issues. In S. Andresen et al. (Eds.), *Children and the*

good life: New challenges for research on children (pp. 75–89). Dordrecht/Heidelberg/London/New York: Springer.
Biggeri, M., Ballet, J., & Comim, F. (2011). *Children and the capability approach.* Basingstoke/New York: Palgrave Macmillan.
Brighouse, H. (2002). What rights (if any) do children have? In D. Archard & C. M. Macleod (Eds.), *The moral and political status of children* (pp. 31–52). Oxford: Oxford University Press.
Corsaro, W. (1997). *The sociology of childhood.* Thousand Oaks: Pine Forge Press.
Dewey, J. (1910). *How we think.* Lexington: Heath & Co.
Dixon, R., & Nussbaum, M. C. (2012). Children's rights and a capabilities approach: The question of special priority. The Law School. The University of Chicago. Public Law and Legal Theory Working Paper No. 384, vol. 97, pp 547–594
Freeman, M. (2007). Why it remains important to take children's rights seriously. *The International Journal of Children's Rights, 12*, 5–23.
Gasper, D. (2003). Nussbaum's capabilities approach in perspective: purposes, methods and sources for an ethics of human development, Institute of Social Studies, Working Paper Series No. 379, The Hague, The Netherlands. http://repub.eur.nl/pub/19137). Accessed 11 Dec 2013
Hartas, D. (2008). *The right to childhoods: Critical perspectives on rights, difference and knowledge in a transient world.* London, New-York: Continuum International Publishing Group.
James, W. (1910). *Philosophie de l'expérience.* Paris: Flammarion.
James, A., & Prout, A. (1990). *Constructing and reconstructing childhood: Contemporary issues in the sociological study of childhood.* Basingstoke: Falmer Press.
James, A., Jenks, C., & Prout, A. (1998). *Theorizing childhood.* Cambridge: Polity Press.
Matthews, H. (2003). Children and regeneration: Setting an agenda for community participation and integration. *Children and Society, 17*(4), 264–276.
Nussbaum, M. (2000). *Women and human development. The capabilities approach.* New York: Cambridge University Press.
Nussbaum, M. (2011). *Creating capabilities. The human development approach.* Cambridge: Harvard University Press.
Qvortrup, J., Bardy, M., Sgritta, G., & Wintersberger, H. (1994). *Childhood matters.* Aldershot: Ashgate Publishing.
Poretti, M., Hanson, K., Darbellay, F., & Berchtold, A. (2014). The rise and fall of icons of 'stolen childhood' since the adoption of the UN Convention on the Rights of the Child. *Childhood, 21*(1), 22–38.
Sen, A. (1992). *Inequality reexamined.* Oxford: Oxford University Press.
Sen, A. (1993). Capability and well-being. In M. Nussbaum & A. Sen (Eds.), *The quality of life* (pp. 30–53). Oxford: Clarendon Press.
Sen, A. (1999). *Development as freedom.* New York: Alfred Knopf.
Sen, A. (2002). *Rationality and freedom.* London/Cambridge: The Belknap Press of Harvard University Press.
Sen, A. (2009). *The idea of justice.* London/Cambridge: The Belknap Press of Harvard University Press.
Sirota, R. (2006). *Eléments pour une sociologie de l'enfance.* Rennes: Presses Universitaires de Rennes.
Stoecklin, D. (2013). Theories of action in the field of child participation. In search of explicit frameworks. *Childhood, 20*(4), 443–457.
Stoecklin, D. (2014). Transformation of children's lives through their rights. A new approach to agency. In L. Chisholm & K. Deliyanni-Kouimtzi (Eds.), Changing landscapes of childhood and youth in Europe. Cambridge: Cambridge Scholars Publishing.
UNCRC. (1989). *UN convention on the right of the child.* New York: United Nations.

Veerman, P. E. (1992). Towards a more integrated basis for the children's rights movement: The aims and outcome of the first International Interdisciplinary Study-Group on Ideologies of Children's Rights'. In M. Freeman & P. E. Veerman (Eds.), *The ideologies of children's rights* (pp. 357–63). The Hague: Martinus Nijhoff.
Weber, M. (1968). *Economy and society (1921)*. New York: Bedminster Press.
Weber, M. (1992a). L'objectivité de la connaissance dans les sciences et la politique sociales (1904). In J. Freund (Ed.), *Essais sur la théorie de la science*. Paris: Plon, Pocket (Collection Agora).
Weber, M. (1992b). Essai sur le sens de la "neutralité axiologique" dans les sciences sociologiques et économiques (1917). In J. Freund (Ed.), *Essais sur la théorie de la science*. Paris: Plon, Pocket (Collection Agora).
Zermatten, J., & Stoecklin, D. (2009). *Le droit des enfants de participer. Norme juridique et réalité pratique: contribution à un nouveau contrat social*. Sion: IUKB/IDE.

Chapter 2
Transforming Children's Rights into Real Freedom: A Dialogue Between Children's Rights and the Capability Approach from a Life Cycle Perspective

Mario Biggeri and Ravi Karkara

2.1 Introduction

Despite progresses, the long-standing material and immaterial deprivation of the children in many parts of the world has remained extraordinarily strong (UNICEF 2005; Trani et al. 2013). In particular, children are denied their rights including their right to participate to institutional changes.

In this paper we argue that a synergic dialogue between the Human Rights (HR) paradigm and the Human Development (HD) paradigm could be pivotal to rethink policies and actions.

In the last two decades the interchange between the HR and HD has increased substantially: a synthesis of this debate was found in the Millennium Development Goals (MDGs) most of which are indirectly connected to children issues. However, apart from this very important process aiming at settling a 'common vision of future goals and targets', much is still to be done from a theoretical, practical and empirical perspective. In the case of children this means to find synergies mainly between the United Nations Convention on the Rights of the Child (UNCRC) and the Human Rights Approach (HRA) – which has been used by UNICEF as a theoretical and practical framework for analysis on children issues – and the capability approach (CA), which was developed by Amartya Sen (1985, 1999, 2009a) and Martha Nussbaum (2000, 2010) and other scholars (see for instance Comim et al. 2008; Deneulin and Shahani 2009), and provides the intellectual foundation for the HD paradigm of the UNDP.

M. Biggeri (✉)
Department of Economics and Management, University of Florence, Florence, Italy
e-mail: mario.biggeri@unifi.it

R. Karkara
Youth (Global), United Nations Human Settlements Programme, Youth and Livelihoods, Urban Economy Branch, UN-HABITAT, New York, USA
e-mail: ravkarkara@gmail.com

D. Stoecklin and J.-M. Bonvin (eds.), *Children's Rights and the Capability Approach*, Children's Well-Being: Indicators and Research 8, DOI 10.1007/978-94-017-9091-8_2,

Therefore, the aim of this paper is twofold. On the one hand we explore the relationships and synergies between the CA and the HRA in the case of children. On the other hand we investigate if it is possible to analyse and to translate into practice this relationship using an equity, participatory and life cycle perspective.

The chapter is structured into five sections. In the second section, following Sen (2007) and Nussbaum (2006) we bridge the CA and the HRA, through the exploration of the main complementary relationships and synergies. Since both approaches are fully discussed in other chapters of this book, in this section we concentrate on links and synergies between the HRA and the CA. In the third section we focus on the role of participation and the life-cycle to combine and reinforce these two approaches. The analysis shows the potential positive synergies between rights and capabilities. In the fourth section we outline briefly some of the main policy implications of these findings. In the fifth section main conclusions are reported.

2.2 Bridging the CA and the HRA

In being both opportunity oriented the HRA and the CA can complement each other quite well from several perspectives.[1] In this section, we depart from identifying the strengths and weaknesses of each approach and how, by complementing and bridging each other, the main limits of both are overcome.

On the one hand the HRA is the main framework for national and international policies aimed at benefiting children. It is based on the 1989 UNCRC, some relevant ILO conventions, and on more recent other documents such as the Convention of the Rights of Persons with Disabilities (UNCRPD 2007) (with a supplementary document with reference to children), which has covered further areas of concerns. At the core of the HRA there are several principles and core articles. Two of them, Articles 5[2] and 12 of the UNCRC, are central for bridging the two approaches. In particular, Article 5 refers to children's "evolving capacity" for decision-making – a revolutionary concept in international law that has profoundly influenced the practice of organizations working in the field. The UNCRC Article 12 and the UN document, "A world fit for children" (UN 2002), already present a

[1] For proposals and discussions on how to complement the two approaches see, for instance, Sen (2004, 2005) and Nussbaum (2003). Attempts to link the CA and the HRA have been developed for adults by Nussbaum (1997), UNDP (2000), White (2002), OHCHR (2004), Alexander (2004) and Vizard and Burchardt (2007, 2011). For a tentative attempt to include participatory methods in the HRA, see Jonsson (2003). Recently, see the papers of Dixon and Nussbaum (2012) and Stoecklin and Bonvin (2014).

[2] Being able to influence decisions that affect an individual is one of the defining characteristics of human rights principles. When it comes to designing opportunities for them to participate, conditions need to be adjusted in accordance with a child's age and maturity (Article 5, UNCRC 1989).

new ethical attitude towards children in which children are no longer recipients of services or beneficiaries of protective measures, but subjects of rights and participants in actions affecting them. Thus, the right of children and young people to participate is a fundamental component of respecting them as holders of their own rights. Participation is one of the guiding principles of the UNCRC, yet it is arguably taken less seriously than the other key principles of universality, the best interests of the child, and survival and development (Karkara 2011).

On the other hand the main message of the CA is that social arrangements should aim to expand children's capabilities (opportunities and capacities) – their freedom to achieve valuable beings and doings.[3] Following Aristotle, the capabilities of a person have been associated with human flourishing, which suggests they can be realized in many different ways (Nussbaum 2000, 2011). This reflection helps to depict the multidimensional nature of child development and their aspirations (Hart 2012). The emphasis on well-being's multidimensionality is a key factor of the CA with respect to the most standard approaches to poverty analysis and it is particular relevant for children (Biggeri and Mehrotra 2011; Trani et al. 2013). Indeed, during the childhood the salience of each critical domain evolves over time resulting in a complex process of capabilities expansion (that children and their parents have reason to value) and that is connected to other elements such as goods and services available and the individual and societal conversion factors (see later, for more details). Thus, the child's flourishing from a CA perspective is an intrinsically multidimensional phenomenon. Moreover, by extending the capability approach to children (Biggeri 2004; Biggeri et al. 2011a) we recognize that children are social actors endowed with agency and autonomy (according to their maturity) who are able to express in different ways their points of view and priorities. Sen's capability approach considers human well-being, participation and freedom to be central objectives of economic and social policies (Sen 1999). However, if the CA offers a framework for the evaluation of social arrangements more broadly based on opportunity freedom and values, on the other hand it has limited capacity to facilitate process freedom which is well captured by a HRA. The relevance of the HRA in terms of advocacy, awareness and reasons for action is fully acknowledged in the literature and by Sen (2004, 2005, 2006, 2007, 2009a) and Nussbaum (1997, 2000, 2003, 2006). Sen also emphasizes that the CA can help to promote human rights (Sen 2004, 2005). Indeed, even if basic capabilities and basic rights are interchangeable, the CA still provides a more comprehensive framework for analysing and interpreting child development and well-being, as it allows us to explore the consequences of promoting rights (Ballet et al. 2011).

Therefore, in order to build a solid bridge it is useful to recognize both positive aspects (many) and the limits that are few but relevant. In particular, the HRA presents some limitations in terms of a comprehensive tool for understanding

---

[3] Capability is defined as "the various combinations of functionings (beings and doings) that the person can achieve. Capability is, thus, a set of vectors of functionings, reflecting the person's freedom to lead one type of life or another ... to choose from possible livings" (Sen 1992, p. 40).

children issues and for policy proposals, which can be fulfilled by the CA. Indeed, apart from few articles, most of the UNCRC articles see children as passive actors, and follow a paternalistic approach, which is typical of the classic human rights approach.[4] In other words, one of the concerns of using the HR discourse is that it runs the risk of focusing solely on lobbying at the expense of practical solutions.

> It may also lead to the inaccurate conceptualisation of impoverishment where there actually is none, simply because the international rights legislation does not reflect the socio-economic realities of children's lives, their relationships with other group members in their communities[5]

Furthermore, the prevalence of legalistic approaches to HR over libertarian (Freeman 1998), does not help the development of people's awareness of themselves as active social agents. In other words, the HR approach risks neglecting the importance of building active social citizens through participatory approaches. This also applies to children participation: its importance is well stated in the Article 12 of the UN CRC (1989) which defends the rights of the child to freedom of association and to peaceful assembly. However, when HR are evoked participatory processes play a residual role.

The CA is an opportunity based framework (similarly to the HRA) but at the same time is also an agency oriented approach. Therefore, the CA is able to take into account values and aspirations of children and their communities in a bottom-up manner. According to Biggeri et al. (Biggeri et al. 2011a, b), this allows for more flexibility and adaptation to different personal capacities (talent, skills and personal characteristics) and different cultural and societal contexts (Biggeri and Ferrannini 2014).

It is widely acknowledged that there is a potential tension between the intrinsic nature of the local communities and the implementation of human rights. HR can be not flexible enough to capture local contexts. Furthermore, when HR are perceived by the communities as the product of top-down political commitment, their fulfilment can be opposed by local norms which are at least apparently in conflict with them.

On the other side of the bridge, the HR can offer a long-term perspective on specific rights and duties and on the allocation of these duties. Following this direction, human rights can be seen as meta capabilities, and they can be seen as an expression of values and "local" human rights: this is the cornerstone. In other words the capability approach can extend the human rights agenda towards notions of secure rights and towards the "localisation" of international rights.

The CA positively addresses human and social diversity capturing the multidimensional and dynamic nature of child development. In particular, the dynamic nature of child development is depicted by the process of *evolving*

[4] In practice, no child has participated in drafting the Convention (Lewis 1998; Feeny and Boyden 2004) and, more generally, the rights international conventions follow a top-down fashion (Harris-Short 2003; Lewis 1998), without roots at local level. Baraldi (2009), for instance, underlines that amongst over 40 articles, only one concerns participation, while all others are about the control of children.

[5] Feeny and Boyden 2004, p. 18.

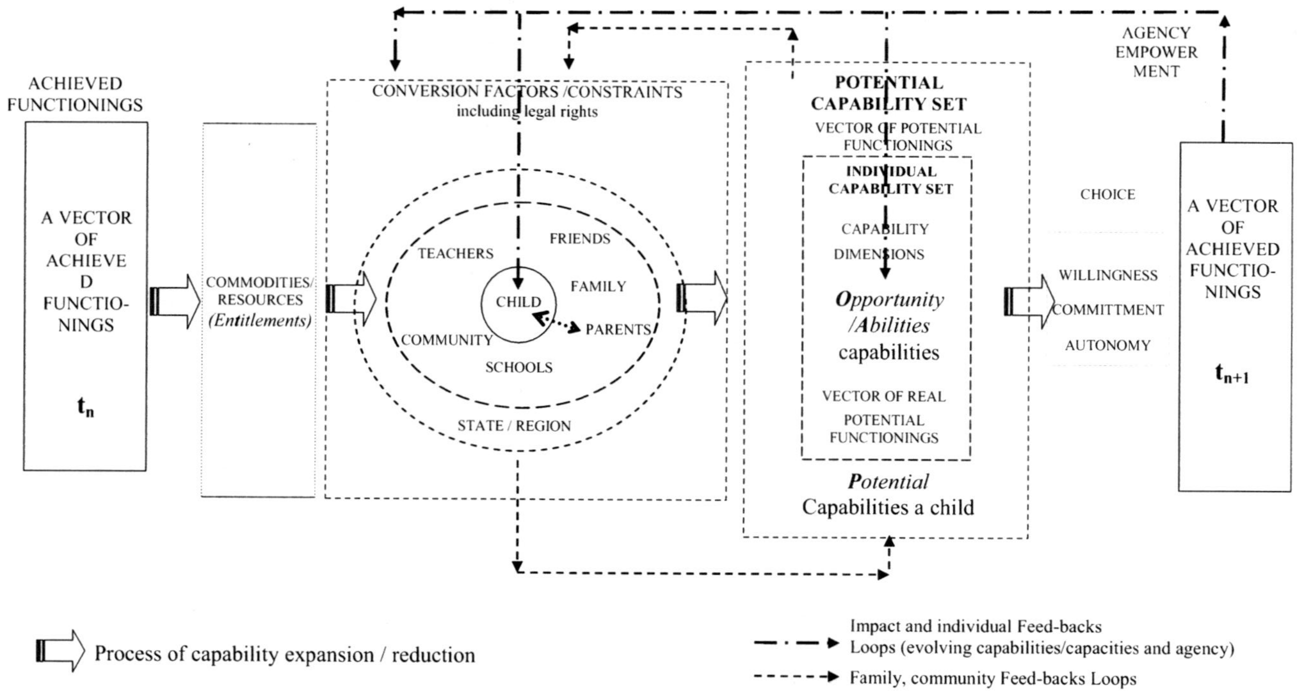

Fig. 2.1 Capability approach framework and the evolving capabilities (Source: Adapted from Trani et al. (2011b, p. 150), Trani et al. (2011a, p. 252), Ballet et al. (2011, p. 24), and Biggeri and Santi (2012, p. 378))

capabilities (Ballet et al. 2011), which incorporates the opportunity concept, the capacity concept (the evolving capacities concept in Art 5. UNCRC; see also Lansdown 2005) and the agency concept that evolve over time.

The evolving capabilities process, illustrated in Fig. 2.1, starts with the initial achieved functionings of a child at time t. The child is at the centre of the an ecology developmental process (Bronfenbrenner 1998), interacting with other agents (peers, teachers, family and community members) and drawing on and using entitlements (the availability of which is mediated through the families, schools, communities and regional/national entities). In the right end of the diagram (Fig. 2.1) the choice results in a functioning vector from the available capability set, which will determine the achieved functionings in the following time period (t + 1).

The dynamic core of the evolving capabilities process is expressed by the feedback loops that re-shape the potential capability set of the child and enhance or reduce agency and interact with conversion factors. The process of resources conversion into children's capabilities and functionings is significantly affected by how different institutions (including education, health services), norms and cultural characteristics interact with personal and household characteristics. In particular, legal rights – which should reflect human rights wisdom and opportunity in actual legislation – highlight entitlements. In the West bank city of Hebron, for instance, where roughly 800 Jewish settlers live surrounded by over 120,000 Palestinians, the visual anthropologist Hester Hertog shows how children' opportunities are denied by social norms and how the children themselves play an active role in discriminating and perpetuating the violence. Also Palestinian children of Hebron have difficulties in moving out and among Palestinian territories. This, in turns, limits children and adults social and geographical mobility.

It is important to notice that the child's capabilities are embedded in the community and affected by the capability set and achieved functionings (as also by their means, i.e. assets, disposable income) of their parents, as an outcome of a cumulative path-dependent process that can involve different generations of human beings. A life cycle perspective helps in understanding better different age barriers to the enjoyment of capabilities. Therefore, converting capabilities into functionings depends also on parents', guardians' and teachers' decisions, implying that the child's conversion factors are subject to further possible constraints. On the one hand parents/caregivers and teachers need to respect children's desires and freedoms but on the other hand they have to assist children to expand or acquire their capacity and further capabilities, even though this may need to be done against children's willingness and desire. This, for instance, "can become relevant to an education capability where parents and tutors can be inspired by different motivations and they can be either autonomy supportive (e.g. giving an internal frame of reference, providing meaningful rationale, allowing choices, encouraging self-perspective) or just controlling (e.g. pressure to behave in specific ways). … Therefore, the degree of autonomy is relevant in the process of choice" (Biggeri 2007).

The interaction between different capabilities and achieved functionings is a key element with important feedback-loops. Education and health are not only basic capabilities with an intrinis values but they are also instrumental for other capabilities.

Sen's approach emphasizes the importance of self-determination, especially when he distinguishes between well-being freedom and the process freedom or agency freedom (e.g. Sen 1985, 1992, 2009b). In the case of children Sen admits that this point could be questionable:

> If rights are interpreted in terms of freedoms that the right-holders should have, their usefulness must depend on how those freedoms are exercised. But can children take their own decisions? If the application of human rights to children must involve the children themselves taking well-considered decisions on the exercise of those freedoms then we would seem to be on the threshold of a manifest contradiction. Can children really take these decisions?[6]

However, this issue evaporates if connected to the concepts of agency and evolving capabilities (Ballet et al. 2011) and evolving capacities of the child, as stipulated in Art. 5. of UNCRC. According to Lansdown (2001):

> There is no lower age limit imposed on the exercise of the right to participate. It extends, therefore, to any child who has a view on a matter of concern to them[7]

Fostering participation since childhood helps the formation of capable agents (Bonvin and Galster 2010) but it needs also to create spaces of dialogue for decision making and for institutional change.

At the same time Sen clearly points out that the CA alone can be in shortfall (Sen 2005), since it is not sufficient to secure neither the opportunity freedom nor the process freedom, which have to be guaranteed by a HRA and legal framework. Sen (2007) argues that the field of human rights plays a crucial role in shaping one's well-being by the adoption of "freedom" as a normative tool. Indeed, many different forms of freedoms, such as freedom from hunger, from escapable morbidity or from premature mortality, can consolidate the obligations that society has towards children. The human rights language reminds us that children have justified and urgent claims to certain types of treatment, wherever they may live. "Human rights generate reasons for action for agents who are in a position to help in the safeguarding or promoting of the underlying freedoms" (Sen 2007).

The diagram reported in Fig. 2.2 shows the centrality of HRA in capabilities expansion as real freedoms and vice versa. Indeed, the acquisition of capabilities which in turns strengthens children's agency enhances the capacity of children to see their rights fulfilled.

The CA can distinguish between three types of capabilities (see Figs. 2.1 and 2.2) – the capacity/ability concept (A-capabilities) and the opportunity concept (O-capabilities) that together remind the standard concept of capabilities as achievable functionings and, finally, the potential concept (P-capabilities) valued capabilities but not achievable at the moment but potentially achievable in the future

[6] Sen 2007, p. 9.

[7] Lansdown 2001, p. 2.

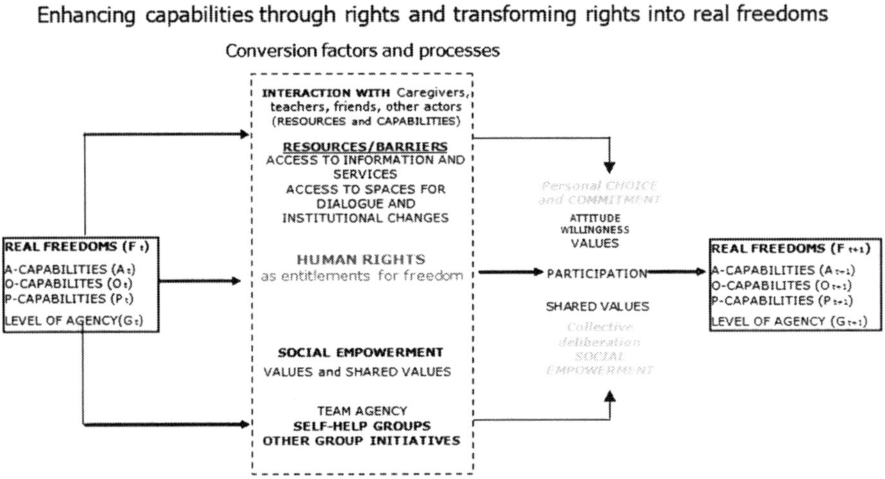

Fig. 2.2 Children's evolving capabilities and human rights at dialogue (Source: Adapted from Biggeri et al. (2011a, b))

(see also Gasper 2002, 2007; Bellanca et al. 2011). Another important concept to disentangle the evolving capabilities is that of agency (Ballet et al. 2011). This distinction is important to capture the dynamic dialogue between human rights and the evolving capabilities concept. It helps also to get a better perspective for complementary policy implications. The capability set, here reported as O-capabilities, is the overall set of achievable functionings, given the available conversion factors for instance social norms and the A-capabilities. For instance, in Pakistan in Swat (a Taleban area) a healthy girl (A-capability) has almost no chance to go to school against her willingness and to be educated and to develop her participation and agency. The school is in theory available but the social norms and fear of Taleban forbid her to be enrolled and attend the class (as well as to female teachers to teach). The girl is deprived of the O-capability to be educated i.e. it was not in her achievable functionings or capability set. However, this capability was in her Potential capability set (P-capabilities) i.e. those capabilities not reachable but considered by the girl (such as such as Malala Yousafzai and by part of the community) of high value. The community has to bring actions and policies to allow these children to get and to do (opportunity to be educated) what they have reason to value. In other words she was denied of her right to be educated.

In this context a two prong strategy needs to be accomplished. The first, and most obvious, is that the HR framework needs to be enforced in the area where the girl lives, while the second needed prong consists in an endogenous change within the society to re-elaborate social norms that do not allow the girl to flourish. These social and individual empowerment processes need time as well as an increased participation in decision making processes, and they need to be accompanied by access to information and spaces and tools for dialogue. All these changes would delineate and make explicit how in the "new" context the girl can receive her

Table 2.1 CRC articles and CRPD vs. capabilities domains

Children's capabilities domains	CRC articles direct	CRC articles indirect	CRPD articles directly correlated	CRPD undirectly correlated
Life and physical health	6, 23, 24, 25, 27, 29	(17), (19), (33), (37), (39)	10, 15, 16, 17, 22, 25, 28, 30	Preamble (l), (9), (12), (24), (26)
Love and care	7, 9, 18, 20, 21, 26, 27	(3), (10), (22)	8, 10, 22, 23	Preamble (x), 23
Mental well-being	23, 25, 27, 29, 37	(17), (19), (33), (39)	15, 16, 17, 25, 30	(9), (12), (24), (26)
Bodily integrity and safety	19, 25, 26, 37	(23), (24), (39)	11, 14, 15, 16, 17, 25, 28, 30	(9), (12) (24), (26)
Social relations	15, 27, 29	(12)	30	(19)
Participation	12, 13, 15, 17, 23, 29	(40)	3, 19, 29, 30	Preamble (o), (7), (9), (21), (24), (27)
Education	13, 24, 28	(32)	24, 27	(8), (9), (30)
Freedom from economic and non-economic exploitation	19, 32, 34, 36	(33), (35)	16, 27	(12)
Shelter and environment	24(c), 27(3), 29(c)		11	(25, (17)
Leisure activities	31	(40)	30	
Respect	16, 19, 23, 30, 39(2)	(2)	3	
Religion and identity	8, 14, 29, 30, 31	(2), (7), (37)	30	(22)
Time-autonomy		(31), (37)	3,19 20	(26), (27), (18)
Mobility		(31), (37)	18, 19, 20	(30)
Mobility (as accessibility)			3, 9, 19	(4), (20), (21), (25), (27), (28), (29), (30)

Source: Our elaboration on Biggeri and Mehrotra (2011) and Biggeri (2004) (Apart from Article 27 the following rights are relevant: right to survival (Article 6); right to health care (Article 24); right to enjoyment of full and decent life for children with disabilities (Article 23); right to social security (Article 26); right to basic education (Article 28); right to protection from economic or sexual or other forms of exploitation (Articles 11, 32–5); right to freedom of expression, thought, conscience, religion, association and information (Articles 12–17 and 30))

education. The results of the first prong (action) without the second prong would be very limited and vice versa.

Operationally the linkages between the HRA and the CA can be captured from a multidimensional perspective. As reported in Table 2.1, capability well-being domains are those conceptualised directly by children (see Biggeri et al. 2006). These domains adequately capture most of the UN CRC articles (and even more, those of the UN CRPD) (for detail see the appendix at the end of the chapter and Biggeri and Mehrotra 2011). The data reported in Table 2.1 are extremely interesting and challenging as they show how it is both possible and fruitful to complement the CA and the HRA. They also help to understand if more rights need to be considered, or which rights enforcement can help to reduce the current capabilities deprivation, especially those indicated by Sen (1985) as basic capabilities.

Therefore, we can follow Nussbaum when she writes that "The capabilities approach is closely allied to the human rights approach" and that, despite their differences, the capabilities approach is in fact "a species of the human rights approach".[8] In fact, she emphasizes that the advantages of the capabilities approach, as she would call it, that lends precision to the language of rights. However, it is also true that many basic capabilities, as they appear in Nussbaum's list, overlap with core human rights, such as those concerning political liberties and free choice of leisure time (among others).[9]

2.3 Participation, Rights and the Life-Cycle of Capabilities

As we have argued elsewhere individual and social empowerment and participation are key elements to favour children agency. From a life cycle perspective it is also important to consider the age and maturity of the child in defining the relevance of a capability approach and the level of participation. This means that a careful timing of interventions for children's well-being is required, including different types of education objectives and socialisation according to the age and the maturity of the child and to the child aspirations (Hart 2012). Children, from this point of view, by becoming part of the decision making processes, can also contribute to shaping future conversion factors and be considered as a vehicle of change.

Rights have a central role in guaranteeing the opportunity freedom as well as the process aspects of freedom. However, as we have argued in the previous section, human rights discourse does not automatically translate into social change. The most crucial way to realize human rights is through creating opportunities,

[8] Nussbaum (2006, p. 284).

[9] In the end, both perspectives refer to basic standards of humanity that should be fulfilled in the process of development and that need to be secured for the most vulnerable (Nussbaum 2006). Very important linkages between the HRA and the CA in the case of children have recently been outlined in the paper of Dixon and Nussbaum (2012).

capacities and participation. By participation we mean the process of sharing decisions that affect one's life and – in a broader sense – the dynamics of the community individuals live in. We argue that participation is not only a right ("right to participate"), it is also central for the process and agency freedom and it is instrumental to capabilities expansion and facilitating the fulfillment of the rights.

Therefore, capabilities expansion through participation works on realizing human rights and vice versa through focusing on available opportunities and values. Thus the CA and participation help in a certain sense to actualize and localize the HRA.

According to Karkara (2011):

> Supporting children and youth to be active right holders is central to the understanding of inclusive participation. Girls/young women and boys/young men from all backgrounds and diversities have their human right to participate in the realization of their rights based on their evolving capacities and age of maturity[10]

The framework presented by Karkara (2011) can be reinterpreted inserting the elements related to the capabilities expansion and agency as reported in Fig. 2.3.

Taking this holistic perspective requires a multi-sectoral and multidimensional response throughout the life cycle. This is to ensure that child and young people's participation is seen as cross cutting in all aspects of child rights programs, ranging from social budgeting, national plans of action in fields like protection, health, education, environment, water and sanitation, etc. (Karkara 2011). A life cycle analysis can help to identify the main capabilities according to the age, the talents and the maturity of the child. It also emphasizes that a careful timing of the interventions for children's well-being and well-becoming is required, including different types of education objectives.

The rights and capabilities enjoyed have an intrinsic value as well as an instrumental value in determining life trajectories of children and young adults. Figure 2.4 shows how HRA and the CA together can have an impact at individual and at community level.

Participation varies according to a child's evolving capabilities (opportunity, capacity and agency). Children can participate in different ways since the earliest ages. Competence comes through experience, and is not suddenly enjoyed at a certain age (Ballet et al. 2011). According to Karkara:

> Our earliest interactions establish our sense of who we are and the confidence and skills to express ourselves and negotiate our rights[11]

Thus, it is not just competences arising from experiences: adult perception of themselves is built upon early childhood experiences. For instance, boys and girls who are born into societies that practice discrimination, oppression and non-participation learn and may practice prejudicial behaviour during childhood. Some children easily bully other children and are likely to exclude certain groups of

[10] Karkara 2011, p. 17.

[11] Karkara 2011, p. 23.

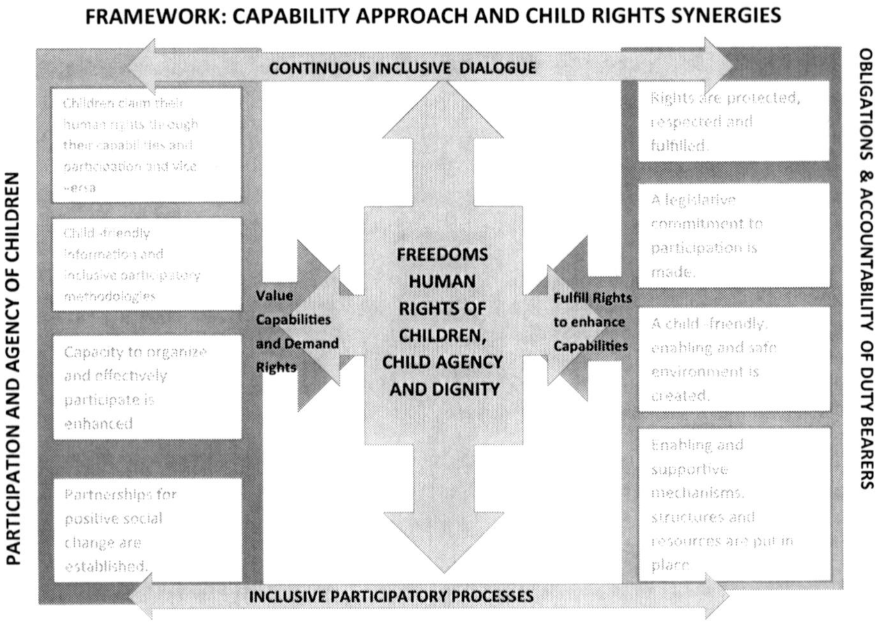

Fig. 2.3 Child rights, capabilities and participation (Source: Our elaboration)

children in their game, for example girls, children with disability and children from minority groups. If they go unchallenged, a young person may act on the basis of these stereotypes; this becomes discriminatory behaviour as they move into adulthood. A cycle of oppression and exclusion results in transmitting the same practices to the next generation and generally discourages participation and democratic processes. However, children experiencing exclusionary processes are not passive agents. They can progressively re-build a sense of personal worth and therefore they can break the cycle of oppression and exclusion. Being engaged in participatory processes since childhood might thus strengthen the capacity to resist exclusionary practices.

Building on work with children in the early years, a life cycle approach to children and young people's participation can be explored, enabling girls' and boys' participation at different ages and abilities. Therefore, a life cycle approach in a multidimensional perspective encourages building upon their strengths and abilities to participate. In practice, we need to access the childhood culture (James et al. 1998; Baraldi 2009) and to understand what 'childhood' means for girls and boys in each particular context and at different stages of the life cycle. What are girls and boys encouraged to do or not to do? What active role can girls and boys play?

It has to be acknowledged that, in recent years, UNICEF has attempted to increase children's participation substantially (see UNICEF 2002). Children's social participation needs to be visible in public contexts, being conducted through

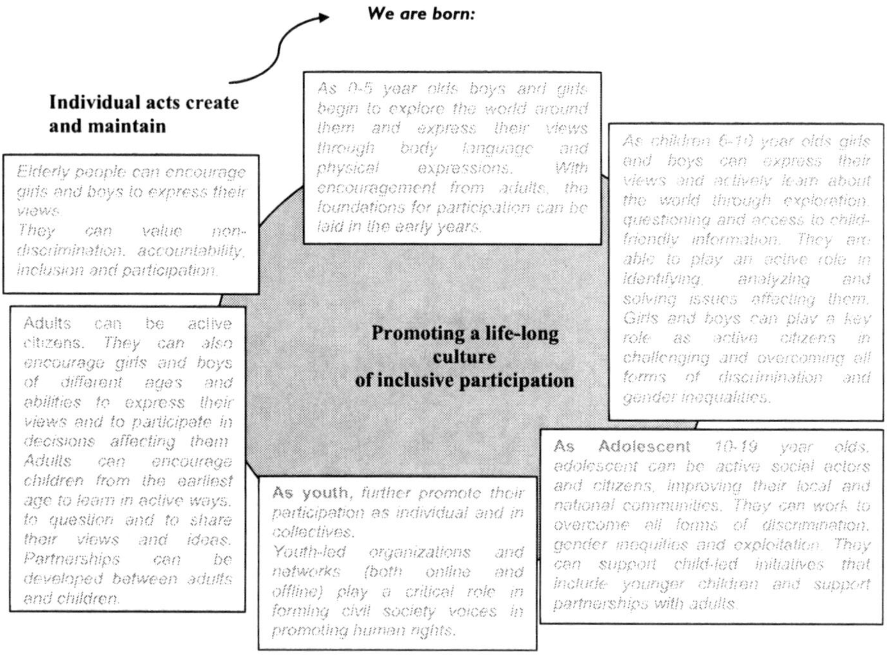

Fig. 2.4 A life-cycle perspective (Source: O'Kane (2003, p. 9) and Karkara (2011, p. 24) both adapted from Karkara (2003))

a clear manifestation of their citizenship and inclusion in a society that provides a full range of rights and opportunities (Biggeri et al. 2011b).

All these aspects have profound policy implications that will be addressed further below.

2.4 Policy Implications and Recommendations

Bridging between the CA with the HRA for transforming children's rights into real freedom requires a systematic understanding of the process of capabilities expansion and the role within this of human rights and legal rights. This analysis has a series of important and self-reinforcing policy implications.

Reducing the level of abstraction, the capability dimensions can be linked to previous works on human capabilities (see for instance Nussbaum 2000; Nussbaum 2003; Robeyns 2003) and to conceptualisation of children as subjects (Biggeri et al. 2006), and then establishing a link with the articles of the UNCRC as in Table 2.1.

The articles – or part of them – are recalled in Box 2.1 for each capability dimension only if they are directly or indirectly (reported in parenthesis) linked to each capability (Detrick 1999; Santos Pais 1999).

Box 2.1: Bridging Between Capabilities' Dimensions and CRC Articles

Life and physical health: being able to be born, being able to be physically healthy and enjoy a life of normal length. For instance, according to the UNCRC this is an inherent right to life (Art. 6) and a full and decent life. The child should be able to enjoy the highest attainable standard of health and access to facilities for the treatment of illness and health rehabilitation. States Parties shall strive to ensure that no child is deprived of his or her right of access to such health care services (Art. 23 and 24). Articles of the UN CRC 6, (17), (19), 23, 24, 25, 27, 29, (33), (37) and (39).

Love and care: being able to love and being loved by those who care for us and being able to be protected. This is fundamental in accordance with the age and maturity of the child.

The child shall be registered immediately after birth and shall have the right from birth to a name, the right to acquire a nationality and as far as possible, the right to know and be cared for by his or her parents (Art. 7). Care and protection of children in the areas of safety, health, competent supervision and appropriate assistance and protection (Art. 3). Both parents have common responsibilities for the upbringing and development of the child. The best interests of the child will be their basic concern (Art. 18). As a girl put it "Parent's must realise that they are responsible for their children's welfare" (girl -from Indonesia- UNICEF, Voice of Youth, 2003). Articles of the UN CRC (3), 7, 9, (10), 18, 20, 21, (22), 26 and 27.

Mental well-being: being able to be mentally healthy. Such as all forms of mental violence, injury or abuse, neglect or negligent treatment, maltreatment or exploitation, including sexual abuse. Articles of the UN CRC (17), (19), 23, 25, 27, 29, (33), 37 and (39).

Bodily integrity and safety: being able to be protected from violence of any sort. Such as all forms of physical or mental violence, injury or abuse, neglect or negligent treatment, maltreatment or exploitation, including sexual abuse. Articles of the UN CRC 19, (23), (24), 25, 26, 37 and (39).

Social relations: being able to be part of social networks and to give and receive social support. In accordance with the age and maturity of the child. Family friendship affiliations. Articles of the UN CRC (12), 15, 27, 29.

Participation: being able to participate in and have a fair share of influence and to receive objective information. In accordance with the age and maturity of the child. Children should not be voiceless. At least they must participate initially within the family and among friends and later with the community. Articles of the UN CRC 12, 13, 15, 17, 23, 29, (40).

Education: being able to be educated. Freedom of expression; this right shall include freedom to seek, receive and impart information and ideas of all kinds, regardless of frontiers, either orally, in writing or in print, in the form

(continued)

Box 2.1 (continued)

of art, or through any other media of the child's choice (Art. 13). Furthermore, the right of all children to relevant and good quality education (Art. 28). The development of the child's personality, talents and mental and physical abilities to their fullest potential. Articles of the UN CRC 13, 24, 28 and (32).

Freedom from economic and non-economic exploitation: being able to be protected from economic and non-economic exploitation. The Article 32 of the Convention recognizes "the right of the child to be protected from economic exploitation and from performing any work that is likely to be hazardous or to interfere with the child's education, or to be harmful to the child's health or physical, mental, spiritual, moral or social development" (UNICEF 2000: 62). Articles of the UN CRC 19, 32, (33), 34, (35), 36.

Shelter and environment: being able to be sheltered and to live in a safe and pleasant environment. Articles of the UN CRC 24 (c), 27 (3) and 29 (c).

Leisure activities: being able to engage in leisure activities and undertake projects. As reported in the article 31: 1. States Parties recognise the right of the child to rest and leisure, to engage in play and recreational activities appropriate to the age of the child and to participate freely in cultural life and the arts. 2. States Parties shall respect and promote the right of the child to participate fully in cultural and artistic life and shall encourage the provision of appropriate and equal opportunities for cultural, artistic, recreational and leisure activity. Articles of the UN CRC 31, (40).

Respect: being able to be respected and treated with dignity. Articles of the UN CRC (2), 16, 19, 23, 30, 39 (2).

Religion and identity: being able to choose to live or not to live according to a religion. In accordance with the age and maturity of the child. Freedom of thought, conscience and religion. States Parties undertake to respect the right of the child to preserve his or her identity, including nationality, name and family relations as recognised by law without unlawful interference (Art. 8). The development of respect for the child's parents, his or her own cultural identity, language and values, for the national values of the country in which the child is living, the country from which he or she may originate, and for civilisations different from his or her own (Art. 29). Articles of the UN CRC (2), (7), 8, 14, 29, 30, 31, (37).

Mobility: being able to be mobile. Articles of the UN CRC (31), (37).

Time-autonomy: being able to exercise autonomy in allocating one's time Articles of the UN CRC (31), (37).

Furthermore, following Trani et al. (2011b) it is possible to highlight (Fig. 2.5) the potential actions that could be undertaken and thus the role of policies within the CA framework. Human rights (on the left side) are determinant in.shaping, together with other factors, a common vision which is going to influence the community

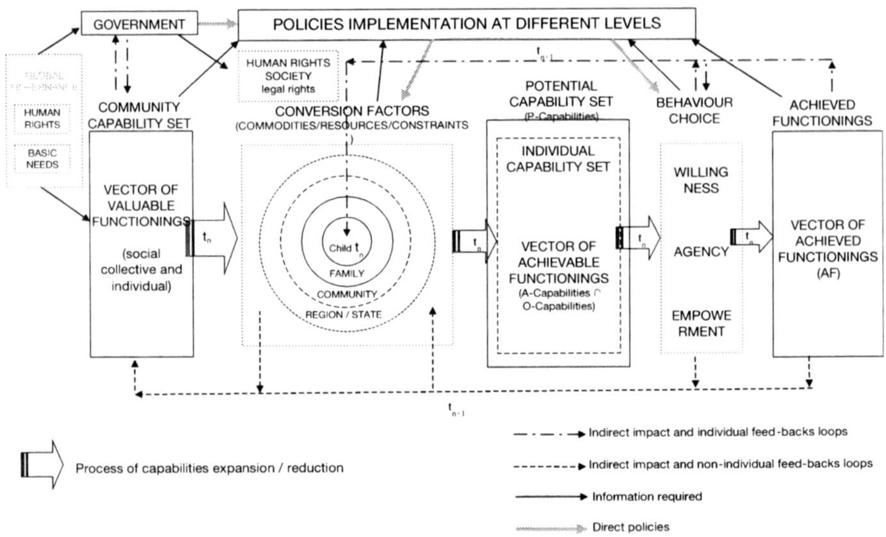

Fig. 2.5 Children evolving capabilities and policy makers' strategies according to values and human rights (Source: Own elaboration on Trani et al. (2011a, p. 252; b, p. 150) and Ballet et al. (2011, p. 24))

valuable functionings and capabilities – i.e. the community capability set that is composed of individual, collective and social capabilities – as well as government actions and, hence, the final achieved functionings or final outcomes. The community capability set (Fig. 2.5, large box at the far left) includes all potentially valuable functionings that should be guaranteed for members of the community, and that can be considered the starting point for policies implementation. These include the potential capability set of the children. More in detail, the diagram shows that policies can affect children well-being using the basic capabilities and human rights discourse by influencing three main aspects: public resources availability, the conversion factors (including legal framework and entitlements) and through services enhancing the capacities of the child. In this direction, Sen affirms that

> human rights should motivate the vision and the law, but they have to be distinguished from legal rights, since these human rights exist whether or not the makers and interpreters of law have had the wisdom and opportunity to reflect these rights in actual legislation. The legal relevance is posterior rather than prior to ethical reasoning, and legal use is not the only field of application of the ethical and political idea of human rights. This is not to deny that there can be very important legal connections that make the ideas of human rights more effective and consequential. Legislation can indeed, often enough help to promote the ethical claims reflected in human rights, and many concerned citizens and many NGOs have been intensely involved in promoting fresh legislation.[12]

[12] Sen 2007, p. 8.

At the same time however, although legislation is important, it is possible to protect and advance human rights through channels other than legislation. As mentioned in the previous sections, some human rights cannot be easily translated into legislation, thus some other instruments may be necessary to achieve social change (Sen 2007). Children capabilities thus depend on the capabilities of other persons. In synthesis:

> What opportunities children have today and will have tomorrow, in line with what they can be reasonably expected to want, is a matter of public policy and social programmes, involving a great many agencies.[13]

Human and sustainable development relies on people's freedom to make decisions and to advance key objectives as agents of change. Children and the youth (according to their age and maturity) will need the freedom to be educated, to be loved and cared for, to participate in community life, to be respected and to have freedom of expression and association (amongst many other capabilities and basic functionings). Therefore, it is also by being capable agents that people (including children and youth) can contribute to the environment in which they are educated, loved and cared for, as well as be able to speak freely, and participate in decision-making processes (amongst other things) (Biggeri and Santi 2012).

Therefore several policies and actions can be implemented at different stages of life and levels as reported in Figs. 2.3, 2.4 and 2.5. In practice, in this dialogue between the HRA and the CA, the synergies between the two are the basis for an advancement of capabilities and rights i.e. real freedoms. Following Karkara (2011) several actions and policies can become central. However, there are no linear processes on child and young people's participation; processes must be based on bottom up structures, with upstream advocacy and downward flow of commitment.

Here, we recall the central elements of this framework as a set of recommendations.

- Putting children at the centre, recognizing them as rights-holders as well as social actors (Biggeri et al. 2011a, b). This means a shift from skill-based childhood education to building their capacities to participate, promoting capable agents and enhancing critical, creative and caring thinking for active citizenship (Biggeri and Santi 2012; Nussbaum 2011). Children should be then taught not just cognitive skills, but also how to imagine new ways of connecting experiences and how to deal with emotional and motivational dimensions during reasoning and argumentation (Biggeri and Santi 2012).
- Recognising governments as primary duty-bearers accountable to their citizens – including children and youth – and to the international community. Creating structures and mechanisms where rights holders have continuous dialogue with duty bearers. This facilitates the connections between capabilities and functionings and the legal framework.

[13] Sen 2007, p. 5.

- Recognising parents and families as primary care-givers, protectors and guides – and supporting them in these roles (Comim 2011) by insuring resources as means for household capabilities satisfaction. Ensuring parenting programs are for both father and mother with clear focus on encouraging children, especially girls and young women, to express themselves and participate in decisions that affect them, based on their evolving capacities and maturity.
- Giving priority to young people and to creating a child and youth friendly environment (including spaces for dialogue among children). An environment that is based on respect, mutual trust and safe, so that children can engage and dialogue with key actors at all levels (local, sub-national, national, regional and global) and in all settings (family, community, school, media, internet, etc.) i.e. promoting their civic engagement. Integrating participation, civic engagement and citizenship education in school systems and informal education systems (primary, middle and secondary school, based on the principle of evolving capacities).
- Addressing horizontal inequalities and unequal power structures (class, gender, ethnicity, age, caste, religion, sexual preference, HIV status, etc.). Ensuring that while working with children/youth this power structure does not hinder child and young people's participation processes. For instance, being gender sensitive, tribal sensitive and disability sensitive and seeking inclusive solutions that involve a focus on those boys and girls who are at risk and who are discriminated against. "Policy makers and programmes must ensure a non-discriminatory and inclusive response that ensures the participation of girls, children/adolescent/youth with disabilities, indigenous and minority children/youth, young people living with and affected by HIV and AIDs, street children, children forced into prostitution, children on the move, etc. As applicable, work with boys/young men in various stages of their life cycle on gender equality" (Karkara 2011, p. 19)
- Holding a holistic vision of the rights of the child/youth while making strategic choices and taking specific actions. Setting goals in terms of the fulfilment of rights, as well as in terms of capabilities deprivation. At the same time, building partnerships and alliances for the promotion of human rights of children and youth. Developing inter-government working groups across various Ministries to ensure that child and young people's participation is institutionalised.
- Establishing a long-term goal, which clearly sets out international legal frameworks that are shared with governments, donors and civil society. Promoting implementation of General Comment 12, counting on international co-operation. Furthermore, aiming at sustainable results for children by focusing not only on the immediate, but also on the root causes of problems. It is crucial to address social norms and values that discourage participation and expression of women and children. Patriarchal structures and hegemonic norms of masculinities need to be made more inclusive. Establish an independent human rights institution like an Ombudsman office that supports child and young people's participation and other spaces of dialogue for children and among children to develop a

childhood culture, i.e. this means also to form their own organisation, networks and initiatives for social transformation.
- Using participatory, non-discriminatory, inclusive and empowering approaches, particularly with regard to children and young people. In particular, develop inclusive and participatory communication tools and channels that support children and young people to actively participate in social action. Apply an inclusive approach to use of progressive technology like social networking, etc.
- Encouraging legal and other reforms, such as regular monitoring mechanisms that create a much greater likelihood of sustainable change. Develop and adopt a child and young people's participation law with children and young people. In the meantime, establish local to global structures that are bottom up and promote children/youth's voices and partnerships with them in development. It is crucial to see community action to policy advocacy at national and international levels on child and young people's participation.
- Evidence and results on impact of children's and young people's participation is crucial. Develop young people centred knowledge management, monitoring and evaluation systems that promote active role of children in knowledge creation and knowledge management. Develop child led indicators.

2.5 Final Remarks and Future Challenges

"The promotion of human development and the fulfilment of human rights share, in many ways, a common motivation, and reflect a fundamental commitment to promoting the freedom, well-being and dignity of individuals in all societies." (UNDP 2000, p. 19). The CA and the HRA provide a different vision from the economic growth strategy, since they are opportunity based theories. Bridging the HRA and CA is one of the key goals of this chapter that is devoted to build up a synergic and fruitful dialogue among the two approaches. The capability approach is per se a powerful framework for understanding children's well-being in terms of capabilities since it forces us to think about the complexities that characterize their lives (from opportunity freedom to agency freedom). Yet, without an operative legal framework based on HRA, the CA is incomplete.

On the one hand the human rights approach can be used as the main argument for defending relevant capabilities for children. On the other one, the capability approach can become a framework for normative evaluation and policy implementation. Therefore, it seems that the libertarian HRA and the CA can dialogue and complement each other quite well, with the first calling attention to the deprivations, while the second can concentrate on their causes and assessment. Together, they can produce a cogent set of policy prescriptions and policy evaluation.

One critical point is that the *capability to be an agent* means being able, to a varying extent (according to the maturity and the age of the child), to influence his/her life and/or general rules in the society. Democratic societies should therefore aim to produce capable agents (Bonvin and Galster 2010; Nussbaum 2011;

Stoecklin and Bonvin 2014) and communities. Hence, the development of a democratic society implies the promotion of critical, creative and caring thinking among its citizens, so as to enhance their autonomy and at the same time, open their minds to confrontation and cooperation with different perspectives and points of view (Biggeri and Santi 2012).

Furthermore, an authentic and meaningful participation requires a radical shift in adult thinking and behavior from an exclusionary to an inclusionary approach for children and their capabilities, from a world defined solely by adults to one in which children contribute to build the kind of world they want to live in (UNICEF 2002, p. 5). This means that the on-going discussion on the post-2015 development agenda needs not only to ensure that children remain at the heart of the agenda but to make them part of these processes for institutional changes.

Acknowledgements This chapter is the fruit of an encouraging and ongoing debate with several scholars. During this period we have been privileged to receive comments and suggestions from a large number of people, all of which have been very useful to us. In particular, we would like to thank: Caterina Arciprete, Jerome Ballet, Nicolò Bellanca, Sara Bonfanti, Sandra Boni, Jean-Michel Bonvin, Enrica Chiappero-Martinetti, Federico Ciani, David A. Clark, Flavio Comim, Michela Da Rodda, Francesca D'Erasmo, Alex Apsan Frediani, Cristina Devecchi, Diego Di Masi, Maria Laura Di Tommaso, Jean-Luc Dubois, Andrea Ferrannini, Alex A. Frediani, Des Gasper, Caroline Hart, Vittorio Iervese, Leonardo Menchini, Ayacx Mercedes, Giuliana Parodi, Altair Rodriguez, Marina Santi, Daniel Stoecklin, Lorella Terzi, Elaine Unterhalter, Polly Vizard and Melanie Walker. Furthermore, organisers of the workshops within the Thematic group on Children Capabilities of the Human Development and Capability Association are thankfully acknowledged.

We have benefited of comments and suggestions by the participants of two relevant conferences on these issues where we both were invited as keynote speakers: the International Conference on "Human Development and Human Rights: Two decades of advancement, What's next for Children and youth? Agency and participation for enhancing equity", organised jointly by UNICEF and UNDP at Santo Domingo, Dominican Republic, 27–29th October 2011 and the Scientific Meeting on "Children rights and children capability approach: standpoints and prospects" at IUKB – Institut Universitaire Kurt Bösch, Sion, Switzerland 5–6th July 2012.

References

Alexander, J. M. (2004). Capabilities, human rights and moral pluralism. *The International Journal of Human Rights, 8*(3), 451–469.

Ballet, J., Biggeri, M., & Comim, F. (2011). Children's agency and the capability approach: A conceptual framework. In M. Biggeri, J. Ballet, & F. Comim (Eds.), *Children and the capability approach* (pp. 22–45). Basingstoke: Palgrave Macmillan.

Baraldi, C. (2009). *Dialogue in intercultural communities*. Amsterdam: John Benjamins.

Bellanca, N., Biggeri, M., & Marchetta F. (2011). An extension of the capability approach: Towards a theory of dis-capability. *ALTER. European Journal of Disability Research.*

Biggeri, M. (2004). Capability approach and child well-being. In *Studi e Discussioni*, 141, Dipartimento di Scienze Economiche, Università degli Studi di Firenze, Florence.

Biggeri, M. (2007). Children's valued capabilities. In M. Walker & E. Unterhalter (Eds.), *Amartya Sen's capability approach and social justice in education, Chapter 10* (pp. 197–214). New York: Palgrave.

Biggeri, M., & Ferrannini, A. (2014). Capability approach as a framework for development initiatives: A procedure for practical planning. *Journal of Human Development and Capabilities, 15*(1), 60–78.

Biggeri, M., & Mehrotra, S. (2011). Child poverty as capability deprivation: How to choose domains of child well-being and poverty. In M. Biggeri, J. Ballet, & F. Comim (Eds.), *Children and the capability approach*. Basingstoke: Palgrave Macmillan.

Biggeri, M., & Santi, M. (2012). Missing dimensions of children's well-being and well-becoming in education systems: Capabilities and philosophy for children. *Journal of Human Development and Capabilities, 13*(3), 373–395.

Biggeri, M., Libanora, R., Mariani, S., & Menchini, L. (2006). Children conceptualizing their capabilities: Results of the survey during the first children's world congress on child labour. *Journal of Human Development, 7*(1), 59–83.

Biggeri, M., Ballet, J., & Comim, F. (Eds.). (2011a). *Children and the capability approach*. Basingstoke: Palgrave Macmillan.

Biggeri, M., Ballet, J., & Comim, F. (2011b). Final remarks and conclusions: The promotion of children's active participation. In M. Biggeri, J. Ballet, & F. Comim (Eds.), *Children and the capability approach*. Basingstoke: Palgrave Macmillan.

Bonvin, J. M., & Galster, D. (2010). Making them employable or capable; social integration policy at the crossroads. In H. U. Otto & H. Ziegler (Eds.), *Education, welfare and the capabilities approach* (pp. 71–84). Opladen: Barbara Budrich Publishers.

Bronfenbrenner, U. (1998). The ecology of developmental processes. In U. Bronfenbrenner, P. Morris, W. Damon, & R. M. Lerner (Eds.), *Handbook of child psychology*. Hoboken: Wiley.

Burchardt, T., & Vizard, P. (2011). 'Operationalizing' the capability approach as a basis for equality and human rights monitoring in twenty-first-century Britain. *Journal of Human Development and Capabilities, 12*(1), 91–119.

Comim, F., Quizilbash, M., & Alkire, S. (Eds.). (2008). *The capability approach: Concepts, measures and applications*. Cambridge: Cambridge University Press.

Comim, F. (2011). Parenting style. In M. Biggeri, J. Ballet, & F. Comim (Eds.), *Children and the capability approach*. Basingstoke: Palgrave Macmillan.

Deneulin, S., & Shahani, H. (Eds.). (2009). *An introduction to the human development and capability approach: Freedom and agency*. London: Earthscan.

Detrick, S. (1999). *A commentary on the United Nations convention on the rights of the child*. The Hague: Martinus Nijhoff.

Dixon, R., & Nussbaum, M. (2012). Children's rights and a capabilities approach: The question of special priority. Public Law and Legal Theory Working Paper Series, Univ. Chicago.

Feeny, T., & Boyden, J. (2004). Acting in adversity – Rethinking the causes, experiences and effects of child poverty in contemporary literature. Working Paper Series, WP 116. Oxford: QEH.

Freeman, M. (1998). The sociology of childhood and children's rights. *The International Journal of Children's Rights, 6*(4), 433–444.

Gasper, D. (2002). Is Sen's capability approach an adequate basis for considering human developing? *Review of Political Economy, 14*(4), 435–461.

Gasper, D. (2007). What is the capability approach? Its core, rationale, partners and dangers. *The Journal of Socio-Economics, 36*, 335–359.

Harris-Short, S. (2003). International human rights law: Imperialist, inept, and ineffective? Cultural relativism and the UN Convention on the Rights of the Child. *Human Rights Quarterly, 25*(25).

Hart, C. S. (2012). *Aspirations, education and social justice: Applying Sen and Bourdieu*. London: Bloomsbury.

James, A., Jenks, A., & Prout, A. (1998). *Theorizing childhood*. Cambridge: Polity Press.

Jonsson, U. (2003). *Human rights approach to development programming*. New York: UNICEF.

Karkara, R. (2003, February). Children's participation and oppression. Presentation in Save the Children meeting on corporal punishment, Cairo

Karkara, R. (2011). *Essential reader on strengthening meaningful and ethical participation of children and youth – Social coherence and human rights*. Istanbul: International Training Program.

Lansdown, G. (2001). Promoting children's participation in democratic decision-making. *Innocenti Insight*. Florence: UNICEF Innocenti Research Centre.

Lansdown, G. (2005). The evolving capacities of the child. *Innocenti Insight*. Florence: Save the Children-UNICEF Innocenti Research Centre.

Lewis, N. (1998). Human rights, law and democracy in an unfree world. In T. Evans (Ed.), *Human rights fifty years on: A reappraisal* (pp. 77–104). Manchester: Manchester University Press. Mehrotra (2002).

Nussbaum, M. (1997). Capabilities and human rights. *Fordham Law Review*, *66*(2).

Nussbaum, M. (2000). *Women and human development*. Cambridge: CUP.

Nussbaum, M. (2003). Capabilities as fundamental entitlements: Sen and social justice. *Feminist Economics*, *9*(2–3), 33–59.

Nussbaum, M. (2006). Education and democratic citizenship: Capabilities and quality education. *Journal of Human Development*, *7*(3), 385–398.

Nussbaum, M. (2010). *Not for profit. Why democracy needs the humanities*. Princeton: Princeton University Press.

Nussbaum, M. (2011). *Creating capabilities: The human development approach*. Harvard: Harvard University Press.

O'Kane, C. (2003). *Children and young people as citizens: Partner or social chance, learning from experience*. Kathmandu: Save the Children.

OHCHR. (2004). *Human rights and poverty reduction. A conceptual framework*. New York/ Geneva: United Nations.

Robeyns, I. (2003). Sen's capability approach and gender inequality: Selecting relevant capabilities. *Feminist Economics*, *9*(2–3), 61.

Santos Pais, M. (1999). *A human rights conceptual framework for UNICEF* (Innocenti essays). Florence: ICDC/UNICEF.

Sen, A. K. (1985). Well-being, agency and freedom: The Dewey lectures 1984. *Journal of Philosophy*, *82*(4), 169–221.

Sen, A. K. (1992). *Inequality re-examined*. Oxford: Clarendon.

Sen, A. K. (1999). *Development as freedom*. Oxford: Oxford University Press.

Sen, A. K. (2004). Elements of a theory of human rights. *Philosophy and Public Affairs*, *32*(4), 315–356.

Sen, A. K. (2005). Human rights and capabilities. *Journal of Human Development*, *6*(2), 151–166.

Sen, A. K. (2006). What do we want from a theory of justice? *The Journal of Philosophy*, *CIII*(5), 215–238.

Sen, A. K. (2007). Children and human rights. *Indian Journal of Human Development*, *1*(2), 1–11.

Sen, A. K. (2009a). *The idea of justice*. London: Allen Lane.

Sen, A. K. (2009b). Capability: Reach and limits. In E. Chiappero-Martinetti (Ed.), *Debating global society: Reach and limits of the capability approach* (pp. 15–28). Milan: Fondazione Giacomo Feltrinelli.

Stoecklin, D., & Bonvin, M. (2014). The capability approach and children rights. In C. Hart, M. Biggeri, & B. Babic (Eds.), *Agency and participation in childhood and youth: International applications of the capability approach in schools and beyond*. London: Bloomsbury.

Trani, J.-F., Bakhshi, P., & Biggeri, M. (2011a). Re-thinking children's disabilities through the capability lens: A framework for analysis and policy implications. In M. Biggeri, J. Ballet, & F. Comim (Eds.), *Children and the capability approach* (pp. 245–270). Basingstoke: Palgrave Macmillan.

Trani, J.-F., Bakhshi, P., Bellanca, N., Biggeri, M., & Marchetta, F. (2011b). Disabilities through the capability approach lens: Implications for public policies. *ALTER. European Journal of Disability Research*, *5*(3), 143–157.

Trani, J-F., Biggeri, M., & Mauro, V. (2013). Child poverty and its multidimensional character: An empirical investigation on children of Afghanistan. *Social Indicators Review. Special Issue*.

UN (2002). A world fit for children. A/S-27/19/Rev.1. 12 July 2002, United Nations Children's Fund, http://www.unicef.org/specialsession/documentation/documents/A-S27-19-Rev1E-annex.pdf
UNCRC. (1989). *UN convention on the right of the child*. New York: United Nations.
UNCRPD (2007). *United Nations convention on the rights of persons with disabilities*. http://www.un.org/disabilities/convention/conventionfull.shtml. Retrieved on 30 June 2014.
UNDP. (2000). *Human development report: Human rights and human development*. Oxford: Oxford University Press.
UNICEF. (2000). *Monitoring progress towards the goals of the world summit for children: End-decade multiple indicator survey manual*. New York: United Nations Childrens Fund, Division of Evaluation, Policy Planning.
UNICEF (2002). *State of the world children 2003*. New York: UNICEF.
UNICEF. (2003). *Voices of Youth. The Bimonthly Newsletter*. www.unicef.org/voy/
UNICEF (2005). *State of the world children 2005*. New York: UNICEF.
Vizard, P., & Burchardt, T. (2007). Developing a capability list: Final recommendations of the equalities review steering group on measurement. *Centre for Analysis of Social Exclusion*, Mimeo.
White, S. C. (2002). Being, becoming and relationship: Conceptual challenges of a child rights approach in development. *Journal of International Development, 14*(8), 1095–1104.

Chapter 3
Observing Children's Capabilities as Agency

Claudio Baraldi and Vittorio Iervese

3.1 Introduction

In the past 10 years, the capability approach (Sen 1999a) has increased its importance as a theoretical framework aiming to define and measure individual well-being and used in different fields of human development (Robeyns 2006). In many areas, the capability approach has enhanced various and different research methodologies, both quantitative and qualitative, as well as dialogue among disciplines.

This chapter aims to enrich this interdisciplinary dialogue with two concepts originating from the sociology of childhood (hereafter SC), i.e. children's participation and children's agency. The use of these concepts established potential elements of convergence with the basic concepts of the capability approach (hereafter CA). Drawing on some empirical examples of promotion of children's participation and agency, the chapter shows that these two concepts can fruitfully support the CA in approaching the issue of children's well-being.

The significance of childhood depends on narratives built in societies, which are constructed in different ways. In modern Western societies, the mainstream narrative of children is an individualistic and developmental narrative. In a large number of papers and books, including the studies of James and Prout (1997) and Qvortrup et al. (2009), the SC has observed that the focus on the future of children overlooks the importance and characteristics of their present life, actions, and views of the world. The focus on development regards the "becoming" of children rather than their "being" children; in other words, children are important because they will become adults. The narrative of children's becoming has produced many methods and techniques of children's education and protection.

The CA is influenced by the narrative of children's becoming. Sen (1999b: 4) states that "capabilities that adults enjoy are deeply conditional on their experience

C. Baraldi (✉) • V. Iervese
Department of Studies on Language and Culture, University of Modena and Reggio Emilia, Largo Sant'Eufemia 19, Modena 41121, Italy
e-mail: claudio.baraldi@unimore.it; vittorio.iervese@unimore.it

D. Stoecklin and J.-M. Bonvin (eds.), *Children's Rights and the Capability Approach*, Children's Well-Being: Indicators and Research 8, DOI 10.1007/978-94-017-9091-8_3,

as children". Adopting this perspective, the CA has focused more on future outcomes of children's socialisation than on observation of children's wellbeing. This perspective is based on the combination of liberal theories and psycho-pedagogical theories. Liberal theories do not consider children in their conceptual framework for their inability to make choices for themselves. Psycho-pedagogical theories are based on a "socialization paradigm emphasizing children's development towards becoming mature human beings in the future" (Kjørholt 2002: 70). Therefore, the CA generally pays more attention to children's development and children's protection than to the promotion of children's participation, although it considers participation in social settings as a key element. This preference is clearly stated in Dixon and Nussbaum (2012):

> When people talk about children and children's rights, they often talk about the vulnerability of children (p. 573). When it comes to a vulnerability principle, for example, an important component to a CA (...) is that it recognizes human frailty and vulnerability as central parts of the human condition for adults as well as for children (p. 584).

However, many doubts have been expressed about the adequacy of methods and techniques based on the narrative of becoming in promoting children's participation. The main problem is that negative or insufficient expectations about children's participation create important barriers to the achievement of children's capabilities. For example, as Twun-Danso (2010: 136) notes, in Ghana, children' passivity depends on their expectations that they should rely on their parents' actions in their best interests; however, there is evidence that parents are retreating from their responsibilities, thus preventing the development of their children's capabilities. As Lansdown (2010) writes:

> children are denied opportunities for participation in decision making and the exercise of responsibility in many areas of their lives, because of extended social and economic dependency and an enhanced perception of the need for protection. This, in turn, reduces opportunities for developing the capacities for emerging autonomy, which then serves to justify their exclusion from decision making. A downward spiral is thus created (p. 16).

In this chapter, we aim at observing how children's participatory practices can enhance children's capabilities, i.e. freedoms and opportunities to act, and functionings, i.e. ways of doing and acting.

On the one hand, participation can be considered as a fundamental right in itself, on the other hand, it is also a means to achieve other rights. Participatory practices can involve a transfer of power to children and can therefore have an important impact in terms of socio-cultural change, improving respect for children as citizens and holders of rights.

We will first clarify the concepts of participation and agency in the CA and the SC. Then, we will highlight how the concepts of conversion processes and factors, which originate in the CA, can be analysed in the perspective of Conversation Analysis and Social Systems Theory. The former involves the observation of interactions as organised sequences of actions, whereas the latter observes social systems as communication systems. Both approaches can be applied to promotion of children's rights to agency, i.e. to children's rights to participate in decision making. In particular, we will consider the social conversion processes and factors in the education system, looking at the social structures of this system. We will analyse some adult-children interactions, which were videotaped during interventions of facilitation with the explicit aim to promote children's participation. Finally, we will discuss the general features of facilitation as a social conversion factor and promotion of children's rights to participate in decision making.

3.2 Children's Participation and Agency

According to Sen (1999a), participation means the possibility for individuals to make decisions about their own life freely; therefore, participation is considered fundamental in human development processes. The CA conceives participation as both a way to achieve individual development and as part of a capability set. According to Sen (1985, 1993) and Crocker (1998), a capability set should be evaluated in terms of quality as well as quantity of available opportunities. Therefore, a capability set is linked to variety of options; on the other hand, ways of doing and acting (i.e. functionings) are linked to the individual use of these opportunities (Clark 2006). Decision making is the activity that translates the abstract concept of participation in empirical reality, and it is the process in which we can observe how capabilities are managed. Nigel Thomas (2007) suggested that it is possible to distinguish between two competing visions of children's participation, focusing respectively on (1) children's and adults' sharing of the process of decision making, or (2) on shifting power from adults to children, as an outcome of decision making.

Against this backdrop, some studies have conceptualised capabilities as freedom to choose (e.g. Schokkaert and Van Ootegem 1990), or human talents and skills (e.g. Jasek-Rysdahl 2001). Sen (1999a) draws a distinction between "well-being freedom" and "agency freedom", the latter implying the individual capacity to exercise free will:

> the capability set would consist of the alternative functioning vectors that she can choose from. While the combination of personal functionings reflects her actual achievements, the capability set reflects the freedom to achieve: the alternative functioning combinations from which this person can choose (p. 75).

Sen (1992) has stressed the importance of self-determination. However, children are excluded from self-determination as they are not considered rational and reasonable beings. According to Nussbaum (2000: 78), rationality and reason consist in "being able to form a conception of the good and to engage in critical reflection about the planning of one's life". This way of analysing the development of capabilities implies an individualistic approach and a primary interest in the future of children as adults. In this perspective, children are usually observed as lacking 'agency freedom', and children's functionings are considered fundamental in determining the full development of children's future capabilities as adults. According to Saito (2003: 26), "when dealing with children, it is the freedom they will have in the future rather than the present that should be considered". However, it is possible to apply the CA to children, although they are not mature enough to take decisions for themselves.

In the SC, children's participation is associated with children's agency in their present life (James 2009; James and James 2008; James et al. 1998). Agency can be defined as "the capacity of individuals to act independently" (James and James 2008: 9). In this perspective, agency means that a course of action is one among various possibilities (Giddens 1984; Harré and van Langhenove 1999) and implies the availability of a range of choices of action for the individual. However, the concept of agency does not only indicate an individual competence, but also the social relationships in which individuals are involved (Alanen 2009; James 2009). Observing social relationships, it is possible to find out if and how individual competences can be converted in capabilities. Children's participation can regard formal decision making (Percy-Smith and Thomas 2010: 357), as well as social relationships that characterise their everyday practices.

It is possible to understand agency as the capability of individuals to both shape their own lives, and to influence their social contexts. However, children's agency can be observed only in specific forms of social participation, which highlight children's right of choosing and making decisions. Agency means opening up different courses of action in communication processes. By opening up these different courses of actions, agency can also enhance social change; therefore, agency can be defined as a specific form of active participation that enhances unpredictable social change, thus showing children's capabilities as opportunities to achieve functionings, i.e. to achieve ways of acting. Hence, the meaning of children's agency is closely associated with change and unpredictability in social processes, particularly in interactions, in which children's actions always affect their interlocutors' actions; more specifically, agency means that individual actions can also enhance the transformation of the structures of interactions.

The SC claims that in many social practices, participation is seen primarily as an instrument for the smooth functioning of society, unilaterally designed for adults (Craig 2003; Jans 2004; Matthews 2003). The institutional attention continues to be focused much more on the contribution of social systems to children's development rather than on children's active contribution to social systems (Prout 2003). Therefore, children are expected to fit into adult ways of participating in institutional contexts. In this context, the goal of changing the societal status quo through children's participation is observed as prominent. Participation is primarily observed as an involvement in decision making (Blanchet-Cohen and Rainbow 2006; Hill et al. 2004; Sinclair 2004; Thomas 2007) through which children can feel influential (Holland and O'Neill 2006). This approach supports the recognition of children's rights to participate in decision making concerning social systems.

To sum up, agency can be observed by analysing three aspects. Firstly, agency can be observed as participation in social processes rather than as individual freedom. Agency is visible in communication processes, in particular in interaction as a specific social system, i.e. communication system. According to Niklas Luhmann (1984), a social system is composed by a series of communicative events, and reproduces itself through recursive communication processes, in which each communication event refers to other communication events (e.g. "how are you?", "Fine thanks and you?", "I'm fine" etc.). Interaction is a specific type of communication system, which exists when the participants perceive one another, i.e. when participants' mutual perception is relevant for communicating. If capabilities are observed as a display of agency, they are visible (and therefore *exist*) only if they are displayed in communication. Therefore the interplay of individual capabilities and social structures can be explained by observing how children's actions are included in communication systems. This approach thus highlights children's multiple competencies in social contexts by stressing the importance of children's agency in communication, e.g. in educational interactions (e.g. Baraldi 2008; Baraldi and Iervese 2010).

Secondly, agency does not only imply individual competence in acting, which is displayed in communication systems, but also specific social conditions promoting the expression of this competence. If for some children participation may open up new opportunities, choices and rights to take decisions, for others, who live in situations of conflict and poverty, participation may simply be essential to assure their right to survive, e.g. in conditions in which children need to work (Biggeri et al. 2006; Liebel 2003). Therefore, children's agency cannot be achieved without the establishment of particular social conditions, i.e. particular structures in social systems.

Thirdly, agency can be seen as a way of promoting change of social structures (Giddens 1984); children's agency can be seen as right to promote structural transformation, e.g. planning the urban environment (Baraldi 2003). Children's participation in difficult situations can also be seen as a key strategy in transforming their relationships with adults, e.g. the relationships with parents in the case of working children (e.g. Abebe and Kjørholt 2009).

Ultimately, observing children's agency means looking at (1) the structures that promote agency in communication processes, and (2) the ways in which agency modifies the structures of communication processes. Against this backdrop, our main questions are: To what extent can children's agency enhance social change? What kind of social change is possible through children's agency? How is this social change achieved?

3.3 Social Conversion Processes and Factors

Already in the early 1990s, Rogoff (1990: 22) stated that: "children are not separate entities, that become capable in the future", but they are "inherently engaged in the social world". In the last years, the CA has increased its interest in children as autonomous social agents. In particular some recent studies, mobilizing the CA, have conceptualized children as capable agents (Babic 2011; Biggeri et al. 2011; Biggeri et al. 2006). This interest has been translated into research that considers: (1) children's activation of capabilities through their participation in social contexts (interacting with peers and adults); (2) children's capabilities as the result of a social coordinated process, not only as individual skills.

In relation to these two aspects, the CA asserts that children's ability to convert resources and commodities into capabilities and functionings depends on *conversion factors*. Both individual freedom and group freedom may be enhanced or constrained by access to resources, i.e. by "entitlements" (Sen 1981, 1984). The ways in which these resources can be used depend on "conversion factors" (Burchardt and Vizard 2011). The CA accounts for interpersonal variations in the conversion of resources and commodities into capabilities and functionings. These interpersonal variations depend on different kinds of conversion factors: *personal* factors (e.g. metabolism, physical condition, sex, reading skills, intelligence); *social* factors (e.g. public policies, social norms, discriminating practices, gender roles, societal hierarchies, power relations); *environmental* factors (e.g. climate, infrastructure, institutions, public goods). Conversion factors affect individual abilities to transform means into achievement, i.e. what is generally called the individual conversion rate (Sen 1992); conversion factors are "technical" constraints determining conversion rate, which indicates the conversion factors affecting and determining individual abilities in transforming resources into achievements.

We have looked at communication systems promoting children's active participation seen as the social conversion processes of children's human resources (or human capital), including rights, into capabilities as agency. In this perspective, the social conversion factors of agency can be observed in communication systems – in particular in adult-children interactions – which shape policies, practices and roles and which break the 'generational order' of children-adults social relationships (Alanen 2009), based on power relations and societal hierarchies. On the basis of the existing generational order, children participate in hierarchically structured communication within social systems, which restricts their agency. For this reason, in social systems, children's agency is less developed and is observed as less relevant than adults'.

The achievement of children's agency needs the construction of specific opportunities, in particular it needs specific adults' promotional actions. Given the mainstream narrative of children, adults' actions have frequently the only aim of stimulating children's actions as responses to adults' questions or instructions. Children's agency requires specific conditions of promotion, not just elicitation of actions. In particular, the promotion of children's agency requires that adults' actions aim to enhance unpredictability of children's active participation. The paradox here is that actions showing children's agency are promoted by adults' actions; therefore, the incidence of children's agency in social systems is proportional to and interdependent with the incidence of adults' agency. The social relevance of children's agency is proportional to the relevance of its social promotion. However, the promotion of children's agency is not achieved through adults' individual actions; it is achieved in communication systems, as the interplay of adults and children's actions.

Against this backdrop, the promotion of children's agency cannot mean building consensus or searching for an agreement, but opening, accepting and managing differences and conflicts in communication processes (Baraldi and Iervese 2010). One of the most challenging narratives in the past few years (and probably one of the most stimulating for the future) has been the importance of children's active participation not only in terms of having the right to be heard (art. 12, UN Convention on the Rights of the Child) and to expression (art. 13, UN Convention on the Rights of the Child), but also the right to choose among alternatives in communication systems, i.e. in terms of practicing agency rather than simply having voice. For example, children can be heard and can express their rights by asking for more time to play or for less homework, but the real difference regarding their rights is their possibility to decide rules and time for play and homework. Supporting and improving children's capabilities means promoting children's participation beyond their right to speak and to be heard, to a wider concept of active citizenship, which means rights to contribute to the structuring of social systems. In this approach, therefore, children's capabilities are displayed in social forms, i.e. as forms of agency in communication systems.

The methodological problem in researching children's agency is to observe the interplay between children's active participation and adults' actions enhancing participation rights, thus investigating the ways in which children's agency is promoted and children's choices are supported in communication processes (Baraldi and Iervese 2012). An analysis of this kind regards the ways in which:

1. Children and adults' actions are interrelated (e.g. certain answers follow certain questions or proposals);
2. Each action influences another one, making it relevant or likely (e.g. certain questions or proposals influence certain answers);
3. The chains of these actions constitute interactions as communication processes;
4. These interactions are part of wider communication systems (e.g. education, families, healthcare);
5. Communication systems highlight the meanings of children's active participation. Children's active participation can be highlighted in communication systems, through: (a) the production of information (what children say) and the ways of acting (how children say it); (b) the change that this production of information and these ways of acting introduce in specific communication processes, (c) the change that this production of information and these ways of acting promote for social structures (e.g. of education, families, healthcare) that are visible in communication processes, i.e. agency.

This kind of analysis offers two important advancements in the study of social conversion processes. Firstly, it makes it possible to observe how children and adults' actions are coordinated, as both children and adults are responsible and competent interlocutors in interaction. This clearly does not mean that there are no social differences between adults' actions and children's actions, but that we need an "analytically symmetrical" approach (Christensen and Prout 2002) to make them visible. Secondly, this analysis makes it possible to observe interactions within wider communication systems, such as the education system (Luhmann 2002). Therefore, it enables the observation of children's capabilities and rights to participate in decision making in both interactions and wider social systems, as a result of a 'participation chain' (ib.) that involves both children's actions and adults' actions. The observation of the participation chain, and the ways in which it affects social systems, enables the empirical description of conversion processes.

The analysis of interactions, as specific communication systems included in wider communication systems (e.g. education system, family, healthcare system), provides a way of understanding and describing children's capabilities as agency. This analysis requires a methodology to closely observe how children and adults' actions are interrelated in the interaction, and how children's agency can enhance social change. An effective methodology of this kind is Conversation Analysis (Sacks et al. 1974). Conversation Analysis observes interaction as a sequence of actions (turns) produced by the participants. This sequence is organised, as any action reduces the range of possible next actions (Goodwin and Heritage 1990) and new actions show their being in tune with former actions. Conversation Analysis regards participants' ways of taking turns (acting) in the interaction and organising sequences of turns. Agency can be analysed as displayed through the design of turns and in the sequence organisation in which these turns are included (Heritage and Clayman 2010). Turn design indicates how agency is displayed, i.e. it indicates the ways in which children take initiatives and make decisions, and sequence organisation affects the success of agency, as children's initiatives are intertwined with their interlocutors' actions and reactions, which condition their success; participants' agency can be observed through the ways in which their actions 'project', i.e. influence, the content and the design of next actions.

Conversation Analysis also highlights that sequence organisation in the interaction is based on particular social structures. One interesting example of these structures is epistemic authority (Heritage and Raymond 2005), i.e. authority in the management of rights and responsibilities for knowledge and information. For example, in the education system, the teacher's role implies rights and responsibilities for teaching, and in the healthcare system the doctor's role implies rights and responsibilities for diagnosis and therapy. Epistemic authority depends on the social construction of participants' epistemic status (Heritage 2012), i.e. the social construction of their autonomous access to knowledge and information. In the interaction, children's participation can be described as recognition of epistemic status and display of epistemic authority, for example in the interplay between children's talk initiatives, and adults' reactions to these initiatives, which can be either assessments of children's performances or recognition of children's rights of access to knowledge. In particular, the recognition of epistemic status and the level of epistemic authority are made visible in the interplay of children and adults' actions that upgrade (recognition) or downgrade (assessment) rights and responsibilities for knowledge.

The analysis of structures of interactions is not sufficient to explain children's agency and its promotion, as specific interactions cannot ensure stable conditions for children's active participation. The analysis of the structures of wider social systems, in which these conditions are established, is needed. This analysis can include the following structural presuppositions: (1) coding, i.e. a basic distinction between positive and negative values guiding and structuring communication systems (Luhmann 2000); (2) positioning, i.e. the forms of roles or personal expression created and established in the social systems, in which children and adults' participation is made meaningful and their actions are made intelligible (Harré and Langhenove 1999); (3) forms of expectations (Luhmann 1984), originating from coding and positioning and defining the ways in which adults and children are expected to act in the interaction. In the case of the education system, coding is evaluation, which distinguishes between correct and incorrect children's positioning, observed as students' role performances, and expectations have a cognitive form, i.e. they are expectations of change of children's personalities. Based on these structural presuppositions, agency is not adequately enhanced (James and James 2004) in the education system.

To sum up, the possible indicators of agency and promotion of agency in communication processes are:

1. Turn design (e.g. questions, assessments, minimal responses, such as "okay", "yes", "mm");
2. Sequence organisation (positions, combinations and alternations of different turns);
3. Structures of the interaction (e.g. epistemic status and authority);
4. Structural presuppositions of the social systems in which the interactions are included (coding, positioning, forms of expectations).

The structural presuppositions of these social systems (education system, healthcare system, etc.) can be considered as the most important social conversion factors from resources and rights of choosing into capabilities as agency, as we will see for the case of the education system in the next section.

3.4 The Analysis of Social Conversion Factors in the Education System

The present analysis draws on a long-term research project based on video-recorded classroom interactions involving children and adolescents. In particular, we have analysed data regarding special forms of education, such as education to dialogue, positive relationships, respect of cultural difference, peace and memory of war and violence. Data were collected in different settings and geographical areas; the investigated interactions were based on different methodologies, but "facilitation" of communication was their common form. Facilitation is interesting because it aims to create adequate conditions for children's agency.

In the present and following sections, we shall present some examples of sequence organisation, which show the ways in which facilitation of children's participation was achieved in some of the recorded interactions. In particular, we shall analyse some unpublished data, collected in a research project, regarding the facilitation methodology, known as Methodology of Narrative and Reflection (hereafter MNR). MNR is employed by an association of teachers working as facilitators in many schools of an important Italian town (Genoa). The research project analysed interactions in ten classrooms, for a total of 42 meetings between facilitators and students, and about 84 h of recorded and transcribed interaction. In what follows, we shall analyse three extracts from this huge corpus. The analysis of these extracts aims at showing some social conversion processes and factors regarding capabilities as agency. For this purpose, in our analysis we shall distinguish between the general presuppositions of the promotion of children's active participation and the specific presuppositions of the promotion of children's rights to agency, i.e. specific right to participate in decision-making in social systems. The general presuppositions of active participation consist in those social structures that promote children's actions without important consequences for social change, i.e. for decision-making. The specific presuppositions of rights to agency consist of those social structures that allow children to participate actively in social change, by participating in decision-making in social systems.

This analysis shows that social change can be enhanced through children and adults' turns, but it is determined only in the self-organisation of a communication system. Adults and children's actions enhance the building of specific structures of interaction, e.g. particular forms of epistemic status and authority, reducing the range of interlocutors' actions; these interactional structures can trigger structural changes in the wider social system. Therefore, social change may concern both the structure of the interaction (e.g. epistemic status and authority), and the structures of social systems including the interaction (i.e. coding, positioning and forms of expectations).

The main sequence organisation in classroom interaction between teachers and students is the IRF sequence (Mehan 1979), which is made up of teacher's Initiation (often questions), student's Reply, and teacher's Feedback (evaluation). Each of these actions is designed in such a way as to project the next one. This form of IRF sequence is based on the social structures of teacher's superior epistemic status and authority, evaluation (coding), positioning of teachers and students in role performances, and cognitive expectations. These structures work as social conversion factors of a very limited children's participation, because children are positioned in the role of responders, and in the uncomfortable position of being evaluated for their replies. The IRF sequence indicates a hierarchical structure of the adult-children interaction and of the wider education system in which this interaction is placed; this hierarchical structure restricts the opportunities of conversion from children's resources to children's capabilities.

This form of IRF sequence has been observed as persistent in classroom interactions, although with some variations and mitigations (e.g. Farini 2011; Margutti 2010; Walsh 2011). Our data do not confirm that this form of IRF sequence is generalised. Rather, they highlight the existence of other forms of IRF sequences, which are enhanced by the specific structure of facilitation. Facilitation is activated in situations in which adult's evaluation of children's actions is discouraged, and the interaction is based on mitigations of hierarchical structures, and favours dialogue, positive relationships, and respect of different perspectives.

The analysis of our data shows that facilitation frequently includes IRF sequences in which facilitators ask questions and give feedback. However, these sequences are structured differently from the traditional ones. Extract 1 concerns the interpretation of Saverio's behaviour. Saverio is the protagonist of a written text, including a narrative concerning children, which was handed out to the students and commented on in small groups, following a recurrent procedure in the MNR. In extract 1, the facilitator asks a question in turn 1, about Saverio's needs as they emerged from the text. A student (M1) answers in turn 2, and the facilitator gives a feedback in turn 3. This feedback is not an evaluation of turn 2, rather it is a formulation (Heritage 1985), which glosses the meaning of turn 2 and thus acknowledges understanding and acceptance.

Extract 1

1. `FAC: quindi quale esigenza dimostra questo Saverio o chiunque sia?`
   `So, what kind of necessity does Saverio or whoever show?`
2. `M1: desiderio di compagnia comunque`
   `Desire of company anyway`
3. `FAC: quindi al gruppo non si rinuncia`
   `So you can't renounce the group`

Formulations summarise, gloss, or develop the gist of an earlier statement; they "advance the prior report" by "shifting its focus, redeveloping its gist, making something explicit that was previously implicit in the prior utterance, or by making inference about its presuppositions or implications" (Heritage 1985: 104), projecting a direction for subsequent turns by inviting new responses from answerers. Formulations, as third-turn feedback, seem to be particularly useful to enhance children's active participation in interactions. They can both show understanding and acceptance of the previous turn(s), and project further turn(s), in which students can actively participate. Formulations reveal that first-turn questions are referential questions which look for students' autonomous perspectives. Therefore, IRF sequences that include formulations can facilitate (i.e. promote and support) children's active participation.

Here, however, we are interested in children's initiatives and in their (potential) agency, rather than in facilitators' initiatives. Therefore, we shall comment on sequences in which: (1) children initiate the sequence through a turn design that displays potential agency (I); (2) facilitators reply through a turn design that either promote or does not promote opportunities for children's agency (R); (3) children give some feedback, either exploiting or not exploiting the opportunity they are given, thus projecting facilitators' subsequent actions with their own actions (F). We are interested in these forms of IRF sequence because they may potentially promote children's agency (and capabilities). In the following section, we shall describe three examples of IRF sequences; all of them are initiated by children and show the interplay between children's participation, the self-organisation of facilitation interactions, and wider social systems.

3.5 Forms of IRF Sequences and Facilitation

In this section, we will show how different forms of IRF sequences, which are achieved through facilitation of classroom interactions, can lead to different results in terms of rights to children's agency.

In extract 2, the children introduce some relational problems with their teachers. The facilitator tries to stop their claims by diverting the topic of conversation. Extract 2 shows that the children's initiatives may be blocked in the interaction, preventing the achievement of both children's agency and change of epistemic authority in the interaction.

Extract 2

1. `M1:` `In questa classe no va beh non lo dico, magari qualcuno sta più zitto di un altro, cioè che non disturba il professore, allora se quello che è stato zitto e fa una verifica da schifo, cioè l'aiuta e magari gli dà lo stesso voto di quello che fa più casino anche se ha fatto le cose più giuste.`

   `In this classroom no ok I won't say it, maybe someone is more silent than others, I mean he doesn't disturb the teacher, so if the one who was silent does really bad on a test, I mean he helps him and maybe he gives him the same mark as the one who disturbed even if this did better.`
2. `FAC:` `e diciamo che umanamente possono succedere queste cose, ma ma voi stavate dicendo invece, mi pare, che emergesse un concetto, vorrei capire se è condiviso, che l'insegnante se deve aiutare tutti, deve aiutare il singolo.`

   `And let's say that it is human that these things can happen, but but you were saying that, instead, it seems to me that a concept emerged, I would like to understand if it is shared, that if the teacher must help everybody, he must help the individual.`
3. `M2:` `Se se lo merita.`

   `If he deserves it.`

In turn 1, M1 (a male student) introduces the topic of the difficult relational situation in the classroom, showing direct access to knowledge, i.e. a high epistemic status. In turn 2, the facilitator makes a quick comment about the complaint introduced by the student (*let's say that it is human that these things can happen*), then she changes the topic, although with some embarrassment, as shown in the repetition of "but" and in the use of "it seems to me" (*but but you were saying that instead it seems to me*). In turn 3, M2 aligns with the new topic proposed by the facilitator, although with an autonomous comment (*If he deserves it*) that shows some reluctance to accept the facilitator's positioning.

In this case, the student (M1) initiates the sequence, showing his epistemic status (autonomous access to knowledge about the relationship with the teachers) and upgrading his epistemic authority (right and responsibility in producing knowledge about this relationship). However, the facilitator blocks the student's initiative, restoring her own epistemic status and therefore the normatively expected organisation of the interaction, by upgrading her own epistemic authority. Firstly, she upgrades the level of abstraction of the argument (*let's say that it is human that these things can happen*); secondly, she combines her formulation (*you were saying*) with an indirect question (*I would like to understand if*), positioning herself as questioner. Another student (M2) aligns with the facilitator's positioning, accepting her upgrading, although showing some degree of autonomy in his epistemic status, by restricting the facilitator's formulation. The hierarchical structure of the interaction is preserved through the facilitator's positioning in the second place of the triplet. The students' agency is not promoted, and no change is visible in the hierarchical structure of both the specific interaction and of adult-children communication. However, the students' attempts to upgrade their status and the facilitator's hesitation in rejecting these attempts, show that this form of hierarchical structure creates some problems of communication: this structure is not smoothly accepted, as the students show their interest in upgrading their epistemic authority, and the facilitator shows her interest in avoiding impositions or directions.

Extract 3 concerns a discussion about the ways of dealing with difficult, and possibly violent, situations, which was enhanced by the reflection on the text in the handout (the numbers in the extract represent the seconds of pause).

Extract 3

1. M1: perché lei cioè se uno si fa avanti cos'è giusto? È giusto darsi o allontanarsi? Secondo lei chiedo.
   because you I mean if someone makes a step forward what is the right thing to do? Should you accept or go away? In your opinion I mean.
2. FAC: non non non ti rispondo perché è una scelta personale, è una scelta personale, è una scelta personale.
   I won't won't won't answer because it's a personal choice, it's a personal choice, it's a personal choice.
3. ((hubbub))

4. M2: sì va beh.
   Yeah right.
5. FAC: è sempre difficile rispondere.
   It's always hard to answer.
6. M1: discutere.
   Discuss.
7. FAC: io ne ho sempre buscate molte.
   I always got beatings.
8. M3: eh?
9. FAC: ne ho sempre buscate e ci sono delle persone che danno botte e in questo caso era mia sorella, e non c'era verso, era fatta così cosa fai? Questo era il suo modo di comunicare capito? Quindi io telavo (2) telavo però bisogna vedere chi è vincente e chi perdente.
   I always got beatings and there are people who hit you hard and in my case it was my sister, and there was no way, that's how she was what should you do? That was her way to communicate you know? So I would leave (2) I would leave but we should see who's the winner and who's the loser.
10. M3: era più grande sua sorella?
    Was your sister older?
11. FAC: era più grande e più forte e quindi chiedevo giustizia a chi doveva, a chi doveva farla giustizia.
    She was older and stronger and so I would ask for justice to those who were supposed to do justice.
12. M1: i genitori.
    Parents.
13. FAC: eh in questo caso Saverio (2) Saverio può chiedere giustizia a qualcuno?
    Eh in this case Saverio (2) Saverio can ask anyone to do justice?

Extract 3 shows that children's initiatives can lead to a contingent, but unstable change. In turn 1, M1 takes the initiative and asks a question about the facilitator's personal positioning regarding the topic of the conversation. In turn 2, the facilitator refuses to answer this question (*I won't won't won't answer*), trying to avoid introducing her personal positioning in the interaction (see extract 2). However, this reaction provokes evident, although not explicit, perplexities among the students (turns 3, 4). Therefore, in turns 5, the facilitator mitigates her refusal (*It's always hard to answer*), and in turn 7 she changes her positioning, reporting a personal story, thus violating the same rule that she said she would follow. This change in the facilitator's positioning projects interest among the students. Firstly, it projects surprise (turn 8: *Eh?*), then it projects upgrading of a student's epistemic status as questioner (turn 10), a status that very frequently applies to facilitators. In turns 9 and 11, the facilitator adapts to this new structure of the interaction, continuing in her unusual narrative; however, at the end of turn 11, she changes her positioning from responder to questioner, changing the topic of conversation, and announcing the restoration of her prominent epistemic status. In turn 12, M1 aligns with the facilitator's question, and in turn 13 the facilitator stabilises her usual positioning, neutralizing students' further attempts to display agency.

In this case, the student initiates the sequence, upgrading his epistemic status as questioner. Initially, the facilitator replies by adapting to the student's initiative and positioning, thus downgrading her own status and supporting the student's upgrading. The students support this change with their positive feedback. However, the facilitator re-positions herself as soon as possible, upgrading her authority and restoring the organisation of the IRF sequence. The IRF sequence is expanded by the facilitator in order to restore the hierarchical structure of the interaction. In this case, the students' agency is *contingently* promoted, as the facilitator, after an hesitation, decides to answer the students' question; this choice leads the facilitator to a contingent and unstable change of her positioning, from questioner to answerer, and from leading the interaction to leaving more opportunities for the children's participation. However, this change is promptly reversed in the facilitators' coordination, through a reference to Saverio, the protagonist of the story.

Extract 4 shows how facilitation can create the opportunity for more radical and coherent change in the interaction.

Extract 4

1. F1: A me è piaciuto intanto molto perché abbiamo potuto dire le nostre opinioni liberamente, senza la preoccupazione del voto, come se fossimo delle persone che possiamo dire le nostre cose liberamente insieme ad un gruppo e questo mi è molto piaciuto.

   I liked it a lot first because we could express our opinions freely, without any concern about marks, as if we were people who can freely express in a group and I liked that a lot.
2. Fac: qualcun altro vuol dire cosa pensa del lavoro fatto insieme.

   Does anyone else want to say what they think of the work we did together.
3. M1: Per me quello che ha detto F1 è vero che anche a me mi è piaciuto molto questa idea e mi chiedevo un po' come mai gli adulti vogliono capire dai bambini.

   I think what F1 said is true that I also liked this idea a lot and was kind of wondering why adults want to understand from children
4. Fac: Eh! Che carino!

   Eh! How nice!

5. M1: Eh, di solito l'adulto spiega al bambino, giusto? Però una volta siamo noi che con la nostra opinione possiamo spiegare agli altri. Questa idea mi è piaciuta perché vedendo gli altri non è piaciuta solo a me ma anche agli altri.

   Eh, usually adults explain things to children, right? But for once it's us with our opinion explaining to others. I liked this idea because seeing the others it was not just me but the others who also liked it.
6. Fac2: vai avanti abbiamo bisogno che tu continui.

   Go on we need you to go on.
7. M1: perché questa idea mi è piaciuta, perché vedendo gli altri non è piaciuta solo a me ma a tanti altri.

   Because I liked this idea, because seeing the others it was not just me but many others who liked it.
8. M2: è stata interessante, entusiasmante.

   It was interesting, exciting.
9. Fac2: *lui ha fatto una domanda, come mai gli adulti vogliono sapere dai bambini. Qualcuno di voi riesce a rispondere?*

   He asked a question, why adults want to know from children. Can anyone reply?
10. F2: Secondo me perché vogliono sapere come si sentono loro e le loro e le loro opinioni in questo lavoro, cosa abbiamo fatto, se hanno capito il senso del-

    In my opinion because they want to know about their feelings and opinions about this work, what we did if they have understood the meaning of-
11. M1: oppure per aiutarci.

    Or to help us.
12. M3: Perché sì che hanno studiato e sono andati a scuola, ma vogliono sapere dai bambini cose che non sapevano, opinioni.

    Yes because they studied and went to school, but want to know from children things they didn't know, opinions.
13. Fac: Quello che ho capito da M3 sembra che i grandi vadano a scuola e i ragazzini sono le maestre.

    As far as I can gather from M3 it sounds like adults go to school and children are the teachers.
14. M4: Io volevo dire anche che gli adulti vogliono sapere da noi le cose, perché ai loro tempi non ci sono le cose che ci sono adesso e quindi ci sono molte più cose.

    What I meant is that adults also want to know things from us, *because when they were children there were not the same things there are now and so there are many more things.*

15. M1: anche per me.
I think so too
16. M2: e vogliono saperne di più per sapere come comportarsi e aiutarci.
And they want to know more to know what to do and how to help us.

In turn 1, a student (F1) stresses her satisfaction for the interaction with the facilitator, as it allowed students' free expression of opinions, without evaluation and personal positioning. In turn 2, the facilitator invites the other students to express their opinions. In turn 3 M1 confirms the narrative of F1, adding a question on the reasons of adults' interest in understanding from children (*was kind of wondering why adults want to understand from children*). In this turn, M1 is not only expressing his opinion, he is also upgrading his epistemic status, by proposing a new interpretation of the meaning of the interaction with the facilitator. In turn 4, the facilitator shows her appreciation for this status, stressing her personal positioning (*Eh! How nice!*). Her appreciation projects the continuation of M1's discourse, in which the student upgrades his epistemic authority, which originated from his confirmed epistemic status, through the explanation of his point of view. The student's explanation is rather complex, in that it includes three parts. Firstly, M1 asks a question to receive confirmation of the typical structure of adult-children interaction (*Eh, usually adults explain things to children, right?*); he does not wait for an answer to this question, continuing with the second part, in which he observes the novelty of the present situation (*But for once it's us with our opinion explaining to others*); finally, he adds a comment about the importance of children's overall satisfaction for this change (*I liked this idea because seeing the others it was not just me but the others who also liked it*).

In turn 6, the second facilitator (who is positioned as an observer in the interaction) invites M1 to continue; it is interesting to observe that, in order to explain her request, she does not stress her "interest", but her "need", confirming the importance of dismissing the hierarchical structure; the facilitators need the children's views in order to understand the meaning of the interaction. However, M1 simply repeats the third part of his previous turn, showing that in fact he has completed his narrative. His positioning does not conclude the conversation, as M2 intervenes to stress his interest in the interaction, using the empathic term "exciting" to describe it. In turn 9, the second facilitator asks a question to the whole classroom, formulating the focal point in the interaction, i.e. the reason for adults' interest in children's views. Three children answer this question, expressing different opinions, and in turn 13 the facilitator picks the last answer, formulating a gloss of the third child's explanation; she glosses it as a way of dismissing the hierarchical structure of positioning between adults and children, thus showing understanding and justification for the change introduced by the students. This formulation projects three new comments, thus enhancing the reflection on the change in the structure of the educational interaction.

In this case, a student (F1) initiates the sequence, upgrading her own epistemic authority. The facilitator supports the student's initiative, positioning and display of expectations, downgrading her own epistemic authority. In this way, she enhances feedback from other students, and encourages their positioning and display of expectations as capable agents, thus upgrading their epistemic status. The same structure is repeated in the following turns. In these turns, the facilitators ask questions and formulate the gist of previous turns, as usually happens in this form of facilitation. However, this situation is peculiar in that the usual design of facilitators' turns is promoted by children's agency; therefore, facilitators stress children's agency by promoting their epistemic status and authority. This promotion is particularly relevant as the conversation focuses on the dismissal of the hierarchical structure of education: in promoting the right to children's agency, not only do facilitators enhance a different structure of the interaction, but also an explicit reflection on this different structure. In this case, the paradox of agency, i.e. the fact that actions showing children's agency are promoted by adults' actions, is very evident in the interplay of facilitators' promotion and students' active participation.

3.6 Discussion

In both teaching and facilitation, IRF sequences are based on specific social structures (structures of epistemic status and authority, coding, positioning, and form of expectations). Different IRF sequences are based on different social structures and have different consequences for children's agency. In this chapter, the analysis of facilitation in classroom interactions has highlighted social conversion processes and the corresponding social factors converting children's human resources and rights of choosing into capabilities as agency.

In particular, the analysis has highlighted three different forms of facilitation, which, at a first glance, can be observed through facilitators' positioning aiming to promote children's participation:

1. Mitigated hierarchical positioning (extract 2). This form of positioning is "mitigated" because it does not try to control or direct a communication process; rather it diverts this process, on the basis of the facilitator's re-positioning in the interaction. This form does not upgrade children's epistemic status and authority.
2. Contingent personal positioning (extract 3). This form of positioning is "contingent" because it provisionally adapts to children's initiatives as well as to their epistemic status and authority; however, this initial positioning is followed by the facilitator's hierarchical re-positioning.
3. Stable personal positioning (extract 4). This form of positioning is "stable" because it is not followed by any re-positioning. It affects the hierarchical structure of the interaction and upgrades children's epistemic status and authority.

The facilitators' turns, which steadily affect the hierarchical structure of the interaction, are second-turn feedback, which depend on and adapt to children's initiatives; these turns are designed as minimal responses, invitations to talk, promotional questions, and formulations glossing children's first turns. These forms of second turn can project and support children's third turns, which continue the narrative initiated by children in first turns.

Positioning, however, is only a component of the various forms of facilitation. Therefore, we need to observe the differences among these forms, in order to fully understand promotion of rights to agency. We have observed: mitigated hierarchical facilitation, which rejects children's positioning through feedback (extract 2); personal facilitation, which is forced by the children's initiatives and contingent, as it is followed by quick recovery of a mitigated hierarchical form (extract 3); and personal facilitation, which steadily dismisses the hierarchical structure of the interaction (extract 4). The latter is based on the following structural presuppositions: (1) coding as distinction between positive, equal active participation and negative, unequal participation; (2) form of positioning, which gives primary value to personal expressions; (3) affective form of expectations, which is a form of expectations regarding participation as personal expression, rather than role performance (Baraldi 2008, 2009). Therefore, personal facilitation is based on a coding that substitutes evaluation with the distinction between equal participation (positive value) and hierarchical participation (negative value), and on personal positioning and affective expectations.

The analysis has highlighted that different forms of facilitation have different consequences for the promotion of rights to children's agency, i.e. rights to participate in decision-making:

1. Mitigation of hierarchical structure downgrades children's capabilities as agency, although without any explicit negative evaluation;
2. Contingent personal positioning, followed by hierarchical re-positioning, enhances unstable facilitation of children's capabilities as agency, followed by its downgrading through questioning;
3. Stable personal positioning enhances the successful upgrading of children's capabilities as agency, by dismissing the hierarchical structure of the interaction.

The upgrading of children's capabilities as agency changes the meaning of children's rights, from the right to say what they think when adults take decisions for them (art. 12 UNCRC) or the right to free expression (art. 13 UNCRC), to the right to participate in decision making regarding social systems, therefore participating in their structural change. Articles 12 and 13 of the CRC imply that all children are entitled to be informed, to express their views and to have their views taken into account, but they do not extend rights to children's decision making. The recognition that children can exercise their rights to decision making implies a transfer of epistemic authority and responsibility for decisions from adults to children, and a correspondent change in adults' way of acting: adults need to negotiate capabilities with children. This shift could lead the CA to consider that (1) children have their own capabilities *as children*, (2) children attach their own relevance to capabilities and (3) children's capabilities influence adults' capabilities in social systems.

Coding as distinction between positive equal participation and negative hierarchical participation, personal positioning, and affective form of expectations are the successful social conversion factors from children's resources and rights to children's capabilities displayed as agency. These conversion factors cannot be produced only in specific, contingent interactions, but should be produced as stable structures of wider social systems. These social conversion factors upgrade children's epistemic status and authority, by (1) eliciting the introduction of particular issues by children, (2) creating opportunities for children's telling of their own stories, and (3) enhancing the construction of new, alternative narratives concerning children as social agents. Under these circumstances, children can be co-promoters of structural change in social systems: coding, positioning and form of expectations are created in the interplay of facilitators and children's actions.

The social conversion factors described are not frequently observed in classroom interactions, for two reasons. Firstly, it is difficult to drop the traditional form of IRF sequence, as students are used to it and display expectations regarding facilitators' questions and feedback, and position themselves as responders in the interaction. Secondly, this difficulty influences the meanings of facilitators' actions, which can be interpreted as different ways of asking questions and giving feedback, without considering the importance of children's initiatives, as initiations and feedback. Therefore, an interesting and not sufficiently explored analysis is about the extent to which facilitation of children's agency can become a stable form in the education system The right to agency and the corresponding facilitation process cannot be guaranteed by any Convention; they require a change regarding structural presuppositions of social systems that involve children's participation. For this reason, at present, it seems rather difficult to change conversion processes and factors in the education system, towards an effective promotion of children's rights to agency. In order to promote a structural change of this kind, newly, systematically structured curricular activities would probably be necessary, e.g. facilitating interactions among children in a "classroom context mode" (Walsh 2011) or, more radically, withdrawing from claiming any superior epistemic authority in interactions with children (Edwards et al. 1998).

References

Abebe, T., & Kjørholt, A. T. (2009). Social actors and victims of exploitation. Working children in the cash economy of the Ethiopia's South. *Childhood, 16*(2), 175–194.

Alanen, L. (2009). Generational order. In J. Qvortrup, G. Valentine, W. Corsaro, & M. S. Honig (Eds.), *The Palgrave handbook of childhood studies* (pp. 159–174). Basingstoke: Palgrave.

Babic, B. (2011). Ohne intellektuelle Redlichkeit kein Fortschritt. Kritische Anmerkungen zum Umgang mit dem Capability Approach aus erziehungswissenschaftlicher Sicht. In C. Sedmak, B. Babic, R. Bauer, & C. Posch (Eds.), *Der Capability Approach in sozialwissenschaftlichen*

Kontexten. Überlegungen zur Anschlussfähigkeit eines entwicklungspolitischen Konzepts (pp. 75–89). Wiesbaden: VS Verlag.
Baraldi, C. (2003). Planning childhood: Children's social participation in the town of adults. In P. Christensen & M. O'Brien (Eds.), *Children in the city. Home, neighbourhood and community* (pp. 184–205). London: Falmer Press.
Baraldi, C. (2008). Promoting self-expression in classrooms interactions. *Childhood, 15*(2), 239–257.
Baraldi, C. (Ed.). (2009). *Dialogue in intercultural communities. From and educational point of view*. Amsterdam: John Benjamins.
Baraldi, C., & Iervese, V. (2010). Dialogic mediation in conflict resolution education. *Conflict Resolution Quarterly, 27*(4), 423–445.
Baraldi, C., & Iervese, V. (Eds.). (2012). *Participation, facilitation, and mediation: Children and young people in their social contexts*. London: Routledge.
Biggeri, M., Libanora, R., Mariani, S., & Menchini, L. (2006). Children conceptualizing their capabilities: Results of the survey during the first children's world congress on child labour. *Journal of Human Development, 7*(1), 59–83.
Biggeri, M., Ballet, J., & Comim, F. (Eds.). (2011). *Children and the capability approach*. Houndsmill: Palgrave.
Blanchet-Cohen, N., & Rainbow, B. (2006). Partnership between children and adults? The experience of the international children's conference on the environment. *Childhood, 13*(1), 113–126.
Burchardt, T., & Vizard, P. (2011). 'Operationalizing' the capability approach as a basis for equality and human rights monitoring in twenty-first-century Britain. *Journal of Human Development and Capabilities, 12*(1), 91–119.
Christensen, P., & Prout, A. (2002). Working with ethical symmetry in social research with children. *Childhood, 9*(4), 477–497.
Clark, D. A. (2006). Capability approach. In D. A. Clark (Ed.), *The Elgar companion to development studies* (pp. 32–45). Cheltenham: Edward Elgar.
Craig, G. (2003). Children's participation through community development. In C. Hallett & A. Prout (Eds.), *Hearing the voices of children, social policy for a new century* (pp. 39–56). London: Routledge Falmer.
Crocker, D. A. (1998). Consumption, well-being and capability. In D. A. Crocker & T. Linden (Eds.), *Ethics of consumption: The good life, justice and global stewardship* (pp. 366–390). New York: Rowman and Littlefield.
Dixon, R., & Nussbaum, M. (2012). Children's rights and a capability approach: The question of special priority. Cornell Law Review, vol. 97, Public Law Working Paper No. 384.
Edwards, C., Gandini, L., & Forman, G. (Eds.). (1998). *The hundred languages of children*. Greenwich: Ablex Publishing Corporation.
Farini, F. (2011). Cultures of education in action: Research on the relationship between interaction and cultural presuppositions regarding education in an international educational setting. *Journal of Pragmatics, 43*, 2176–2186.
Giddens, A. (1984). *The constitution of society*. Cambridge: Polity Press.
Goodwin, C., & Heritage, J. (1990). Conversation analysis. *Annual Review of Anthropology, 19*, 283–307.
Harré, R., & Van Langenhove, L. (Eds.). (1999). *Positioning theory*. Oxford: Blackwell.
Heritage, J. (1985). Analysing news interviews: Aspects of the production of talk for an overhearing audience. In T. Van Dijk (Ed.), *Handbook of discourse analysis, vol. 3. Discourse and dialogue* (pp. 95–117). London: Academic.
Heritage, J. (2012). Epistemics in action: Action formation and territories of knowledge. *Research on Language and Social Interaction, 45*(1), 1–29.
Heritage, J., & Clayman, S. (2010). *Talk in action. Interactions, identities, and institutions*. Chichester: Wiley-Blackwell.
Heritage, J., & Raymond, G. (2005). The terms of agreement: Indexing epistemic authority and subordination in talk-in-interaction. *Social Psychology Quarterly, 68*(1), 15–38.

Hill, M., Davis, J., Prout, A., & Tisdall, K. (2004). Moving the participation agenda forward. *Children & Society, 18*, 77–96.
Holland, S., & O'Neill, S. (2006). We had to be there to make sure it was what we wanted. Enabling children's participation in family decision-making through the family group conference. *Childhood, 13*(1), 91–111.
James, A. (2009). Agency. In J. Qvortrup, G. Valentine, W. Corsaro, & M. S. Honig (Eds.), *The Palgrave handbook of childhood studies* (pp. 34–45). Basingstoke: Palgrave.
James, A., & James, A. (2004). *Constructing childhood. Theory, policy and social practice*. Houndmills: Palgrave.
James, A., & James, A. (2008). *Key concepts in childhood studies*. London: Sage.
James, A., & Prout, A. (Eds.). (1997). *Constructing and reconstructing childhood*. London: Falmer Press.
James, A., Jenks, C., & Prout, A. (1998). *Theorizing childhood*. Oxford: Polity Press.
Jans, M. (2004). Children as citizens. Towards a contemporary notion of child participation. *Childhood, 11*(1), 27–44.
Jasek-Rysdahl, K. (2001). Applying Sen's capability approach to neighbourhoods: Using local asset maps to deepen our understanding of well-being. *Review of Social Economy, 59*(3), 313–329.
Kjørholt, A. T. (2002). Small is powerful. Discourses on 'children participation' in Norway. *Childhood, 11*(1), 27–44.
Lansdown, G. (2010). The realisation of children's participation rights: Critical reflections. In B. Percy-Smith & N. Thomas (Eds.), *A handbook of children and young people's participation. Perspective from theory and practice* (pp. 11–24). London: Routledge.
Liebel, M. (2003). Working children as social subjects: The contribution of working children's organisations to social transformations. *Childhood, 10*(3), 265–285.
Luhmann, N. (1984). *Soziale systeme*. Frankfurt a.M: Suhrkamp.
Luhmann, N. (2000). *Art as a social system*. Stanford: Stanford University Press.
Luhmann, N. (2002). *Das erziehungssystem der gesellschaft*. Frankfurt a. M: Suhrkamp.
Margutti, P. (2010). On designedly incomplete utterances: What counts as learning for teachers and students in primary classroom interactions. *Research on Language and Social Interaction, 43*(4), 315–345.
Matthews, H. (2003). Children and regeneration: Setting and agenda for community participation and integration. *Children and Society, 17*, 264–276.
Mehan, H. (1979). *Learning lessons*. Cambridge: Harvard University Press.
Nussbaum, M. (2000). *Women and human development: The capabilities approach*. Cambridge: Cambridge University Press.
Percy-Smith, B., & Thomas, N. (Eds.). (2010). *A handbook of children and young people's participation. Perspective from theory and practice*. London: Routledge.
Prout, A. (2003). Participation, policy and the changing conditions of childhood. In C. Hallett & A. Prout (Eds.), *Hearing the voices of children, social policy for a new century* (pp. 11–25). London: RoutledgeFalmer.
Qvortrup, J., Valentine, G., Corsaro, W., & Honig, M. S. (Eds.). (2009). *The Palgrave handbook of childhood studies*. Basingstoke: Palgrave.
Robeyns, I. (2006). The capability approach in practice. *Journal of Political Philosophy, 14*(3), 351–376.
Rogoff, B. (1990). *Apprenticeship in thinking: Cognitive development in social context*. Oxford: Oxford University Press.
Sacks, H., Shegloff, E., & Jefferson, G. (1974). A simplest systematic for the organization of turn-taking for conversation. *Language, 50*, 696–735.
Saito, M. (2003). Amartya Sen's capability approach to education: A critical exploration. *Journal of Philosophy of Education, 37*(1), 17–33.
Schokkaert, E., & Van Ootegem, L. (1990). Sen's concept of the living standard applied to the Belgian unemployed. *Recherches economiques de Louvain, 56*(3–4), 429–450.

Sen, A. K. (1981). *Poverty and famines: An essay on entitlement and deprivation*. Oxford: Clarendon Press.
Sen, A. K. (1984). *Resources, values and development*. Oxford: Blackwell.
Sen, A. K. (1985). *Commodities and capabilities*. Oxford: Elsevier Science Publishers.
Sen, A. K. (1992). *Inequality re-examined*. Oxford: Clarendon Press.
Sen, A. K. (1993). Capability and well-being. In M. C. Nussbaum & A. K. Sen (Eds.), *The quality of life* (pp. 30–53). Oxford: Clarendon Press.
Sen, A. K. (1999a). *Development as freedom*. New York: Knopf.
Sen, A.K. (1999b). Investing in early childhood: Its role in development. Paper presented at: Conference on breaking the poverty cycle. Investing in early childhood, Inter-American Development Bank, Washington, DC.
Sinclair, R. (2004). Participation in practice: Making it meaningful, effective and sustainable. *Children and Society, 18*, 106–118.
Thomas, N. (2007). Towards a theory of children's participation. *International Journal of Children's Rights, 15*, 199–218.
Twun-Danso, A. (2010). The construction of childhood and the socialisation of children in Ghana: Implications for the implementation of Article 12 of the CRC. In B. Percy-Smith & N. Thomas (Eds.), *A handbook of children and young people's participation. Perspective from theory and practice* (pp. 133–141). London: Routledge.
Walsh, S. (2011). *Exploring classroom discourse: Language in action*. New York: Routledge.

Chapter 4
From Evolving Capacities to Evolving Capabilities: Contextualizing Children's Rights

Manfred Liebel

4.1 Introduction

My starting point is to understand Children's Rights (hereafter CR) as Human Rights (hereafter HR) in the sense that they are valued as unconditional and interconnected.[1]

CR are explicitly connected with the principle of 'evolving capacities'. The 'evolving capacities' principle of the United Nations Convention on the Rights of the Child (hereafter UNCRC) is codified in Article 5 as follows:

> States Parties shall respect the responsibilities, rights and duties of parents or, where applicable, the members of the extended family or community as provided for by local custom, legal guardians or other persons legally responsible for the child, to provide, in a manner consistent with the **evolving capacities of the child**, appropriate direction and guidance in the exercise by the child of the rights recognized in the present Convention. (UNCRC 1989; bold words underlined by the author)

This principle raises the question whether the rights of the child, as codified in the UNCRC, can be really understood as unconditional HR and if they gain equal relevance for all children, or only for those children, to whom are attributed the 'capacities' considered (by adults) as relevant for enjoying the rights themselves.

I will discuss whether the Capability Approach (hereafter CA) and particularly its concept of 'capabilities' can contribute to re-conceptualize the CR in such a way that they might become an entitlement or instrument in the hands of children, or become relevant as 'agency rights' (Brighouse 2002) that are at reach for children

[1] I would like to thank Rita Nunes, Rebecca Budde, Janica Hundacker and Ortrud Leßmann as well as the editors for their comments and their support to express my thoughts in English. Of course, I am responsible for the text myself.

M. Liebel (✉)
Fachbereich Erziehungswissenschaft und Psychologie, Freie Universität Berlin, Berlin, Germany
e-mail: mliebel@ina-fu.org

D. Stoecklin and J.-M. Bonvin (eds.), *Children's Rights and the Capability Approach*, Children's Well-Being: Indicators and Research 8, DOI 10.1007/978-94-017-9091-8_4,

and can be influenced and used by them.[2] In this context, it seems helpful to refer to the idea of 'evolving capabilities', first phrased by Biggeri et al. (2010: 81), and to reflect it in the concrete living context(s) of children. Regarding the CA, I will discuss whether this approach considers children as subjects of HR and how do the main authors of the CA understand the CR and the role of children in society, particularly with regard to children's agency.

4.2 Understanding CR: The Ambivalence and Risks of the HR/CR Discourse

Taking into account that CR are understood as HR which are applicable as absolute rights to children as all other human beings I understand CR as 'agency rights', i.e. as 'subjective' rights or entitlements for personal actions. CR should not be understood only as 'welfare rights', 'well-being rights' or 'objective rights', i.e. as an exclusive task or obligation of States or adults in favour of children.

Such different understandings correspond to different currents in the history of CR: on the one hand there is a protectionist or paternalistic tendency, on the other hand an emancipatory or liberationist tendency (see Hanson 2012; Liebel 2012: 29–42). Both tendencies are represented in the UNCRC, nevertheless with a protectionist bias and emphasis on the responsibility of States/adults (see Liebel and Saadi 2012a).

The 'right to have rights' is in accordance with Hannah Arendt (1951/2004) a fundamental HR. At least since the UNCRC, this also applies to children worldwide. The essence of HR consists of protecting humans from arbitrary actions and to extend their possibilities towards a 'good human life', e.g. to reach more freedom and better living conditions – instead of stabilizing the existing social order and its power structures. Nevertheless, the HR/CR discourse is not free from risks and ambivalences.

Firstly, there is the risk to use HR in an *ideological* sense. In this case, the reference to rights could suggest a 'freedom' that would actually exist, implying that social justice can be reached by the personal use of rights and that this is possible under all circumstances. By this, structural reasons for social inequality, unequal power relations or violence are underestimated or denied, and HR may be used to justify structural injustice by emphasizing individual responsibility. This vision corresponds to the liberal understanding of rights already questioned by Marx and other sociologists or philosophers of rights. Such a vision corresponds also to the lack of reflection on the 'structural' limitations of human agency.

Secondly, following Hannah Arendt's (1952/2004) assumptions on the '*aporias*' or '*perplexities*' of human rights (see Gündoğdu 2012), having rights does not automatically means their fully enjoyment, for instance, in the case of 'stateless'

[2] The concept of *agency* refers to the capacities for action as well as to the opportunities of the subjects to make use of their capacities (see James 2009).

refugees, or in the case of marginalized children, due to their powerless status. Enjoying HR/CR always depends on certain conditions that allow and make sense to claim such rights oneself (see Liebel 2012: 43–59 – on the example of 'street children' in Guatemala and India, and children living in 'child-headed households' in southern Africa). The understanding or re-conceptualization of HR needs to 'contextualize' them and go hand in hand with a critical analysis of the corresponding social and political structures of a given society. Such risks and ambivalences hold true particularly in the case of the 'evolving capacities' principle as codified by the UNCRC.

4.3 The Ambivalence and Risks of the Evolving Capacities Principle

The notion of the child's evolving capacities (Art. 5 UNCRC) is also reflected in Article 12.1, which reads as follows:

> States Parties shall assure to the child **who is capable of forming his or her own views** the right to express those views freely in all matters affecting the child, the views of the child being given due weight **in accordance with the age and maturity of the child**. (UNCRC 1989; bold words underlined by the author)

The 'evolving capacities' principle can be understood in two contrary ways: as a limitation of the rights exercised by children (a pretext to deny the use of rights, which means conditioning CR as HR), or as a stimulant for the recognition of the special capacities of children and their promotion (taking into account that children are in a process of development, but not understanding these capacities in a hierarchical sense). However, as long as adults possess the definition power on capacities, the principle will be used in the sense of a limitation for children.

It is important to reflect which kinds of capacities we have in mind when speaking of 'evolving capacities' and for what reasons they are to be developed. The UNCRC 'evolving capacities' principle is up to now understood mainly as a question of 'subjective' abilities without taking into account the 'objective' living conditions as relevant for gaining and using them. Furthermore, there is only little discussion on the criteria used to determine what may count as a capacity (or the opposite) and who may decide about it.

According to Lansdown (2005: 15, see also Alderson 2008: 82), capacities are not simply fixed personal characteristics of children, but their evolution is seen as the result of different circumstances (living conditions), or of children's own activities (in different socio-cultural settings). For Lansdown the "evolution of the capacities" can be based in different conceptual frames that have a complex relation to each other:

1. As a *developmental* concept, recognizing the extent to which children's development, competence and emerging personal autonomy are promoted through the realization of the rights contained in the UNCRC.

2. As a *participatory or emancipatory* concept, denoting children's right to the respect of their capacities and shifting the responsibility for exercising rights from adults to children in accordance with their levels of competence.
3. As a *protective* concept, which acknowledges that because, throughout childhood, children's capacities are still evolving, they have rights to protection from exposure to activities likely to cause them harm both by parents and the State.

These are important considerations on the different ways how the 'evolving capacities' principle may be understood or performed in the CR practice. Nevertheless, the question what is or should be recognized as capacities is seen completely from the adults' or authorities' perspective. In my opinion it remains unclear:

(a) What might be understood as capacities in general and in the special case of children?
(b) In which way children could gain definition power on this issue?
(c) What conditions must be given for the children to use their capacities for the exercise of CR and to give them real power to take decisions on all affairs affecting them?

Therefore my objective is to understand whether the concept of 'capabilities' as represented by the CA may help to overcome the risks and ambivalences included in the 'evolving capacities' principle and re-conceptualize and use it in an emancipatory sense.

4.4 Understanding Capacities and Capabilities

Although under semantic aspects there is no difference between the English terms 'capacities' and 'capabilities' one should look precisely into these because of the special and sometimes different and changing understandings of the term 'capabilities' within the CA. While the terms 'capacities' and 'capabilities', in everyday language, are commonly used in the sense of personal attributes or abilities of subjects, the term 'capabilities' as used in the CA refers particularly to its relevance for realizing personal options in a given or aspired society. Therefore I would like to refer to Amartya Sen and Martha Nussbaum as two of the CA's main advocates.

Sen (1992, 1993, 1999) defines capabilities as an answer to the question regarding what a person is really able to do or to be. He understands capabilities as *opportunities* to choose or to act, calling them 'substantive freedoms'. According to him, a person's 'capability' refers to the alternative combination of 'functionings' that are feasible for a person in a particular living situation which he calls 'capability set'. In Sen's words: "Capability is, thus, a set of vectors of functionings, reflecting the person's freedom to lead one type of life or another [...], to choose from possible livings" (Sen 1992: 40). As 'functionings' he understands the various beings and doings a person can achieve such as being nourished, being healthy, riding a bike, walking, reading, appearing in public without shame, etc. Thus, they range from rather elementary to complex ones.[3]

In Sen's approach the term capability refers to the styles of living (understood as different combinations of 'functionings') a person can really access. Such 'functionings' can be potential or realized. He argues that capabilities, as a fundamental ethical category, are not just equal but superior to the 'functionings' because capabilities express one's freedom to choose. In this sense he sees a great difference between the ownership of an object X, if no possible alternative can be found, and the conscious decision in favour of X, if actual alternatives exist.

As for Nussbaum (2011) capabilities "are not just abilities residing inside a person but also the freedoms or opportunities created by a combination of personal abilities and the political, social, and economic environment" (op. cit.: 20), she updates Sen's concept of 'substantive freedoms' as 'combined capabilities' distinguishing them from 'internal capabilities'.

Nussbaum explains the importance of distinguishing both dimensions of capabilities referring to what she calls a 'decent society' or a society which recognizes the human dignity. For her, the differentiation corresponds to two tasks of a decent society. The dichotomy relies on the fact that a society may be efficient producing 'internal capabilities' but it may be intercepting the opportunities to function in conformity to these internal capabilities (ibid.: 21).[4]

In this sense, 'capacities' or 'internal capabilities' can be understood, generally, as innate or acquired abilities (or powers) to influence the circumstances and to transform given realities; in other words, to open up new possibilities and to amplify the scope of action. Transforming realities can be understood in a double sense: on the one hand to transform the outside ('objective') reality (societal development), on the other hand to transform oneself as a person (personal development), including the ability to understand what is happening and for what reason (see Sedmak 2011).[5] The fact that children always ask 'why?' may serve as an

[3] I admit to feel uncomfortable with the CA because its main authors use for key concepts a structural-functional language which, from my point of view, distorts their emancipatory intentions. This applies principally to the term 'functionings' but also to others, like 'conversion factors' which indicate the functions of the capabilities.

[4] In a similar way another author (Gasper 2002) makes a difference between 'S-capabilities', on the one hand, which indicate internal enabling skills as well as faculties, abilities, aspirations and attitudes and, on the other hand, 'O-capabilities', which entail the control over resources, opportunities or options available to a person respectively the socially structured set of a person's attainable life-paths. These 'O-capabilities' or 'social conversion factors' are further subdivided into 'socio-structural and cultural conversion factors' (such as social norms, gender roles or power relations) and 'institutional conversion factors' (such as entitlements, welfare and educational arrangements or collective provisions). Also see Leßmann et al. (2011): 10–11.

[5] This refers to an article written by Sedmak in German. The German term '*Fähigkeiten*' used by Sedmak can be understood in the sense of the term 'internal capabilities' used by Nussbaum. Nevertheless, Nussbaum (2011: 23) includes, in a wider sense, also elements "such as education, adequate information, and confidence" while mentioning that the "distinction between internal and combined capabilities is not sharp, since one typically acquires an internal capability by some kind

example for my further focus but might also have consequences for the other kind of transformations.

Such internal capabilities are structured from 'inside' and 'outside'. 'Inside' means: by internal, subjective resources, attitudes, motivations, aims and convictions. 'Outside' means: by the opportunities of what is possible, and the social and cultural values dominating in a given society (such values 'co-decide' what is recognized as a capacity or, by contrast, perhaps a 'disability'). According to Sedmak (2011: 36–41), we can distinguish the following aspects of capacities or internal capabilities:

1. They are *related to the subject* in two ways: as the capacities contribute to mould the individual identity, and as the subject produces his/her capacities.
2. They are '*anchored*': a capacity never happens isolated but within a bundle of capacities; capacities and their opposites are mutually related and cannot be absolutely separated.
3. They are *valued*, or, more precisely, socially and culturally valued in different ways; some are highly appreciated, others not; some may serve for 'functioning', but others may be understood as a 'handicap' and are not recognized as capacities (e.g. creativity in a repetitive working set). The question is whether certain capacities in a given society can be understood as 'minimal' or 'fundamental' capacities, i.e. as indispensable for living in this society (e.g. to be able to read and write). Other differentiations may be: socially neutral capacities which do not bring advantages or disadvantages (e.g. to be able to answer to quiz questions); highly valued rare capacities (e.g. to manage difficult mathematical operations or to show musical virtuosity at a special instrument); but also 'paradoxical' capacities, which are seen as 'out of place' and bring disadvantages (e.g. 'witch-hunting'). This variety of interpretations tells us that what is understood as a capacity or a lack of capacity depends on cultural factors.
4. They are *dynamic*, that means they do not simply exist, but are developing.
5. They are *potentially competitive*; in other words, the appropriation of one capacity can lead to the loss of other ones.[6]

Continuing the analysis of capabilities discussion between the CA's two main advocates it is important to refer that Sen emphasizes the cultural dependency of the freedom of choice removing Nussbaum's attempts to define a set of universally significant 'central capabilities' (see the newest version of this list in Nussbaum

of functioning, and one may lose it in the absence of the opportunity to function". But she sees the distinction as "a useful heuristic in diagnosing the achievements and shortcomings of a society" (ibid.).

[6] Sedmak's explanation remains unclear concerning the question whether capacities or internal capabilities should be understood only as individual, or as collective ones, too. His thoughts do not consider the childhood status either. The subordinated status of childhood is the reason why the capacities of children are *a priori* measured on adults' standards and therefore inferior. Thus, special capacities of children may be even turned into no-capacities, e.g. de-qualifying their mimetic capacities or imaginations as irrational or dysfunctional.

2011: 33–34). For Sen, the opportunity to have public discussions is crucial, as much as the implementation of certain liberties, for instance the extension of actual freedom through education or uncensored media. His arguments are based on the principle of equality: every human life has the same value and everyone has the same rights regardless of gender, skin colour, etc.

This last point is object of criticism by Graf (2011) who believes Sen's conception "involves an ethical individualism: The individual and not the group, such as family or other institutions of society, defines the core and the origin for further thoughts" (op. cit.: 25). Taking this into consideration it is evidently necessary to specify which capacities are relevant in the particular context and "how a good life in a certain socio-cultural context would look like" (op. cit.: 27; the notion 'ethical individualism' was phrased first by Robeyns 2006).[7]

We can summarize that there is a difference between the common understanding of capacities (particularly in the context of HR and CR) and the understanding of capabilities by the CA. While capacities are understood as attributes or abilities of a subject (on a subjective level), the term capabilities also takes into account the conditions and reasons for the development and the use of capacities. Within this logic, even 'innate capacities' receive the status of 'capabilities' if they are appropriate to achieve wanted or recognized aims or outcomes. This means that they are perceived and only become visible as capacities in a certain context. The fundamental idea of the CA is that capacities (on a subjective level) always depend on certain living conditions beyond the subject's reach or which exist independently of the individual subject.

The CA could really contribute to a better understanding and re-conceptualization of the 'evolving capacities' principle, by advocating to look not only at the attributes or abilities of the subjects, but also at the available opportunities. Likewise, it is important that the CA emphasizes the centrality of the subject's autonomy and value-oriented own decisions. In this way the CA can also help to overcome the paradoxes and risks of the HR/CR discourse by placing it in the concrete living context. The CA strongly invites to contextualize this discourse. Nevertheless, it remains unclear how HR/CR are understood and connected with the capabilities by the main advocates of the CA. This will be discussed first with regard to HR and later with regard to CR.

4.5 Human Rights in the Light of the Capability Approach

The reference to HR can be found particularly in Sen's work. He identifies "human rights as entitlements to capabilities" (Sen 2005: 152) while he defines capability as "the opportunity to achieve valuable combinations of human functioning – what a person is able to do or be" (op. cit.: 153). He argues that HR are understood as rights

[7] All quotes from German literature are translated by the author.

to "certain specific freedoms" which is correlated to what others "can do to safeguard and expand these freedoms". Since capabilities can be seen, broadly, as freedoms of particular kinds, this would seem to establish a basic connection between the two categories of ideas" (op. cit.: 152). However, distinguishing 'opportunity' and 'process' as two aspects of freedom, has difficulties, as Sen himself admits:

> While the opportunity aspect of freedoms would seem to belong to the same kind of territory as capabilities, it is not at all clear that the same can be said about the process aspect of freedom. [...] Capabilities and the opportunity aspect of freedom, important as they are, have to be supplemented by considerations of fair processes and the lack of violation of people's right to invoke and utilize them. (op. cit.: 152 and 157)

Sen concludes that both human rights and capabilities function well together but shall not be included in each other concept because "there are many human rights for which the capability approach has much to offer" as well as many human rights "cannot be adequately analyzed within the capability approach" (op. cit.: 163). In a later published text, Sen (2009) emphasizes:

> Capability is basically a concept of freedom. But freedom has different aspects, including what can be called 'the opportunity aspect' reflecting the actual opportunities a person has, and 'the process aspect' (such as equality of treatment), which deals with having arrangements and institutions that can be seen to be components of procedural freedom. While the idea of capability has considerable merit in the assessment of the opportunity aspect, it cannot possibly deal adequately with the process aspect of freedom. Capabilities are characteristics of individual advantages, and they fall short of telling us enough about the fairness or equity of the processes involved, or about the freedom of citizens to invoke and utilize procedures that are equitable. (op. cit.: 27)

According to Sen, the 'process aspect' may be involved in a theory of HR, or in a theory of justice:

> A theory of justice – or more generally an adequate theory of normative social choice – has to be alive both to the fairness of the processes involved and to the equity and efficiency of the substantive opportunities that people can enjoy. [...] But neither justice, nor political or moral evaluation, can be concerned only with the overall opportunities and advantages of individuals in a society. The subject of fair process and fair deal goes beyond overall advantages of persons into other – mainly procedural – concerns, and these concerns cannot be adequately addressed through concentrating on capabilities only. (op. cit.: 27–28)

Sen's arguments are object of criticism, also of self-criticism. Referring to a critical comment by Susan Okin (2003), he admits himself that his idea of freedom may be too inclusive and overextended (Sen 2005: 154). Okin argued: "It is hard to conceive of some human functioning, or the fulfilment of some needs and wants, such as good health and nourishment, as freedoms without stretching the term until it seems to refer to everything that is of central value to human beings" (Okin 2003: 292).

The question whether capacities or capabilities are valued as such depends on what is seen as 'good' and 'indispensable' for human life in a certain context. One shall consider that neither capacities nor capabilities are neutral towards social judgments, which develop from implicit or explicit conceptions of the 'good'.

Just the determination of one's ability as a 'capacity' opens a deep insight into the conceptions of the good life. As an example it could be referred to the capacity to work or the lack of the capacity to work. Within the capitalist economy the functionality of this capacity depends on its usefulness towards the accumulation of capital which is devaluated as no-capacity (in case it does not work towards that, for instance social competencies or altruistic attitudes). There are not isolated individuals who cultivate or lose capabilities, but people who always are involved in relationships. Capabilities are not placed on the same level but in a hierarchic order corresponding to social values (see Sedmak 2011: 41–42).

In Sen's version of the CA the basis of the values development policy is not precise and hardly argumented. He "only affirms that policies have to be judged in the space of capabilities or freedoms" (Deneulin 2009: 5). Deneulin considers Sen's version of the CA absent of a detailed analysis of values without any reference to its definition, development and modification (ibid.: 7). According to Deneulin, values have two core characteristics: they refer to what is believed to be good and they guide human action applicable to individuals and social groups denominated by the author as "drivers of values" (op. cit: 11; see also Stewart 2005). The analysis of groups as 'agents of value change' has remained absent from the human development and CA literature so far. Deneulin (2009: 12) explains "The human development and the CA would need a more careful analysis of the relational spaces which shape people's values, and the groups which dominate them." She exemplifies this with the link to religious communities, the education system, global corporations or the media.

In a critique of the 'individualism' of the CA, another author (Evans 2002) cites, for instance, the empires of Coca-Cola and MTV as shaping people's values and what they consider as 'valuable'. Thus, according to Evans, it is necessary to analyse groups or communities "which foster or nurture certain kinds of values" and "to analyse the conflicts between them as these may lead in a change of values (op. cit: 12–13). The same shall be analysed in terms of social movements, particularly because "the promotion of human freedoms is often not a peaceful enterprise" (op. cit.: 14). This is also relevant with regard to what is understood as freedom and HR. "The human development and CA need to provide, in addition to an evaluative framework for states of affairs – the capability space, an analysis of the dynamics of value formation, of the different groups which shape these values, of the degree of power they command, and their consequent influence on policy" (op. cit.: 15).

Up to now Amartya Sen as well as other advocates of the CA do not take into account in which way the capabilities (which are relevant for the use of HR) may be acquired during the life course and in which way they are influenced by or interconnected with the value system or the production of values within a given society. Over the next paragraphs I will discuss the meaning of the CA for children and for CR.

4.6 Children's Rights in the Light of the Capability Approach

With regard to CR the leading authors of the CA postulate a fundamental difference between children and adults while not considering children as agents properly. They only mention children briefly.

Martha Nussbaum (2000) holds that in relation to children it is "perfectly legitimate" to require certain types of functionings instead of looking at their capabilities because "exercising a function in childhood is frequently necessary to produce a mature adult capability" (op. cit.: 89–90). In a similar way Amartya Sen (2007) argues that the promotion of children's "freedom may well have to be, often enough, in the hands of others" (op. cit.: 243). He sees the task of public policy mainly in providing and maintaining opportunities to young people in line with what they "can be reasonably expected to want" (ibid.). Leßmann et al. (2011) conclude that "there is a theoretical capability gap concerning justice for the young to be filled" (op. cit.: 21; see also Leßmann 2014).

Considering the basic relevance of HR for human beings, Sen (2007) regards that there is

> [. . .] a special problem in the case of children, since they do not, frequently enough, take their own decisions. If rights are interpreted in terms of freedoms that the right holders should have, their usefulness must depend on how these freedoms are exercised; but can children take their own decisions? If the application of human rights to children must involve the children themselves taking well-considered decisions on the exercise of those freedoms then we would seem to be on the threshold of a manifest contradiction: Can children really take these decisions? But is that the right question? (op. cit.: 243)

In the case of children, Sen does not see any sense in the distinction of the 'opportunity aspect' and the 'process aspect', which otherwise seems to him essential for a theory of justice and HR. He argues:

> Insofar as the process aspect of freedom demands that a person should be making his or her own choice, that aspect of freedom is not particularly relevant to the human rights of children, except in some rather minimal ways (such as a child's freedom – and perhaps right – to get attention when it decides to scream the house down). But the opportunity aspect of freedom is immensely important for children. What opportunities children have today and will have tomorrow, in line with what they can be reasonably expected to want, is a matter of public policy and social programmes, involving a great many agencies. (op. cit.: 244)

In this connection Sen does not distinguish between two possible meanings of the 'process aspect'. If we consider the institutional requirement to make use of one's personal HR and to let opportunities become real we would relate to the question of contextualizing rights. In this case the 'process aspect' would be closely connected to the 'opportunity aspect'. This argument would be important to avoid the ambivalence or 'aporias' of HR and to place them into a more concrete context. However, if we consider the subjective capacity to make use of one's rights this would imply taking the subjective ability to act as the only benchmark to implement HR. Sen seems to follow the second argument with regards to children. With regard to them he only focuses on the lack of subjective capacities. He implies, in an abstract and static manner, that children do not have the necessary capacities, nor will they be able to gain them (as children). That means, he understands CR solely in a paternalistic way, as described in the beginning of this paper, without allowing children the opportunity to use rights themselves, to claim their rights or to execute them.

The same line of thought is reinforced by Babic (2011: 82) who indicates that Sen seems to have "a fairly undifferentiated understanding of children and childhood". Babic criticizes Sen for "not allowing children to make decisions. There doesn't seem to be any recognition of the fact that children won't just turn into an adult all of a sudden but need to go through processes of development and growth till they reach adulthood (which is hard to define), to also become more experienced and capable to make decisions" (op. cit.: 83; similar Graf et al. 2011).

Another author criticising Sen is Leßmann (2009) who points out that in Sen's model of processes of development and growth "any description of temporal interactions" is missing (op. cit: 453). According to her, Sen has limited his view with his "comparative static model" on "choice situations but does not link them" (ibid.). Because of his orientation in consumer choice models in economics, Sen seems to be satisfied "with modelling the 'process aspect' by allowing for choosing one functioning bundle out of the capability set" (ibid.).[8]

So far, Amartya Sen does not consider children as social subjects with personal needs of autonomy, but only as *future* citizens who will have to develop capabilities regarding this citizenship.[9] He emphasizes the capabilities that *shall* be gained. Although he admits that children have or want a certain variety of options to choose from, he claims that these liberties only become relevant with regard to the future. Opinion confirmed by Saito (2003): "When dealing with children, it is the freedom they will have in the future rather than the present that should be considered" (op. cit.: 26).

This also holds true for Martha Nussbaum, the other leading author of the CA. She considers children's participation and decision-making in certain situations as possible and desirable, particularly in order to prepare them for citizenship (see e.g. Nussbaum 1999: 198). In a recent publication, Nussbaum and her co-author Rosalind Dixon (2012) suggest to grant younger children "at least certain

[8] Referring to questions of 'moral powers' and the 'sense of justice', MacLeod (2010) invites to get a more differentiated look at the *moral* capacities of children and their imaginations of the 'good'. He points out: "In virtue of their less fully developed moral powers, children, and even young adolescents, lack full authority to set their own ends. This does not imply, however, that children, even young children, are passive subjects to whom childhood goods are simply delivered. Even without the powers of full agency, children are active participants in the creation of goods because the character of the good they experience when some facet of their faculties is engaged or challenged will depend partly on their own tastes and idiosyncratic responses to challenges they face" (ibid.: 190–191). On the development of children's sense of justice see Liebel (2013b: 217–230) for more details.

[9] See Invernizzi and Williams (2008) and Liebel (2012: 183–195) on different concepts of children's citizenship and corresponding capacities and capabilities.

decisional rights". This is based on the argument that "the right to make certain decisions provides an important opportunity to practice thinking, and making decisions, within certain protected bounds, so as to develop their *future* capacity for meaningful agency" (op. cit.: 560; italics added by ML). Nussbaum highlights the need to bring out *future* capabilities of children, principally by obligatory school attendance (opinion shared by Sen who indicates the importance of compulsory education for developing capabilities). She emphasises the restriction of children's self-determination in favour of their supposedly better life in future. Such restrictions conflict with the assumption that the above mentioned 'central capabilities' have to be guaranteed for *all* human beings as indispensable prerequisites for a 'decent life' (see Schweinitz 2012: 31–35).

Only in the last few years, thoughts and research approaches have evolved, like the question how children's views, interests and rights can be included in the CA. The central question that arises is what basic needs have to be fulfilled to live a worthy and equitable life during childhood and which capabilities and entitlements have to be accessible. In the following paragraph I will focus on the so far empirical studies which have been conducted.

Using the perspective of the CA, some empirical studies have been conducted which aimed to estimate the possibilities and limitations children face in achieving capabilities, which will be meaningful for children's current and future life. In some of these studies children have been asked about their goals and values (Graf et al. 2011) or their well-being is assessed (Kellock and Lawthom 2011; Alkire and Roche 2012). Other studies are centred on the agency of small children (Volkert and Wüst 2011). Most studies focus on 'street children' (Anich et al. 2011; Horna Padrón and Ballett 2011; Serrokh 2011; Camfield and Tafere 2011) or 'child labour' (Biggeri et al. 2010, 2011) and try to estimate children's personal views on their capabilities. In a study the attempt was made to define universal criteria of children's specific capabilities in 'developing countries' (Di Tommaso 2007).

Even though these studies have continuously proven children's agency, it remains indistinct to what extent children are actually understood as stakeholders with personal subjective rights or are just seen as potential beneficiaries of welfare laws. They mainly restrict themselves to identifying criteria of well-being or conditions for the development of capabilities, without going into detail about how children could influence the definition of these criteria and conditions. Moreover, the agency perspective remains focused on children as individuals, without involving the experiences and possibilities of children's organised and collective actions. An example for such collective agency is the social movements of working children and adolescents that come into being in some parts of the majority world since the eighties of the last century (see e.g. Liebel 2004, 2013a).

In another paper, Clark and Eisenhuth (2009) deal with the CA's advancement regarding children and youth. In their view "the early stages of life are not considered as intrinsically valuable, but tend to get reduced to instruments for later adulthood" (op. cit.: 3). They see a contradiction between this exclusively instrumental view and the CA fundamental requirement not to define the individual as an instrument of society (e.g. for the community or the economy), but as an individual in his/her own right. Both authors understand children explicitly as stakeholders, whose competences might be age-related, but who are able to take an active part in conflicts of justice. They shall be entitled to co-decide regarding issues that matter to them or what a good childhood shall consist of. "Consequently children should not only be seen as passive recipients of schooling, welfare, social services, but should be allowed to realize a capability for voice, in order to recognize them as current subjects of moral concern, instead of future citizens" (op. cit.: 7; similar Clark and Eisenhuth 2011). In a further paper, Clark and Eisenhuth (2010: 72) suggest to advance the CA in a way "that the same metric of human dignity applied to adults should also be addressed to children, even though it might need to be specified in a certain age-dependent way". These authors do not analyse this aspect in further detail (see also the chapter by Clark and Ziegler in this volume).

The theoretical chapters of a textbook edited by Biggeri et al. (2011) pursue this perspective, which emphasizes the meaning of the CA for children. In order to use the CA towards the analysis of children's life situations, the authors find it necessary to overcome the 'static' conceptualization (as in Sen's and Nussbaum's work) of capabilities and its definition of an ideal and grown-up understanding of rationality. From a capability perspective it is not only necessary to ask about children's ability (to be well educated, healthy, etc.) but to ask about the "the process of freedom itself" (Comim et al. 2011: 13). Children are explicitly defined as "co-producers of their capabilities" (op. cit.: 5), and as "active actors and agents" (ibid.). Children's agency can be confirmed by their participation which shall be seen in conjunction with their specific capacities. "Participation is the autonomy's expression and the individual expresses itself in autonomous ways by participating. Autonomy has sense only *in* social participation" (op. cit.: 11; italics in original work).

The field of studies on capabilities cannot disregard possible ways to encourage children's active participation in various social settings. In favour of this, the authors point out three main reasons:

> (1) the competencies, resources and capabilities of a subject, in particular of children, are tied to the possibility of being acted, understood and being recognized as significant. In other terms, capabilities are strictly dependent on the forms (social and individual) and by the possibilities (environment) of agency; (2) the different forms of participation and the environmental conditions that enable its expression need to be valorized and sustained to enable them to reproduce over time: there are no 'natural' *capabilities* (understood as opportunities) but only those socially built; and (3) different cultures and many social contexts that denote, and in which capabilities are built, can be considered only if they become visible along with the practices and the orientations that inspire them. (op. cit.: 12)

If these three conditions were disregarded, the CA would remain captured in a conventional understanding of childhood and would be incapable of doing justice to cultural differences, different ways of expression and of taking account certain social, political and environmental conditions all of which are relevant for children's concrete life. There is a strong demand for the CA to overcome the "individualistic approach" regarding children (Ballet et al. 2011: 36) and children's rights, and to understand and seize them in a non-paternalistic way. However, this programmatic challenge has until now rarely been put into practice by empirical studies that use the CA as an orientation.

4.7 Perspectives of Evolving Capabilities by Children

If we want to get a deeper understanding of children's possibilities to make use of their rights, the idea of 'evolving capabilities' as articulated in the above mentioned interpretations and enhancements of the CA, can be helpful. This allows us to contextualize CR with children's concrete living situations and experiences. Nevertheless a more dynamic and differentiated look at the different aspects and representations of childhood is needed as well as it is important to observe the lived realities of children and how to understand and deal with their agency.

First, it needs to be taken into account that the term 'child' as used in the UNCRC refers to a broad variation of ages (from birth to the age of 18). This goes hand in hand with different manifestations and potentials of agency as well as it is linked to different scopes of action and autonomy in taking decisions on one's own life. Such differences are not simply the 'natural' result of the chronological age or corresponding physical or mental attributes, but also strongly influenced by the children's life experiences. Furthermore, what is called "maturity and the ability to live an independent life is not something that is simply given or not. It has to be seen as a process, as something that develops and grows over time" (Graf et al. 2011: 270), which depends on the opportunities available to the children to develop the relevant capacities for a self-understanding and realization of their agency.

Secondly, the evolution of capacities and capabilities must not be understood – as suggested by the concept of 'maturity' – as a process which leads necessarily and always from lower to higher levels. What we may understand as a certain level of capacity is always a question of definition and depends on those who have the corresponding definition power, for which reason this process must be reflected in regards to how decisions are made and who is in charge of deciding which capacities and capabilities are relevant for children especially. As demonstrated in former chapters, what is recognized as capacity or qualified as a certain level of capacity there is always a 'relation' to the question of what it is understood as 'functional'. In a hierarchical sense the capacities of children are usually seen as 'lower' or 'less developed' than those of adults. The criteria for these types of judgement remain a mystery to those who have the definition power, and are usually adults. Their basis is a special kind of rationality that seems to be 'normal' in a society where adults are accustomed to see themselves as dominating or actually are. In other words: it is an adult-centred rationality that devaluates all kinds of thinking and reasoning by children as 'irrational', 'immature' or with less value. There is no doubt, we can observe certain differences between the capacities of adults and children but we are in need to recognize the capacities of children as 'differently equal' to those of adults and respect them as likewise valuable and important within society (see Moosa-Mitha 2005; Liebel 2012: 188–195). Moreover, children's particular capacities, notably where they are articulated in collective forms, might even be understood as 'drivers of value' (Deneulin) to the point of stimulating social transformations (see Liebel 2012: 199–225). At least, children can be protagonists of new social relations and forms of communication.

Thirdly, as meanwhile broadly recognized within the developmental psychology, children's capacities are not simply a 'passive' result of interventions by adults, but likewise co-produced by themselves (see e.g. Woodhead 2009; Smith et al. 2011). From an early age on already, "children choose and select their developmental aims. Additionally they choose, design or influence their environment" (Sadlowski 2011: 228). If we recognize that children as social subjects (under the 'being' aspect as well as the 'becoming' aspect) are able to influence the social conditions relevant for the *evolution*, for the *recognition*, and finally for the *use* of their capacities, we must *recognize* them as co-producers of capabilities in the widest sense of the CA. Of course, not all children can perform this in the same way or without limitations, set by their limited capacities as well as by the structural conditions of their living, but they are able to and in fact do contribute in modifying those limitations.

Fourthly, the status of childhood as a subordinated and marginalized 'social group' must be considered as well as the inequality between different 'groups' of children themselves, for instance between children living in poverty and those living in wealth, or between working children and non-working children. Such inequalities as much that they are not 'natural' but structurally conditioned, can have strong impacts on children's scope of agency and their access to CR (see Freeman 2007). Furthermore, it must be taken into account that there are rather different concepts of childhood in different parts of the world which imply different visions of what is 'good' for children or how far and in which way the participation of children is accepted or expected (see Liebel and Saadi 2012b). On the other hand, the intuitive *sense of justice* that can be observed particularly in children who are living under extremely disadvantaged conditions (see Liebel 2013b: 217–240), may be understood (and should be recognized) as a 'driver of value' in the above mentioned sense that can become a strong part of the children's 'capability set'.

Finally, we need to become aware what kind of social relations and which ways of transformation the intended capabilities shall stand for. From my point of view, it is not enough to set the focus on 'freedom' as far as it is understood principally as the number of opportunities for individual choices or the equality of chances. It seems necessary to me to get an understanding of 'freedom' that goes beyond 'individual choices' onto fundamental participation in decision-making on all aspects of human life, individually as well as collectively. This includes the vision of a 'just society' where people can enjoy a maximum of social equality, equity, social recognition and equal access to HR, children as well as adults. CR should not be understood any longer only in a 'negative' sense to be, as children, protected against or provided for (usually by institutionalized authorities), but in a 'positive' sense to be able to live in dignified social conditions and get the power to use the rights by the will of their own. To such ending, not only capacities but capabilities would have been 'evolved'.

References

Alderson, P. (2008). *Young children's rights* (2nd ed.). London: Jessica Kingsley.

Alkire, S., & Roche, J. M. (2012). Beyond headcount. The Alkire-Foster approach to multidimensional child poverty measurement. In I. Ortiz, L. M. Daniels, & S. Englibertsdóttir (Eds.), *Child poverty and inequality: New perspectives* (pp. 18–22). New York: UNICEF Division of Policy and Practice.

Anich, R., Biggeri, M., Libanora, R., & Mariani, S. (2011). Street children in Kampala and NGO's actions: Understanding capabilities deprivation and expansion. In M. Biggeri et al. (Eds.), *Children and the capability approach* (pp. 107–136). Basingstoke: Palgrave Macmillan.

Arendt, H. (1952/2004). *The origins of totalitarianism*. New York: Schocken.

Babic, B. (2011). Ohne intellektuelle Redlichkeit kein Fortschritt. Kritische Anmerkungen zum Umgang mit dem Capability Approach aus erziehungswissenschaftlicher Sicht. In C. Sedmak et al. (Eds.), *Der Capability-Approach in sozialwissenschaftlichen Kontexten* (pp. 75–89). Wiesbaden: VS Verlag für Sozialwissenschaften.

Ballet, J., Biggeri, M., & Comim, F. (2011). Children's agency and the capability approach: A conceptual framework. In M. Biggeri et al. (Eds.), *Children and the capability approach* (pp. 22–45). Basingstoke: Palgrave Macmillan.

Biggeri, M., Ballet, J., & Comim, F. (2010). The capability approach and research on children: Capability approach and children's issues. In S. Andresen et al. (Eds.), *Children and the good life: New challenges for the research on children* (pp. 75–89). Dordrecht: Springer Netherlands.

Biggeri, M., Ballet, J., & Comim, F. (Eds.). (2011). *Children and the capability approach*. Basingstoke: Palgrave Macmillan.

Biggeri, M., Bhukuth, A., & Radja, K. (2011). Re-examing children's economic and Non-economic activities using the capability approach. In M. Biggeri et al. (Eds.), *Children and the capability approach* (pp. 286–303). Basingstoke: Palgrave Macmillan.

Brighouse, H. (2002). What rights (if any) do children have? In D. Archard & C. M. Macleod (Eds.), *The moral and political status of children* (pp. 31–52). Oxford: Oxford University Press.

Camfield, L., & Tafere, Y. (2011). "Good for children?" local understanding versus universal prescriptions: Evidence from three Ethiopian communities. In M. Biggeri et al. (Eds.), *Children and the capability approach* (pp. 200–221). Basingstoke: Palgrave Macmillan.

Clark, Z., & Eisenhuth, F. (2009). *Beyond well-becoming, towards well-being: Young people and the capabilities approach*. Paper at the Human Development and Capability Association International Conference, Lima. http://www.capabilityapproach.com/pubs/ClarkEisenhuth_Beyond%20Wellbecoming.pdf. Accessed 30 June 2013.

Clark, Z., & Eisenhuth, F. (2010). The capability approach and research on children. In S. Andresen et al. (Eds.), *Children and the good life: New challenges for the research on children* (pp. 69–73). Dordrecht: Springer Netherlands.

Clark, Z., & Eisenhuth, F. (2011). Beyond futurity – a capabilities perspective on childhood and youth. In O. Leßmann et al. (Eds.), *Closing the capabilities gap* (pp. 277–285). Opladen: Barbara Budrich.

Comim, F., Ballet, J., Biggeri, M., & Iervese, V. (2011). Introduction – theoretical foundations and the book's roadmap. In M. Biggeri et al. (Eds.), *Children and the capability approach* (pp. 1–21). Basingstoke: Palgrave Macmillan.

Deneulin, S. (2009). *Advancing human development: Values, groups, power and conflict*. WeD Working Paper 09/49. Bath: University of Bath.

Di Tommaso, M. L. (2007). Children capabilities: A structural equitation model for India. *The Journal of Socio-Economics, 36*, 436–450. http://www.de.unito.it/web/member/ditommaso/JA/J_Socio_Economics_JA6.pdf. Accessed 30 June 2013.

Dixon, R., & Nussbaum, M. C. (2012). *Children's rights and the capabilities approach: The question of special priority*. Chicago Public Law and Legal Theory Working Paper No 384: 548–594. Chicago: The Law School, University of Chicago.

Evans, P. (2002). Collective capabilities, culture and Amartya Sen's development as freedom. *Studies in Comparative International Development, 37*(2), 54–60.

Freeman, M. (2007). Why it remains important to take children's rights seriously. *The International Journal of Children's Rights, 15*, 5–23.

Gasper, D. (2002). Is Sen's capability approach an adequate basis for considering human development? *Review of Political Economy, 14*(4), 435–461.

Graf, G. (2011). Der Fähigkeitsansatz im Kontext von Informationsbasen sozialethischer Theorien. In C. Sedmak et al. (Eds.), *Der Capability-Approach in sozialwissenschaftlichen Kontexten* (pp. 11–28). Wiesbaden: VS Verlag für Sozialwissenschaften.

Graf, G., Germes-Castro, O., & Babic, B. (2011). Approaching capabilities with children in care – an international project to identify values of child and young people in care. In O. Leßmann et al. (Eds.), *Closing the capabilities gap* (pp. 267–276). Opladen: Barbara Budrich.

Gündoğdu, A. (2012). "Perplexities of the rights of man": Arendt on the aporias of human rights. *European Journal of Political Theory, 11*(1), 4–24.

Hanson, K. (2012). Schools of thought in children's rights. In M. Liebel et al. (Eds.), *Children's rights from below: Cross-cultural perspectives* (pp. 63–79). Basingstoke: Palgrave Macmillan.

Horna Padrón, M., & Ballet, J. (2011). Child agency and identity: The case of Peruvian children in a transitional situation. In M. Biggeri et al. (Eds.), *Children and the capability approach* (pp. 162–174). Basingstoke: Palgrave Macmillan.

Invernizzi, A., & Williams, J. (Eds.). (2008). *Children and citizenship*. Los Angeles: SAGE Publications.

James, A. (2009). Agency. In J. Qvortrup, W. A. Corsaro, & M.-S. Honig (Eds.), *The Palgrave handbook of childhood studies* (pp. 34–45). Basingstoke: Palgrave Macmillan.

Kellock, A., & Lawthom, R. (2011). Sen's capability approach: Children and well-being explored through the use of photography. In M. Biggeri et al. (Eds.), *Children and the capability approach* (pp. 137–161). Basingstoke: Palgrave Macmillan.

Lansdown, G. (2005). *The evolving capacities of the child*. Florence: UNICEF Innocenti Research Centre.

Leßmann, O. (2009). Capability and learning to choose. *Studies in Philosophy and Education, 28*, 449–460.

Leßmann, O. (2014). Child poverty from a capability perspective. In C. S. Hart, M. Biggeri, & B. Babic (Eds.), *Agency and participation in childhood and youth: Developing capabilities in schools and beyond*. London: Bloomsbury Academic.

Leßmann, O., Otto, H.-U., & Ziegler, H. (2011). Introduction: Closing the capability gap and renewing social criticism. In O. Leßmann et al. (Eds.), *Closing the capabilities gap* (pp. 7–24). Opladen: Barbara Budrich.

Liebel, M. (2004). *A will of their own: Cross-cultural perspectives on working children*. London: Zed Books.

Liebel, M. (2012). *Children's rights from below: Cross-cultural perspectives* (with contributions by Karl Hanson, Iven Saadi and Wouter Vandenhole). Basingstoke: Palgrave Macmillan.

Liebel, M. (2013a). Do children have a right to work? Working children's movements in the struggle for social justice. In K. Hanson & O. Nieuwenhuys (Eds.), *Reconceptualizing children's rights in international development: Living rights, social justice, translations* (pp. 225–249). Cambridge: Cambridge University Press.

Liebel, M. (2013b). *Kinder und Gerechtigkeit*. Über Kinderrechte neu nachdenken. Weinheim and Basel: Beltz-Juventa.

Liebel, M., & Saadi, I. (2012a). Children's rights and the responsibility of states: Thoughts on understanding children's rights as subjective rights. In M. Liebel et al. (Eds.), *Children's rights from below: Cross-cultural perspectives* (pp. 108–122). Basingstoke: Palgrave Macmillan.

Liebel, M., & Saadi, I. (2012b). Cultural variations in constructions of children's participation. In M. Liebel et al. (Eds.), *Children's rights from below: Cross-cultural perspectives* (pp. 162–182). Basingstoke: Palgrave Macmillan.

MacLeod, C. M. (2010). Primary goods, capabilities, and children. In H. Brighouse & I. Robeyns (Eds.), *Measuring justice: Primary goods and capabilities* (pp. 174–192). Cambridge: Cambridge University Press.

Moosa-Mitha, M. (2005). A difference-centred alternative to theorization of children's citizenship rights. *Citizenship Studies, 9*(4), 369–388.

Nussbaum, M. C. (1999). *Gerechtigkeit oder das gute Leben*. Frankfurt/M: Suhrkamp.

Nussbaum, M. C. (2000). *Women and human development: The capability approach*. Cambridge: Cambridge University Press.

Nussbaum, M. C. (2011). *Creating capabilities: The human development approach*. Cambridge MA: The Belknap Press of Harvard University Press.

Okin, S. (2003). Poverty, well-being, and gender: What counts, who's heard? *Philosophy and Public Affairs, 31*, 280–316.

Robeyns, I. (2006). The capability approach in practice. *Journal of Political Philosophy, 14*(3), 351–376.

Sadlowski, I. (2011). A capability approach fit for children. In O. Leßmann et al. (Eds.), *Closing the capabilities gap* (pp. 215–232). Opladen: Barbara Budrich.

Saito, M. (2003). Amartya Sen's capability approach to education: A critical exploration. *Journal of Philosophy of Education, 37*(1), 17–33.

Sedmak, C. (2011). Fähigkeiten und Fundamentalfähigkeiten. In C. Sedmak et al. (Eds.), *Der Capability-Approach in sozialwissenschaftlichen Kontexten* (pp. 29–52). Wiesbaden: VS Verlag für Sozialwissenschaften.

Sen, A. (1992). *Inequality re-examined*. Oxford: Oxford University Press.

Sen, A. (1993). Capability and well-being. In A. Sen & M. C. Nussbaum (Eds.), *The quality of life* (pp. 30–53). Oxford: Clarendon.

Sen, A. (1999). *Development as freedom*. New York: Anchor Books.

Sen, A. (2005). Human rights and capabilities. *Journal of Human Development, 6*(2), 151–166.

Sen, A. (2007). Children and human rights. *Indian Journal of Human Development, 1*(2), 235–245.

Sen, A. (2009). Capability: Reach and limits. In E. Chiappero-Martinetti (Ed.), *Debating global society* (pp. 15–28). Milan: Giangiacomo Feltrinelli Foundation.

Serrokh, B. (2011). Micro-finance, street children and the capability approach: Is micro-finance an appropriate tool to address the street children issue? In M. Biggeri et al. (Eds.), *Children and the capability approach* (pp. 175–199). Basingstoke: Palgrave Macmillan.

Smith, P. K., Cowie, H., & Blades, M. (2011). *Understanding children's development*. Oxford: Wiley-Blackwell.

Stewart, F. (2005). Groups and capabilities. *Journal of Human Development, 6*(2), 185–204.

UNCRC. (1989). *UN convention on the right of the child*. New York: United Nations.

Volkert, J., & Wüst, K. (2011). Early childhood, agency and capability deprivation – a quantitative analysis using Germen socio-economic panel data. In O. Leßmann et al. (Eds.), *Closing the capabilities gap* (pp. 179–198). Opladen: Barbara Budrich.

von Schweinitz, C. (2012). *Kinderarbeit aus wirtschaftsethischer Perspektive*. Bachelor thesis, Universität St. Gallen, Hochschule für Wirtschafts-, Rechts- und Sozialwissenschaften.

Woodhead, M. (2009). Child development and the development of childhood. In J. Qvortrup, W. A. Corsaro, & M.-S. Honig (Eds.), *The Palgrave handbook of childhood studies* (pp. 46–61). Basingstoke: Palgrave Macmillan.

Chapter 5
Reconstructing Children's Concepts: Some Theoretical Ideas and Empirical Findings on Education and the Good Life

Sabine Andresen and Katharina Gerarts

5.1 Introduction

One basic assumption in new social childhood studies is the need to take an orientation toward the present when studying children. This is then frequently contrasted with the future-oriented perspective that adults stereotypically associate with children and childrearing. It seems to be precisely educational science along with pedagogic practice that are particularly susceptible to take such a future orientation and view children as incomplete adults. Recent approaches in childhood studies, in contrast, emphasize the strengths and actor status of children, problematize the power hierarchy in the relation between the generations, and view the childhood phase as a social concept that is also shaped by specific interests (Betz 2008). Research on child well-being also proceeds from a paradigmatic shift in perspective from well-becoming to well-being as well as from a focus on adults to a focus on the child (Ben-Arieh 2010). This orientation toward children in the here and now and children as autonomous actors links up in terms of the theory of children's rights with the maxims of the Polish pediatrician and educator Janusz Korczak who called for recognition of children's right to live in the present (Korczak 1929, 1999). However, any examination of children's rights and their justification in the theory of childhood soon reveals the insufficiency of any one-sided concentration on only the future or only the present. Children are able

---

Translated from the German by Jonathan Harrow.

S. Andresen (✉)
Institut für Sozialpädagogik und Erwachsenenbildung, Goethe University Frankfurt, Grüneburgplatz 1, 60323 Frankfurt am Main, Germany
e-mail: S.Andresen@em.uni-frankfurt.de

K. Gerarts
World Vision Institute für Forschung und Innovation, Am Zollstock 2-4, 61381 Friedrichsdorf, Germany
e-mail: institut@worldvision.de

D. Stoecklin and J.-M. Bonvin (eds.), *Children's Rights and the Capability Approach*, Children's Well-Being: Indicators and Research 8, DOI 10.1007/978-94-017-9091-8_5,

as children, and they have a right to participation as children, to their existence as children in the here and now. However, they also have a right to education, which is always linked to the future (Robeyns 2000), as well as a right to protection. One question of this chapter is how the rights of participation, education and protection take part within the concepts of children themselves (Doek 2014). How children focus on participation, education and protection as rights in their all-day life and what they miss should be more reflected by the theory of childhood. Another issue here is the possible hierarchy children maybe make between the principle rights.

In general this chapter argues that it is necessary not to lose sight of this tension between well-being and well-becoming in either theory or empirical research but to address it systematically.

The realization that childhood is constructed in social contexts was and continues to be a major insight in social-constructivist childhood studies (Qvortrup 2014). At the same time, however, it is necessary to recognize the child's vulnerability and need for protection along with a right to not only the here and now but also to a future perspective. This question of the tension between the two forms the basis for this chapter.

We shall start by taking a sociology of science perspective on a childhood studies oriented toward educational science. To express it pointedly, educational science is a discipline obligated to "intervene" in children by rearing and educating them. It possesses corresponding concepts of childrearing, it has foundations in childrearing theory and education theory, and it positions the child in what is finally a hierarchically structured generation difference. Childhood studies with an educational orientation have to take this into account while simultaneously acknowledging central evidence of new social childhood studies such as that of the child as a competent actor. This means that children not only participate in their world and make different experiences, they creates worlds. But childhood studies needs more research on the meaning of what we claimed 'competent' with respect to children's different developmental stages and their abilities and control over themselves. And also is research needed to figure out much more deeply the relations between adults as "actors" e.g. in schools and children as "actors". The Sect. 5.2 will examine how an educationally oriented research on childhood can be conceived and how it could negotiate with empirical and systematical challenges.

Then, we have to clarify how one can systematically focus on the relation between well-being and well-becoming when carrying out childhood studies (Sect. 5.3). We shall attempt to do this with the theory of the "good life." One aspect of the concept of a good life according to Martha Nussbaum (1999, 2000) is being in any way able to have ideas about what this may be. To develop ideas about a good life, people need to possess abilities and possibilities. We could also ask who disposes of which living conditions in order to be able to think about a good life going beyond the real conditions of existence and to develop plans, wishes, and dreams. This is covered in the Sect. 5.3 that focuses on the possibilities for children to form their own ideas about a good life.

Following the theoretical consideration of the tension sketched above, we shall discuss empirical findings from our own studies that we consider to contribute to an educational-science-oriented childhood studies. Both empirical sections include a description and reflection on our methodological approach. Analogue to Sect. 5.2, Sect. 5.4 presents and analyzes the childrearing concepts of those for whom being reared is simply part of their daily lives of which they are more or less aware. The analysis of childrearing concepts is based on qualitative data gathered by Katharina Gerarts for her doctoral thesis and examined in more depth in this chapter. In sum, Sect. 5.6 can thereby be viewed as a first empirical test of the "negotiation" of the tension described above. This is followed by Sect. 5.5 with a description and analysis of the concept of the "good life" based on findings from the World Vision Children Studies (World Vision 2007, 2010, 2013) combined with asking the children themselves what they understand by freedom. The latter also forges a link to the ideas on childrearing, because children are aware of and appreciate both the care and the freedom they experience when being reared by their parents (Andresen et al. 2012).

From our perspective, it is necessary to distinguish between those questions that are more theoretical and more empirical. One fundamental theoretical research question—and not just in childhood studies—addresses the differences between children's and adults' ideas of the "good life", "freedom", and "childrearing/care". This can be examined by assessing how the development of children's concepts relates to the power relations within the generational order. It ties in with what we consider to be the more far-reaching question in a theory of childhood, namely that of the relation between the here-and-now and the future, or between well-being and well-becoming. It is precisely child well-being research that calls for a concentration on the here-and-now of the child. But there is a lack of research how children experience the present and how they reconstruct past and figure out ideas of the future. Our impression is that this relation has to be clarified more intensively. However, in systematic terms, it is doubtful whether one can think about the "good life" without considering the future as well. Hence, we shall call for a stronger fusion of well-being and well-becoming in childhood.

5.2 Cultures of Disciplines: The Tension Between Educational Perspectives and Childhood Studies

In our field of research, we first have to negotiate with different disciplines such as psychology, mental health, philosophy, sociology, or education and their understandings of concepts. Our question here is: Do these have an impact on our conceptual framework? To give an example, educational science with its focus on not only learning and education but also on the development of children and on institutional settings requires a different concept compared to, for example, the new sociology of childhood. Why? First of all, there is only a minor debate on child well-being in educational science (Andresen 2014). Second, the social theory of childhood with its contrasting ideas of constructivism versus the autonomous actor has much to offer for our research contexts. From this perspective, one important starting point is the social-constructivist assumption that childhood is shaped by social institutions, by legal regulations of the relation between the generations, by educational and other practices, by cultural ideas on what constitutes a good childhood and good parent–child relations, and by society's ideas regarding what kind of education should be acquired during childhood. Viewed historically, the idea of actively defining childhood as a distinct life phase is based on a welfare-state notion of child well-being and the minimization of risk. Over the last 20 years, this has been reinforced by the UN Convention on the Rights of the Child. However, it is still necessary to ask whether the ways in which childhood is shaped can themselves have negative effects and, for example, contribute to or even heighten social inequality in this life phase.

Nonetheless, from an educational point of view, it is necessary to reflect more on adults' responsibilities together with children's dependencies and vulnerabilities. Therefore, what, in general, is important in our eyes is an interdisciplinary reflection and intensive discourse over the central terms such as autonomy, the subject, or the "generational order."

This leads us to the idea of talking about education-science-oriented childhood studies that maintain their focus on the development of the child while simultaneously recognizing the status of the child as actor.

In his book *Entwurf einer Theorie der Kindheit* [Proposal for a Theory of Childhood], Michael-Sebastian Honig explains childhood as being organized and conceived as a childrearing childhood (Honig 1999).[1] As a result, childhood and childhood studies cannot be conceived with no reference at all to pedagogic and educational science. In his article *Weder Hexen noch Heilige* [Neither Witches nor Saints], Michael Winkler addresses the "relation between pedagogic and recent sociological research on childhood". He reaches the conclusion that childhood studies are trying to "depedagogize" research through their desire to "conceive pedagogic as a control structure" (Winkler 2006: 99). In contrast, Winkler calls explicitly to relate childhood studies to pedagogic, because it is particularly progressive teaching approaches that closely match the arguments in the theory of childhood. Likewise, Karin Bock points out that "the methodological argument that childhood studies should be understood as being ultimately a 'study of the generational order' . . . [throws] childhood studies back to its beginnings . . . [because] the generational order [was] the starting point of ideas in pedagogic, sociology, and the humanities and not its quintessence" (Bock 2010: 33, translated).

Bearing this in mind, our understanding in both the World Vision Children Studies (World Vision 2007, 2010, 2013) and the doctoral research thesis reported in this chapter comes from the new sociology of childhood that focuses on the child as an actor, as a subject with her or his own rights. However, it also reflects the challenge that the child is also vulnerable as a child both within hierarchies and in

[1] In her postdoctoral habilitation thesis *Kinderalltag—Kinderwelten* [Children's everyday life—Children's worlds], Karin Bock (2010) points out that Honig nonetheless goes far beyond viewing childhood as just a childrearing childhood and determines that the generational order is an object of research in childhood studies.

comparison to adults. The child is dependent and lacking in power. We focus on the concept of well-being by combining subjective with social aspects and trying to conceptualize childhood from both perspectives: from the perspective of a rights-based autonomy, resources, and capacities and from the perspective of vulnerability.

5.3 Well-Being and Well-Becoming: The "Good Life" Approach

Talking about the "good life" in childhood studies means negotiating theoretical complexity. Questions on what a good life may be and what may define it always address the image of humanity and the conditions for a fulfilling human life—what Martha Nussbaum (2000) calls "human flourishing." Especially questions about children and the good life require not only normatively based responses, ethical reflections, and sound theories but also differentiated empirical findings.

In this context, we view the tension between autonomy and dependence as being the main challenge to research on the good life. This links up with further questions such as:

- How can we achieve respectful caregiving while simultaneously ensuring the freedom to choose between different options and lead a self-determined life?
- How can we link together social policies, which focus particularly on the vulnerability of children, with child-appropriate policies directed toward participation and agency (see Andresen et al. 2010)?

In general, the Capability Approach focuses on the latitudes of possibility and freedom and the accompanying chances that people have to realize their ability to lead a good life (Andresen et al. 2010). Hence, the concern is to examine which abilities, conditions, and freedoms people require in order to be able to realize this good life. This approach includes a theory of justice, which is receiving increasing attention internationally; it distinguishes between forms of being, known as functionings, and chances of their realization, known as capabilities (Sen 2009). Whereas functionings focus on whether people are or do something specific, capabilities focus on the objective set of possibilities of bringing about various combinations of specific qualities of functionings.

Capabilities are more than the possession of certain goods or the knowledge of specific cultural techniques and so forth; they are expressions of actual possibilities of being that individuals may choose "for good reasons." The Capability Approach systematically links together freedom—in the sense of social, political, and cultural framing conditions—with individual abilities—in the sense of an unfolding of potentials, competencies, and education. The theoretical potential of this approach lies in developing responsibility as an issue addressing the conditions for a good life and examining the necessary processes of negotiation to allow responsible participation for all.

This also permits what could be a new order of the social-philosophically based relation between rights and duties and the sense of responsibility for childrearing.

In her variant of the Capability Approach, Martha Nussbaum (1999) has compiled a list of factors that make it possible to live a life according to one's own wishes and needs. Nussbaum is not interested exclusively in rationally justified decision-making and behavior. She also explicitly addresses the importance of feelings, namely, the moral feelings of respect and empathy. Both are acquired through interaction with others—not only directly but also in the form of art, myth, and literature (Nussbaum1999).

Martha Nussbaum (1999) developed her "strongly vague" list of the good life over a long period of time and in a series of analytical steps. She drew strongly on Aristotle's philosophy and the liberal justice theory of John Rawls (1971). Nussbaum declares that people must have the chance to make their own free choice regarding what their concept of the good is like. This should not be imposed paternalistically. She is in no way concerned with a perfectionist concept as many have criticized, but with defining *capabilities* as "rights" and not as "duties". She also emphasizes the need for consensus and democratic negotiation over the list of factors that always have to be renegotiated and, if necessary, modified. It is essential to also include children in these "negotiations".

Nussbaum's list is based on the following assumptions: Fundamental human abilities are not innate properties that develop by themselves (Clark/Ziegler in this volume). They require nurturing, the provision of resources, and education. According to Nussbaum, society has to provide the necessary conditions and make them available in a socially just way. Every individual has the right to the same opportunities and conditions for self-fulfillment. Hence, Nussbaum refers to a universal ethics in which freedom (of choice), equality, and human dignity serve as central guidelines.

However, what is decisive both at this point and for our central research question is the importance of negotiating dimensions of the "good life" with children. Necessary is a clear description and reconstruction of children's perceptions. This offers a view on the tension between well-being und well-becoming, and this is why Nussbaum's perspective offers an approach to more far-reaching ideas on a theory of childhood.

Within the frame of the Capability Approach we can focus on childhood as a concept in the generational order and characterized by autonomy and vulnerability. Besides this theory of childhood can combine present and future perspectives and well-being and well-becoming. This offers new empirical perspectives: The list has been referred to international childhood studies and it has also been used in empirical research by, for example, Paul Anand (2008) when examining the situation of children in Great Britain; Jérome Ballet et al. (2004) when looking at the identity-forming processes in street children; and Sabine Andresen and Susanne Fegter (2011) in a study of child poverty. The potentials of the Capability Approach for assessing social work and childrearing measures have also been emphasized with discussions focusing on possible ways of testing its application empirically (Andresen et al. 2008).

The Italian economist Maria Laura Di Tommaso (2006) has used quantitative empirical surveys to examine how the well-being of children may be assessed with the help of the Capability Approach. She has studied the well-being of children in developing countries such as India as well as in Italy. Nussbaums studies concentrate on the *capabilities* "Senses, imagination, and thought: Being able to use the senses to imagine, think, and reason" (Nussbaum 2011: 33), along with leisure-time activities and play. Her surveys, which are performed with methods taken from economics, are both theoretically and methodologically inspiring and relevant for childhood studies.

Mario Biggeri takes a qualitative, participation-oriented approach to research. Using different research designs and types of research, he has asked children and adolescents to report which are the most important opportunities that a child should have in life and how significant these are in their own lives (Biggeri et al. 2010). They argue that children not just the subjects of capabilities but, that they have different capabilities than adults have. An important here is also the question we focused on with the empirical research, do children give different degrees of relevance to capabilities as well as to rights. Biggeri et al. conclude with respect to the potential of the Capability Approach: "The dynamic of the Capability Approach is indeed expressed by the feedback loops that reshape the potential capability set of the child." (Biggeri et al. 2010: 82).

Besides the theoretical impact we have to show how children link together present and future and possibly also the past in their concepts and also what significance is attached to well-becoming here. This also includes an understanding of childhood as an element in the generational order of societies, and this requires a two-sided outlook on the child, because, on the one side, children are equipped with an enormous potentiality that enables them to be autonomous, to focus on past, present and the future; whereas, on the other side, they are vulnerable and dependent on care. A concept of childhood oriented towards children's rights, tries to do justice to both: the granting of autonomy and the right to protection. The following section is an example for research on how children are actors in their lives, how they actively handle the generational order and how they build concepts around all day experiences.

5.4 Children's Concepts of Childrearing: Reconstructions

Now we will start with the empirical parts of this chapter and focus first on children's childrearing concepts as a path to the right of protection as well as the right of education. So the following section will introduce into some results that were taken while a doctoral thesis on familiar childrearing (in German: Erziehung) out of the perspective of children between 5 and 10 years. The term "Erziehung" can be used in different ways and meanings. Winfried Böhm (2005) writes the following about the variety of understandings of childrearing: "In the German language, it covers both a process and its outcome, an intention and an activity (of the childrearer and the *educandus*), a state of the school child and the conditions of this state" (Böhm 2005: 186, translated). This shows the diversity of this concept and—in the meaning of participation rights—the necessity to research on children's views on this childrearing process. We understand children as actors in their life and understand them as actors in the childrearing process as well. The following results are only taken out of the group discussion and represent the views of the 9–10 year old participants, which means that this is only a part of the whole interpretation of the doctoral thesis.

5.4.1 Methodology

As part of the doctoral thesis, a qualitative study surveyed how children aged 5–10 years view family childrearing. This involved one group discussion with ten children aged 9–10 plus narrative interviews with single children and pairs of children (another ten children). The data were analyzed with triangulation and on the basis of Grounded Theory (Strauss and Corbin 1996). One of the things that became clear when analyzing the group discussion on the basis of Grounded Theory, was that the children talk about a kind of 'ideal childrearing conception' that can be labeled 'childrearing as metamorphosis'. In the following, we shall discuss this key category generated from the group discussion in more detail.

5.4.2 Reconstruction: Childrearing as Metamorphosis

In the group discussion the children reach a meta-level while talking about parenting. That means they discuss childrearing in their family not only by talking about *what* childrearing *is* but also by *how* it *works*. They develop a conception of childrearing. The interpretation allows to call this conception as 'childrearing as metamorphosis'. Children are presented in a dichotomous relation to adults, for example, as immature versus mature. They accordingly have to pass through a 'civilizing process' in order to attain the stage of mature adulthood. Within this conception of 'childrearing as metamorphosis', various childrearing goals are striven toward over childrearing as a teleological process. From a child perspective, these goals can be summarized as (secondary) virtues.[2] They include good manners, politeness, patience, and obedience. Once these childrearing goals are attained, the child as minor has passed successfully through a process of maturation—the

[2] Secondary virtues mean characteristics of a person which help him or her to cope with the all day tasks but which do not have any ethical contents.

metamorphosis—into being a responsible adult. Children consider that parents are responsible for accompanying the child's maturation process or even initiating and guiding it actively. Within this ideal conception of childrearing, children seem to adopt and internalize the perspective of adults. The many repeated variations of the statement by the children that their parents "have my best interests at heart. I know that," nonetheless indicate the presence of another perspective on the 'reality of childrearing' that contrasts with the 'ideal conception'. Although the children show a great theoretical and conceptual understanding of the goals and procedures of parental childrearing activities by adopting their parents' argumentations, the tensions and dissonances as well as resistant practices to be found in familial childrearing show how the children actively process parental childrearing activities and thereby negotiate not only reactively but also progressively.

5.4.3 *The Civilizing of the Child*

In the group discussion, the children differentiate clearly between the status of children and that of adults, and they attribute dichotomous properties and abilities to these two groups. The children's statements suggest that they view children as having an incompleteness that is guided through a process of maturation, the metamorphosis, to change into the status of the mature adult. An example of this is the way Johanna[3] explains:

> **Johanna**: Yes, and I also think it's good that our parents taught us how to talk and walk and everything that you have to do here like that you shouldn't knock things over or the like.

Evidently, Johanna is referring to infancy here. It is only through the process of being taught by parents that infants become able to communicate through speech and to move around through walking. Johanna does not see any active role for the children themselves here that would first make this parental teaching process possible and then make it successful. Moreover, she considers it to be a part of the parental teaching process for children (infants) to learn "everything that you have to do here." By this, she is referring to learning a set of social rules that will be explained below. In sum, children enter this world without knowing this set of rules, and they first have to learn which behaviors are appropriate and desired "here," that is, in this world, in the social community; and this quite clearly includes "that you shouldn't knock things over or the like." Hence, Johanna attributes adults with the power to teach children fundamental abilities, with possession of the necessary knowledge, and with the ability to ordain what duties and rules have to be passed on to the younger generation. What Mathis says also fits in with Johanna's explanation:

> **Mathis**: And that they set rules for good manners that we do not misbehave so much then so that we know the rules.

[3] All names are anonymized by Katharina Gerarts.

Children seem to enter the world almost as incomplete, one could even say uncivilized beings, at least ones who do not yet know the rules in society; they first have to be taught the set of rules for life. Mathis then addresses this set of rules explicitly.

> **Mathis**: Well, my parents want want only that I **then** when I am grown up that I just keep to the rules as well like driving in traffic or the like and that I also finish doing everything that is, for example, difficult that I **then** just understand yes that I am also ready **then** (bold put by the authors).

He explains that his parents want that *then*, when he is an adult, he will follow the rules like driving in traffic and finish doing everything that is difficult because he will *then* understand [the rules] and *then* be ready.

Here Mathis is referring to "rules" that are comparable with those for driving in traffic. These have to be learned even when this learning process may be arduous. When children eventually grow up, this learning process should bear fruit. It is *then*, for example, that the rules that have been learned can also be applied. Hence, at the latest when Mathis becomes an adult, he should have learned so much that he will be able to stand among adults; he will not break the rules, and will thereby contribute to making society work. Here as well, the child is described as being incomplete compared to the adult. It is only through the maturation process, the metamorphosis, that the child will become an able and knowledgeable adult. *Then* the child will understand the rules that apply in the world; *then* the child will be ready. The repeated use of the adverb "then" also reveals how this childrearing focuses on the future. In this perspective, rearing strengthens children for the future, that is, for when they have attained the status of adulthood.

Children see another aspect of childrearing in the fact that they are being prepared for "real life." As Renate says:

> **Renate**: And that I also know a bit about what life is like out there as well, and not only just like a child, because you have to pay taxes.

The status of the child seems to be an incomplete one. From the children's own perspective, they are going through a developmental process and are therefore in a kind of moratorium. This seems to be shaped by adults and above all, by parents. In her first statement, Renate distinguishes between two worlds: the one out there and the one in which she lives. She believes that, as a child, she lives in her own, apparently protected world. In this statement, the difference between child and adult along with the accompanying abilities and responsibilities become very clear: Adults can survive in the world out there. They know the rules; they know how they have to behave; they seem to possess certain skills that make them "able to survive." The statement "not only just like a child" seems to judge the child somewhat disparagingly. Children are namely *not yet* ready, they *still do not* know the rules, they are *still not* grown up, and they are *not yet* able to survive in the world out there. In other words, they are incomplete, they are small, they are ignorant, and they are weak. Children seem to know about these differences that exist between adults and children. Further analyses of the group discussions reveal that the children locate a developmental process in childhood itself. For example, Mathis says:

> **Mathis**: I have several brothers and sisters and I **previously** always played a few jokes on my brothers and sisters that they didn't like at all I didn't know that **before** and that and then my parents kept on telling me you shouldn't do that and so on and **nowadays** I have learned properly that I should not do that (bold put by the authors).

The temporal adverbs marked in bold indicate that Mathis distinguishes between a "before" and "after" the learning process. This makes it clear that he is looking toward the past and to the future from the child's present perspective. Mathis explains that he has already learned something compared to before. However, his previous explanations of, for example, the set of rules emphasize that he still has a long path in front of him on which there is more to learn.

This shows how children are aware that adults expect them to pass through a civilizing process. The process starts with the infant and his/her inabilities (lack of speech, mobility, knowledge of the rules of society). With the help of parents, the infant passes gradually through a maturation and developmental process that finally leads to the consummate status of being an adult. We shall consider the parents' responsibility for this metamorphosis as well as the intentional nature of this childrearing process in more detail below.

5.4.4 Childrearing as a Teleological Process

Above, under the concept of 'childrearing as metamorphosis', we have shown that children report having to pass through a civilizing process to successfully attain the maturity of a civilized adult. Further analysis of the group discussion shows that the parental childrearing that guides this maturation process is, according to the children's statements, a goal-directed procedure. Hence, childrearing is of an intentional nature. For example, for Laurin, childrearing is an activity that will **lead him to** being a good child. From his perspective, the childrearing activity can be viewed as being intended by parents. Hence, parents seem to engage in childrearing in order to pursue certain intentions or goals. This is supported by a further statement from Laurin in which he explains that his mother wants to raise him so **that** he should no longer do this (Laurin makes a screeching noise with his lips), because she freaks out when he does it.

Laurin reports on a habit of making a noise that seems to upset his mother greatly. In this statement, Laurin assigns his mother the intention of wanting to rear him so that he no longer makes this noise. Through this, Laurin attributes not only an intentional component to childrearing, but also the possibility of shaping the child and the child's behavior. This statement makes it clear that children assume that *their parents rear them intentionally*, and thereby want to guide their children in specific directions or encourage learning processes in them. The following quotation from Mathis is used again because we will interpret it with another focus. So it can also be reinterpreted in this way:

> Mathis: Well, my parents want want only **that** I then when I am grown up **that** I just keep to the rules as well like driving in traffic or the like and **that** I also finish doing everything that is, for example, difficult that I then just understand yes **that** I am also ready then (put bold by the authors).

The emphases in bold point to the very frequent use of the pronoun "that". The parents of Mathis want him to comply with the rules or also persevere with everything that is difficult. Hence, according to Mathis, the parental intention in the childrearing process is linked to various goals. A subsequent phase in the group discussion accentuates the goal directedness of parental childrearing somewhat more strongly when Mathis states:

> **Mathis**: Now they want to rear me only so **that** I know the rules better (bold put by the authors).

Here Mathis defines the rearing by his parents through the way that it is goal-directed, working toward a consequence, and thus also performed intentionally and thoughtfully. The childrearing by his parents has clear goals in sight. These goals refer—as presented here—to concrete behaviors in the child (e.g., being good) as well as to the need to extend the knowledge of children. As already implied above, it is clear that the parents are assigned attributes that make them seem powerful in relation to their offspring. Adults possess the abilities to guide children in their behavior and their learning processes. According to the children's statements, they can teach the children these various things (see below), and are thereby equipped with knowledge that grants them the power to decide in which directions the developmental processes in children can and should be directed. In this ideal childrearing conception, children thereby have an image of powerful, knowledgeable, and thereby hierarchically higher ranking adults. We shall consider how far children handle this perspective on adulthood and process it constructively in the following section.

5.4.5 *Childrearing Goals: Virtues*

The goal-directedness of childrearing described above can extend to various domains. For Mathis, it is particularly the rules he mentions that are important. Children have to learn a certain set of rules so that they can adapt to the given norms as adults and be aware of the cultural standards. However, we can also identify a degree of social conformity as a childrearing goal of parents. For example, Talea says:

> **Talea**: Tere as well, them too, that is, my parents have also taught me that you don't hit and spit and the like.

That Laurin should also be such a good child (see above) also indicates a desire for a degree of social conformity. As synonyms of "good," we also find the following attributes: lovable, charming, attractive, popular, decent, compliant, well-behaved, wished for, obedient, dutiful, well-bred, well-raised, and amenable. These are all attributes that make the person who possesses them easy to deal with. They are well received and make it possible to conclude that a relationship is "uncomplicated." The German language even has a saying *sich lieb Kind machen* meaning to put oneself into a good child's shoes, even ingratiate oneself, and offer the least possible resistance. Hence, Laurin's statement shows that from his perspective, the childrearing goals of parents include socially acceptable behavior in their children and thus their adaptation to the structures of society.

However, being polite and learning certain manners are also considered to be essential aspects of childrearing according to the children. Martha starts off by explaining:

> **Martha**: I think that childrearing is that you don't bang your feet on the table when you come home [quiet laughter] or the like.

At this point, Martha does not declare childrearing to be a procedure or process. It is already reflected in certain behaviors. Accordingly, the childrearing process has already been passed through, and has now become an action pattern. Renate also considers that politeness is an important aspect that has to be learned during childrearing:

> **Renate**: wanted to add something to Martha um and banging your feet on the table and when you are then invited to a very refined person or the like and then you suddenly put your feet on the table and then and then and then it's not at all polite and how you also that you know what being polite is.

Hence, children have to learn how they should behave in certain situations. If you are invited to visit a "refined" person, then it's bad manners to "put your feet on the table." And it is also bad manners to "bang" your feet on the table when you come home every day as well. Hence, from the children's viewpoint, childrearing is when parents teach their children that certain behaviors are taboo or frowned upon. Accordingly, there are certain rules—especially for good manners. Mathis explains explicitly that these are set by adults (see above). Children do not (yet) know these rules; they first have to get to know them. Once again, it becomes clear here that childrearing from the child's perspective is a procedure that is intended and thought out by adults. Through childrearing, children should learn the rules and manners ordained by parents.

Renate finds it "embarrassing" that children do not yet know these social rules or manners. As she says:

> **Renate**: Or somehow also just being polite because that is and also using *Sie*[4] I find as well because I sometimes actually say *Du* to an adult or the like *Duhu*[5] and that is somehow totally embarrassing [laughter].

---

[4] *Sie* and *Du* are the formal and informal forms of address in German. *Sie* is used for all strangers and superiors; *Du* for the family and close friends.

[5] "Duhu" is the trivialized form of the German "Du".

For Renate, being polite also means using the *Sie* form to address adults and not using *Du*. Sometimes Renate forgets this rule, and then she appraises her own childish behavior as embarrassing. This also once more reveals parallels to the category of childrearing as metamorphosis addressed above in which children and their childish behavior are appraised as being immature and children first have to grow into mature and knowledgeable adults.

Alongside the childrearing goals of learning social conformity, the set of rules in society, and good manners, childrearing also has the goal, according to the children's statements, of teaching children patience and obedience. According to Renate:

> **Renate**: I mean my mother and father also want me to learn to be patient because sometimes I am really impatient and then I simply want to do something STRAIGHT AWAY [she stresses these two words]. . .then they also want us to be patient and that we are also obedient because sometimes I am really disobedient I simply go there and although I shouldn't at all.

Patience, obedience, good manners, and politeness can be summarized as virtues that are among those to be found in the so-called "civil catalogue of virtues."[6]

5.4.6 *Parental Responsibility in the Childrearing Process*

Children view their parents as being accountable for the success of the childrearing process, that is, their metamorphosis or maturation. As soon as the researcher asked what the children thought childrearing was, they immediately talked about parents. Hence, childrearing is related directly to the children's parents. In addition, parents are responsible for setting the above-mentioned rules, they have the above-mentioned virtues in mind as childrearing goals, and they are considered to be responsible for meeting a child's basic needs. Renate says:

> **Renate**: In any case, I think that it's good that I have parents who look after me, cook, or because and I am also happy that we have a home.

According to the children, parents are also responsible for other childrearing activities such as arbitrating disputes between siblings. Martha points to the responsibility that parents have for the success of the child's metamorphosis:

> **Martha**: Mostly I think that that childrearing is that you don't bang your feet on the table when you come home [quiet laughter] or the like and if I and if and **if my parents didn't just say stop** then perhaps I would carry on doing it and get used to doing it and if you have done it for a long time you also don't really have any more chance to start from the beginning again.

[6] For a detailed analysis of the position of the discourse on virtues in educational science, see Timo Hoyer (2005).

The first part of this quote was already introduced earlier and points to the children's postulated childrearing goal of good manners. As Martha's narration continues, however, it becomes clear—in line with the proverb "A tree must be bent while it is young"—that the foundation for successful childrearing, that is, learning good manners and certain rules, has to be laid *by the parents* during childhood. If parents fail to pass on this set of rules and the accompanying behaviors to their children and do not point these out to them, then the child—according to Martha—will have no chance of learning the norms of society and, in the worst case, she will also not get rid of her bad habits. Here, the parents are being made responsible for passing on their knowledge, their social and cultural habitus, to their children so that they can successfully metamorphize into mature and responsible adults. Children themselves make their parents responsible for education and welfare, like article 5 of the UNCRC demands. The parents serve as a model here, and they are designated by the children as being essential for the metamorphosis to succeed. However, as Mathis points out with the following statement, there always remains an individual nuance, that of the specific child:

> **Mathis**: Yes just like my parents I learn that from my parents and when they're not there I do a bit of childrearing in my way I do that a bit as well yes.

Here Mathis is referring to looking after or rearing his siblings. He says "I learn that from my parents." In other words, he follows his parents' example of how children should be reared. However, when his parents are absent, he does this in his own way. His parents serve as models. Mathis adopts their knowledge and their abilities while simultaneously pointing to his own constructive activity: He does not adopt his parents' attributes unquestioningly and not one to one, but implements his own kind of childrearing. This delivers a first insight into how children engage in constructive activities within the childrearing process. They adopt an active role going beyond the childrearing concepts they develop and beyond what they have to say *about* childrearing. This active role of the children, which may well take the form of contrary and resistant practices, frequently contains a critical view of parental behaviors. As Renate says: "Parents can also be pretty stupid." In addition, during the group discussion, the children repeatedly uttered slight variations of one single sentence, namely: "I know that my parents only want to do their best for me", "she [the mother, KG] means well," or "and when they [the parents, KG] tell me off a bit, I know that they only intend it to be for my own good." This type of sentence should be conceived as a bridge between the "childrearing conception" and the "childrearing reality." Such statements show not only that the children adopt the adult perspectives on childrearing but also that the child perspective does not necessarily match that of the parents. The narrations in which children defend their parents always also reveal a "but" or an "actually." This becomes particularly clear when children describe dissonances and tensions in the childrearing process and their practices to resist them.

5.5 Theorizing

The detailed interpretation of the group discussion shows that children have a highly complex notion of childrearing. Their *childrearing conception* is shaped initially by adult images and discourses. Here, children unquestioningly adopt the idea of a difference between adults and children and thereby make their contribution to *doing generations* (Kelle 2005).

Especially their understanding of education as an outcome and not as a process permits to make a link to the comprehension of Berger and Luckmann about their "primary socialization" (Berger and Luckmann 1966). As they say human beings are not born as a member of society but they have to become one. They call this "internalization" (Berger and Luckmann 1966: 139). In the phase of the primary socialization the human being becomes in the time of childhood a member of the society (Berger and Luckmann 1966: 141). The child takes the role and the preferences of the "significant other" (Berger and Luckmann 1966, S. 142), in this case of the parents who are the first socialization instance of the children. This become very clear when Mathis talks about rules which children have to learn from their parents or when Johanna expresses her gratitude to her parents that they taught her to walk and to speak. Children seem to need these significant others, especially their parents, for this primary socialization, they really want them to play this role for them. For that they acknowledge the differences in the generational order. This is also confirmed by Berry Mayall's research on childhood in Great Britain. In her book, *Towards a sociology for childhood*, she states: "One of the main characteristics of childhood offered by young people is its difference from parenthood. ... Parental definitions constitute them as children" (Mayall 2002: 45). The children in our group discussion show the greatest understanding for these fundamental differences between children and adults. Initially, they willingly adopt the parental perspectives and argumentations. This also includes recognizing the power of their parents that is elicited and maintained by the intergenerational relation between adults and children. Mayall comes to a similar conclusion: "Parents had authority over their children. Many young people also provided justification for parental authority" (p. 46). In her study of unequal childhoods [*Ungleiche Kindheiten*], Tanja Betz also determines that children accept the relationships of inequality between the generations. She draws on the French sociologist Bourdieu and his "symbolic power concept" (Betz 2008: 160) to explain that children are a dominated group in society with less economic, social, and cultural capital than adults, and she uses this to point to the relationships of inequality that exist between the generations. She goes on to state that "the children themselves conform to this view of the world. The existing relationships become a part or a component of how they see both themselves and the world." With reference to Bourdieu, she goes on to ask "which power of negotiation is really available to children?" (Betz 2008: 161, translated). In her secondary analysis of the German Youth Institute's 2005 Children longitudinal study, she comes to the significant conclusion that "the intergenerational positions of power are distributed unequally, and all parties involved consider this to be legitimate" (Betz 2008: 259, translated). The results of the group discussion go even further than this: Children actively demand this parental power by assigning parents responsibility for a successful child metamorphosis or—as to say it in Bergers and Luckmanns words—to become a member of society through primary socialization. They claim their right on education and welfare, their right on education by their parents.

At the same time, however, the children also question the power of parents in the generational order, and confront it powerfully from their own side. Accordingly, in summary, children switch between, on the one side, adopting the adult perspective on childrearing, which is conceived here as an ideal childrearing conception; and, on the other side, adopting a child perspective on the reality or practice of childrearing in the family. They finally do this actively by confronting these relationships between the generations through a negotiation that also includes resistant practices. Mayall also reaches a similar conclusion: "Thus young people subscribed to the socialization thesis—childhood is in part preparation for adult life, and childhood is a journey during which one learns—but they also ascribed themselves agency in their own socialization" (Mayall 2002: 47). Hence, children gain an active role in the childrearing process in the form of an *autopoiesis*.[7] Thereby childrearing must "whether it so chooses or not, accept that the development of the child takes the form of a sustained autopoiesis" (Liegle 2006: 204, translated). This means that children are in no way the products of their parents or other educators, but that they play an active role in an interactive process in which childrearing and self-socialization are interlinked.

5.6 Children's Concepts on the "Good Life" and "Freedom": Reconstructions

The former part of the chapter focused on empirical results on children's perceptions and experiences on childrearing and education. The emphasis lay more on the rights of protection and education. Now the reconstruction of children's ideas on the "good life" combined with perceptions on freedom and autonomy argues more on the right of participation.

[7]The term autopoiesis comes from ancient Greek (αὐτός"self" and ποιέιν"create, build") and means the self-creation and self-maintenance of a system. While originating in biology, it became a key term in Luhmann's systems theory in the 1980s (see Böhm 2005).

5.6.1 Methodology of the Surveys on "Children in Germany"

The following analyses is based on a survey, which combined quantitative and qualitative methods. The reconstruction of the concept of a good life and, in particular, the ideas of freedom is based on data from the World Vision Children Studies: first, qualitative data from the second study (2010); and, second, surveys of 100 children during the pretest for the questionnaire in the third study (2013). We shall start with an overview of the general procedure used in this research. The first, second, and third World Vision Children Surveys in 2007, 2010, and 2013 were based on representative samples and qualitative interviews. In 2007, the representative part included 1,600 children aged 8–11 years. In 2010, we expanded the size of this sample to 2,529 children aged 6–11 years, and in 2013 we once again surveyed 2,600 children aged 6–11 years. The survey took the form of personal oral interviews in the children's homes. The underlying population is 6- to 11-year-old children living in Germany. While carrying out the first *World Vision Survey* in 2007, it soon became apparent that our approach was also suitable for interviewing children from the age of 6 years onward. As a result, the second *World Vision Survey* in 2010 also included 6- to 7-year-olds. Nonetheless, among these 6-to 7-year-olds, we surveyed only those who were already attending school, because the everyday worlds of school and preschool (*Kindergarten*) children differ greatly—even when both are of the same age.[8] This aspect was taken into account in the design and weighting of all three studies. Alongside German children, we also assessed children with migration backgrounds—particularly in 2013. The qualitative part of the study also included 6- to 11-year-old German and non-German children.

The quantitative part of the survey was based on two different instruments. The first was a personal oral interview with the children carried out by well-trained interviewers working with a fixed, standardized assessment instrument. This was computer-assisted, and the interviewer entered the children's answers directly into a laptop. The second instrument was a short paper-and-pencil questionnaire that one parent was asked to complete while the child was being interviewed. This questionnaire was used to gather basic sociodemographic information on the child's family background.

Both questionnaires contained about 65 questions and were structured by the different spaces of children's experiences: family, leisure time, school, friends, media, and time use. However, they also included questions about hopes and fears, political ideals (in 2007), self-efficacy and satisfaction (in 2010), and feelings of inequality and justice (in 2013). We also added some questions on the feelings and everyday life experiences children have when they are poor.

The qualitative interviews in 2010, which are important for the reconstruction of the good life, addressed experiences with time use and the children's possibilities of

[8] Although compulsory education starts at the age of 6 years in Germany, there is a degree of variation in the age at which children first attend elementary school.

self-determination. At the end of the interview, we asked the children to count five "things" that are important for every child to live a good life.

5.6.2 *Description and Reconstruction of the "Good Life"*

The research on child well-being is working with different dimensions and indicators, and there are some studies which includes like the World Vision Studies the concept of the "good life". The British studies asked adolescents about their ideas on a good life. We shall refer only to these briefly in order to permit comparisons. The survey from "The Children's Society" asked 14- to 16-year olds: "What do you think are the most important things that make for a good life for young people?"

In the eyes of these adolescents a good life means:

- Having close friends, a loving family, a nice home, enough money for food and things wanted, and doing well at school.
- Having freedom in what you think, say, and do.
- Having a good and safe environment, having a place to go and play, and enjoying themselves.
- Being treated with respect and fairly, particularly in school or at home (Rees and Lee 2005; Rees et al. 2011).

When the younger children in the German study are asked to name five indispensable resources for living "a good life," they express very similar concrete ideas. In compiling their personal "hit list," they think about their immediate life world: a home, mother and father, friends, and leisure-time opportunities. To give a special example, Sammy is an 8-year-old child who was living in a children's home at the time of the survey. His perception of a "good life" differs in some ways from the others:

I: *Good, then just tell me! And I'll write them down.*

S: Food ... drinks. What a child needs to stay alive?

I: *What a child needs to feel good.*

S: Freedom. Privacy when he doesn't feel good. How many is that?

I: *Shall we call food and drink one? I think that food and drink is one thing, then we've got freedom and privacy.*

S: Then it's four, three. Three.

I: *We've got three now.*

S: A school. Even though I personally don't like it at all, never mind, but I need it in order to learn. And ... and lots of luck in life.

At first glance, it is surprising that an 8-year-old child talks about freedom and privacy. Probably, the children had been talking about this in group discussions with their childcare worker. It stands to reason that this is an important topic in a children's home, and Sammy seems to consider that privacy is also desirable for other children (World Vision 2010: 283).

Almost all the children also link their own concrete world to ideas on which basic needs have to be satisfied. They consider food and drink to be just as indispensable as protection from the cold and harm. What is particularly conspicuous here is the children's need for security—in older children just as much as in 6- to 7-year-olds.

We found the images drawn by young children to be extremely interesting. For example, 6-year-old Cora drew a banana, her bed, a tube, a house with windows and a light. When we asked her what the light meant, she explained the need for a light when a child has had a bad dream at night and wants to find her mom or a doll. Or 6-year-old Ben who wrote his own name "BEN". For him, a child's name is the symbol of individuality and singularity. Based on the analyses of the qualitative interviews we can figure out two central dimensions: the extent and quality of care and the type and quality of freedom that children perceive in different domains such as the family, school, and leisure time. The analysis of the data showed that children consider both to be important, and that what seems to matter most is to achieve the right balance. In the third survey (World Vision 2013) we tried to specify care and freedom clearly when developing our qualitative and quantitative assessment instruments.

From the children's perspective, their good life is structured by the substantial balance: that between care and freedom. Hence, the subjective situation of the children can be viewed as a balance between structure, care, and security on the one side and freedom of movement and autonomy on the other. This offers a systematic link to the reconstruction of the childrearing concepts as an issue of care.

5.6.3 Reconstruction of Freedom

The relation between care and freedom seems to play a key role for well-being in general for the children in this age group. This makes it particularly interesting to find out what children understand by freedom. In the second World Vision Children Study, we operationalized freedom with the indicators codetermination in daily family life and experiencing that one's own opinion is taken seriously and valued.

For the 2013 study, 100 children were given a pretest in which they were asked to report their understanding of freedom in an unstructured way.

Results showed that the 6-, 7-, and 8-year-olds think about freedom in terms of:

- Playing outside the house
- Going to a shop or ice café without an adult
- Watching TV
- Being able to choose which friends they play with

The 9-, 10-, and 11-year-olds come up with similar ideas, but they also have other ideas connected with freedom such as:

- Making own decisions about time use
- Independent media consumption
- Unsupervised Internet access
- Staying overnight with friends

There are some small differences between girls and boys: For boys, media consumption is more related to freedom than for girls. And 6- to 11-year-old girls combine the idea of freedom with nature and spending time outside in, for example, the forest. For both boys and girls, friends are an important indicator for freedom. What nobody mentions in terms of freedom is school and other learning activities.

5.7 Conclusion

The experiences and lessons learnt of the conducted surveys lead us to the idea of talking about education-science-oriented childhood studies that maintain their focus on the development of the child while simultaneously recognizing the status of the child as actor. In regard to the participations rights "Including children's perspectives may help get an accurate picture of their activities and experiences and capture important aspects of their lives, such as children's contributions to their own well-being and the well-being of the significant others" (Doek 2014: 213/214). Protection, education and participation as children's rights form a perspective for a theory of childhood, which methodically interlaces well-being and well-becoming. To expound the problems of the separation between well-being as a present and well-becoming as a future question was a concern of the article. In order to do that, the Capability Approach was followed closely. The concept of "Good Life", voiced by Nussbaum, admits a methodical observation of the child as a being capable of autonomy but at the same time dependent on care. This dual view is vital for a further development of the theory of childhood inside educational science. The empirical findings provide indication of how children themselves conceptualize capabilities and rights.

In childhood studies, and particularly in child well-being research as well, both quantitative and qualitative methods are being applied increasingly in a mixed-method approach like that taken in the World Vision Children Studies (World Vision 2007, 2010, 2013). Our reconstructive analyses of children's concepts of childrearing, child well-being, and freedom were able to show that children see themselves in the here-and-now, and that they actively negotiate concepts of "childrearing" and that they argue for the "good life" and "freedom". At the same time, they see themselves as being in a condition of development and becoming. They are in a stadium of negotiating permanently between these two poles to reach finally autonomy and go through a process which ends in the birth of their autonomy.

In relation to children's studies as well, this means that well-being and well-becoming should be conceived together. In a childhood studies oriented toward educational science, this means focusing on the developing child, the child's dependence on and integration in a generational relationship of power, and the child's actor status.

References

Anand, P. H. (2008). *Homo Faber: The happiness and capabilities of very young children*. Unpublished manuscript, Open University, Milton Keynes, England.
Andresen, S. (2014). Educational science and children's well-being. In A. Ben-Arieh, F. Casas, I. Frones, & J. E. Korbin (Eds.), *Handbook on child well-being. Theories, methods and policies in global perspective* (pp. 249–278). Dordrecht: Springer.
Andresen, S., & Fegter, S. (2011). Children growing up in poverty and their ideas on what constitutes a good life: Childhood studies in Germany. *Child Indicators Research, 1*, 1–19.
Andresen, S., Otto, H.-U., & Ziegler, H. (2008). Bildung as human development: An educational view on the capabilities approach. In H.-U. Otto & H. Ziegler (Eds.), *Verwirklichungschancen und Befähigungsgerechtigkeit in der Erziehungswissenschaft. Zum sozial-, jugend- und bildungstheoretischen potential des capability approach* (pp. 165–197). Wiesbaden: VS Verlag.
Andresen, S., Diehm, I., Sander, U., & Ziegler, H. (Eds.). (2010). *Children and the good life. New challenges for research on children*. New York: Springer.
Andresen, S., Hurrelmann, K., & Schneekloth, U. (2012). Care and freedom. Theoretical and empirical aspects of children's well-being. *Child Indicators Research, 5*, 437–448.
Ballet, J, Bhukuth, A., & Radj, K. (2004).*Capabilities, affective capital and development application to street children in Mauritania*. Paper presented at the 4th International Conference on the Capability Approach "Enhancing Human Security". Pavia, Italia.
Ben Arieh, A. (2010). Measuring and monitoring children's well-being: The policy process. In A. Ben-Arieh & R. Goerge (Eds.), *Indicators of children's well being: Understanding their role, usage and policy influence* (Social indicators research series, Vol. 27, pp. 21–32). Dordrecht: Springer.
Berger, P. L., & Luckmann, T. (1966). *The social construction of reality*. New York: OpenRoadMedia.
Betz, T. (2008). *Ungleiche Kindheiten. Theoretische und empirische Analysen zur Sozialberichterstattung über Kinder*. Weinheim: Juventa Verlag.
Biggeri, M., Ballet, J., & Comim, F. (2010). The capability approach and research on children: Capability approach and children's issues. In S. Andresen, I. Diehm, U. Sander, & H. Ziegler (Eds.), *Children and the good life* (pp. 75–90). Dordrecht: Springer.
Bock, K. (2010). *Kinderalltag—Kinderwelten. Rekonstruktive Gruppendiskussionen mit Kindern aus Sachsen*. Opladen: Barbara Budrich.
Böhm, W. (2005). *Wörterbuch der Pädagogik*. Stuttgart: Alfred Kröner Verlag.
Di Tommaso, M. L. (2006). *Measuring the well-being of children using a capability approach: An application to Indian data*. CHILD Working Papers wp05_06, CHILD (Centre for Household, Income, Labour and Demographic economics), Torino, Italy.
Doek, J. E. (2014). Child well-being: Children's rights perspective. In A. Ben-Arieh, F. Casas, I. Frones, & J. E. Korbin (Eds.), *Handbook on child well-being. Theories, methods and policies in global perspective* (pp. 187–217). Dordrecht: Springer.
Honig, M.-S. (1999). *Entwurf einer Theorie der Kindheit*. Frankfurt: Suhrkamp.
Hoyer, T. (2005). *Tugend und Erziehung. Die Grundlegung der Moralpädagogik in der Antike*. Bad Heilbrunn: Klinkhardt.
Kelle, H. (2005). Kinder und Erwachsene. Die Differenzierung von Generationen als kulturelle Praxis. In H. Hengst & H. Zeiher (Eds.), *Kindheit soziologisch* (pp. 83–108). Wiesbaden: VS Verlag.

Korczak, J. (1999). Das Kind in der Familie. In *Sämtliche Werke Bd. 4. Wie man ein Kind lebt. Erziehungsmomente, das Recht des Kindes auf Achtung, Fröhliche Pädagogik*. Gütersloh: Gütersloher Verlagshaus. (Original work published 1929).
Liegle, L. (2006). *Bildung und Erziehung in früher Kindheit*. Stuttgart: Kohlhammer.
Mayall, B. (2002). *Towards a sociology for childhood: Thinking from children's lives*. London: Open University Press.
Nussbaum, M. (1999). *Gerechtigkeit oder das gute Leben*. Frankfurt: Suhrkamp.
Nussbaum, M. (2000). *Women and human development: The capabilities approach*. New York: Cambridge University Press.
Nussbaum, M. (2011). *Creating capabilities: The human development approach*. Cambridge, MA: Harvard University Press.
Qvortrup, J. (2014). Sociology: Societal structures, development of childhood, and the well-being of children. In A. Ben-Arieh, F. Casas, I. Frones, & J. E. Korbin (Eds.), *Handbook on child well-being. Theories, methods and policies in global perspective* (pp. 663–708). Dordrecht: Springer.
Rawls, J. (1971): A Theory of Justice. Harvard University Press.
Rees, G., & Lee. (2005). *Still running II: Finding from the second national survey of young runaways*. London: The Children's Society.
Rees, G., Pople, L., & Goswami, H. (2011). *Understanding children's well-being. Links between family economic factors and children's subjective well-being: Initial findings from Wave 2 and Wave 3 quarterly surveys*. The Children's Society. http://www.phru.net/mhin/childandyouth/Child%20and%20Youth%20resources/Understanding%20childrens%20wellbeing.pdf
Robeyns, I. (2000). *An unworkable idea or a promising alternative? Sen's capability approach re-examined*. Discussion paper 00.30. Center for Economic Studie, Leuven. Retrieved from http://www.econ.kuleuven.ac.be/ces/discussionpapers/Dps00/DPS0030.pdf
Sen, A. (2009). *Development as freedom*. Oxford: Oxford University Press.
Strauss, A., & Corbin, J. (1996). *Grounded theory: Grundlagen Qualitativer Sozialforschung*. Psychologie Verlags Union: Weinheim.
Winkler, M. (2006). Weder Hexen noch Heilige—Bemerkungen zum Verhältnis von Pädagogik und der neueren soziologischen Kindheitsforschung. In S. Andresen & I. Diehm (Eds.), *Kinder, Kindheiten, Konstruktionen. Erziehungswissenschaftliche Perspektiven und sozialpädagogische Verortungen*. Wiesbaden: VS Verlag für Sozialwissenschaften.
World Vision. (2007). *Kinder in Deutschland 2007. 1. World vision survey*. Wissenschaftliche Leitung: Klaus Hurrelmann und Sabine Andresen. Frankfurt: Fischer Taschenbuch Verlag.
World Vision. (2010). *Kinder in Deutschland 2010. 2. World vision survey*. Wissenschaftliche Leitung: Klaus Hurrelmann und Sabine Andresen. Frankfurt: Fischer Taschenbuch Verlag.
World Vision. (2013)."*Wie gerecht ist unsere Welt?*" *Kinder in Deutschland 2013. 3. World vision survey*. Wissenschaftliche Leitung: Sabine Andresen und Klaus Hurrelmann. Weinheim: Beltz.

Chapter 6
Children's Councils Implementation: A Path Toward Recognition?

Dominique Golay and Dominique Malatesta

6.1 Introduction

The city of Lausanne, Switzerland, which was recently certified as a Child-friendly City by UNICEF, promotes children's participation in public governance by implementing children's councils. Councils, which can be defined as political and educational devices, seek to involve children in the public sphere and to encourage a citizenship apprenticeship. As a matter of fact, this citizenship education closely relates to civicism and civility, or in other words, to a civilisation policy (Murard and Tassin 2006). As such, participation processes within institutionalised bodies aim to produce "good citizens", that is to say, socially integrated subjects. In the same time, these "forums" enable children to express their views on the city they inhabit and on urban planning, which in turn, may give them visibility and social existence. Providing access to councils, enabling effective participation in debates and decision-making, improving children's empowerment at the local level – through giving them social visibility for example – can be considered key indicators of the recognition provided to children by the councils. Setting it in the framework of the capability approach, we can ask the following question: if the "forums" were created in order to allow children's expression and to promote children's participation, how and to what extent can the experience of these "forums" be seen as a tool for expanding real freedoms?

On the basis of research data, mainly collected between 2005 and 2009 (Malatesta and Palazzo 2005; Malatesta et al. 2006; Malatesta and Golay 2010), we discuss in this chapter the opportunities and hindrances that result from councils implementation in order to show whether certain devices lead to children's empowerment and social recognition. Social recognition being a key aspect of political justice (according to Honneth 1995), we assess here the value of councils

D. Golay (✉) • D. Malatesta
Haute école de travail social et de la santé, EESP, Lausanne, Switzerland
e-mail: dominique.golay@eesp.ch; dominique.malatesta@eesp.ch

D. Stoecklin and J.-M. Bonvin (eds.), *Children's Rights and the Capability Approach*, Children's Well-Being: Indicators and Research 8, DOI 10.1007/978-94-017-9091-8_6,

as a mean to sustain a sensible implementation of articles 12 and 13 of the UN Convention on the Rights of the Child (United Nations 1989) considering in particular the way inequalities are dealt with. Thus, from our point of view, children's rights implementation goes beyond learning about formal rights and procedures to give birth to a concrete experience of rights. To do so, three variables will be considered: (1) the role the institution plays in defining the frame and the goals of the participation processes; (2) the opportunities and the barriers that stem from councils implementation, including class and gender inequalities, rules and norms; (3) the sense of belonging the councils create.

To discuss councils implementation through the prism of recognition and social justice, this paper will be divided in three parts. The first one reviews three major theoretical contributions stemming from political philosophy and social justice, the capability approach (Sen 1985), Fraser's account on either redistribution and recognition (Fraser 1997; Fraser and Honneth 2003), and Honneth's conception of recognition (Honneth 1995; Fraser and Honneth 2003). The second part presents the different stages of data collection, the methodology used and the implementation contexts. Finally, the third part discusses to what extent children's councils can sustain effective participation for all and promote children's recognition as well as an understanding of their rights (as living rights rather than strictly formal). More specifically, the implementation of children's councils will be analysed convoking social justice and recognition theoretical frames to highlight how institutional and professional goals relates with the way children participate, build a feeling of group belonging and deal with the resources and the opportunities offered. In that matter, two major pedagogical trends, child oriented and city oriented councils, emerging from our study will be developed and compared here to assess their potentials regarding children's recognition as social actors.

6.2 The Capability Approach and Children's Participation

From Sen's perspective, the capability approach suggests switching from a human development approach, based on economics, to a focus on freedom as a more accurate way to promote valuable beings and doings (Alkire 2005). According to this point of view, what people are able to do and to be in a specific environment is considered as an indicator of quality of life and basic justice. Sen defines "*capabilities* [*as*] *a set of* (*usually interrelated*) *opportunities to choose and to act*" (Sen, cited by Nussbaum 2011, p. 20). The concept of capability therefore refers to "*the opportunities created by a combination of personal abilities and the political, social and economic environment*" (Nussbaum 2011, p. 20). When applied to children, this definition of capability implies considering the councils as social arrangements, located in a Swiss city, that are willing to improve children's participation through the creation of specific "meeting places" dedicated to debates and facilitating their voicing. If a clear political agenda of promoting children's expression and participation can be highlighted, the councils achievements, where and when they can be identified, suffer from a lack of visibility. As such, this questions their ability (1) to produce effective changes outside the forum setting itself and (2) to offer valuable opportunities. That raises the following question: how can a child or a group of children benefit from participating as far as decision-making, projects attainments or self-assertion are concerned? In that matter, the Capability Approach offers a frame in which to evaluate the potentials and hindrances of the councils insofar as it sheds light on individual resources as well as on the relations between children and their social environment.

As Sinclair (2004, p. 116) argues, the challenge is to move to

> a position where children's participation is firmly embedded within organisational cultures and structures for decision-making – to offer genuine participation to children that is not an add-on but an integral part of the way adults and organisations relate to children.

We, then, could state that the participation processes should become part of children's socialisation, and thus provide them with substantial freedoms, in addition to developing their skills and to producing changes in the social, educational, economical and political context they inhabit. However, since we are dealing with children, aged 9–12, the definition of capabilities should be seen as an evolving process.

> [...] the Capability Approach and the capability concepts, which, in a certain sense, incorporate the opportunity concept, the capacity concept and the agency concept, evolve over time. The dynamic process of the three components of capabilities can be captured by the notion of evolving capabilities. (Biggeri et al. 2010, p. 82)

The opportunity concept refers to the possibility that children, as council participants, have to produce valuable achievements considering their individual characteristics and external factors. In other terms, the opportunity concept accounts for the real freedom children have to participate as peers, to define the goals to be achieved, to choose the topics to be discussed and/or to realise the projects they value for example. The capacity concept outlines what children are able to do according to their age and maturity as well as the resources provided by the councils. Pedagogical means are quite central in that matter insofar as they tend to sustain or impede children's participation. The agency concept provides a frame to assess for the control children have over the process, their active participation in the changes that may occur in their surroundings, and for the possibility the councils gives them to decide about what really matters for themselves. In brief, the agency concept shed light on their actual empowerment.

According to Biggeri et al. (2010), conceptualising capabilities as evolving enables to consider the child both as a human being (a social actor or an agent of his own life) and as a human becoming (an individual situated in the centre of a development process). The concept of evolving capabilities correlates with the UN Convention on the Rights of the Child (UNCRC) that recognises children as active agents who are entitled to certain rights; namely, to be heard, to express themselves, to participate in decision-making and to be protected. Moreover, evolving capabilities show, according to the age and maturity of the children, that the conversion of resources and commodities into functionings and capabilities may well depend on the type of assistance the adults provide as well as on the nature of social arrangements (Biggeri et al. 2010).[1] If capabilities are to be considered as indicators of quality of life and basic justice, pinpointing what individuals are able to do and to be in a specific environment, then children's recognition as social actors becomes a key issue in analysing participation processes as supports of collective action. In this sense, children's councils, because they are meant to encourage children's expression and participation, are a means that might develop their empowerment and autonomy. However, according to Biggeri et al. (2010), the assistance of adults is likely to be central in the way children translate resources and commodities into functionings and capabilities. When applied to children's councils, the recognition of children as social actors cannot be isolated from the given assistance of the professionals in charge. It should also integrate a three-dimensional analysis which includes the opportunities they offer, the capacity they help to develop and the agency they promote or sustain according to children's age and maturity.

Moreover, defining councils as a form of collective action implies, first, taking into consideration the effects or consequences each council has on the children's environment and, second, considering three aspects of possible changes occurring through the participation processes. These aspects are: the relations to other children, the relations to professionals and organisations, and the inclusion of the children's point of view in the governance of the city. On these grounds, considering the participants (boys and girls, aged 9–12), as well as the settings investigated (children's councils situated in low income neighbourhoods), we will analyse the degree of children's recognition deriving from their participation by leaning on Fraser and Honneth's social justice critical theories (Fraser 1997; Honneth 1995; Fraser and Honneth 2003).

6.3 Social Justice: A Matter of Redistribution and Recognition

Fraser's conception of justice is based on the acknowledgement that, nowadays, claims of recognition predominate as redistribution demands recede. Reflecting on social as well as cultural inequalities, Fraser argues that the principles of redistribution and recognition should be articulated in an attempt to conceptualize social justice (Fraser 1997). She pleads for a justice capable of remedying socio-economic injustices by redistribution (providing universal access to goods) and cultural injustices by recognition (giving positive value to devaluated groups). To do so, Fraser insists on the principle of "parity of participation" which means that all adult members of society should be able to interact with one another as peers (Fraser and Honneth 2003).

[1] It should be mentioned that this interpretation of the capabilities is linked to a specific understanding of the concept and is not necessarily shared by all the tenants of the capability approach.

> In the case of recognition, the objective is to remove the cultural barriers which prevent some from being others' peers and thus to fulfil (...) the intersubjective condition of parity of participation. (...) In the case of redistribution, the objective is to remove the economic barriers which prevent some from being others' peers, and so to fulfil (...) the objective condition of parity of participation. (Thompson 2005, p. 90)

Even though Fraser's principle of parity of participation do not integrate children as member of society, it gives an interesting insight to assess the way councils work and deal with social inequalities. In other words, it is important to specify who are the participants and what credit is given to their opinion according to their socio-economic and/or socio-cultural backgrounds. If Fraser's theory of social justice consider both the redistribution and the recognition principles, it is mainly because the collectivities she analysed are virtually two-dimensional (in particular those defined by race and gender).

> They are defined both by economic and cultural characteristics, where neither set of characteristics is reducible to the other. (Fraser, cited by Thompson 2005, p. 89).

From that standpoint, recognition is insufficient to remedy social injustices and therefore to provide a theoretical framework capable of analysing capitalist societies. Moreover, Fraser's conception of recognition differs from Honneth's insofar as she relates it to groups' status and their (re)evaluation which is quite detached from psychological bonds or intersubjective relations. Therefore, Fraser's framework is fruitful to shed light on the differentiated value accorded to specific groups, namely, in councils assessment, the distinct weight given to the participation of girls and of boys. This raises two fundamental questions: Are all children equally able to participate as peers? How can economical and cultural barriers be overcome by councils monitoring?

For Fraser and Honneth (2003), on the contrary, recognition is linked to identity and to the construction of self. According to him, recognition is the very base of social justice involving public attribution of positive value by one party to another. Recognition is, in Honneth's perspective, embedded in intersubjective relations and has three components (love, rights and esteem[2]). Honneth argues that, without care and love, children's personalities do not develop. In this regard, the experience of affective recognition plays a central role in the construction of human identity. Moreover, love, as the first stage of recognition, is a necessary ground to build the "*individual self-confidence indispensable for autonomous participation in public life*" (Honneth 1995).

The second component refers to rights, and implies the respect each individual is entitled to in modern society.

> In such a system, one can be respected as a legal person with the same rights as all other members of society. (Honneth, cited by Thompson 2005, p. 91)

[2] The three components of recognition are also defined as love, rights and solidarity (Thomas 2012).

Legal recognition comprises civic, political as well as social rights. More specifically, the rights component of recognition is related to a definition of individuals as morally responsible which raises the problem to determine if children can be considered as morally responsible persons.

> Just as, in the case of love, children acquire, via the continuous experience of 'maternal' care, the basic self-confidence to assert their needs in an unforced manner, adult subjects acquire, via the experience of legal recognition, the possibility of seeing their actions as universally respected expression of their autonomy. (Honneth 1995, p. 18).

Accordingly, children seem to be excluded from the class of morally responsible persons and are not entitled to legal recognition. This may well be explained by the ambiguity of the subject's definition as a morally responsible person on the one hand, and by Honneth's conception of legal recognition on the other. Indeed, legal recognition is intrinsically linked to social respect and self-respect which depends, as he argues, on the "*ability to claim one's rights through a legal process*" (Thomas 2012, p. 456). Hence, if children are rights-bearers, it is not clear to what degree they may be called morally responsible and to what extent they own the ability to claim their rights through a legal process.[3] From our standpoint, though, and more particularly in terms of council assessment, children's rights as well as their recognition remain a key indicator to understand the meaning adults and children give to participation processes.

The third component is governed by the achievement principle, which means that the individual's contribution to society is likely to be appreciated, giving him or her an equal opportunity to earn esteem. Esteem is related to solidarity that Honneth (1995) defines as a form of interaction in which subjects are concerned with others personal route insofar as they share relations of symmetrical esteem. In this regard, esteem is closely linked to group relations because agreement over practical goals offers an "intersubjective horizon of values" sustaining the recognition of others personal characteristics (their capacities and their qualities). Thus, esteem goes beyond the respect component and is, in modern society, detached from legal recognition.

However, the worth accorded to individuals remains dependent on socially defined traits and abilities and consequently "relations of social esteem are subject to permanent struggle" (Honneth 1995, p. 126). If, in Honneth's conception of recognition, children are mainly situated at the first stage (love), the esteem component may nevertheless be convoked to assess councils implementation. More specifically, considering that children contribute to society and culture, as Thomas (2012) suggests, two dimensions will be accounted for: the solidarity emerging through participating in the group of children; the evaluation of children's claims by carers. A series of questions can therefore be raised: do councils encourage a sense of belonging and a recognition of others as peers? Are children's claims

[3] Knowing that the third optional protocole stemming from the Committee on the rights of the child gives the opportunity to children or their representatives to submit a complaint about violations of their rights to the UN Committee.

taken seriously? To what extent do councils sustain children's claims and their social visibility?

6.4 From Councils Assessment to Councils Institutionalisation

From 2001 to 2004, The City of Lausanne launched participation processes dedicated to children in two neighbourhoods. Children were invited to engage in councils through school. Nevertheless, the forums were managed by youth workers and took place outside school hours and curriculum. To decide whether or not to institutionalise children's councils, the Childhood and Youth Office of Lausanne requested an evaluation of the outcomes produced by these participation processes. In order to proceed to council assessment, the Office, in accordance with the researchers in charge of the evaluation process, decided to set up a forum in a low-income neighbourhood. The main goal of this choice was to compare children's needs and claims as well as forums monitoring and outcomes according to socio-economic and socio-cultural backgrounds. This specific council assessment was achieved in 2005 (Malatesta and Palazzo 2005). The evaluation implied regular observations of council' sessions as well as a set of group interviews with children aged 8–13. Observations permitted a close following of the council monitoring and an "immersion" in the events deriving from it (for example museum field trips, swimming pool sessions, and a block party, just to name a few). Group interviews were focused on the way children perceived and experienced the council in which they participated. This evaluation phase highlighted three major issues for the children involved. The first one is related to the publicity and the visibility the council gave to children's point of views and eventually to their claims.

> I liked it because it's a place where children can express themselves and talk about the neighbourhood and it's nice. (girl participant)

The participants enjoyed the possibility to give their insight about what should be done to improve their surroundings. This opportunity, far from being a way to fulfil individual interests, was seen as a mean to work on the well-being of a community of inhabitants.

> And then, if we want to improve things like that, people will also be happy, they're gonna like it. (girl participant)

Participating to a council, for the children involved, is an opportunity to gain local visibility. Therefore, when preparing an event such as a block party, making their presence noticeable became a real issue. Consequently, the children decided to mark their council belonging by creating a logo for the occasion.

> We made T-shirts so everybody would know we are the councillors. (boy participant)

Thus, public visibility took on great importance for the children involved. They did not only enjoy the possibility of self-expression the councils gave them but they also sought after some kind of recognition by participating. In this regard, the gain of social esteem proved to be a key issue when considering the outcomes of the councils.

The second issue emerging from group interviews had to do with councils monitoring by the youth workers. In fact, the perception that children had of group dynamic was closely linked to the enforcement of minimal rules such as listening to each other, talking one at a time, respecting each other. As a matter of fact, children tended to appreciate the secure environment that rules provided. Moreover, rules were seen as indispensable tools to ensure an equality of treatment between children.

> I would put a rule that say that council is reserved to 10–12 years old and that was it, because there were a whole bunch of kids that wanted to come and they couldn't because they were too young, but in the same time a lot of kids that didn't have the age came anyway. That wasn't right for the others.... (boy participant)

Rules fulfil two major functions. They sustain a positive group dynamic from which a sense of belonging could emerge – which can also be analysed as an emerging solidarity between children – and they guarantee a better equality of treatment.

Finally, the third outcome is related to the benefits deriving from participating to a council. In this regard, the children involved insisted on the increase they noticed in their communication skills.

> We learned to express ourselves, to talk about our neighbourhood, to be more free, not to keep our thoughts for ourselves, but to let them free. (girl participant)

They especially valued the opportunity to talk and to express their opinion about the improvements the neighbourhood needed. However, their understanding of rights and/or citizenship were somewhat absent of their discourses. Or, as one of them put it in a rather ironical way, participating to a council does not guarantee a recognition of children as subjects.

> We are no citizens, we are your students, we are only small kids who don't know about anything. (boy participant)

As a participation process dedicated to children, the council studied shed light on issues linked to children's life, preoccupations and understandings of their environmental surroundings. More specifically, children's opinion and analysis of the neighbourhood they inhabit revealed the inequalities they suffered and in particular the gender ones.

> Boys go wherever they want, girls not that much. Boys can go to the field [playing field], wherever, (...). [Talking about the girls] It's not that they can't go, but if they go to the field, it's not worth anything. There are really only a few places where they can go, yes downtown in girls' shops. (girl participant)

Girls' access to a variety of recreational territories as well as the harsh relationships between boys and girls are therefore structuring children's everyday life. This raises the question of the potentialities of councils as devices sustaining children's empowerment but also as social arrangements where inequalities are likely to be challenged.

These findings gave birth to a research project in partnership with the Childhood and Youth Office of Lausanne and with a foundation grouping the local recreational centres (Malatesta et al. 2006). The investigation aimed to analyse councils' implementation in five different settings (three recreation centres and two day-care centres dedicated to schoolboys and schoolgirls). It involved a close collaboration with the seven professionals (social workers) who agreed to participate in the study. In order to launch the participation processes in the five settings in the same period of time[4] and to take into account the specificities of the centres, the project implied a minimal sharing of goals and guidelines.[5] Basically and according to the findings of the council assessment achieved in 2005, three requisites were settled: the professionals valued children's expression and participation as a mainstream of their intervention; the children's voices and actions were to be taken seriously; a monitoring of social inequalities. Then and according to the group of children attending either the centre or the council, specific goals were set in each location giving more or less weight to the apprenticeship of citizenship.

The first council grouping eight children (girls and boys) and situated in a recreational centre worked essentially on food and nutrition. The second one, also belonging to a recreational centre, reunited seven girls preoccupied by the conflicting relationships they observed in their surroundings. The third one, comprised a bigger group of children, around 12, and was clearly aimed towards improving what the neighbourhood had to offer to the children as users and inhabitants. The fourth one related to a day-care centre tried to launch a participation process anchored in the everyday life organisation. This choice implied the inclusion of the younger ones[6] in the process and privileged procedures oriented towards the planning and scheduling of recreational activities. Finally, the fifth one, also situated in a day-care centre benefit from the larger group of children (around 14 altogether). The main goal pursued by the professionals in charge of this specific council was to offer a forum where children can express themselves, choose the themes they want to discuss and realise projects according to their interests.

In terms of data collection, and in addition to regularly observing how the councils set up, we asked the professionals to work with a "diary" in order to collect their own analysis of the process after each session (once every other week) over a period of 4–5 months. We also conducted ten collective interviews with children,[7] five in-depth ones with the social workers and moderated six focus

[4] The councils took place once every 2 weeks during a 4–5 months period.

[5] The guidelines were based on the UNICEF recommendations related to children's participation (Haas 2003).

[6] Several children under 9 years old were included, two were 6, two were between 7 and 8, the remaining six were 9 or 10 years old.

[7] Fifty-one children participated to the councils, 30 girls and 21 boys, from 6 to 12 years old.

groups with all the professionals involved in the research. The analysis we present in the following part rests mainly on the data collected during this particular research.

However, it should be mentioned that the Childhood and Youth Office of Lausanne worked, meanwhile, at a "council concept" somewhat detached from the outcomes of the investigation presented above. Consequently, children's councils were implemented in various neighbourhoods during the time of investigation but were not part of the ongoing assessment. We were commissioned afterwards to participate in two work sessions with the professionals in charge of the "new" councils. This allowed us to complete our data with a documentary analysis of the resources produced by Lausanne's Childhood and Youth Office regarding children's councils and youth parliaments (it included among others a presentation of the children's council, links to websites, references to similar experiences elsewhere, and a video on a specific experience in a day-care centre).

6.5 Councils Implementation as a Social Justice Issue: The Treatment of Gender Inequalities

As the council evaluation of 2005 highlighted, children are sensitive to justice issues and may claim for stricter rules if they perceive inequalities in the way carers address to them. Nevertheless, gender inequalities are so embedded in cultural habits that it may well go unnoticed. In other terms, if inequalities related to age or economic differences are discussed in meetings, gender inequalities are widely ignored. As Bassand (1997) argues, "unequal access to the three basics of social life, namely wealth, culture and power, is an injustice." Yet, in children's councils, the access to cultural goods and power is a central issue which plays itself out in the ways boys and girls relate to each other during councils sessions (Malatesta and Golay 2010). In fact, the observations of several council sessions demonstrate that boys tend to behave differently than girls. The boys tend to raise their voices and to interrupt others. They especially interrupt the girls, whom they may despise, mock and sometimes insult. Since they act and interact in a more visible (that is to say more audible) manner, boys seem to attract all the attention. At least, this seems to be the case in mixed-sex councils. Moreover, when the setting is "a girls-only council", the professionals are the ones who tend to question the council's value, regretting the absence of the boys.[8] Apparently, girls are only girls and as a consequence, their point of view is seen as specific (girl-oriented). Indeed, according to the professionals' representations of participative processes, a girls-only council seems to go against the universality of citizenship. In other words, the professionals do not look at "a girls-only council" as a device that could sustain

[8] No comparison could be made with boys-only councils through the research we conducted. Most of the councils were mixed-sex and one was a girls-only council.

girls' empowerment. As we can see, girls' councils can hardly produce contextual or institutional changes since girls are not really considered as being valuable actors.

The use of Fraser's framework in the analysis of children's councils sheds light on the fact that a universal access to cultural goods (e.g. access to public expression through participation and the acquisition of organisational competences) is not enough to ensure justice. Therefore it is also necessary to consider the cultural norms – incorporated through socialisation – that may impede equal participation in the making of culture, in public spheres and in everyday life (Fraser 1997). If the professionals working in children's councils are not aware of justice issues, they can easily reproduce inequalities between boys and girls insofar as they turn a blind eye to girls' status in relation to boys.

As a matter of fact, in some settings, what the study of children's councils implementation did highlight is that girls suffer from misrecognition (invisibility) and disrespect (malignity or disparaging in children's interactions) (Malatesta and Golay 2010). As one boy said, boys have the right to disparage girls if they feel that the girls are too talkative.

> We insulted each other (. . .) We were right to insult them, they were talking a lot. (A boy aged 12)

As we can see, access to speech time and to self-expression is a real power issue in mixed-sex settings. Universal access to a council is a first step towards promoting participation, but councils prove to be ineffective if the professionals in charge are not conscious of the social forces at play.

The participation promoted by the implementation of children's councils may be qualified as an "ideological" participation insofar as these forums are not considered as a means to empower children, but rather as an end in itself (what is important is participation in itself). Similarly, ideological participation is particularly evident when the participation processes are deemed "neutral" procedures that are embedded in an instrumental perspective, and as such, do not take proper account of social inequalities.

When oriented towards the City (and a normative definition of citizenship), the forums aim at encouraging children's participation in order to establish good habits.

> Through the concept of children's council, there is a drive to promote children's engagement, according to their age, in a participative, active and responsible process. (Ville de Lausanne 2007[9])

According to the councils' concept as it was developed by the city of Lausanne in 2007, the forums implementation should teach children about their rights and duties, as well as promote their participation in the democratic process, which also means that the children have to conform to the decisions deriving from it.

Accordingly, participating in a children's council implies, *de facto*, subordinating oneself to moral and behavioural norms valued positively by professionals and

[9] The translation is ours.

local authorities. However, if that educational goal could be valued positively as it gives children an opportunity to be heard at a local level, so far, these devices are failing to produce effective changes in the children's social status or in the way the professionals relate to them, mainly because children's words and actions are not taken seriously. "It's magic," said one professional during an interview. Participation is actually viewed as something the professionals ought to do with children because it is perceived as a good thing in general. Moreover, participation processes, when dedicated to children, are often performed as a game. In this sense, participation is not for real and has no consequences in "real life". On account of this, children continue to suffer from invisibility and disrespect, which can also be analysed as a disparaged recognition (or a denial of recognition) (Renault 2004). Moreover, this outcome questions the worth of councils regarding the third component of Honneth's recognition, namely the social esteem the children may gain from participating.

Leaning on Fraser's framework once again, from a gender perspective and a social justice point of view, the implementation of participation processes should articulate the principles of redistribution and recognition to be able to remedy social injustices. However, if boys and girls do not have access to the same amounts of oral expression or speech time when participating in the way the situation is defined, boys and girls do not benefit from equal distribution of these participation elements. If professionals do not offer a clear framework (defining goals to be achieved and rules to be followed) and if they do not intervene in the debate (or even sometimes in the making of decisions), then girls, either as individuals or as a group, are impeded from participating as peers. It appears that professionals have to consider simultaneously an open access to speech time, debate, projects and skills and an equal recognition of both sexes, which also includes attention to minorities (as devaluated groups). Furthermore, the recognition conferred by such devices should be questioned. What kind of recognition do children in general gain from participating? Who benefits from it and to what extent? Lastly, considering the age group investigated, what are the conversion factors allowing resources and commodities to turn into functionings and capabilities (opportunity the children have to choose the topics to be discussed, decide about the goals to be achieved and about the projects they value; control given to children over the whole process; changes that occurred through the participation process)?

6.6 Children's Participation: How Might Professional Goals Undermine Recognition?

Since the recent institutionalisation of children councils, studying the ways professionals define the goals of participation processes dedicated to children, leads to two rather contrasting views that can be highlighted: (1) the professionals (social workers) focus on children's social position and their participation to the City affairs. Then they tend to circumscribe their thinking about children's participation in the public sphere (area of debates) and/or in the public space (access to an open physical territory). (2) They primarily focus on children, taking into consideration their preoccupations, their experiences, their expectations in a social setting marked by social inequalities (class, race and gender).

The first set of children's councils can be defined as citizenship-oriented. As such, their main goal is to make "good citizens", responsible human beings engaged in City issues. In order to educate children to citizenship, the professionals tend to teach them democratic procedures, such as voting. The way they teach the children to make decisions resides in the opportunity to vote and to make a choice from a set of suggestions submitted by some of the children (for example what they wish to eat for lunch in a day-care centre). As voting is central in the process, children learn that majority prevails and that minority can be left aside. It could be problematic knowing that the children considered here are likely to belong to minorities and to be excluded from voting when they reach their majority. Furthermore, if democratic procedures are to be taught, the process of participation cannot be reduced to the right to vote (as a neutral procedure excluding a reflection on the existing social forces and inequalities). How, then, could the professionals integrate in the process a genuine concern for social injustices and teach children that democracy also entails a consideration of minorities? How could these devices provide children with a sense of justice if social inequalities are not considered an issue? How, and to what extent, could an instrumental perspective create an experience of recognition, which might provide children with social esteem?

The second set of children's councils can be defined as children-oriented. According to the professionals involved, their main pedagogical goal is creating a "space" dedicated to children's expression by allocating them a meeting time and venue. In doing so, the main objective is to give the children an opportunity to express themselves and to participate in the making of a decision rooted in their daily lives. The professionals' central preoccupation is to sustain children's empowerment (and autonomy) in a secure environment (with clear objectives, rules to be followed by all, regulation of speech time, monitoring of behaviours and interactions). They endeavour to explain what the council is (or can be) and to describe its objectives (related to what children can really do). This set of councils seem to encourage participation, to build a strong sense of peer group membership and to create an experience of social usefulness (social esteem). Nevertheless, the "debate space" emerging from the discussions among peers does not necessarily lead to establishing city-oriented projects. In these particular forums, the citizenship definition is on par with "lived citizenship" (Liebel 2008) as a process oriented towards the understanding the children have of their rights and embedded in a real life experience. The learning of procedures such as voting or project-making comes after the voicing of the children's needs and expectations.

As this set of councils is children-oriented, and endeavours to respect their interests and preoccupations, it does not necessarily give birth to projects or creations that can be made visible in a public space. Moreover, by creating a sense of belonging children-oriented councils can also lead to the exclusion of newcomers. The children involved in these particular settings tend to define strict group borders that impede the outsiders from joining. In one case, the council was renamed "La bande secrète"[10] by the participants and a membership card was designed to reinforce the sense of belonging. As such, "La bande secrète" was perceived as a place reserved to a specific group. The other setting, which can also be analysed as children-oriented, was formed by a small group of eight children situated in a recreational centre that decided to work on food and nutrition. As they became very involved in the project, this particular group refused to admit newcomers who were perceived as potential threats. In these two specific settings, the councils, as experienced by children, constitute not only a reserved space, but they also define a "closed" space. Moreover, in addition to the absence of projects which produces a lack of visibility, the fact that the debate space becomes private[11] puts into question the council's capacity to provide children with social esteem outside of the group and its local organisation. To what extent does this second set of councils provide children with a better social esteem (an understanding of selves as social actors)? Does the environment that the councils help to (re)create, sustain children's capabilities by, for example, improving their opportunities to make choices and to demonstrate their autonomy?

6.7 Institutional Goals: Opportunities and Barriers to Children's Social Recognition

The comparison between the two sets described above in terms of children's participation and empowerment highlights the central role that the institution plays in the process. The institutional role is dependent upon the frame it provides as well as the goals it sets. This frame defines the contextual conditions in which participation processes take place. That is to say that the council's definition and the related institutional expectations about the council's achievements interfere with the way mandates are given to professionals and their monitoring of the forums they supervise. Since the participation processes are clearly influenced by the way institutions define the goals that such devices are supposed to achieve, these institutional frames and goals have a direct impact on the participation procedures and affect if and how social inequalities are taken into consideration.

On the one hand, the making of "good" citizens is thus often embedded in an instrumental perspective where devices and procedures resulting from it can be defined as a-sociological or neutral. In this sense, the way councils are implemented and organised seems to be blind to social (class) and/or cultural inequalities (gender, age, nationality). By ignoring or overshadowing social forces at play and inequalities, they tend to reinforce individual responsibility for the injustices

[10] That can be translated as "The secret bunch".

[11] The privacy of the debate space relates here to the enjoyment of being with well-known peers, to share some intimacy and to the lack of openness due to group frontiers.

suffered. That blindness to social inequalities is well summarized by a social worker involved in a recreational centre.

> Why shall we want to reduce inequalities, what a child experiences in hard times makes him develop plenty of skills and life' strengths. Some of them might even be ten times more performing, performing is not quite the word, but they are going to be more alive, more proactive in life.

From her standpoint, inequalities might be seen as chances or opportunities to develop personal strategies to overcome social and economical obstacles. In other words, children, individually, take responsibility for the social injustices they may suffer. They are called upon to overcome what may impede them in order to fully participate as peers. This perspective, which does not offer any recognition of status, tends to reinforce the social forces at play. It also reproduces the social order without recognising children as "real" social agents.

On the other hand, as these councils tend to privilege some individuals perceived as leaders, they may provide some children, especially boys, with a form of recognition.

> I think it's cool because we have an opportunity to express ourselves pretty good. And also, what is outstanding with children's council, is that we can do all we can usually not do in life. For example we can call "stars" and ask them to come and have an interview. And then it's cool. And we make suggestions for the neighbourhood. Yes, we're like young agents that starts to plan things for the neighbourhood. (Boy participant, 13 years old)

This type of recognition mainly concerns individuals and does not take any group membership into account. In this sense, the council benefits one child or another as an individual, but does not consider the children as a group.[12] In this type of council, the participation process avoids dealing with group issues. It does not include a questioning about those who are really able to participate and those whose participation is impeded. Consequently, the solidarity component of recognition (Honneth 1995) as a relation of symmetrical esteem is clearly absent of the process. That "blindness" to group issues and specificities has direct consequences on the engagement of children in the council. As a matter of fact, they attend the council' sessions inconsistently. Furthermore, in one specific setting, the group finally split up, with the boys developing a video making project (outside the council) and the girls completing a fashion project of their own. On the light of this outcome, creating a sense of belonging seem to be necessary for the children to engage in a collective action oriented towards making effective changes.

On the contrary, the children-oriented councils, because they seek to increase children's autonomy and empowerment as a group, offer a better environment in which to create capabilities. Nevertheless, the experience of recognition that derives from children's participation through the right to self-expression (article 13 UNCRC), emotional security and social esteem, is limited to the confines of the

[12] This can also be questioned according to the general comments stipulated by The Children's Rights Convention Committee about article 12 of UNCRC in which children are entitled to be heard individually and/or in group.

council itself. If children develop a strong sense of peer group membership (and solidarity), allowing them to go beyond social cleavages such as the division between boys and girls, they may not feel the urge to expand their new skills outside of the safe place that they helped to construct through their participation in active discussions and debates.

The recognition derived from the experience of participating in a council consists of two dimensions (or levels) that should be considered when working with children. The first dimension implies that the children recognize each other as peers which also refers to the solidarity component of recognition (Honneth 1995). This first level of recognition is oriented towards the inside (the group in itself); this dimension is necessary and useful for each individual to be able to participate fully in the group. Nevertheless, it is not enough to produce effective changes in the children's environment. As a matter of fact, recognition also needs visibility in order for the children to gain social esteem beyond the confines of specific organisation. This second dimension needs to be worked on if children's councils are to be devices sustaining children's recognition on a wider scale. However, a child-oriented perspective seems to be better suited to children needs by favouring more active and regular participation, and giving them a strong peer-group membership. It seems equally more capable of overcoming social cleavages giving girls and other devaluated groups a better chance to actually participate and be heard.

6.8 Children's Participation: Agency, Capabilities and Living Rights

The implementation of children's councils is, in the major cities of Switzerland, a dominant method, which helps to promote children's participation in decisional processes at a local level (social organisations, city governance). The efficiency of the councils in terms of children's recognition, of children's rights actualization and of capabilities should, thus, be discussed if the goal is to improve children's well-being either at a local level or on a larger scale. As we mentioned previously, the recognition derived from the participation processes does not give full satisfaction because children are still not considered as valuable actors outside of some specific settings reserved to them. To go further in the analysis and to give a better insight into the articulation of these findings, the children's point of view as well as the professionals' understanding of the processes need to be explored.

The children involved in the councils globally appreciated the opportunity they had to express themselves on different matters and eventually to decide on the projects they wanted to pursue. As one boy puts it, council gave them the possibility to express their ideas and feelings, to develop their knowledge (about nutrition in that specific case) and to take an active part on the organisation of activities and projects inside or outside the recreation centre.

> [...] We prepared cocktails and chocolate buns that we made by ourselves... We went to a fieldtrip to a chocolate factory... then we have a lot of fun because we can say...yes we can talk and say how we feel, if we want to change things or something like that... I think it's really super especially at our age. (Boy participant, aged 12)

Nevertheless, their consistent involvement in the participation processes largely depended on the way the professionals presented and regulated the councils.

The city-oriented settings appeared to be quite removed from the children's everyday life experiences or concerns. On account of this, the implementation suffered from children's "resistance". As a matter of fact, children tended not to attend, preferring other activities available in the recreational or day-care centres. The younger children complained about and even rejected the council as it impeded them from playing.

> I don't like councils. It's boring. And then we can never do what we like with the council's project. Sometimes, we'd like to go and play hide and seek at the park. We'd like to stay here [at the day-care centre] but we're always annoyed by the council, we always have to do the project. (Boy participant, aged 7)

The older children came and went, distracted by other events or activities that were happening in the neighbourhood or in the centres (birthdays, video workshops, fieldtrips, and so on.) They reported feeling bored during their participation in the council. According to some children, the council did not offer clear objectives and it did not explain where the discussions were meant to go. As a 13 years old boy explained, he got tired of talking.

> We were talking a lot about the same thing over and over, and we were going around in circles.

This reflects the fact that children lost interest in the participation process since they did not really understand what was expected of them. The children's evaluation of the councils outlines the difficulty that the professionals faced when they implemented a participation process that made little sense from a child's standpoint. If the children understood the opportunity the settings offered them, they were not able to connect it to their life experience, which prohibited the development of potential capacities and the increasing of their autonomy. In terms of agency, the children's analysis of the process showed their reflexivity, but that capacity to reflect on their experience came to justify their limited involvement in the council sessions.

The city-oriented councils continued to privilege education to citizenship procedures over communication skills and debates and they usually did not include a relation-based learning. In fact, children behaved according to their own habits and their interactions relied on the way relations were already settled between them in the neighbourhood. In this sense, the council sessions highlighted the existing conflicts and cleavages in particular between boys and girls. The professionals may even have reinforced conflicts since they were not aware of them or because they chose not to regulate the group for the sake of self-expression. Thus, participation in decision-making was a right reserved for the dominant ones, the others being actually impeded from participating fully as peers. This had consequences not only on children's individual agency, but also on the opportunity to create a pressure group and to launch collective actions. This opportunity was actually never mentioned by the children who primarily saw in the participating process an opportunity for individual gain in status.

However, the city-oriented councils produced, albeit in a limited manner, changes in the social organisations where they occurred (recreational centres, day-care centres). Faced with the difficulty of involving children in the participation process they sought to implement, the professionals tried to understand what went wrong in the process and they chose to integrate the children's points of view, ideas and interests in the making of the activity program they offer on a regular basis. If this option does not interfere with city governance, it can, hopefully, be analysed as a first step toward including children in the decision-making process pertaining to their everyday lives.

In the children-oriented councils, the children experienced greater enthusiasm and a perceptible involvement when they discussed their doings in the sessions. As a matter of fact, they were eagerly expecting the sessions, asking the professionals when the next one was going to take place. They especially enjoyed the debates and activities deriving from the themes they had decided to discuss.[13] They seized the opportunity offered by co-creating with the professional assistance a specific space reserved for them. The professionals didn't actually expect such an investment from the children. They talked endlessly and they exchanged ideas on different matters such as love, conflicts, fears, as well as their other preoccupations of the moment. The children, though, were not interested in working on projects, even though they clearly enjoyed the possibility of discussing and eventually deciding what to do to resolve the problems they encountered.

As we already mentioned, the children-oriented councils created a strong sense of group membership and developed a sense of solidarity between the participants that helped to overpass social cleavages. In terms of capacities, the children developed communication skills, in addition to acquiring some knowledge related to the themes discussed, which then led them to a better sense of themselves and a better understanding of their concrete rights. Therefore, we can say that the councils had a real impact on the relationships between children, at least in the centres. As a matter of fact, their recognition of each other as valuable peers became evident through the feedback they gave about the councils.

Children's agency was noticeable on two different levels. First, all the children interviewed gave a clear idea of what a council was. They were able to deliver explanations and give personal impressions according to their shared experience. In other words, they develop their communication as well as their expression skills. Secondly, their answers highlighted the fact that their opinions and decisions counted and were valued by the professionals in charge of the council. Through the construction of their group belonging, they realised that they were able to act as

[13] The themes derived from collective discussions between children and between children and the professionals in charge.

a group and maybe change some aspects of their everyday life. One group, for example, was very proud of the actions they took to rename a particular location in the neighbourhood. That specific place had been perceived negatively both by adults and children and was called "La colline des drogués".[14] To overcome the fear they felt about that place, they decided, with the professionals' assistance, to rename it and to place a flag on it. After a small ceremony on the hill, they took it upon themselves to inform the inhabitants, contacting children as well as adults, they explained the hill's new name and they tried to convince everybody to switch to a positive representation of that given place. As we can see, children-oriented councils not only encourage children to participate, but they also constitute an interesting ground from which to launch collective action. Moreover, professionals' supervision and monitoring, in these set of councils, apparently provide children with the necessary assistance allowing them to translate resources and commodities into capabilities (Biggeri et al. 2010), even though, councils achievements suffer from a lack of visibility.

Nevertheless, these children-oriented councils have a limited impact on child-adult relations. Indeed, we have to emphasize that the absence of any visible change is largely due to the use of pedagogical methods which rely on a children-oriented perspective. The councils implementation was embedded in educational habits that encourage children's expression and participation. Nevertheless, the sensitivity to children's rights and consequently their recognition as valuable actors was and continues to be, as far as we know, mainly limited to the centres adopting a child-oriented approach. In that sense, the children's councils play a very minor role in the city management and planning. As Baraldi (2005) argues, to be efficient at the city level, children's participation processes need to be embedded in networks that involve all the concerned actors, including the city administrators. This was clearly not the case in our investigation.

6.9 Towards Children's Recognition

Children's councils, as they are implemented in Lausanne, raise fundamental issues in terms of children's social recognition and the affirmation of their rights. The analysis of several stages of councils implementation highlights their failure to extend children's recognition beyond the confines of specific locations and to sustain their empowerment on a long-term basis. Therefore, councils in their institutionalised form are oriented toward a tendency to avoid conflicts and as such to control rather than produce changes. Therefore, they can be seen as domination tools that impose values and norms without offering effective institutional alternatives in order to sustain children's empowerment. These participation processes seek to promote compliance and they can be defined as "add-on", which

[14] That can be translated as the "drug-addicts hill".

actually keeps children out of the decision spheres, namely the political and institutional offices in charge of childhood and youth policies or services.

The capabilities and children's right approaches can offer interesting insight into what has to be done to overcome that denial of recognition. As a matter of fact, the concepts of evolving capabilities and of living rights could be fruitful not only to analyse and evaluate the processes. These approaches also offer a frame in which "best practices" concerning children's rights implementation can be configured. In addition, the three components of capabilities (opportunity, capacity and agency) provide an interesting ground from which to evaluate the opportunities and the barriers emerging from within the councils. The city-oriented councils seem to be less efficient in developing capabilities. If self-expression is at the heart of these forums, they seem to be quite removed from children's everyday life experience which in fact impedes their full engagement in the process. Nevertheless, they can promote a limited experience of recognition that allows some children to take part in decision-making, which directly affects how these children gain a better understanding of themselves as social actors. However, since city-oriented councils largely rest on children's capacities to overcome inequalities on their own, some children may suffer because the professionals' assistance is limited to project monitoring. If children's agency is reserved to specific individuals, who are generally leaders, it is almost never considered as relevant at a collective level.

On the contrary, children-oriented councils supply the participants with a frame where opportunities, capacities and agency are developed and reinforced through clear attainable goals and the belief in children's ability to act as social actors. The assistance provided by professionals is primarily geared towards the creation and the moderating of the group. Time is not devoted to projects that could be potentially visible outside the council. In this sense, if children-oriented councils are better suited to address the interests and preoccupations of the children, the recognition they provide is nevertheless limited to the social organisations (centres) where they are implemented. Their main strength lies in producing real changes in the way children consider each other and how they relate to each other. The group dynamic and the creation of group membership are then central in the process. In this sense, they offer a favourable ground for collective actions and develop relations of solidarity between children.

Regarding the civic dimension, the two sets of councils described illustrate two different conceptions of civic implementation. The city-oriented councils privilege an apprenticeship of formal laws and citizenship procedures without considering the children's life conditions and/or their actual capacity to participate as peers. Thus, they tend to reinforce social inequalities and provide children with an understanding of democratic procedures where the majority prevails over minorities. The children-oriented councils get closer to the notion of living rights as they are anchored in an everyday life perspective which gives great attention to the children's well-being. Self-expression and participation are a means to work on communication skills and therefore on the functioning of the group before undertaking collectively decided projects. To that end, children-oriented councils increase the opportunity for each child to participate in group activities and projects.

The assessment of councils shows that the mutual recognition "supported by an affective confidence in the continuity of shared concern" is mainly ensured by the professional in charge of the forums. It is embedded in the strong belief that children are competent social actors and it constitutes a ground from which solidarity between children can emerge. It also means that children voices, actions and claims need to be taken seriously and considered meaningful. Nevertheless, the rights component of recognition (Honneth 1995) even if it justifies councils implementation demands further considerations. Indeed, children are rights-bearers in accordance to UNCRC but the rights dimension is relatively absent from forums meetings or from children as well as professionals discourses.

If, as we pointed out, the role of the institution as well as the motives of all the involved actors are key issues in the way participation processes and procedures are achieved in terms of children's recognition, the goodwill of competent professionals might not be enough to promote sustainable changes in children's environment. According to some Italian experiences (Baraldi 2005), in order to be efficient and to have an impact on city management and planning, including urban space affectations, the participation processes, when directed to children, need to be embedded in a network capable of bridging professional and administrative segmentations. In light of all this, the living rights concept and the capabilities approach could offer a general frame to reconsider the place and the role that children's councils should play in city management as a means to increase the well-being of its population as a whole.

References

Alkire, S. (2005). *Capability and functionings: Definition and justification*. Human Development and Capability Association. Portable document, HDCA Briefing_concepts. Pdf, URL: http://www.capabilityapproach.com

Baraldi, C. (2005). *La città con i bambini. Città amiche dell'infanzia in Italia*. Firenze: UNICEF Centro di Ricerca Innocenti.

Bassand, M. (1997). *Métropolisation et inégalités sociales*. Lausanne: Presses Polytechniques et Universitaires Romandes.

Biggeri, M., Ballet, J., & Comim, F. (2010). The capability approach and research on children: Capability approach and children' issues. In S. Andresen et al. (Eds.), *Children and the good life: New challenges for research on children* (pp. 75–89). Dordrecht: Springer.

Ville de Lausanne. (2007). *Conseils des enfants*. Lausanne: Service de la jeunesse et des loisirs.

Fraser, N. (1997). *Justice interrupts*. New York: Routledge.

Fraser, N., & Honneth, A. (2003). *Redistribution or recognition? A political-philosophical exchange*. London: Verso.

Haas, E. (2003). *Donner une voix aux enfants*. Zürich: Comité Suisse pour l'UNICEF.

Honneth, A. (1995). *The struggle for recognition*. Cambridge: Polity Press.

Liebel, M. (2008). Citizenship from below: Children's rights and social movements. In A. Invernizzi & J. Williams (Eds.), *Children and citizenship* (pp. 32–43). London: Sage.

Malatesta, D., & Golay, D. (2010). La participation des enfants au débat public: une expression des dominants? *Nouvelles Questions Féministes, 29*(2), 88–99.

Malatesta, D., & Palazzo, C. (2005). *Evaluation des conseils d'enfants de la ville de Lausanne*. Lausanne: Haute école de travail social et de la santé, EESP.

Malatesta, D., Golay, D., & Thommen, E. (2006). *L'enfant dans la Cité. Enjeux de reconnaissance, enjeux de citoyenneté, enjeux de travail social. Les "tweens" (9 – 12 ans) à Lausanne et Bussigny*. Lausanne: Haute école de travail social et de la santé, EESP.

Murard, N., & Tassin, E. (2006). La citoyenneté entre les frontières. *L'homme et la société, 2* (160–161), 17–35.

Nussbaum, M. C. (2011). *Creating capabilities. The human development approach*. Cambridge: The Belknap Press of Harvard University Press.

Renault, E. (2004). Reconnaissance, institutions, injustice. *Revue du MAUSS, 1*(24), 180–195.

Sen, A. (1985). Well-being, agency and freedom: The Dewey lectures 1984. *Journal of Philosophy, 82*(4), 169–221.

Sinclair, R. (2004). Participation in practice: Making it meaningful, effective and sustainable. *Children & Society, 18*, 106–118.

Thomas, N. (2012). Love, rights and solidarity: Studying children's participation using Honneth's theory of recognition. *Childhood, 19*(4), 453–466.

Thompson, S. (2005). Is redistribution a form of recognition? Comments on the Fraser-Honneth debate. *Critical Review of International Social and Political Philosophy, 8*(1), 85–102.

United Nations. (1989). *Convention on the rights for the child*. Portable document, crc.pdf. URL: http://www2.ohchr.org/english/law/crc.htm

Chapter 7
Cross-Fertilizing Children's Rights and the Capability Approach. The Example of the Right to Be Heard in Organized Leisure

Daniel Stoecklin and Jean-Michel Bonvin

7.1 Introduction

This chapter starts with some critical considerations about article 12 UNCRC, which is considered the general principle and masterpiece regarding child participation and which reads as follows: "*States Parties shall assure to the child who is capable of forming his or her own views the right to express those views freely in all matters affecting the child, the views of the child being given due weight in accordance with the age and maturity of the child*" (UNCRC 1989, art. 12.1). The capability approach is very useful to analyse the transformation of the normative framework of the child's rights into children's lived experience. This approach seeks to understand how formal entitlements can (or cannot) be transformed into real freedoms. It suits our intention, which is to see how the formal entitlement to participate, enshrined in art. 12 of the Convention on the Rights of the child (the right to be heard), is converted into a real freedom to participate.

In order to do this, we selected one specific area: the field of organized leisure (also called extra-curricular activities). Our choice is motivated by the fact that studies on the way children take part in decisions about their leisure activities are relatively rare, especially in the French-speaking world (Roucous 2006, p. 235). This may be explained by the dichotomy between a sociology of leisure that ignored children and a sociology of education that neglected leisure activities (Sirota 2006). Meanwhile, it is mainly developmental psychology that provided knowledge and recommendations for recreative and cultural activities. The

D. Stoecklin (✉)
Children's Rights Unit, University Institute Kurt Bösch, P.O. Box 4176, Sion 4 CH – 1950, Switzerland
e-mail: daniel.stoecklin@iukb.ch

J.-M. Bonvin
Ecole d'études sociales et pédagogiques (EESP), University of Applied Sciences Western Switzerland, Chemin des Abeilles 14, Lausanne CH 1010, Switzerland
e-mail: jmbonvin@eesp.ch

D. Stoecklin and J.-M. Bonvin (eds.), *Children's Rights and the Capability Approach*, Children's Well-Being: Indicators and Research 8, DOI 10.1007/978-94-017-9091-8_7,

English-speaking world is better off, with more works on children's leisures in market-oriented economies where leisure time follows the trend towards privatization (Oke et al. 1999; Bai 2005; Naftali 2010), cooperation between children in plays organised in kindergartens (Evaldsson and Corsaro 1998), or influence of parents' social class and occupation over children's leisure activities (Lareau 2000). However, among the publications of NGOs and intergovernmental agencies, children's leisure and play activities only represent 2 % of the literature over the last 20 years (Hanson and Nieuwenhuys 2013). Therefore, our chapter intends to explore intersections between childhood sociology, sociology of leisure, children's rights, and the capability approach.

We try to come closer to the dynamic and evolving process of children's participation in organized leisure. The key to open the door leading to a better understanding of this process lies in listening to participants who depict their involvement in these activities. Therefore, our focus is on the "voices of children rather than on adult perspectives" (Kamerman 2010, p. vii). We first begin by recalling the participation rights of children and our view on them before presenting the capability approach as our theoretical model and the corresponding methodology based on a tool highlighting the recursive nature of the phenomenon. The results allow for important developments in the theory of child participation. In so doing, we build up a critical position towards participative rights by uncovering the "regime of truth" (Foucault 1991) that pervades the field of child participation. We also highlight the cumulative and recursive nature of action which allows us to conceive child participation as a *praxis*. This explains the importance of individual reflexivity in the formation of one's capability set, as the child's capacity to identify and claim for participation rights progressively enters within the range of opportunities available to him/her.

7.2 Participation Rights as They Are Experienced

The "participation rights" contained in the UNCRC are civil and political freedoms as well as economic, social and cultural rights: the right to be heard (art. 12), the right to freedom of expression (art. 13), the right to freedom of thought, conscience and religion (art. 14), the right to freedom of association and peaceful assembly (art. 15), the right to privacy (art. 16), the right to have access to information (art. 17), and the right to participate freely in cultural life and the arts (art. 31). The UNCRC is a holistic framework in the sense that its provisions are bound together and thus participation rights are not only interdependent but also inseparable of the other rights contained in the convention. This means that participation rights can be a goal in themselves but also a means to achieve other rights, like protection rights and provision rights. For instance, Zermatten and Stoecklin (2009) underline wrong connection between the right to be heard (art. 12) and the best interest of the child principle (art. 3), and show that the child's right to be heard, as a general principle of the UNCRC, is a procedural guarantee for the child's participation in decisions made in the best interest of the child. We should bear in mind these connections between rights when considering the ways in which children can participate in the design of extra-curricular activities (organized leisure) and the decisions made within the organized structures where these activities take place. In other words, the question is not just: "is the child being heard within these structures?", but in a more comprehensive manner: "how are the child's participation rights (art. 12–17, and 31) dealt with when it comes to decide about activities that are in the best interest of individual children, and of groups of children?", and also "how do these participation rights impact on, and are impacted by, access to facilities and provisions necessary for these activities?".

The picture that comes out of this holistic approach to children's rights gives an idea of the complexity that should be recognized and researched. This raises the question of the relevance of general frameworks that try to capture or evaluate "levels" of child participation. These are mostly centred on the degree to which children are integrated in the decision-making process. Consequently, the "levels" approach has generated several "ladders of participation" (Hart 1992; Franklin 1997; Thoburn et al. 1995; Treseder 1997; Shier 2001; Thomas 2002). Our own research is closer to a phenomenological approach to child participation, as we are trying to see how children experience their own participation (here in organized leisure activities). We start from a constructionist perspective whereby the understanding of child participation builds on the identification of the processes at play that emerge from interviews with children and which we do not define beforehand. Therefore, we propose to proceed inductively using the empirical results of the exploratory research we have conducted as the basis of our reflection. We do not start from an abstract construction of dimensions (with corresponding indicators) that would be related to each right of the UNCRC, but rather the contrary: we start with the factors appearing to be decisive in children's participation in organized leisure to highlight dimensions that are relevant in children's participation experiences. This gives the possibility of identifying, on a grounded basis, some theoretical questions that are overlooked by the dominant top-down approach, which is entailed by the formal adoption of normative frameworks, as is also the case with the CRC. Our purpose then is not to advocate in favour of the CRC as a normative framework, but to empirically look at some of the rights contained in the convention and to illustrate how they are "experienced" by children in their daily lives. In order to understand children's experiences and choices in the field of organized leisure activities, we use the theoretical model of the capability approach which we present in the next section.

7.3 The Capability Approach as a Theoretical Model

The capability approach holds that children's capacities evolve along both individual and social factors that promote or obstruct the conversion of their formal rights into real freedom. This perspective offers promising insights into understanding the

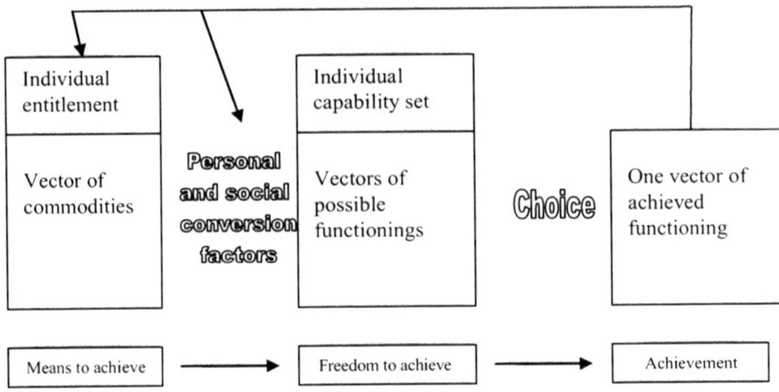

Diagram 7.1 From entitlements and commodities to achieved functionings (Bonvin and Farvaque 2006, p. 125, adapted from Robeyns 2003, p. 12)

decision making process as a complex interplay between children's reflexivity, that of adults and the opportunities offered by actual structures. Therefore, what we have to consider are the factors converting the right to participate into an actual possibility or a capability to participate (cf. Diagram 7.1).

From this perspective, the individual entitlement is the right of the child to be heard (art. 12 CRC) in decisions over leisure activities, and we want to see how personal and social factors help (or not) to convert this right into capabilities in the field of children's leisure. We have added backwards arrows (feed-back loop) in Diagram 7.1 to symbolize the recursivity or cyclical aspect of the process, whereby achieved functionings, in later sequences, retroact on the social definition of individual entitlements as well as they become part of the configuration of personal and social factors that convert these entitlements into an ever evolving capability set.

Among the social factors, we consider public policies regarding children and youth, institutions and procedures through which children can participate and be heard, and especially their accessibility and adaptability to different groups of children (age, gender, ethnicity, geography) possessing different kinds of capital: economic, social and cultural (Bourdieu 1994). The unequal distribution of these forms of capital is however not the sole explanation to children's differential participative capability. One should also look closer to how the social actor perceives reality and gives meaning to his/her actions in relation with others. Actually, the personal characteristics are crucial to see how the child converts the right to be heard into a functioning. To specify the conversion factors and the links among them, we have interviewed children, discussing with them about the influence they think they have over issues that are supposed to be in their reach, like decision-making about their leisure activities.

The capability approach (Sen 1999), and more specifically its application to children (Biggeri et al. 2011) has two important features, that are both assets and challenges and are useful to conceptualize children's citizenship and participation:

- It highlights that factors converting participation rights into real participation are partly social and partly individual and therefore it leaves open the question of "agency within structure" or the reciprocal influence between the collective and the individual.
- It looks at the observable activities or functionings of people as the result of a choice among a set of possibilities; it therefore considers participation not as a duty but as an opportunity. This aspect requires including two complementary parameters in the empirical investigation. On the one hand, the power of dominant ideas and their impact on individual freedoms: are children constrained to comply with the social norm of participation or is participation a genuine choice? Are they allowed not to participate and at what cost? On the other hand, the challenge of assessing freedom to choose forces us to deal with methodological questions about counterfactual deduction: it requires identifying the opportunity set of the children (i.e. what they do and what they could have done, but chose not to do), as it significantly impacts on their degree of freedom to choose.

The child's ability to make sense of the right to be heard and to use and shape the existing means to achieve this right is the focus of our chapter. How and why the actor makes (constrained) choices has to do both with objective socio-cultural influences and subjective perceptions. These aspects have been incorporated in the systemic theory of action and corresponding methodology which will be presented in the next section.

7.4 Methodology

In order to highlight factors that must be considered when observing how formal entitlements, such as the rights of the child, can (or cannot) be transformed into real freedom to participate, we have conducted a small-scale study, which is of exploratory nature, in Switzerland and in France. We are thankful to Pierrine Robin (also a contributor to this volume) and Aline Jacquemet who helped with interviews and coding, and especially Pierrine Robin for participating with inspiring ideas for analysis. Our observations have involved 19 respondents aged 12–15 years in western Switzerland and France. Respondents in France (5) are located in a neighborhood of Montreuil, a small town near Paris, while respondents in Switzerland (14) live in small towns and villages. Random sampling has ensured a certain socio-cultural diversity of respondents. We were not looking for representativity because it would have required data on the mother-population (all youth participants in organized leisure) all of which was not possible in the context of this research. The "projects" attended by respondents were a disco, a rap workshop, a party for students who had just graduated, a music scene, the animation of a leisure center, a youth parliament, and a video library.

Our purpose is to illustrate how participation rights are "experienced" by children in their daily lives. Participation is not observable only through the child's "active

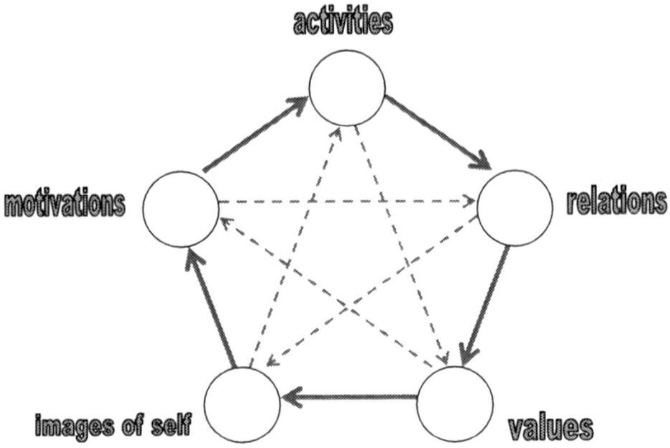

Diagram 7.2 The actor's system (Stoecklin 2013)

presence" in an organized activity but also through understanding how the activity is anchored in the child's reflexive behavior. We must consider how resources in the environment are reflexively interpreted by children and therefore it is through their subjective accounts that we are able to identify the social and individual factors that transform the abstract right to participate into concrete modes of participation. In this respect, we look at how the children interviewed experience their participation in the field of organized leisure activities. We start from the lived experience, as it is conceptualized by children, with a methodology that favours the expression of subjective thoughts and reduces the social desirability of responses.

We do this on purpose, because we could have started with questions that are more evaluative, taking for instance the Recommendation adopted in March 2012 by the Council of Europe regarding the Participation of Children and Young People under the age of 18, in order to develop our questions accordingly. This Recommendation states that:

> Participation is about individuals and groups of individuals having the right, the means, the space, the opportunity and, where necessary, the support to freely express their views, to be heard and to contribute to decision making on matters affecting them, their views being given due weight in accordance with their age and maturity (COE 2012).

If we had strictly followed this definition of participation, we would have ended in a top-down approach, and we probably would have influenced the responses as the way of asking questions would inevitably have induced some degree of compliance of the respondents with the perceived goals of the inquirers.

Respondents were asked to reflect on their activities, relations, values, images of self and motivations in the context of organized leisure to which they participated. Specific questions about the right to be heard (art. 12) were introduced in the conversation. Using such broader concepts reduced the risk of using ethnocentric or adult-centred categories, an asset that has already been confirmed within evaluations of policies regarding child participation in Europe (COE 2011). The methodology rests on a systemic model called the "actor's system" (Stoecklin 2013) which is illustrated in Diagram 7.2:

The model is called the "actor's system" because it is assumed that one's system of action is the constantly evolving outcome of the links between these components of personal experience. Action (*praxis*) is not reduced to activity but encompasses the whole system. The five dimensions are what Blumer (1969) calls « *sensitizing concepts* », open to be defined by the respondents, suggesting only directions to look at and therefore acting as lenses through which the actors may read and give meaning to reality. The way one defines any of the five dimensions will influence the definition of the other elements. With its recursive chain of causality, this model tries to capture and reflect the cumulative nature of experience (Dewey 1910).

This model has been materialized with a concrete tool called the "kaleidoscope of experience", that is a disc made out of paper (format of a CD) with a child-friendly and playful shape (it is reproduced hereunder in its only existing language, which is French) (Diagram 7.3).

Diagram 7.3 The kaleidoscope of experience (Stoecklin 2009)

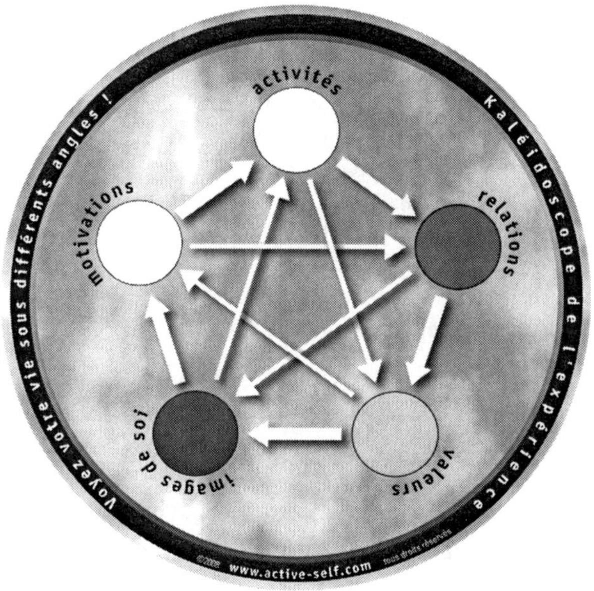

One can turn the colours (red, yellow and blue) and place them alternatively on the five dimensions in order to use the disc in a prospective way (what if?) or in a retrospective way (what explains?). The tool uses common language concepts so that respondents can easily reflect on how they are structuring their own experience. This tool has been used for the interviews. The interviews were semi-structured, with an open phase regarding the five concepts of the "actor's system": young people were asked about their understanding of these five concepts (activities, relations, values, images of self, and motivations) as illustrated in their life in general. In a later phase, they were asked about their appreciation of recreational

Table 7.1 Conversion factors of top-down and bottom-up participation

Conversion factors	Top-down participation	Bottom-up participation
Economical factor	Disposition	Conquest
Political factor	Insertion	Integration
Organisational factor	Selection	Election
Personal factor	Heteronomy	Autonomy

organized activities, particularly those in which they were involved. We then used the kaleidoscope of experience to invite the respondents to reflect about the links among these dimensions of their participation experiences. From these interviews, it was possible to identify "systems of action", namely to understand the typical experience as reported by the actors in their own terms. The observation of these terms and their relationships helps better understand how children "function" and develop their capabilities. This methodology both promoted their active and voluntary participation in the interview process and reduced the bias of the social desirability of responses. A request for parental consent was sent to parents and we made sure that the child was voluntary. We informed the child about his/her right to terminate the interview at any time s/he would wish, the right not to answer certain questions and to have access to research results. Individual interviews were recorded and transcribed verbatim. Data analysis was performed according to the principles of content analysis (Denzin 1990; Pfaffenberg 1988), grounded theory (Glaser and Strauss 1967; Strauss and Corbin 2004) and social constructionism (Berger and Luckmann 1966; Schütz 1987; Moustakas 1994). It was made from a series of encodings done with NVivo.

7.5 Results

The encodings of the interviews led us to progressively cluster the responses and we came out with four sets of factors (economical, political, organisational and personal) that convert or obstruct the child's entitlement to participate in the definition of organized leisure activities. Two ideal types (Weber 1978) – bottom-up participation and top-down participation – have been built along these lines and they are presented in Table 7.1. Bottom-up (rising) participation covers actions initiated by children, whereas top-down participation (downward) refers to actions implemented by adults (Liebel et al. 2010). Of course, the top-down and bottom-up participation processes are only ideal types (Weber 1978), or pure types.

Following Weber's (1978) definition of the ideal type, the "great many diffuse, discrete, more or less present and occasionally absent concrete individual phenomena" that appeared in the interviews with young participants to organized leisure projects have been "arranged according to those one-sidedly emphasized viewpoints into a unified analytical construct". This is how we came to identify aspects like "disposition", "insertion", "selection", and "heteronomy" as qualifying the ideal type of top-down participation, and aspects like "conquest", "integration", "election" and "autonomy" as typical of the bottom-up participation process. We summarize our findings hereunder:

We observe a predominantly downward participation, with activities initiated by adults, and with a purpose to "frame" the occupations of young people who are perceived as potentially at-risk or authors of risky actions if they are not cared.

The range and types of projects appear to be largely guided by adults who tend to reproduce an already existing offer. The interviews highlight the predominance of a logic of providing structures in which young people are supposed to participate. Selection of participants characterizes these projects that adults put to the disposition of young people, at the expense of a logic that would "conquer" support from other people to a project that is primarily conceived by young people. The approach taken is that of an insertion, with the ultimate aim of bringing individuals into existing structures, without discussing their role or function. The project thus has a normalizing function as it would select the participants according to the degree to which they share the values and language of the project.

We find fewer examples of project activities that have been "conquered" by young people. The logic of conquest characterizes projects for which young people had to fight for, progressively obtaining adult attention and recognition. The political context favourable to the emergence of "conquered" projects is also receptive to different claims, points of views, and this is what we qualify with the term "integration". A diversity of voices that can be integrated within the project is the opposite of the logic of insertion which forces people to adhere to a predefined activity with selected participants. In the latter and predominant top-down logic, we have also identified that heteronomy is prevailing.

The heteronomous individual functioning is characterized by the fact that the individual follows what others would tell, in opposition to the autonomous functioning whereby the person is able to set her own priorities and means to achieve them.

The ideal types serve as an "ideal" reference for the understanding of each concrete situation which might be more or less close to it. In other words, real children and real projects can be understood as tendentially closer to some dimensions of the ideal types rather than others. What is especially interesting is to consider that there is a dynamic process which can allow children to move from one ideal type to the other. One can first follow a logic top-down participation before turning to a logic of bottom-up participation. In our interviews, we have been able to identify three elements that are necessary for the child to be able to pass from top-down to bottom-up participation:

1. The expansion of social networking,
2. Cooperation learning,
3. Awakening of critical mind.

These three elements are integrated in subsequent sequences of the participation process. They qualify the feed-back loop (see backward arrows in diagram 7.1) promoting the passage from a heteronomous functioning to a subsequent autonomous functioning. We can thus say that these elements contribute greatly to explain children's agency. The three elements making up such an agentic functioning can be seen as different ways of describing the same phenomenon, namely the birth of autonomy.

7.5.1 *Expansion of Social Networking*

Organized leisure activities promote the expansion of the network of relationships. It is not simply an increase in number, but a real diversification of relations, which is accompanied by a greater recognition. The transition to autonomous functioning is observed when the actor perceives recognition of his or her abilities. This recognition can be found in larger and differentiated audiences, and this entails the cyclical reinforcement of confidence in one's system of action (images of self and motivation in the actor's system diagram).

We have observed that an autonomous functioning within the project is facilitated by diversified relationships, a wider network, contacts with all sorts of people. Many young participants in this situation evoke that the project gave them access to people (like politicians) that they would never have met otherwise. They speak about new possibilities brought by the expansion of their network. Reversely, the latter brings in a more diversified composition of the participants to the project. This contributes to a strengthened sense of autonomy and confirms the fact that self-control is enhanced as the chains of interdependence are longer (Elias 1991): a diversified composition of the group goes along with the inclusion (integration) of more points of views and consequently the elaboration an individual conduct that is actively constructing its own line (autonomy) borrowing from a multiplicity of values and references. It is the logic of recognition, that has more chances to appear when children have access to more diversified groups, that entails motivation to participate in activities that recursively reinforce relationships, values and a positive image of self. On the contrary, a logic of social control, through an undifferentiated social network, maintains children in a downward participation process. It doesn't matter whether the network is objectively small and with undiversified points of view, or if it is just subjectively perceived as such. What is more important is that objective or subjectively perceived recognition of one's competences and points of view is the trigger to bottom-up participation processes.

7.5.2 *Cooperation Learning*

We can consider that any common project requires that participant agree on a number of things and hence a project can be successful only if the participants have learned to cooperate. Therefore, participation in a common project contains some form of obligation to confront others and to negotiate the definition of joint action.

This is possible when the project allows participants to change perspectives and to integrate diversified points of view. Therefore cooperation learning is both a condition and an outcome of participatory projects. It is both a vector of more autonomous functionings, and the result of the child's choice to make use of it and to integrate this element into the actual functioning.

7.5.3 Awakening of the Critical Mind

The collective project to which a child participates can accelerate his or her maturation. This is favoured by the exercise of whole sets of roles across the different worlds of childhood and adulthood. Children have a certain access to the "world of adults" which means that "childhood" and "adulthood" are not to be seen as separated entities, but rather as social constructs qualifying what is supposed to be a world of children and a world of adults. Actually, children and adults come and go between these two abstract worlds. Participatory projects can therefore be seen as transitional spaces (Parazelli 2002). These spaces accelerate the back and forth movements between these two "realities" of the child and adult worlds, and consequently the child's maturation. The transitional space can be seen as a symbolic space, where conflicting norms and values converge. This fosters heightened awareness of contradictions and the necessity of resolutions thanks to higher and more general references. In other words, the critical mind is favoured by the necessity of problem solving.

This process is also linked to the complexification of social interactions, that we have already mentioned when speaking of the longer chains of interdependence (Elias 1991). In other words, more complex and diversified interactions enhances the critical appraisal of one's own behaviours and thoughts: the actor is confronted to more diversified expectations and consequently he or she is looking for a common reference that may regulate the interactions. When interactions diversify, there is a significant increase in individual reflexivity, as the actor is gradually led to understand, adopt, reject of change points of view. Abstract thinking, through the reflexive process of deduction and generalization implies the ability to compare. A normative referent is sought. Our interviews showed that the consciousness of having rights emerges through these more complex interactions. None of the respondents demonstrated an explicit knowledge of the right to be heard (art. 12 CRC), but the more they participated in bottom-up participation processes and the more they referred to the general and diffuse understanding of "rights". The ideal type device (Weber 1978) helped us identify these three aspects of the birth of autonomy.

7.6 Agency Within Structure

These results lead to some critical developments about child participation, and more specifically about the issue of agency within structure. Our observations confirm that the child develops agency as a conquered competence that is both dependent on the child's own skills and on the reactions of others towards his/her performed choices. We therefore consider agency as "*an individual's or a group's capacity to make decisions, act, and interact with other people in a socially competent way*" (Nibell et al. 2009, p. 264). The model "actor's system" (Stoecklin 2013) helps better understand the complex interplay between one's reflexivity and social opportunities to choose and display activities that one has reason to value. Important differences linked to children's evolving capacity and to dynamic contexts are to be addressed if we want to document the range of children's agency. We have to observe children who "*act as agents in various ways at any one time in the course of their development*" and better understand how "*the range of sophistication of their agency changes over time*" (Pufall and Unsworth 2004, p. 9).

The predominantly downward participation we have observed indicates that social relations play a greater role than children's rights in their subjective evaluation of participatory projects. Child participation can be seen as a sequential process whereby the actor's reflexivity plays an important role as a converting factor, and thus enriches the theoretical model used in the capability approach (Bonvin 2008). The results have important implications for the paradigm of the social actor and contribute to the theory of child participation (Thomas 2007).

We see that the three elements making up an agentic functioning (expansion of social networking, cooperation learning, awakening of the critical mind) are actually all linked to the actor's relationships with some group(s). For the child, integration in groups is both a goal and a means to develop one's sense of belonging. This issue is central to understand how and why an actor chooses to participate or not. These two aspects are interdependent: the group has a mediating effect on how the actor perceives the world and, reciprocally, individual reflexivity mediates the actor's engagement with the group. This underlines the impossibility to clearly delineate what is individual and what is social and confirms that the individual/ society dichotomy is a social construct and not a reality (Elias 1991). Following Elias, we want to depart from the concentric vision conceiving society as "surrounding" and the individual as "inside".

In this perspective, the "economical" dimension of organized leisure is not just the question of how many leisure facilities exist in a certain population. Indicators such as the density of such facilities are superficial indicators: they do not account for what is really happening in these facilities in terms of child participation. Our hypothesis is that child participation depends on their subjective assessments of situations and that these cannot be grasped with ladders of participation (Hart 1992; Treseder 1997). Children's agency starts with their own reflexivity about concrete experiences, and the decision not to participate in a given process is also an agency.

Measuring "child participation" therefore requires that processes and not just outcomes are considered.

The results allow us to put the child's evolving capacities (Lansdown 2005) in context and to see that the development of the child's "participatory capability" depends on the dynamic and recursive system made of the interactions between factors conducive to more or less personal and social empowerment. These links between social configurations and individual reflexive control (Elias 1991) allow us to go beyond the problematization of participation in terms of scales or levels toward a multidimensional theory of participation (Percy-Smith and Thomas 2010). This is why we prefer the term "evolving capabilities", as these "should not be viewed within a static (as they usually are) but in a dynamic framework", and as they emphasize the "need to recognise that children are social actors endowed with agency and autonomy (according to their maturity) who are able to express (in different ways) their points of view and priorities" (Biggeri et al. 2010, pp. 81–82).

It is therefore important to distinguish between the child as subject of rights and as a social actor, as it is the capability of the latter who gives meaning and reality to the former. The difference between the child as a subject of rights and the child as a social actor is that the former is an assigned status whereas the second is a conquered competence. The child is both *being* a subject of rights and *becoming* a social actor. Agency, as a conquered competence, is a capability resulting from the interdependence between the actor's skills and the opportunities of the environment. Agency is not acquired by the simple fact that the child is given the status of subject of rights by the UNCRC. One has therefore to observe how the child develops the capacity to influence social dynamics. Our study shows that the child's "participatory capability" is non-linear, context-specific, and bound to individual reflexivity.

The factors that are involved in the transformation of formal freedom into real freedom are interconnected and they form a dynamic system. Therefore, this focus on the interplay between social and individual factors entails new considerations about agency, namely and foremost the systemic nature of agency. The dynamic nature of agency suggests that these social and individual factors cannot be turned into indicators of child participation without first specifying the theory of child participation.

7.7 Theory of Child Participation: Processes not Ladders

Despite the wide range of theoretical sources informing implementation of participation practices there is still a lack of child centred theories (Percy-Smith and Thomas 2010, p. 3). The literature on child participation mostly focuses on several dimensions, namely goals, types, levels, means of participation, as well as participation rights (Sinclair and Franklin 2000; Matthews 2003; Thomas 2007; Percy-Smith and Thomas 2010). The debate mainly focuses on the degree to which children are integrated in the decision-making process and it has generated several models, referred to as "ladders of participation" (Hart 1992; Franklin 1997; Thoburn et al. 1995; Treseder 1997; Shier 2001; Thomas 2002). The benchmarks or standards that are currently being used to measure to which extent children participate in communal activities, such as organized leisure activities, are quantitative outcome indicators whereby limited, moderate and comprehensive day-to-day participation is measured by the proportion of children involved : a small minority (10–30 %) would account for limited participation, a minority (20–50 %) would mean moderate participation, whereas a comprehensive participation requires that the majority of children "volunteers regularly and takes part in social, cultural and environmental activities". On the other side of the spectrum, if less than 10 % children participate in activities within their local communities, this would be qualified as non-participation (Lansdown 2011, p. 19).

But of course, measuring the number of children taking part in these activities is not sufficient, as the quality of participation must also be assessed. On this level, Lansdown makes a matrix regarding the degree of involvement and distinguishes between four levels of participation: children are not involved, consultative participation, collaborative participation and finally child-initiated, led or managed participation (Lansdown 2011, p. 25).

These four levels of participation are put in context according to typical phases of a project which go from situation analysis to strategic planning, programme development and design, implementation and eventually monitoring and evaluation. Lansdown's framework is a valuable alternative to the dominant ladders of participation where the underlying assumption is that the best programmes are the ones that would reach the most comprehensive degree of child participation in all the phases of the project. This maximalist option is not the one recommended by Lansdown who advocates for the optimum rather than for the maximum child participation: "It should not be assumed that all projects must aim for children to be involved throughout, or that child initiated activity is the universal goal" (Lansdown 2011, pp. 24–25). She recognizes that maximal child participation can turn into reverse and negative effects for children: children might be over-burdened when they are not any more participating voluntarily but in a compulsory way just in order to have the programme evaluated by outsiders as a good one.

There are numerous examples where the debate on child participation focuses on the level of involvement, which actually is just another way of putting the qualitative aspect of participation in a kind of quantitative assessment. In doing this kind of "qualitative" evaluation, one runs the risk of describing complex social processes into simple ladders of participation (Hart 1992) embodying a discourse so dominant that it becomes invisible. Situating children at different levels on this ladder is comparable to situating children's evolving capacities within a "ladder" of cognitive development. The social psychologist Valerie Walkerdine argues that "the very lynchpin of developmental psychology, the 'developing child', is an object premised on the location of certain capacities within 'the child' and therefore within the domain of psychology" (Walkerdine 1984, p. 154). This location of the "developing child" as a particular subject position within specific discursive arrangements illustrates Foucault's notion of "regimes of truth" (Oswell 2013, p. 64). As a consequence, we have to identify this regime of truth, its genealogy, as this is the backdrop against which child participation, in discourse and practice, is constructed. In other words, talking about indicators in the field of child participation requires that we deconstruct the regime of truth, supported by numerous people and agencies, that is considered as being the single version of reality identified and acted upon.

In our view, the "levels" of participation are clearly linked to a narrative, or "regime of truth" (Foucault 1991) lying behind participation as a hidden assumption. We think that this has to do with the idea of "growth". The epistomological break requires that we question the dominant evaluative categories with regard to child participation: why has "levels of participation" become a relevant category? We suggest that this attitude of measuring or evaluating something as "big" or "small", "high" or "low", has become the dominant habitus (Bourdieu) because the regime of truth underlying everything we do is a mathematical view of the world (more, less, growth, decline). As "more" and "growth" are positively valued we may call this an "ideology of growth". It pervades fields where numbers can easily be produced, notably the economy, and the market-oriented globalisation is only a proof of this powerful narrative which also stretches to the field of rights and moreover children's rights: the claim for indicators in this field can be seen as a "normalization", because the regime of truth, the ideology of growth, calls for comparable data.

This framing of reality is embedded in a hidden and unquestioned "culture of growth". The idealized image of child development is marked by the ideology of growth whereby the skills and capacities of children should be developed to their maximum extent. The same (hidden) assumptions frame the opposition between children and adults and justify the idea of maturity supposed to reach its climax in adulthood.

Something is clearly missing in the existing models, ladders, measures and theories of child participation, namely the causal factors that explain the very variations of child involvement over time. In the existing literature, the focus is on delineating stages, both in terms of life-cycle analysis as in terms of levels of child involvement at any phase of the project. But there is no attention paid to the dynamics of factors that would explain why and how a given child would have more or less involvement in the collective action at any one stage as compared to another.

The observation of these dynamics would lead us to another conception of "child participation" that would be closer to the child's own rhythm, made of diverse motivations and hesitations. In other words, a child participation theory should be closer to the subjectivity of children, and therefore depart from the dominant tendency of putting the programme itself as the "unit" that has to be observed. The fact that the project itself is cut into several stages (from situation analysis to implementation and evaluation) imposes an underlying frame to analyse child participation from the angle of project-cycle planning.

A more child-centred perspective underlines the relevance of the capability approach that considers subjective choices and achievements people have reason to value. The projective dimension of this approach also helps departing from the centration on "being", that others (Dahmen in this volume, and Reynaert et al. 2009, p. 518) also critically view as a "new norm", and the associated risk to fall into the trap of another ideological perspective in childhood studies. This tendency can be seen as the effect of a rather radical reaction against the adult-child dichotomy, and the related dominance of developmental psychology and functional sociology, whereby the "new sociology of childhood" has underlined that childhood is a social construction and has put particular emphasis on children's competences (James and Prout 1990; see also Oswell 2012). It denounces the paternalistic view on children which considers them only with regard to what they will become as adults. Along this traditional viewpoint, children are seen only as "*becomings*", not yet as "*beings*". On the other side of the spectrum, the liberationists treat children with a presumption of competence. They consider children as independent actual citizens ("*beings*") who make competent and rational decisions, and therefore claim for equal rights to those of adults (Hanson 2012, p. 74).

Our position is to reject the "being/becoming" dichotomy, as this divide is misleading. As we have underlined, children, as adults, are both being and becoming. The interdependence between what is assigned (the child being a subject of rights, or seen as an adult in becoming) and what is conquered (the child heading towards the life he/she wants to live) is simply more acute with children as their agency is more limited by personal skills and by social opportunities. While their "being" is primarily defined by others (parents, neighbours, teachers, etc.) according to different criteria such as the legal status (subjects of rights), the tradition, the culture, their "becoming" is not a deterministic outcome of adults' views and expectations. Therefore the "being/becoming" divide is a poor sociological device that has more to do with ideologies and schools of thoughts than with real children.

Our attempt to come closer to children's experience follows the direction given by Sen in the field of economics, as also a still marginal but promising path in the field of children's rights. The field of children's rights, especially child participation, is still lagging behind the call for a Copernician revolution that the capability approach has made within economical sciences, when Sen has stressed that development cannot be measured in terms of Gross Domestic Product but of the opportunities people have to choose the life they want to live.

Our intention is to identify indicators, and therefore data, that would be detached from current normative claims. Participation to social processes, be it child or adult participation, has roots that are not sufficiently considered in the production of "best practices". They are linked to motivations and identity, which require qualitative understanding that can hardly be translated into the quantitative language of the dominant regime of truth.

We therefore can see that the regime of truth that makes it possible to view the child as a member who "participates" in society is the discourse about rationality whereby self-constraint is an indicator of what Foucault (1977) calls discipline. In this discursive arrangement, discipline is the main indicator of maturity. This regime of truth produces specific behaviors, like a self-fulfilling prophecy, as it advises to behave in ways that can be "recognized" as significant. Therefore, the indicators of child participation take the form of the expectations generated by this discursive arrangement: decision-making, collaboration, consultation... These concepts and corresponding indicators are embedded in a certain regime of truth that sees growth as linked to maturation, or, in other words, development as linked to self-restraint. Taking a foucaldian perspective, we could thus see that disciplining children through participation in projects is more effective than getting their consent and active involvement through punishment. Ironically, what is seen as a "child-led" project may in fact well be the climax of the disciplining practices: there is no need to punish when participants voluntarily incorporate and display disciplining techniques in which they find forms of recognition, like the image of a collaborative decision-maker, that work as avatars of forms of affection that are not (anymore) available.

By including the foucaldian perspective, we can now better situate child participation and children's participation rights in the context of governmentality which in the modern State is associated to reason. Foucault was critical towards enlightment reason, which he considered as dogmatic and despotic. He saw Western rationality's claim to universal validity as "a mirage associated with economic domination and political hegemony" (Foucault 1980, p. 54). Actually, the dominant narrative, or regime of truth, is the discourse on rationality. The States that are parties to the UNCRC and the numerous NGOs and researchers who propose frameworks and tools to measure child participation should be seen as embedded in a wider picture or discourse that considers adults as responsible subjects of rights and children as subjects of rights that are progressively heading towards responsibility. Against this backdrop, mostly invisible, the real children try to make sense of the forms through which expectations and recognition are displayed in diverse contexts, and their effective involvement in participation project is the result of the interaction between the institutionalized discourse and their reflexivity about it. Non-participation in collective projects or alternative participations may thus be seen as indicators of a higher degree of reflexivity. How then can we come to an exhaustive list of child participation indicators?

The dominant indicators found in the literature are still bound to a project-based perspective rather than to a child-centred approach. Does the capability approach offer a different perspective? We think it does, especially because it allows focusing on processes and not only on outcomes. Participation as a means to responsible autonomy is underlined by several scholars. Actually, participation rights are seen as both an end and a means: they have a constitutive dimension because they enrich children's lives (an end in itself), whereas they are instrumental as they are used for in the realisation of other rights (Hanson and Vandaele 2003). Sen also makes the distinction between the "constitutive" and the "instrumental" role of freedom for development (Sen 1999).

Our own observation also shows that participation is instrumental: it expands the child's network, whereby the child can be confronted to other points of views, a process whereby the critical mind and the necessity to deal in cooperative ways are fostered. Participation is therefore instrumental as these factors help the child pass from a top-down to a bottom-up participation. Hence, the child's "own views" and consciousness of rights are pragmatically formed when the child has actively taken part in a collective project. Therefore, the participative capability is caused by individual entitlements (participation rights) and by reflexivity about these entitlements that is generated through concrete experiences of participation.

A big difference lies in the way the dominant approach to child participation considers the constitutive role of participation, compared to the way the capability approach poses the goal of participation. The former sees the enrichment of children's lives in the growing individual and responsible autonomy that participation fosters. The latter leaves it open to individuals to identify the goals (choices and functionings) they have reason to value. Participation is thus seen in terms of the freedom people have to lead the life they have reason to value (Sen 1999). This position requires that we take account of the goals that our respondents are expressing as being theirs. Starting with the children's accounts about the real freedom (or choices) they have in their daily experiences helps uncover how their participative achievements (real freedom) are shaped and construed by the dominant approach to their participation rights (formal freedom).

7.8 Conclusion

We have been tackling the issue of children's participation in organized leisure activities. According to our preliminary findings, the child's right to be heard (art. 12 UNCRC) in organized leisure activities appears in a rather discrete way. Our study shows that participation is experienced as a means rather than as a goal or "value" in itself. It is through participation that the child's "own views" are pragmatically formed.

Thus we can conclude that participation rights become real only through the exercise of participation itself. In other words, it is the praxis of participation which may, progressively, anchor participation rights in the consciousness of children, and not the reverse: children are not born with the UNCRC in mind, they do not participate in social activities and in decision making processes because they know or suddenly discover that the UNCRC gives them the right to do so. It goes rather the other way round: children participate from the moment they are born within configurations that are marked by different combinations of top-down and bottom-up processes, and only progressively become aware of different ways of participating, which eventually are linked, to some extent, to their evolving cognitive capacities of recognizing, naming and claiming their rights (Snodgrass Godoy 1999). We can conclude therefore that the children's participatory capability builds upon their competence to make direct use of the rights they "hold" and that it therefore depends on the abilities of the child actor to use symbolic resources and to take advantage of opportunities.

The child's subjective discourse regarding his/her own experience (Ellis and Flaherty 1992) is therefore a major indicator of the child's participative capability:

how the child identifies and defines the social opportunities to participate or not, tells a lot about his/her appraisal of the rights contained in the UNCRC. The child doesn't need to know how these rights are phrased in the Convention: it is the child's reconstruction of reality that tells whether or not the "spirit" of children's rights is present in his/her mind. This is why the capability approach is very useful to highlight children's rights as they are experienced (living rights; see Hanson et al. in this volume).

By highlighting the recursive nature of action, we stress that it is by observing actual functionings that we can reconstruct the set of potential functionings. We can also see that the methodological difficulty of counterfactual inference can be resolved, at least to some extent, when the respondents are questioned about the links among the dimensions of experience, as this opens up a discussion on what other ways of doing things are or would have been possible. We have been able to do this with the kaleidoscope of experience, as a heuristic tool that stimulates the child's reflexivity. A more inclusive and participatory research methodology (the kaleidoscope of experience, using a child-friendly language) helps understanding children's appraisals of participation processes and their own agency, or capability set, within these systems of action (theoretical model of the capability approach), which is coherent with both the epistemology (agency within structure) and the ethical position (taking children's voices seriously).

Reversely, we can also conclude that children's rights really have an impact only once they are actively used by actors, including children themselves, for the constitution of their opportunities (capability set). In other words, they are not foundational but only an additional resource to capability sets that are mostly formed through praxis. As a consequence, a capability set that would be more rights-based, favouring more equal opportunities, less subject to adult-child power imbalances and to top-down participation habits, is only possible once the children themselves better know their rights. And to bring them this knowledge is an adult obligation.

What has been underlined regarding the dynamic nature of agency is of crucial importance if one wants to identify indicators of child participation. This means that in order to specify indicators to assess the quality of child participation, we first need to specify the conversion factors and their dynamic interplay. What we have to identify are not only outcome indicators but also process indicators. The shortcomings of the ladders of participation are that they focus only on outcomes and not on processes. This reduction of the set of indicators to only outcome indicators ends up in losing the consideration for the interaction among the conversion factors, and actually the global understanding of the social dynamics involved in child participation.

We have deconstructed the regime of truth that underlies discourses and practices around child participation. This helped us situate how concepts and practices that are dominant in the field of child participation are in fact generated by ideas that stem out of relations of power and in turn further impact on them. The genealogy and perpetuation of top-down participation processes stem from the discourse on performance, growth and self-restraint. We may thus identify a recursive system of action (downward participation), a cycle whereby features such as heteronomy, selection, and insertion are favored against autonomy, election and integration, corresponding to the dominant logic of disposition rather than conquest. Conformity and discipline are therefore built through participative devices that obscure the relations of power embedded in the dominant discourse regarding growth and maturity. This cycle is broken only under certain conditions, that would appear as deviant by the regime of truth: when children enjoy transformative factors like expansion of the social network, learning of cooperation and awakening of the critical mind, and especially when these development are made outside organized leisure activities, and so to say outside adult control. Precisely these empowering factors can be found in leisure activities that are negatively labelled such as "roaming around", "messing", "doing nothing", etc.

The child with participation rights is recognized as a social actor as long at s/he heads towards the climax of discipline. The challenge is to accept that children might have other wishes and may contribute to social life in positive ways that cannot be captured through existing indicators.

References

Bai, L. (2005). Children at play: A childhood beyond the Confucian shadow. *Childhood, 12*(1), 9–32.

Berger, P. L., & Luckmann, T. (1966). *The social construction of reality. A treatise in the sociology of knowledge*. New York: Anchor Books.

Biggeri, M., Ballet, J., & Comim, F. (2010). The capability approach and research on children: Capability approach and children's issues. In A. Sabrine, D. Isabell, S. Uwe, & Z. Holger (Eds.), *Children and the good life: New challenges for research on children* (Children's well-being: Indicators and research series, Vol. 4, pp. 75–90). Dordrecht: Springer.

Biggeri, M., Ballet, J., & Comim, F. (2011). *Children and the capability approach*. Basingstoke/New York: Palgrave Macmillan.

Blumer, B. (1969). *Symbolic interactionism: Perspective and method*. Englewood Cliffs: Prentice Hall.

Bonvin, J.-M. (2008). Capacités et démocratie. *Raisons Pratiques, 19*, 237–261.

Bonvin, J. M., & Farvaque, N. (2006). Promoting capability for work: the role of local actors. In S. Deneulin et al. (Eds.), *Transforming unjust structures: The capability approach* (pp. 121–143). Dordrecht: Springer.

Bourdieu, P. (1994). *Raisons pratiques. Sur la théorie de l'action*. Paris: Le Seuil.

Council of Europe. (2011). *Child and youth participation in Finland. A Council of Europe policy review*. http://www.coe.int/t/dg3/children/participation/PolicyReview_en.pdf. Accessed 10 Dec 2013.

COE. (2012). *Council of Europe. Recommendation CM/Rec(2012)2 of the Committee of Ministers to member states on the participation of children and young people under the age of 18* (Adopted by the Committee of Ministers on 28 March 2012 at the 1138th meeting of the Ministers' Deputies). https://wcd.coe.int/ViewDoc.jsp?id=1927229&Site=CM

Denzin, N. (1990). *Interpretive interactionism* (Applied social research methods series, Vol. 16). London: Sage Publications.

Dewey, J. (1910). *How we think*. D.C Heath & Co publishers.

Elias, N. (1991). *La société des individus*. Paris: Fayard.

Ellis, C., & Flaherty, M. (1992). *Investigating subjectivity. Research on lived experience*. London: Sage Publications.

Evaldsson, A.-C., & Corsaro, W. (1998). Play and games in the peer cultures of preschool and preadolescent children: An interpretative approach. *Childhood, 5*(4), 377–402.

Foucault, M. (1977). *Discipline and punish: The birth of the prison*. Harmondsworth: Penguin.

Foucault, M. (1980). The politics of health in the eighteenth century. In C. Gordon (Ed.), *Michel Foucault: Power/knowledge*. Brighton: Harvester Press.

Foucault, M. (1991). Governmentality. In G. Burchell, C. Gordon, & P. Miller (Eds.), *The Foucault effect: Studies in governmentality*. London: Harvester Wheatsheaf.

Franklin, B. (1997). The ladder of participation in matters concerning children. In J. Boyden & J. Ennew (Eds.), *Children in focus: A manual for participatory research with children*. Stockholm: Grafisk Press.

Glaser, B., & Strauss, A. (1967). *The discovery of grounded theory: Strategies for qualitative research*. Chicago: Aldine Publishing Company.

Hanson, K., & Nieuwenhuys, O. (Eds.). (2013). *Reconceptualizing children's rights in international development. Living rights, social justice, translations*. Cambridge: University Press.

Hanson, K., & Vandaele, A. (2003). Working children and international labour law: A critical analysis. *The International Journal of Children's Rights, 11*(1), 73–146.

Hart, R. (1992). *Children's participation from tokenism to citizenship*. Florence: Innocenti Research Center.

James, A., & Prout, A. (1990). *Constructing and reconstructing childhood*. London: Falmer Press.

Kamerman, S. (2010). Preface. In S. B. Kamerman, P. Shelley, & B.-A. Asher (Eds.), *From child welfare to child well-being. An international perspective on knowledge in the service of policy making* (Children's well-being: Indicators and research series, Vol. 1, pp. v–x). Dordrecht: Springer.

Lansdown, G. (2005). *Can you hear me? The right of young children to participate in decisions affecting them* (Early Chilhood Development, Working Papers No 36). The Hague: Bernard Van Leer Foundation.

Lansdown, G. (2011). *A framework for monitoring and evaluating children's participation*. A preparatory draft for piloting. Unpublished draft.

Lareau, A. (2000). Social class and the daily lives of children: A study from the United States. *Childhood, 7*(2), 155–171.

Liebel, M., in collaboration with Robin, P., & Saadi, I. (2010). *Enfants, droits et citoyenneté, Faire émerger la perspective des children sur leur droit*. Paris: L'Harmattan.

Matthews, H. (2003). Children and regeneration: Setting an agenda for community participation and integration. *Children and Society, 17*(4), 264–276.

Moustakas, C. (1994). *Phenomenological research methods*. London: Sage Publications.

Naftali, O. (2010). Caged golden canaries: Childhood, privacy and subjectivity in contemporary urban China. *Childhood, 17*(3), 297–311.

Nibell, L. N., Shook, J. J., & Finn, J. L. (2009). *Childhood, youth, and social work in transformation: Implications for policy*. New York: Columbia University Press.

Oke, M., Khattar, A., Pant, P., & Saraswathi, T. S. (1999). A profile of children's play in urban India. *Childhood, 6*(2), 207–219.

Oswell, D. (2013). *The agency of children. From family to global human rights*. Cambridge: Cambridge University Press.

Parazelli, M. (2002). *La rue attractive. Parcours et pratiques identitaires des jeunes de la rue*. Sainte-Foy: Presses de l'Université du Québec.

Percy-Smith, B., & Thomas, N. (Eds.). (2010). *A handbook of children and young people's participation. Perspectives from theory and practice*. New-York/Oxon: Routledge.

Pfaffenberg, B. (1988). *Microcomputer applications in qualitative research* (Qualitative research methods series 14). Sage Publications: London.

Pufall, P., & Unsworth, R. (2004). *Rethinking childhood*. London: Rutgers University Press.

Reynaert, D., Bouverne-de-Bie, M., & Vandevelde, S. (2009). A review of children's rights literature since the adoption of the United Nations Convention on the Rights of the Child. *Childhood, 16*(4), 518–534.

Robeyns, I. (2003). *The capability approach. An interdisciplinary introduction.* (Paper, revised version 9 December 2003, written for the training course preceding the 3rd international conference on the capability approach, Pavia, Italy, on 6 September 2003).

Roucous, N. (2006). Loisirs de l'enfant et représentation sociale de l'enfant acteur. In R. Sirota (Ed.), *Eléments pour une sociologie de l'enfance* (pp. 235–243). Rennes: Presses Universitaires de Rennes.

Schütz, A. (1987). *Le chercheur et le quotidien. Phénoménologie des sciences sociales.* Paris: Méridiens Klincksieck.

Sen, A. (1999). *Development as freedom.* Oxford: Oxford University Press.

Shier, H. (2001). Pathways to participation: Openings, opportunities and obligations. *Children and Society, 15*(2), 107–117.

Sinclair, R., & Franklin, A. (2000). *Young people's participation* (Quality Protects Research Briefing, No. 3). London: Department of Health.

Sirota, R. (2006). *Eléments pour une sociologie de l'enfance.* Rennes: Presses Universitaires de Rennes.

Snodgrass Godoy, A. (1999). "Our right is the right to be killed". Making rights real on the streets of Guatemala. *Childhood, 6*(4), 423–442.

Stoecklin, D. (2009). L'enfant acteur et l'approche participative. In J. Zermatten & D. Stoecklin (Eds.), *Le droit des enfants de participer. Norme juridique et réalité pratique: contribution à un nouveau contrat social* (pp. 47–71). Sion: IUKB/IDE.

Stoecklin, D. (2013). Theories of action in the field of child participation. In search of explicit frameworks. *Childhood, 20*(4), 443–457.

Strauss, A., & Corbin, J. (2004). *Les fondements de la recherche qualitative. Techniques et procédures de développement de la théorie enracinée.* Fribourg: Academic Press.

Thoburn, J., Lewis, A., & Shemmings, D. (1995). *Paternalism or partnership? Family involvement in the child protection process.* London: HMSO.

Thomas, N. (2002). *Children, family and the state: Decision-making and child participation.* London/Bristol: Macmillan/Policy Press.

Thomas, N. (2007). Towards a theory of children's participation. *International Journal of Children's Rights, 15*, 199–218.

Treseder, P. (1997). *Empowering children and young people.* London: Children's Rights Office/ Save the Children.

UNCRC. (1989). *UN convention on the right of the child.* New York: United Nations.

Walkerdine, V. (1984). Developmental psychology and the child-centred pedagogy: The insertion of Piaget into early education. In J. Henriques, W. Hollway, C. Urwin, C. Venn, & V. Walkerdine (Eds.), *Changing the subject: Psychology, social regulation and subjectivity.* London: Methuen.

Weber, M. (1978). In R. Guenther & W. Claus (Eds.), *Economy and society.* Berkeley: University of California Press.

Zermatten, J., & Stoecklin, D. (Eds.). (2009). *Le droit des enfants de participer. Norme juridique et réalité pratique: contribution à un nouveau contrat social.* Sion: IUKB/IDE.

Chapter 8
The Theoretical Orthodoxy of Children's and Youth Agency and Its Contradictions: Moving from Normative Thresholds to a Situated Assessment of Children's and Youth Lives

Stephan Dahmen

8.1 Children's and Youth Agency Within the New Sociology of Childhood and the Convention on the Rights of the Child (CRC)

While the children's rights approach operates with prescriptive statements, claiming the fulfilment of a threshold of specific rights for children, sociological perspectives on childhood and youth focus on the social construction of the category of childhood and youth. Bourdieu's known quotation "youth is nothing but a word" (Bourdieu 1980, own translation), suggesting that the idea of youth as a unitary social category is above all a social construction, hiding considerable variance within the life worlds according to class lines, is emblematic for this position. Childhood and youth are seen as a social category, framed by particular institutions, especially education, the labour-market and the family, and different social practices, such as getting educated, leaving home, finding a job and forming a family (Fornäs 1995: 3). Historical research on childhood and youth has shown in many ways that the legal age requirements for accessing adult privileges, the separation between adults, youth and childhood is an issue of social conventions and contingent upon specific socio historical developments (Ariès 1962), which cannot be separated from other social institutions like the family, the State or the development of an industrialized economy. The "social institution" of childhood can be seen as the spreading-out of a "separate world for children" (Reynaert et al. 2009). The youth moratorium as a separate space of childhood and youth, serving as a period of preparation for adulthood, is the result of the historical

This work was supported by the Marie-Curie actions of the European Commission, Framework program 7, Initial training network "education as welfare" (EduWel).

S. Dahmen (✉)
École d'études sociale et pédagogiques, University of Applied Sciences Western Switzerland, chemin des abeilles 14, 1010 Lausanne, Switzerland
e-mail: stephan.dahmen@eesp.ch; stephan.dahmen@googlemail.com

D. Stoecklin and J.-M. Bonvin (eds.), *Children's Rights and the Capability Approach*, Children's Well-Being: Indicators and Research 8, DOI 10.1007/978-94-017-9091-8_8,

"detachment" of children and youth from the sphere of production and from the adult world (see also the chapter by Reynaert and Roose in this volume). The children rights movement, the development of child protection legislation but also the compartmentalization of the modern life-course in different age-groups bear witness of this process. The construction of a "youth land", of a separated spatio-temporal moratorium has been criticized, especially from specific strands of the new sociology of childhood (thereafter NSCH) in the UK. The conception of childhood and youth as a moratorium, so it goes, would politically position children in a "pre-citizenship" space, and not pay sufficient attention to their voices, their capacity to be agentic and their status as social actors (Moran-Ellis 2010: 186). The actual discussion in the NSCH strongly reminds earlier controversies in the children's rights movement, in which the discussion revolved around the question whether children should be conceived as particularly vulnerable, not-yet citizens or if the confinement of children in their "moratorium" is an outcome of an potentially oppressive social relation, as children's liberationists movements argued (Purdy 1994). Some proponents of the new sociology of childhood contest the distinction between "adults" and "children", and position the child "as a social and political actor, a person with opinions, a decision-maker" (James and Prout 1998: 41). As they remind us, children should not be seen as "just passive subjects of social structural determinations" (ibid.). Freeman identifies a convergence between the new sociology of childhood and the children rights discourse:

> studied as passive beings structured by the social context of the family or the school, now research should focus on children's agency, on the ways that children construct their own autonomous social worlds. (Freeman 1998: 436)

Accordingly, in a literature review on the children rights discourse, Reynaert et al. (2009) even identify "Autonomy and participation rights as the new norm in children's rights practice and policy" (Reynaert et al. 2009: 518). A similar normativity can be identified with the focus on "being" instead of "becoming" (see Stoecklin and Bonvin, in this volume). The NSCH has largely endorsed a perspective which highlights children's status as political and social actors. However, the desirability of the shift towards autonomy for children is under discussion. Recently, various scholars have pointed out the risks of a rights tradition that emphasizes individuality and autonomy (Freeman 2000; Bühler-Niederberger and König 2011), because in such a conception children's agency "tends to be naturalized rather than analysed" (Prout 2000), and the difficulty with too great an emphasis on concepts like children's agency and voice, is

> that they are not well suited to grasp differences and distinctions between children, especially class differences. (Bühler-Niederberger and Van Krieken 2008: 148)

The strong recourse to conceptions of the "agentic" child/youth must be seen in the context of the immoderate recourse to Beck's and Giddens theories of modernization and individualization (Brannen and Nilsen 2007) in childhood and youth studies. The centring on young persons as "active agents" constructing their own social worlds strongly resonates with ideas of a "reflexive modernity"

(Beck et al. 2003) in which individuals reflexively construct their own "choice biographies" (Beck and Beck-Gernsheim 2002). Such an approach conceptualizes young persons agency as the ability to navigate trough risky environments, often to the detriment of analysing the structural conditions that lead to the emergence of these risky environments. While on the one hand, the focus on children's agency, their status as social actors and as "beings" versus "becomings" seems to have become the new common denominator of the NSCH and the CRC (Freeman 2000), on the other hand, an increasing range of scholars points to the dangers and quandaries of such an approach.

The first part of the chapter describes that the conception of children and youth as autonomous agents does not only derive from a current research conjecture in research on childhood and youth, but that it is intimately linked to the political-discursive construction of children and youth as policy-subjects. The following part argues that this trend – particularly when trapped within a juridical-legal conception of the child – is at risk of dismissing important dimensions of inequalities, which prove to be highly sensitive with regard to the deliberative, reflexive capacities that supplant a the vision of a "agentic" child. The third part discusses the differences between the CRC and the capability approach and argues that the capability approach provides solid grounds for moving from juridical norms and thresholds to a "situative assessment" of children's and youth lives. The last part establishes a link between current issues in youth research and the capability approach and shows, by means of a research project on transitions from school to work, how such an approach can be operationalized. Research results indeed suggest the crucial role of processes of preference formation and the way in which cultural patterns and symbolic-semantic resources frame the range of available options. The chapter concludes with a brief outline of lessons to be learned from the capability approach.

8.2 Contradictions of the Discourse on Children's and Youth's Agency

The risks and dilemmas of stressing youth and children's agency become apparent if we consider the development of economic and social contexts and their impact on the youth phase. The emergence of "youth" as a phase of the modern life-course goes back to the institutionalized tripartioning of the life-course into childhood and youth (preparation for work) adulthood (work) and old age (retirement) (Kohli 1994). The crisis of industrial times comes with a crisis of the youth phase itself, which becomes increasingly de-institutionalized, de-standardized and it's boundaries become increasingly blurred (Schroer 2007). While on the one hand, this increasingly releases young people from the youth moratorium, it also increases social risks and social pressures and comes with new inequalities. The agenda of youth research was since it's beginnings, strongly influenced by politico-administrative concerns (Cicchelli and Pugeault-Cicchelli 2006) and the political agenda-setting within different policy fields. Youth research has, in the wake of the deterioration of industrial times, moved from a focus on young people's lifestyles, subcultures and forms of resistance towards a more economic perspective focusing on their transitions from school to work (Geldens et al. 2011). All the same, childhood is increasingly addressed as a period of social investment in children's development for the sake of later outcomes in human capital. The more recent focus on young people's agency within the scholarship of youth and childhood can be interpreted as an adjustment of youth research to the fact that transitions are increasingly requiring self-oriented planning-like activities (Giddens 1990), but this happens at the risk of brushing aside important dimensions of inequality. Celebrating the "agentic" side of transitions may "very well create wrong messages to policy makers about action potential of young women and men, as producers of their biography who can be made responsible for not putting their agentic capacity to work" (Heinz 2009: 397). Young people may be firmly inscribed in the discourse of having the opportunity to be the "author" of their personal lifestyle and life-course. However they are also regarded as responsible for the failures and successes that result from the choices they make (Furlong and Cartmel 1997; du Bois-Reymond 1995). This becomes increasingly important when considering that the "construction" of childhood and youth happens mainly through the construction of target groups within social and educational policies, the definition of social problems and the different modes of knowledge production about young people. When for instance, the European Union is rescaling its youth policies towards the notion of "NEETs[1]" (Eurofound 2012; European Commission 2012), highlighting the "costs" of economic inactive young persons for society, these categories of public action creep into the policy vocabulary and in the ways we think about young persons. The "NEET" concept, insofar it "places an undue and often misleading emphasis on voluntarism" (Furlong 2006: 553) also stresses the agency of children and youth. As such, youth and childhood studies play a central role in this process of rendering the addressees of public policies "thinkable by being made visualisable, inscribable, and assessable" (Rose 1998: 112). These classifications, as technically neutral they may seem, are socially constructed categories reflecting specific societal interests.

This is exemplified in proclamations of a "new era of youth policies" by the European commission, which under the heading "investing and empowering" places emphasis on the "youth as a (..) dwindling (..) and precious resource" and highlights the "need to nurture young human capital" (European commission 2009). These discourses typically construct children and youth in instrumentalist terms as profitable investments who represent "citizen-workers of the future" (Lister 2006: 697). On the one side, children and youth are mainly seen as "becomings", whose lives require intervention in the case they are at risk of producing costs to the welfare State at a later point of their life-course. An investment in children and

[1] Neets is an abbreviation for not in employment, education or training, a policy category which plays a central role within the European strategies against youth unemployment.

youth is meant to pay off in terms of crime rate reduction, later income or prevention of later unemployment. On the other side teenagers, young adults as well as parents and caretakers are increasingly addressed within a new "rights and responsibilities" discourse. The reassessed distribution between rights and responsibilities between the State and the citizen within European welfare capitalism, highlighting individual responsibility, applies particularly to teenagers, young persons and adolescents in transition from school to work. The discourse of individual responsibility, shifting the obligation for realizing one's transition from the State to the individual operates with a strong idea of personal autonomy. As a "citizen" and future worker, the individual (youth) is conceived as an autonomous participant and producer of his own human capital, expected to guide and optimize his own learning and integration trajectory. The elusive reference to personal autonomy has also been analysed as a switch of intervention rationalities within institutional discourses of child and youth welfare. These would increasingly follow a logic of governmentality (Kessl 2006), aiming at inducing a "desirable self regulation" (Dean 2007) and targeting the creation of (economically) independent and autonomous citizens, rather than securing adequate living conditions for young persons. These new logics of State-intervention, imputing Agency to the individual consist "of establishing a '*de jure*' autonomy (though not necessarily a *de facto* one)" (Bauman 2001: 3).

The academic discourse of "children (and youth) as social actors" – insofar it pays no particular attention to social inequalities and the life-worlds of children and youth – is at risk of purporting an overly optimistic and inappropriate image of the child-youth citizen. Such and Walker (2005) have convincingly shown that the complex and contradictory ways in which children's participation is represented in the 'rights and responsibilities' discourse translates – within the field of family policy – into a stronger delegation of responsibilities to the family and the private sphere. One can expect that this increases inequalities, as parents are bound to rely on their often scarce resources rather than being provided with adequate support. The current switch to the active welfare state increases rather than prevents circles of deprivation (see Grundmann 2011). For the case of anti-social behaviour policies, young persons are increasingly called into responsibility themselves (Such and Walker 2005: 44). The policy discourse on children's agency thus comes with an ambivalent turn, in which "children appear only to be granted agency and autonomy in the context of wrong-doing: children are able to be wilfully irresponsible but not wilfully responsible" (Such and Walker 2005: 46).

8.3 Unequal Childhoods, Unequal Youth?

The conception of children and youth as competent, agentic and self-reliant is omnipresent in the children' s rights discourse, in the new sociology of childhood and youth studies, and last but not least, in the political-discursive framing of youth issues. The question whether and to what extent young person's can be seen as reflexive agents and to what extent social structures and social dispositions influence individual's agency is ultimately an empirical question. In sociological literature, this is problematized as the relation between the socially constructed, pre-reflexive nature of identities, and the possibility of reflexive agency. In order to be able to talk about reflexivity, agents have to be able to exercise reflexivity, thus to "consider themselves in relation to their (social) contexts and vice versa" (Archer 2007: 4). The main problem with the straightforward assertion of agency is that these theories often ignore the class, race, gender and age bases of such a reflexivity. And in fact, an impressive amount of studies have proven the influence of social contexts. Research on young persons' conceptions of their "future selves" has shown that these strongly differ according to class background (Oysermann and Markus 1990). Zarca (1999) has shown that the "sense of one's place" (Bourdieu 1997) develops between the ages 7 and 12. As children develop their social identity, they also develop a "social sense" according to which they evaluate their relative position in the social space and their social position within class categories. Similar findings have been described by Lareau (2011) who analyses how lower and middle-class families differ in their child-rearing styles and how these differences lead to a "sense of entitlement" for the upper- and middle class, and a "sense of constraint" for the lower-class children. In addition, recent research shows that children's aspirations prove to be class-sensitive (Bühler-Niederberger and König 2011). The experience of the youth moratorium itself strongly differs according to class background (Zinnecker 1988). These strands of research show that children and youth actually *are* social actors, insofar they act within a socially predefined frame at a very young age, and that there exist differences within the experience of being a child or a young person, with considerable impact on their agency. Alanen's call to analyse "agency in the interconnection of class and generational categories" (Alanen 2010: 170) thus points to a central and important claim, especially if we want to analyse inequalities in terms of capabilities.

Nevertheless, within the Convention on the Rights of the Child (hereafter CRC), such differences are at risk of disappearing beneath a "universalist" conception of the child. The CRC is providing an overarching prescriptive standard for the assessment of children's rights but is hardly able to take into account these differences. While the CRC refers to a "universal, free-standing, individual child; a child who is on a particular developmental trajectory" (Mayall 2000: 245), the new sociology of childhood has convincingly shown that

> childhood cannot be understood outside the context of other variables, such as class, gender, ethnicity and culture. If childhood is a social construction, then there are 'childhoods', rather than a single, universal, cross-cultural phenomenon. (Freeman 2000: 438)

But the new sociology of childhood, with its stress on children's individuality and autonomy is at risk of "naturalizing rather than analysing" (Prout 2000) children's and youth agency. For youth research, the focus on young persons' agency, often within an individualized discourse of "choice biographies", can be seen as a "current pervasive theoretical orthodoxy" (Brannen and Nilsen 2007), which rests on weak empirical grounds.

I will now argue that the capability approach provides important clues when it comes to appropriately assess children's lives, and allows to overcome some of the shortcomings of the CRC (that is, a strong focus on the universalist conception of the child) and of the new sociology of childhood operating with inadequate agency assumptions of children and youth. Focusing on children's capabilities – that is what they actually are able to do and to be – requires to look at the social embeddedness of children's and youth's lives and to take into account their perspectives. A perspective focusing on rights is confined to obligations between individual (young) citizens and the state in the legal sphere. Such a perspective is necessarily based on a abstract conception of the child, separate from individual ends or personal attributes. Trough opening the perspective to inter-individual differences, agent-relative values and the non-material social constraints on choice, the capability approach may provides a conceptual bridge between "prescriptive" approaches, coming with normative and legally enforceable thresholds (such as the CRC), and more analytical approaches, which focus on the adequate evaluation of social states and inequalities.

8.4 Sen's Capability Approach and the Issue of Children's Participation

The capability approach provides theoretical grounds on which children's voices have to be taken seriously. More particularly, Amartya Sen defends a particular position regarding the procedure and content when it comes to the definition of "normative thresholds" such as a list of "rights", but as well for the choice of informational bases in other evaluative exercises.

Drawing on Sen's writing about human rights, one is able to show how the CA can help to overcome important critiques that have been issued towards the convention of children rights. For Sen, human rights are founded on individual capabilities that meet threshold conditions. But unlike Nussbaum, who proposes a list of basic capabilities (Nussbaum 2003), Sen explicitly rejects the idea of a predefined list, favouring the role of public deliberation on the basic capabilities or rights to be included in such a list. With this position, Sen parallels important critiques pointed towards the CRC. For instance, Freeman objects that

> there is no evidence that children or children's groups as such participated or were consulted on drafting, or had any real influence in preliminary discussions. (Freeman 2000: 439)

Correspondingly, the set of rights encoded in the CRC are drawn from the "perspective of the adult world looking almost as an external observer on the world(s) of children" while

> the Convention, had it used insights derived from the social world of children, might have made significant additions and amendments. (Freeman 2000: 439)

Sen, despite being in favour of human rights, is sceptical about the possibilities to establish a one and for all valid threshold (citing as an example the declaration on human rights). As Sen describes, one

> cannot 'freeze' a list of capabilities for all societies for all time to come, irrespective of what the citizens come to understand and value. (Sen 2005: 158)

He argues that drawing a list should not be "divorced from the particular social reality that any particular society faces" (ibid.). With his conception of capabilities, Sen argues for a normative foundation based on ethical demands identified by public reasoning rather than on universal claims based on a pre-specified list, or on ontological claims about the human condition (Sen 2004). He argues that

> (t)he implementation of human rights can go well beyond legislation, and a theory of human rights cannot be sensibly confined within the juridical model in which it is frequently incarcerated. (2004: 319)

For Sen the focus should then be on the spaces of public deliberation in which these "ethical demands" are made, discussed and deliberated. This is also one of the reasons why research on and with children inspired by the capability approach is often focusing on participatory approaches in which children "conceptualize their capabilities" (Biggeri et al. 2006), analyze the conceptions of the "good life" of children (Andresen et al. 2011) or take up the issue of how dimensions of valuable capabilities should be established (Alkire 2007). Sociology of childhood and youth is thus relevant for the CA for the critical examination of the structures, operations and contestations of power in policy and practice and of how different contexts make up the lives and the capabilities of children and youth. Moreover, it allows to extend the knowledge on their "ethical demands", their experiences of injustice and the way they read the world in which they live. For research guided by the capability approach this means that instead of drawing on abstract principles when assessing a situation, one has to "examine the agents' opinion of the justice of their situation and the world they live in" (Dubet and Caillet 2009: 21, own translation). As Boltanski and Thevenot write, this implies that one might have to take "the sense of justice (of actors) seriously" and to "construct a model in which the normative views of persons could be fully considered" (Boltanski and Thevenot 2000: 207).

Sen's argument rests on a specific extension of liberal theories of justice, which allows for children's perspectives to be taken into account. Sen's model differs from liberal theorists who usually exclude children from the sphere of citizenship by distinguishing "between those who have the rational capacity to consent to political authority (adults) and those who do not (children)" (Purdy 1994: 2). This can for instance be seen in Rawls' liberal theory of justice, in which free and equal persons decide on the basic structure of the society behind a "veil of ignorance", which prevents the parties to the contract to know their position in society. The agreement on the "just" procedures of society is made by adults as free citizens, who base their choices on rational enlightened self-interest. This position presumes a conception of an abstract, adult and autonomous moral subject. Sen describes the elaboration of collective choices through "just" procedures in Rawls' conception as a

> drastic simplification of a huge and multi-faceted task – that of combining the operation of the principles of justice with the actual behaviour of people – which is central to practical reasoning about social justice. (Sen 2009: 69)

According to Sen,

> the relationship between social institutions and actual – as opposed to ideal – individual behaviour cannot but be critically important for any theory of justice. (2009: 69)

The problem with Rawls' theory is that it is based on a model of "the person or moral subject (...) as an abstract agent of choice, completely separate from her ends, personal attributes, community or history" (Sandel 1998). Sen, on the contrary, argues that the assessment of justice has to include perspectives from already situated, socially embedded human beings with certain experiences, feelings, social positions, which should not be cancelled out by a "procedural transcendentalism" (Sen 2010). Thus, in the view of Sen, the "justice claims" to be taken into account for agreeing on a principle are (using Thomas Nagel's famous expression) not formulated from the "view from nowhere" (Nagel 1989) but from a "situated somewhere". According to Sen (1993), this "positionality" which would be seen as a bias in a Rawlsian perspective, aiming at reaching an impartial consensus, is highly significant, and should not be left aside. A Rights discourse, with a conception of juridical, legal subject is "conceptually ill equipped" (Arneil 2002: 70) to describe the formulation of these ethical claims. Such a juridical conception of a subject is standing in stark contrast to the real, empirical "situated subjects" (Taylor 1985) in the capability approach. The former conceives persons as empty vessels, without an identity who one hardly imagines articulating their situated, positional views on justice. In contrast to such a position, Sen's approach does not aim at providing an "impartial consensus", but defines justice as something procedural, in which empirically embedded and situated persons enter into a deliberative process. Sen argues that "observations are unavoidably position-based" (Sen 2002: 467). But Sen provides another argument against the Rawlsian conception of the "veil of ignorance". Rawls' conception is seen as being exposed to the risk of "exclusionary neglect". Sen means here that the Rawlsian restriction of the contractarian group to people from the same political community excludes people from other countries or parts of the world. The same applies to children which in classical liberal theory are not seen as apt to participate in the sphere of citizenship. For Sen, this is a problem of global justice, as actions within one country may severely impact on stakeholders outside of the contractarian group. Sen therefore advocates to

> take note of voices beyond the membership of the contractarian group, either to take note of their interests, or to avoid our being trapped in local parochialism. (Sen 2009: 70)

This argument to include "voices" beyond the membership of the contractarian group can equally be applied to children. Sen's capability approach thus provides three central arguments for the inclusion of children's voices and perspectives within the sphere of citizenship.

Firstly, the need for the incorporation of "situated knowledge" (Haraway 1988), or in Sen's words, knowledge which comes from a "situated somewhere" rather than a "view from nowhere" as a requirement for an appropriately defined informational basis of judgment in justice. Secondly, independently of whether children are presented as "citizens in waiting" (Arneil 2002) or as full citizens, Sen's vision does not allow to simply exclude them from the "polity" in which ethical claims are to be made: as their voices have an "enlightenment relevance" (Sen 2009: 108), they are of value for public discussion independently from the fact that children are part (or not) of the "contractarian group" in liberal political philosophy. Thirdly, the political construction of the informational basis about children and youth's needs can be critically assessed within the capability approach, thus providing a practical application to contemporary issues of childhood and youth studies.

8.5 Entitlements, Social Realizations and Real Freedoms

It is clear that the universalist stance of the CRC may have particular benefits, as it provides legal yardsticks and incentives to implement children's rights. But the confinement to juridical norms leaves a high number of inequalities untackled. Here, the capability approach may provide important tools to overcome some of the restrictions of the de-contextualized and universalist conception of the child. As Hynes writes in relation to the capability approach for human rights scholarship, Sen has a

> major role to play in encouraging human rights scholarship which is too closely aligned to human rights practice to contextualize and analyse human rights struggles in the full context of social inequalities. (Hynes et al. 2010: 824)

In a nutshell, the CA states that when assessing the quality of a social arrangement, the well-being of a person or the state of development of a country, one should focus on what people are able to do and be, on the quality of their life, and judge it according to the freedom to "live the kind of life that, upon reflection, they have reason to value" (Sen 1999). The important distinction lies in making a difference between the access to certain goods, resources or entitlements (such as rights), functionings (which designate actual beings and doings of a person) and capabilities (which is the real freedom of a person to choose for or against the realization of a certain set of functionings). This distinction is crucial as it introduces the actors' valuations and preferences, which within a pure focus on resources, functionings or rights are not taken into account. Sen makes a point in favour of this distinction by referring to the difference between "agency freedom" and "wellbeing freedom". He invokes the example of two persons, one suffering from starvation because she lacks access to food, and the other fasting because of her religious beliefs. While an assessment in terms of functionings would not grasp this important distinction (both persons lack the functioning of being well nourished), a capability perspective would have to differentiate between these two states along the agency aspect. As Sen puts it, in order to take into account this "agency aspect", one has to "recognize(ing) and respect(ing) his or her (the agent's) ability to form goals, commitments, values, etc." (Sen 1987: 41). The person is taken as an agent "whose achievements can be judged in terms of her own values and objectives" (Sen 1999: 19). The distinction between functionings (doing something) and capabilities (being free to do a certain thing) is crucial here (see the general framework of the capability approach in the chapter by Stoecklin and Bonvin in this volume). Sen pays particular attention to human diversity in terms of "conversion factors". Conversion factors are defined as the degree to which a person can transform a resource into a functioning. For Sen the sole focus on rights is prone to bias, as "equality in holdings of primary goods or resources can go hand in hand with serious inequalities in actual freedoms enjoyed by different persons" (Sen 1999: 115). This can be exemplified by focusing on the "right for play and leisure". While many children may "officially" be granted this right, in reality the lack of appropriate playgrounds, the presence of a highly travelled dangerous road, or the burden of care responsibilities may effectively inhibit the functioning of playing. The CA thus provides conceptual grounds from which we may take into account, "not simply (...) the distribution of resources or formal rights, but (...) the social conditions that are necessary for their effective exercise" (Bonvin et al. 2005: 24).

The concern for the situated diversity of persons and their effective scope of action and "agency" allows switching from a prescriptive threshold of rights to the analysis of social realizations, i.e. what persons are actually able to do and to be. It thus may help to overcome the criticisms of the NSCH towards the CRC on the "de-contextualized" and universal conception of childhood and youth within prescriptive approaches. It is important to highlight that the capability approach, albeit mostly operationalized for research on indicators for human development and within existing quantitative data sets, provides important venues for qualitative participatory research as it can often be found in childhood and youth studies. For the "just distribution of life-chances is not only bound to the means provided by institutions for a *hypothetical* realization of different life-perspectives, rather this comes to the fore only through taking into account biographies and life-conduct of concrete, *empirical* individuals" (Ziegler 2011 own translation). Ziegler specifies "self-interpretations, motives, aspirations, but also emotional, practical, and cognitive competences as relevant aspects" (Ibid.) – aspects for which a comprehensive, interpretative approach is needed (Zimmerman 2006: 447). While the CRC would set thresholds based on a "universalist" conception of the child (Mayall 2000; Freeman 1998), the capability approach would advocate to take a "situated evaluation", looking at what children are effectively able to do or to be, including material opportunities and the possibilities to choose, conversion factors, as well as their own valuations. It acknowledges the capacity of the child to "examine one's values and objectives and choose in the light of those values and objectives" (Sen 2002: 36).[2]

Last but not least, the capability approach pays particular attention to what is commonly referred to as "adaptive preferences". As Sen has shown, people adapt their preferences and expectations to their life-situation, and their well-being is conditioned by previous experiences. People may therefore, even in very marginal life situations, express a considerable degree of satisfaction but mostly on the basis of "preferences that have adjusted to their second-class status" (Nussbaum 2003: 33). Therefore, a simple assessment of subjective well-being as preference fulfilment, as purported by some approaches in the assessment of children's and youth wellbeing, is problematic (Ziegler 2010). The capability approach proposes that an assessment in terms of capabilities requires "a critical scrutiny of preference and desire that would reveal the many ways in which habit, fear, low expectations, and unjust background conditions deform people's choices and even their wishes for their own lives" (Nussbaum 2000: 114). If we want to account for children's status as "social actors" and go beyond the ambiguous celebration of their "agency" (in the NSCH) and the presumption of a "universalist childhood" (in the CRC), the analysis of processes of preference formation and the way in which cultural patterns and symbolic-semantic resources frame the range of available options is of crucial importance. The capability approach accounts for the formation of preferences and the impact of social and moral norms, which are "not taken for granted or assumed away, but analysed up-front" (Robeyns 2003: 203).

One can summarize the claims of the capability approach as a call for a broad informational basis for the assessment of social inequalities, going beyond the politically established constructions of children and youth as target groups of public action, while taking into account the actors' situated perspectives on their lives. This would necessarily imply going beyond rights and as Robeyns (2003) suggests, taking into account issues of recognition. As Anderson and Honneth state, "it is clear that the medium of rights is inadequate to address the full vulnerability of humans" (Anderson and Honneth 2005: 136). This necessarily includes a perspective on youth as "social actors":

> equipping people with a certain array of goods and resources *alone* will not suffice to enhance their capabilities and life chances, (...) this can be avoided by concentrating additionally on the actual processing of their agentic orientations, on the multifarious ways people – especially those with a different sociocultural background – reflect upon, make

---

[2] Sen, as well as Nussbaum are ambiguous about the possibility to the use of capabilities as an evaluative framework for Children: "since children are not mature enough to make decisions for themselves" (Saito 2003: 25), Sen proposes to focus instead on functionings, and to" (...) *not only* consider "the child's freedom now, but *also* the freedom in the future" (ibid., emphasis added). Similarly, Nussbaum argues that "Education is one area in which the usual deference to choice is relaxed: governments will be well advised to require functioning of children, not simply capability" (2011: 156). I argue that despite this partial (and appropriate) restrictions, Sen's claims on "positionality", "exclusionary neglect" and the importance of taking into account "real lives" in the evaluation of justice are equally applicable to children (see for a more thorough discussion on the "choice" issue and the application of capabilities as a evaluative framework for children: Clark and Eisenhuth 2011; Ballet et al. 2011).

sense of, and utilize the human and nonhuman resources and sociocultural schemas available to them. (Grundmann and Dravenau 2010: 94)

8.6 Operationalizing the Capability Approach for Analyzing Transitions from School to Work

The aim of this research project was to analyse how young persons from different social backgrounds experience their transition from school to work and how they react towards the institutional and societal demands. We conducted 20 interviews with youngsters aged 15–22 who, after their obligatory schooling did not find an apprenticeship and therefore had to draw back on a scheme of the unemployment insurance. Cases were selected on the basis of "theoretical sampling" (Glaser and Strauss 1967), in order to cover a maximum variation of situations and facilitate the development of theoretical concepts trough systematic comparison. In addition, case selection was done on the basis of an adequate representation in terms of parental background, educational level, migration status and gender. Interviews were conducted in a non-directive way, starting with one narrative stimulus at the beginning and more specific questions at later stages of the interview. All interviews have been fully transcribed. In a first step, the interviews were analysed in a purely factual way, tracing the sequences and positions, as well as important life-events of each case. In a second step, the narrative structure (and the reflexive assessment of these factual events) was analysed. The different cases were compared in order to systematically find differences/convergences and develop a typology. Our choice for a "biographical approach" resulted from the informational needs of the capability approach. In fact, the definition of capabilities required to take into account how persons perceived, assessed their situations and how they evaluated the different options between which persons could choose. For Sen, "the rejection of alternatives that were available but not chosen is part of what happened" (Sen 2002: 593), and the "circumstances of choice" as well "problem of the 'identity' of a person, that is, how the person sees himself or herself" (Sen 2002: 215) is of crucial importance.

Biographical interviews are the appropriate methodological tool to gather such data: Howard Becker describes that "in order to understand the behaviour of a person, one has to know how it perceived the situation, the barriers the individual expected to encounter, and the alternatives that were opening" (Becker 1970: 106). Farvaque proposes to utilize the capability approach "in a biographical perspective in order to analyse choices in the past and the underlying reasons. This means to analyse an individual trajectory from the perspective of choices taken (or not taken) and the possible alternatives that were accessible at this point" (Farvaque 2008: 72, own translation). The transition from school to work is thus not only to be analysed within a quantitative framework, looking at the sequences and positions of young persons' trajectories, but also has to take into account "how young persons, with their different experiences, resources and endowments relate to the unequally distributed options and action possibilities" (Heinz 1995: 2 own translation). Remember that "biography" does not refer to the "real" life-course, in terms of factual transitions, dates and life-course markers, but to subjective representations through which individuals continually construct, for themselves as for others, the mental and verbal form and meaning of their existence. This aspect is crucial as it allows to conceive young persons as social actors, with certain reflexive capabilities, negotiating their identities in different value-laden cultural worlds, without operating with excessive agency assumptions. On the one side, "courses of action are produced through the reflexive deliberations of agents who subjectively determine their practical projects in relation to their objective circumstances" (Archer 2010: 135). An analysis of reflexive deliberations of agents is thus required to account for the agency aspect of the capability approach: as people are thought to act on the basis of own "value commitments", it is important to be able to account for these valuations. In difference to rational choice approaches which presuppose stable preferences our approach aims at analysing how culture and structure enter into preference formation, and how agents, through undergoing certain experiences, reflect on their past preferences, and scrutinize their decisions and plans. For Sen, actors are not "rational fools" (Sen 1977) which are "pre programmed by a fixed preference schedule", but are able to "to reflect morally on his preference set" (Archer 2000: 77). On the other side, and, as for instance the extensive research conducted by Stephen Ball and his colleagues show, "perceptions and choices of prospective HE (higher education – the author) students are constructed within a complex interplay of social factors that are underpinned by basic social class and ethnic differences" (Ball et al. 2002: 53). That is to say, the pre-reflexive dimensions of Identity, cultural, social and material constraints as well as social perceptions and distinctions are all at work in these processes. These broad social influences are explicitly mentioned by the CA. As Sen writes, the "concern with peoples ability to live the kind of life they have reason to value brings in social influences both in terms of what they value (...) and what influences operate on their values" (Sen 2010: 244–245). Furthermore, due to the predominance of a quantitative operationalization of the CA, it is often overseen that Sen's idea of "reflexive" human beings requires identity as a "native capability" (Davis 2004). Processes of identity formation thus play a crucial role in the analysis of transitions from school to work. The Question – as formulated by Ian Hacking is then "how is the space of possible and actual action determined not just by physical and social barriers and opportunities, but also by the ways in which we conceptualize and realize who we are and what we may be, in this here and now?" (Hacking 2004: 287). It is in fact, not only about the material constraints of choosing between different capability sets, but about the constitution of "subjectivity" defining what we want (thus our preferences) in the first place. Social influences are active as (pre-reflexive) practically intelligible options for what is available in a given social environment. This accounts for the fact that young persons are neither simple utility maximizers, nor "cultural dopes" (Garfinkel 1967), thus over-socialized actors, but biographical actors "who attempt to link their experiences to transitional decisions and interpret their options not only in respect to subjective utilities and norms, but in terms of the legacy of their personal past" and "who construct their life-courses by deciding between options and by negotiating and self-monitoring reasonable causes" (Heinz 2009: 478). This is particularly important for a Life-course approach within the transition from school to work. Here, own characteristics and tastes have to be connected with a specific labour-market situation and with a specific, socially structured opportunity space.

8.7 From the Universal Youth Moratorium to Socially Embedded Actors

The idea of a homogeneous youth moratorium is defeated by a highly differentiated experience of the transition phase, which is structured along differences within conversion factors. The experience of the "youth moratorium" differs according to the economic resources of the parents, the integration into a network of social relationships, and different factors of "employability" (school grades,. . .). All of these can be seen as "conversion factors", as they impact on the ways in which young persons experience the youth moratorium. For instance, having supportive parents with sufficient economic resources allows to escape the need to fall back on public support, which is characterized by a strong rights and responsibilities regime. The analysis has shown that there are considerable differences within the ways of doing and acting in, in relation to the institutionalized demand to conceive one's integration trajectory as an individualist self-project. The analysis describes the effects of institutional practices and the influence of different endowments and conversion factors on the experience of the youth-moratorium.

The cases investigated during our study could be attributed to one of the three categories described below, which differ according to their experience of the youth phase, their biographical actions in relation to their transition and to some extent, their ways of engaging and disengaging with their future.

The first category comprises those youngsters experiencing the youth phase as an extended phase, which mainly served as an exploratory period with no pressure in relation to "adult" responsibilities. The simple disposal of more time (and the fact of not being exposed to temporal pressures) leads to the availability of more options. Their biographical actions were characterized by experimentation and self-exploration, and they were able to postpone the decision for a certain apprenticeship or educational pathway to a later point in time, either through choosing something which leaves them with more later options, or by relying on the possibility to "take a gap year" or going to a private school paid by their parents. The postponement of decisions, and the ability to maintain spaces of indecision, was strongly related to the access to other resources. These young persons described their job choices in terms of largely intentional choices, in which they linked, in a self-evident way, their own capacities to a specific job or educational pathway.

On the other hand, young people with lesser resources experienced the youth moratorium as a limited phase of education and disciplined preparation to becoming adults, guided by attempts to maintain and secure a social position. Here transitions were seen as risky, but in most cases manageable. Nevertheless, their narratives were much more often characterized by a "working-out" (Bühler-Niederberger and König 2011) between own preferences and aspirations and the structure of opportunities, in which choices are negotiated. The injunction to conceive oneself as an individual self project and to describe their biographical pathways as outcomes of an autonomous biographical planning process is not as straightforward as for those of the previous category. Most expressed a precarious balance between an identification with their choices and the realizeability of these choices within a restricted labour market. The biographical choices resulted often into a scaling down of aspirations in order to maintain control over one's future trajectory. This led, in some cases, to a self-exclusion of more ambitious job choices, or to choosing "something" in order to avoid risks and overcome the transition period as fast as possible.

The last category grouped young persons experiencing the youth moratorium as characterized by strenuous efforts aiming towards the access to a minimally secure social position. The relation to biographical time was geared towards the immediate experience without direct orientation towards the future. In this case, the narratives seemed to bear witness of a "line of sight navigation" rather than an individualized self-project. These narratives often showed a switch from "intentional" to "practical" choices, motivated by the fear of social exclusion rather than by reasons linked to the activity itself. These young persons showed different forms of non-conformity and disengagement within their biographical strategies. One example was that they often refused a self-conception based on work. While they endorsed the same societal values as the majority of society, particularly the high value of autonomy through work, they saw themselves as not being entitled to these features. Their own possibilities, restricted to occupational futures with low social status stand in contrast with the standards they have incorporated from the wider society. These standards, according to which outcomes of the transition phase are perceived as a result of personal individual biographical projects attribute responsibility for failure to the individual. Accordingly their biographical actions towards their transition are often characterized by strategies aiming to avoid "moments of truth" in which they are confronted with institutional agents who re-affirm their marginal position on the labor market. These young persons, just like those of the first category, adhere to the meritocratic judgment but this leads in their case to an individual attribution of failure. Some of them develop a "counterculture of dignity" (Sennett and Cobb 1972), in which they internalize the stigma of a "bad student", allowing them to find alternative sources of value and self-respect within a school counterculture and in peer-activities. While this allows them to maintain a positive self-image, it also leads to strategies of avoidance, of "not playing the game anymore" (Dubet 2004, own translation) and exit from those games that threaten the own feeling of dignity. However, "drop-out" trajectories are not the results of choice but of individual coping with previous negative experiences during their transition. In these cases, agency is also inhibited by a withdrawal from the possibility of seeing oneself as a legitimate source of reasons for action. How can I project myself, narrate my trajectory as emerging from my own actions if this "self" is considered as "useless" and without any qualities. Accordingly, the strategies of engagement with one's future are characterized by a feeling of passive processing within institutions, a self-elimination from more prestigious educational pathways and an experience of the semantic of individualized self-project as a form of symbolic violence. In a culture of individualism, failure can only be attributed to the individual.

8.8 Avenues for a Sociology of Youth and Childhood Inspired by the Capability Approach

These short insights in the research results show that the straightforward assumption of youth as autonomous social actors, as represented in some discourses within the NSCH, but as well within the political construction of youth as policy addressees, does not take into account the social preconditions of their agency. It has furthermore been shown that the institutional discourse about young persons as autonomous actors can have detrimental effects on their self-interpretations and identities. As Bourdieu has shown, the reflexivity that is presumed within the idea of individualized choice biographies is dependent on the "withdrawal from practical necessity" and the "objective and subjective distancing from practical urgencies" (Bourdieu 1984). The interviews with the young persons showed a strong contrast between models of agency influential in policy design and their lived experience. It seems as if the construction of youth as "autonomous agents" leads to an "autonomy gap" describing a "discrepancy between the capacities for choice that are presupposed by public policies, (. . .) and the capacities that people actually have or will develop" (Anderson 2009). The call to conceive oneself as an individual self project, implying the ability for long term temporal horizons and a certain security on the outcomes of one's actions, is effectively reduced by situations of crisis and a lack of reliable expectations about the future. The results also shed light on the differences and convergences between children and youth rights-discourse and the capability approach. While the analysis was not directly pointed towards children rights, it has proven that legal prescriptions are an insufficient medium for securing individuals' ability to pursue their own conception of a good life. While the CRC does not claim that one should focus on rights only, it is at risk of being entrapped within a fundamentally individualistic conception of the person as we find it in liberal theories of Justice. As Christman describes

> the picture of the citizen of the just polity includes no specific reference to the marks of social identity, such as race, gender, sexuality, culture, and so on, that many actual individuals might immediately mention when describing themselves. The model person, in the liberal tradition, is characterized without essential connections with past or present others or social factors external to him. (Christman 2009 : 2)

In contrast, and in line with our interpretation of the capability approach, "an adequate approach must start out from the broader range of social institutions and interpersonal contexts within which one finds the recognitional relations crucial for autonomy" (Anderson and Honneth 2005: 136). A capability approach, with its broad informational basis, which is sensitive to the situated knowledge of the respondents and takes into account what persons have reasons to value, conversion factors and the impact of social norms and socialization on preferences, provides some promising avenues for future research, both in the field of children rights and the sociology of youth and childhood(s). In relation to children's rights, the analysis describes that the new rights and responsibilities regime within European welfare capitalism, paired with a "social investment approach" to children and youth, constructs young persons and children primarily as policy objects, rather than providing a recognition of children and youth as citizens. The critical remarks pointed towards the CRC, as well as those concerning approaches claiming the unambiguous status of children as political and social actors, are not meant to delegitimize children's and youth rights approaches *per se*, but highlight the need to take into account the quandaries that such approaches may hide. The chapter thus calls, from the background of the capability approach, for a conception of children's and youth citizenship which goes beyond a bundle of rights and accounts for the situated diversity and the social embeddedness of children and youth within different social and institutional contexts.

References

Alanen, L. (2010). Editorial: Taking children's rights seriously. *Childhood, 17*(1), 5–8.

Alkire, S. (2007). *Choosing dimensions: The capability approach and multidimensional poverty*. Working Paper (88) Manchester, IDPM/Chronic Poverty Research Centre (CPRC).

Anderson, J. H. (2009). Autonomy gaps as a social pathology: Ideologiekritik beyond paternalism. In R. Forst (Ed.), *Sozialphilosophie und Kritik*. Frankfurt: Suhrkamp.

Anderson, J. H., & Honneth, A. (2005). Autonomy, vulnerability, recognition, and justice. In J. Christman & J. H. Anderson (Eds.), *Autonomy and the challenges to liberalism: New essays* (pp. 127–149). Cambridge: Cambridge University Press.

Andresen, S., Diehm, I., Sander, U., & Ziegler, H. (2011). *Introduction. Children and the good life: New challenges for research on children* (Children's wellbeing: Indicators and research, Vol. 4, pp. 1–6). Heidelberg: Springer.

Archer, M. S. (2000). *Being human: The problem of agency*. Cambridge: Cambridge University Press.

Archer, M. S. (2007). *Making our way through the world: Human reflexivity and social mobility*. Cambridge: Cambridge University Press.

Archer, M. S. (2010). *Conversations about reflexivity*. New York: Routledge.

Aries, P. (1962). *Centuries of childhood. A social history of family life*. New York: Mac Millan.

Arneil, B. (2002). Becoming versus being: A critical analysis of the child in liberal theory. In D. MacLeod (Ed.), *The moral and political status of the child* (pp. 70–96). Oxford: Oxford University Press.

Ball, S., Davies, J., David, M., & Reay, D. (2002). 'Classification' and 'judgement': Social class and the 'cognitive structures' of choice of higher education. *British Journal of Sociology of Education, 23*(1), 51–72.

Ballet, J., Bigerri, M., & Comin, F. (2011). Children's agency and the capability approach: A conceptual framework. In J. Ballet, M. Bigerri, & F. Comin (Eds.), *Children and the capability approach*. New York: Palgrave MacMillan.

Bauman, Z. (2001). Identity in the globalizing world. *Social Anthropology, 9*(2), 121–129.

Beck, U., & Beck-Gernsheim, E. (2002). *Individualization: Institutionalized individualism and its social and political consequences*. London: SAGE Publications.

Beck, U., Bonss, W., & Lau, C. (2003). The theory of reflexive modernisation: Problematic, hypotheses and research program. *Theory, Culture and Society, 20*(2), 1–33.

Becker, H. S. (1970). The life history and the scientific mosaic. In H. S. Becker (Ed.), *Sociological work* (pp. 63–73). Hawthorne: Transaction Books.

Biggeri, M., et al. (2006). Children conceptualizing their capabilities: Results of a survey conducted during the first children's world congress on child labour. *Journal of Human Development, 7*(1), 59–83.

Boltanski, L., & Thévenot, L. (2000). The reality of moral expectations: A sociology of situated judgement. *Philosophical Explorations, 3*(3), 208–231.

Bonvin, J., Dean, H., Vielle, P., & Farvaque, N. (2005). Developing capabilities and rights in welfare-to-work policies. *European Societies, 7*(1), 3–26.

Bourdieu, P. (1980). La jeunesse n'est qu'un mot. *Questions de sociologie, 143–154*.

Bourdieu, P. (1984). Espace social et genèse des" classes". *Actes de la recherche en sciences sociales, 52*(1), 3–14.

Bourdieu, P. (1997). *Méditations pascaliennes*. Paris: Seuil.

Brannen, J., & Nilsen, A. (2007). Young people, time horizons and planning a response to Anderson et al. *Sociology, 41*(1), 153–160.

Bühler-Niederberger, D., & König, A. (2011). Childhood as a resource and laboratory for the self-project. *Childhood, 18*(2), 180–195.

Bühler-Niederberger, D., & van Krieken, R. (2008). Persisting inequalities childhood between global influences and local traditions. *Childhood, 15*(2), 147–155.

Christman, J. P. (2009). *The politics of persons*. Cambridge: Cambridge University Press.

Cicchelli, V., & Pugeault-Cicchelli, C. (2006). Les recherches sociologiques sur la jeunesse en France et leurs liens avec les préoccupations politico-administratives. *Revista de Sociologia, 79*, 101–120.

Clark, Z., & Eisenhuth, F. (2011). The capability approach and research on children. In S. Andresen, I. Diehm, U. Sander, & H. Ziegler (Eds.), *Children and the good life: New challenges for research on children* (Children's wellbeing: Indicators and research, Vol. 4, pp. 69–74). Heidelberg: Springer.

Davis, J. B. (2004). *Identity and commitment: Sen's conception of the individual, speech held at the workshop on rationality and commitment*. University of St. Gallen, Switzerland, 13–15 May.

Dean, H. (2007). The ethics of welfare-to-work. *Policy & Politics, 35*(4), 573–589.

du Bois-Reymond, M. (1995). *Childhood and youth in Germany and the Netherlands: Transitions and coping strategies of adolescents*. New York: Walter de Gruyter.

Dubet, F. (2004). Pourquoi la motivation des élèves est-elle un problème? *Bulletin de l'APMEP, 454*, 628–640.

Dubet, F., & Caillet, V. (2009). *Injustice at work*. Boulder: Paradigm Publishers.

Eurofound. (2012). *NEETs – Young people not in employment, education or training: Characteristics, costs and policy responses in Europe*. Luxembourg: Publications Office of the European Union.

European Commission. (2009). *A new era of youth policies*. Press release, 27th April 2009, Brussels. http://europa.eu/rapid/press-release_IP-09-644_en.htm. Accessed 11 Nov 2013.

European Commission. (2012). *Commission staff working document, proposal on the establishment of a Youth guarantee.* Brussels. http://eurlex.europa.eu/LexUriServ/LexUriServ.do?uri=COM:2012:0729:FIN:EN:PDF. Accessed 11 Nov 2013.

Farvaque, N. (2008). "Faire surgir des faits utilisables" Comment opérationnaliser l'approche par les capacités? In J. De Munck & B. Zimmermann (Eds.), *La liberté au prisme des capacités. Amartya Sen au delà du libéralisme* (pp. 51–80). Paris: Editions de l' EHESS.

Fornäs, J. (1995). Youth, culture and modernity. In J. Fornäs & G. Bolin (Eds.), *Youth culture in late modernity* (pp. 1–11). London: Sage.

Freeman, M. (1998). The sociology of childhood and children's rights. *The International Journal of Children s Rights, 6*(4), 433–444.

Freeman, M. (2000). The future of children's rights. *Children & Society, 14*(4), 277–293.

Furlong, A. (2006). Not a very NEET solution: representing problematic labour market transitions among early school-leavers. *Work, Employment & Society, 20*(3), 553–569.

Furlong, A., & Cartmel, F. (1997). *Young people and social change. Individualisation and risk in late society.* Buckingham: Open University Press.

Garfinkel, H. (1967). *Studies in ethnomethodology.* Englewood Cliffs: Prentice-Hall.

Geldens, P., Lincoln, S., & Hodkinson, P. (2011). Youth: Identities, transitions, cultures. *Sage Journal of Sociology, 47*(4), 347–353.

Giddens, A. (1990). *The consequences of modernity.* Cambridge: Polity.

Glaser, B. G., & Strauss, A. L. (1967). *The discovery of grounded theory: Strategies for qualitative research.* New York: Aldine de Gruyter.

Grundmann, M. (2011). Kinderarmut und Wohlfahrtsproduktion. In K. Böllert (Ed.), *Soziale Arbeit als Wohlfahrtsproduktion* (pp. 167–182). Heidelberg: VS Verlag für Sozialwissenschaften.

Grundmann, M., & Dravenau, D. (2010). Class, agency and capability. In H. U. Otto & H. Ziegler (Eds.), *Education, welfare and the capabilities approach. A European perspective* (pp. 87–100). Opladen: Barabara Budrich Publishers.

Hacking, I. (2004). Between Michel Foucault and Erving Goffman: Between discourse in the abstract and face-to-face interaction. *Economy and Society, 33*(3), 277–302.

Haraway, D. (1988). Situated knowledges: The science question in feminism and the privilege of partial perspective. *Feminist Studies, 14*(3), 575–599.

Heinz, W. R. (1995). *Arbeit, Beruf und Lebenslauf: eine Einführung in die berufliche Sozialisation.* Weinheim: Juventa-Verlag.

Heinz, W. R. (2009). Status passages as micro-macro linkages in life course research. In W. R. Heinz, J. Huinink, & A. Weymann (Eds.), *The life course reader: Individuals and societies across time* (pp. 473–486). Frankfurt: Campus-Verlag.

Hynes, P., Lamb, M., Short, D., & Waites, M. (2010). Sociology and human rights: Confrontations, evasions and new engagements. *International Journal of Human Rights, 14*(6), 811–832.

James, A. C., & Prout, A. (1998). *Theorising childhood.* New York: Wiley.

Kessl, F. (2006). Aktivierungspädagogik statt wohlfahrtsstaatlicher Dienstleistung? Das aktivierungspolitische Re-Arrangement der bundesdeutschen Kinderund Jugendhilfe. *Zeitschrift für Sozialreform, 2*, 217–232.

Kohli, M. (1994). *Work and retirement: a comparative perspective.* Oxford: Wiley.

Lareau, A. (2011). *Unequal childhoods: Class, race, and family life.* Berkeley: University of California Press.

Lister, R. (2006). Investing in the citizen-workers of the future: Transformations in citizenship and the state under new labour. In C. Pierson & F. G. Castles (Eds.), *The welfare state reader* (pp. 455–471). Cambridge: Polity.

Mayall, B. (2000). Sociology of childhood in relation to children's rights. *The International Journal of Children's Rights, 8*, 243.

Moran-Ellis, J. (2010). Reflections on the sociology of childhood in the UK. *Current Sociology, 58* (2), 186–205.

Nagel, T. (1989). *The view from nowhere.* Oxford: Oxford University Press.

Nussbaum, M. (2000). *Women and human development.* Cambridge: Cambridge University Press.

Nussbaum, M. (2003). Capabilities as fundamental entitlements: Sen and social justice. *Feminist Economics, 9*(2–3), 33–59.

Oyserman, D., & Markus, H. R. (1990). Possible selves and delinquency. *Journal of Personality and Social Psychology, 59*(1), 112–125.

Prout, A. (2000). Childhood bodies: Construction, agency and hybridity'. In A. Prout (Ed.), *The body, childhood and society* (pp. 1–18). New York: Macmillan, St. Martins Press.

Purdy, L. M. (1994). Why children shouldn't have equal rights. *The International Journal of Children's Rights, 2*, 223.

Reynaert, D., Bouverne-de-Bie, M., & Vandevelde, S. (2009). A review of children's rights literature since the adoption of the United Nations convention on the rights of the child. *Childhood, 16*(4), 518–534.

Robeyns, I. (2003). Is Nancy Fraser's critique of theories of distributive justice justified? *Constellations, 10*(4), 538–554.

Rose, N. (1998). *Inventing our selves: Psychology, power, and personhood*. Cambridge: Cambridge University Press.

Saito, M. (2003). Amartya Sen's capability approach to education: A critical exploration. *Journal of Philosophy of Education, 37*(1), 17–23.

Sandel, M. J. (1998). *Liberalism and the limits of justice*. Cambridge: Cambridge University Press.

Schröer, W. (2007). Zum Verschwinden der Jugend – Die Lebenslage Jugend im Zeichen der Humankapitalpolitik. In S. Hering (Ed.), *Bürgerschaftlichkeit und Professionalität, Wirklichkeit und Zukunftsperspektiven Sozialer Arbeit* (pp. 145–149). Heidelberg: Springer.

Sen, A. (1977). Rational fools: A critique of the behavioral foundations of economic theory. *Philosophy & Public Affairs, 6*(4), 317–344.

Sen, A. (1987). *The standard of living*. Cambridge: Cambridge University Press.

Sen, A. (1993). Positional objectivity. *Philosophy & Public Affairs, 22*(2), 126–145.

Sen, A. (1999). *Development as freedom*. Oxford: Oxford University Press.

Sen, A. (2002). *Rationality and freedom*. Cambridge: Harvard University Press.

Sen, A. (2004). Elements of a theory of human rights. *Philosophy and Public Affairs, 32*(4), 315–356.

Sen, A. (2005). Human rights and capabilities. *Journal of Human Development, 6*(2), 151–166.

Sen, A. (2009). *The idea of justice*. Cambridge: Harvard University Press.

Sennett, R., & Cobb, J. (1972). *The hidden injuries of class*. London: Cambridge University Press.

Such, E., & Walker, R. (2005). Young citizens or policy objects? Children in the 'rights and responsibilities' debate. *Journal of Social Policy, 34*(1), 39–57.

Taylor, C. (1985). What's wrong with negative liberty. In *Philosophy and the Human Sciences. Philosophical Papers 2*, Cambridge, U.K: Cambridge University Press (pp. 211–230).

Zarca, B. (1999). Le sens social des enfants. *Sociétés contemporaines, 36*(1), 67–101.

Ziegler, H. (2010). Subjective well-being and capabilities: Views on the well-being of young persons. In S. Andresen, I. Diehm, U. Sander, & H. Ziegler (Eds.), *Children and the good life: New challenges for research on children* (Children's wellbeing: Indicators and research, Vol. 4, pp. 91–101). Dordrecht: Springer.

Ziegler, H. (2011). Soziale Arbeit und das gute Leben – Capabilities als sozialpädagogische Kategorie. In C. Sedmak, B. Babic, R. Bauer, & C. Pasch (Eds.), *Der Capability-Approach in sozialwissenschaftlichen Kontexten* (pp. 117–137). Wiesbaden: VS Verlag für Sozialwissenschaften.

Zimmerman, B. (2006). Pragmatism and the capability approach: Challenges in social theory and empirical research. *European Journal of Social Theory, 9*(4), 467–484.

Zinnecker, J. (1988). Sozialstruktur – Klassenkultur – Jugendkultur. In Mitte (Hg.), *Jugendarbeit und Kulturarbeit* (pp. 14–27). Stuttgart.

Chapter 9
Children's Rights and the Capability Approach: Discussing Children's Agency Against the Horizon of the Institutionalised Youth Land

Didier Reynaert and Rudi Roose

9.1 Introduction

"Agency" is a fundamental notion in both the frameworks of children's rights and the capability approach. The social movement for children's rights helped to shape a new paradigm of childhood, putting agency at centre stage (Archard 2004; Verhellen 2000). In doing so, proponents criticised the common idea asserting that children are just passive objects in need of protection. As an alternative, they strived to consider children as active agents with entitlements to self-determination and participation rights. Within the capability approach, agency is considered to be a core concept, understood as a measure for autonomous action (Deneulin 2008; Nussbaum 2011). It is recognised that a person pursues the goals and values that he or she has reason to value. But how can we understand agency, and how can it be supported accordingly in order to guarantee that children can live with dignity? This concern is the central point of this chapter, where we will discuss children's agency in the light of both the frameworks of children's rights and the capability approach.

A discussion of children's agency cannot be done without taking into account the historical and socio-cultural structuring of childhood in our society. This structuring can be grasped under what has been appointed as the "youth moratorium" or the "institutionalised youth land" (Verhellen 2000; Zinnecker 2000). The notion of "youth land" or "youth moratorium" refers to the institutionalisation of childhood into *"(...) preparatory arenas that implement a principle of integration*

D. Reynaert (✉)
Faculty of Education, Health and Social Work, University College Ghent, Voskenslaan 362, 9000 Ghent, Belgium
e-mail: didier.reynaert@hogent.be

R. Roose
Faculty of Psychology and Educational Sciences, Ghent University, Dunantlaan 2, 9000 Ghent, Belgium
e-mail: rudi.roose@ugent.be

D. Stoecklin and J.-M. Bonvin (eds.), *Children's Rights and the Capability Approach*, Children's Well-Being: Indicators and Research 8, DOI 10.1007/978-94-017-9091-8_9,

by means of separation." (Honig 2008: 201). Following Giddens's (1984) structuration theory, this process of institutionalisation is both the result of actions by individual agents as well as the condition under which action is possible. It can be considered as the result of a historical process in which children are gradually separated from the adult world with the aim to prepare them for adult life. At the same time, children's actions and processes of appropriation contribute to transforming this social structure (James 2009). Until today, the institutionalised youth land remains the horizon against which childhood in the western world takes place.

Since children's rights and the capability approach are both frameworks to study social justice, it is interesting to link these frameworks to the debate on the institutionalised youth land, and to analyse the meaning of this youth land in contemporary thinking on children and childhood. Indeed, children's rights offer a framework of formal entitlements and resources (Nussbaum 1997; Sen 2005), while the capability approach can be considered as a framework to transform these entitlements and commodities into concrete functionings, thereby making use of individual and social conversion factors. The entitlements, resources and conversion factors are for, in the case of children, an important part situated in the institutionalised youth land. Facilities such as schools, childcare and youth protection services are all institutionalised arrangements that have historically segregated children from adults. Nevertheless, the way in which children's agency has to be understood in the converting process, transforming resources and commodities embedded in the youth moratorium into functionings, in a way that contributes to respecting the human dignity of children, remains an under-theorised question.

Throughout this chapter, the argument will be developed that both the frameworks of children's rights and the capability approach are characterised by a strong egalitarian individualism, which supports an understanding of agency as the individual responsibility of people. However, in the application of the capability approach to children, the basis of egalitarian individualism seems to be abandoned in favour of a rather ambiguous position. What this means for children and childhood will be evaluated successively for the framework of children's rights and the capability approach. The consequences of the construction of the institutionalised youth land will be equally addressed. In particular, the issue of whether the historically developed socio-cultural structuring of childhood is subjected to erosion or consolidation will be discussed, including the question of what the effects can be for realising the human dignity of children. Some suggestions will ultimately be made for a different understanding of children's agency, highlighting the importance of interrelatedness and solidarity.

9.2 Children's Agency: Different Understandings

Since the 1970s, children's agency has become a central notion in the ideas surrounding childhood. The interdisciplinary field of "childhood studies" has contributed to developing a new paradigm that recognises the social and political significance of children's meanings and ideas. This stemmed from the critique of the awareness that children are merely "passive receivers of society's messages" (James and James 2012) characterised by either their structural or biological determinism, which was widely accepted until the paradigm shift. These ideas are indebted to developments in the "reform pedagogy" or the progressive education movement at the end of the nineteenth century. Individuals such as Adolphe Ferrière and Ellen Key in Europe as well as John Dewey in the United States formed the basis for "the inception of the myth of the autonomous child" (Coussée 2008: 29). Although agency has become a central notion within childhood studies, according to Valentine (2011), the term remains inadequately understood. This is consistent with Stoecklin's (2013) observation that *"There is a need to specify concepts like actor and agency, which sometimes sound like slogans rather than notions grounded on empirical evidence"* (Stoecklin 2013: 443). Agency is indeed often used as a premise to study childhood without explaining or analysing what the concept entails exactly. For this reason, childhood studies have demonstrated divergent understandings of agency (Valentine 2011).

A first line of thought along which the discussion on agency can be grasped is the "personal versus relational" dimension. Agency as a personal trait can be defined as an individual capacity to act autonomously, led by rational reasoning. This understanding of agency seems to be suggested in the definition proposed by James and James (2012: 3): "The capacity of individuals to act independently." It highlights children's individual capacities to make choices and to express their own ideas. Agency as a personal characteristic is in line with what Valentine (2011) defined as a liberal model of agency. This model is tailored for adults since it requires rationality, self-awareness and a sense of futurity. She argues that *"such a model of agency has historically excluded children and to some extent, children are still excluded from it"* (Valentine 2011: 350). Mayall made an important contribution to the discussion that sharpens our understanding of agency. She pointed at the importance of distinguishing "agency" from an "agent." According to Mayall, while the latter is an individual disposition, the former is an interactive process that happens with others in a given context (as cited in James 2009). Likewise, Stoecklin's (working) definition of agency is sensitive to its inter-relational trait. He refers to Nibell et al. for whom agency is *"an individual's or a group's capacity to make decisions, act, and interact with other people in a socially competent way"* (Nibell et al. 2009: 264).

The latter part of the definition points to a second important line of discussion, i.e. the "social reproduction versus social transformation" dimension. The wording "socially competent way" might suggest that agency needs to go in a particular direction, one that accords with dominant values and norms in society. Agency, then, is mainly an instrument for the reproduction of the prevailing social order. However, within childhood studies, the socialization process is not focused primarily on reproduction in the sense that there is a passive subject incorporating the existing culture in order to reproduce it. While highlighting agency, reference is made to the fact that children also actively process the existing culture. This is what Valentine's "social model" of agency suggests. Agency is considered as an interactive characteristic, such that in a given context, one learns the prevailing social order, positions oneself in relation to the existing social order and even learns to change or transform it (Mollenhauer 1993). From this point of view, agency should be considered as a *practice*, surrounded by power (Valentine 2011). Following Giddens, Valentine argued that agency is constituted by the social and at the same time constitutes the social. Because of this intertwined characteristic, it should be recognized that children's agency is a complex, multidimensional and ambivalent practice:

> the actions and dispositions that constitute agency, including 'choice' and 'competence,' are not politically empty or neutral categories. Instead, the actions and dispositions of children become, in this approach, mutable, contingent and meaningful: revealing both the role of individual agency in reproducing social norms and the potential for individual agency to disrupt them. (Valentine 2011: 355)

We endorse Valentine's position that such an account of agency is sensitive to differences between children based on class, race, gender and disability. We will further develop our understanding of agency by linking it successively to the framework of children's rights and the capability approach.

9.3 Children's Rights and Agency

With the adoption of the United Nations Convention on the Rights of the Child (UNCRC) in 1989, children's rights have become a significant framework for rethinking the social position of children in society. Generally, children's rights are considered as entitlements, i.e. moral as well as formal or legal claims that can be enforced when necessary. These claims concern the recognition of children as active agents and autonomous persons who construct their lives in their own right (James and James 2004; King 2007). With the recognition of their agency, children were acknowledged as meaningful subjects in the present, as "beings" and no longer as mere passive objects that are only significant as "becomings" (Hemrica and Heyting 2004). In this way, the children's rights movement as the social movement mobilising for the rights of children was part of a paradigm shift in understanding childhood. This was a shift that, in terms of images of childhood, depicted a transformation from the "incompetent child" towards the "autonomous child" (Reynaert et al. 2009). Hanson (2012) however explains that there are different "schools of thought on children's rights". These different schools are based partly on how they relate to the discussion on the competence of children.

The institutionalisation of the framework of children's rights is commonly valued as a step forward in the way of dealing with children more respectfully, as it highlights the interests of a group in society that for a long time has been ignored (Freeman 2007). However, the children's rights agenda is not free from "critique." Such critique, according to Evans (2005), should be understood as the practice of questioning, analysing and trying to understand the underlying logic that shapes children's rights. However, Alanen (2011) rightly argued that the framework of children's rights lacks critique. In this sense, Minow's (1995: 287) observation that *"(...) the movement for children's rights had failed to secure a coherent political or intellectual foundation"* is still valid. The children's rights movement indeed demonstrates a lack of internal reflection and is insufficiently open to external judgment (Reynaert et al. 2012). Due to a lack of critique in academic work on children's rights, many questions and issues of discussion remain unanswered, not in the least how children's rights are constructed in daily social practices and what the consequences of these constructions are in terms of the human dignity of children. Do children's rights contribute to a greater respect for children, and if so, in what sense? Answers to this maybe somewhat provocative, but nevertheless fundamental question could help tackle some major issues of scepticism related to a rights-based approach. Aside from the issue of children's rights and agency that we will subsequently elaborate on, it is also important to point out some other relevant matters. The framework of children's rights is often implemented only at the formal level by the adoption of new legislation that aims at moving the children's rights agenda forward. Nussbaum (2011) argues that "human rights" remain words on paper if they are not accompanied by government intervention. In this sense, Robeyns (2006) suggests that a rights-based discourse is often overtly rhetorical. Furthermore, an overemphasis on the formal function of children's rights would risk reducing those rights to *legal* entitlements only (Robeyns 2006) and would threaten to underestimate the social function of children's rights, considering rights as a lever for social change. A tendency towards over-juridification of social/educational relations can indeed be observed in the field of children's rights. For instance, Huntington (2006) explains that a "myopic focus" on rights, focusing on legal translations, ignores the social contexts in which these rights have to be realised (on the question of translations, see also the chapter by Hanson et al. in this volume).

Although arguments could be presented on each of these topics – something that, as we argue, should be taken more seriously in scholarly work on children's rights – in the scope of this chapter, we are mainly interested in the agency of children, and the question of how agency from a children's rights perspective can be understood.

9.3.1 The Orthodoxy of Egalitarian Individualism

While children's rights were the object of deliberative discussion during the 1970s and 1980s, with liberationists opposing protectionists/welfarists (Archard 2004;

Roose and De Bie 2007), it seems that with the adoption of the UNCRC, a consensus on the nature and interpretation of children's rights has been reached. As we have argued elsewhere (Reynaert et al. 2009), in the "global human rights industry," children's rights are not under discussion. Within the children's rights discourse, they are presented as new norms for child-rearing, which have to be implemented in a variety of educational practices. These norms have been taken for granted, with the consequence that the practice of critique has made way for a technocratic discourse (Fernando 2001). The focus is on *"the schism between the provisions of the Convention and children's rights in practice"* (Pupavac 2001: 96). As such, a "pensée unique" ("ideological orthodoxy") closed the debate on how to understand children's rights. The discussion on the position of children in the family illustrates this thought. Vandenbroeck and Bouverne-De Bie (2006) observed that negotiation between parents and children has become the new norm in family education. This norm was set forward, inspired by the UNCRC, as the *desirable* norm that needed to be stimulated. Whether or not negotiation is indeed the most desirable norm was not questioned. Neither were the consequences of presenting negotiation as a new norm the subject of debate. Vandenbroeck and Bouverne-De Bie (2006) pointed at the fact that negation might favour certain groups of children and parents but at the same time might exclude families who cannot achieve this new norm. It is important to notice that this consensus can be observed at the level of the children's rights *discourse* (i.e. the way we talk and write about children's rights at the macro level). This does not mean that constitutive social action at the micro level, which aims to realise children's rights, would show a very divers image. However, we lack empirical evidence on how children's rights are used in micro-practices to know whether this is indeed the case. In this sense, scholarly work on children's rights is an under-theorised field in academia.

Within the children's rights discourse, a consensus can be noticed relative to the idea of agency. The understanding of agency within the children's rights movement can primarily be attributed to the liberationists (Mortier 2002). These so called "kiddie libbers" aimed towards granting the same rights to children as to adults. This position starts from an egalitarian doctrine emphasising equal treatment, freedom and rights to self-determination. In terms of the 3P-typology of children's rights, i.e. protection, provision and participation (Quennerstedt 2010), the children's rights movement has been mobilising for participation rights over protection rights (e.g. discussion on negotiation household). Agency from this point of view is primarily an individual characteristic of the child and understood as individual responsibility. Although it could be argued that a focus on *egalitarian individualism* relative to children's rights has the merit of contributing to more freedom for children at the expense of the state or parental paternalism, caution remains regarding (the *effects* of) this egalitarian individualism for children. We shall consecutively highlight three points for discussion.

First of all, on an ontological level, one can wonder whether an understanding of the agency of children from the perspective of egalitarian individualism can sustain the test of reality. The childhood image of the autonomous, rational and free child is probably a myth that does not correspond with the reality of everyday life. As Saito

(2003: 25) correctly stated, *"Adopting an extreme libertarian position vis-à-vis children is irrational."* Mortier (2002) argued that people in general, including children, hardly correspond to the ideal of the autonomous human being. Instead, they very often act from interconnectedness with others. Following this position, several authors, including Dean (2009), defended a view on human beings that acknowledged social relationships and interdependency from the perspective of "an ethics of care," especially in the context of child-rearing and education (Cockburn 2005).

Secondly and more recently, some scholars observed that agency as an individual trait can sometimes have negative outcomes for children. In the context of neo-liberal social regimes that emphasise activation and individual responsibility, children's rights-based social and educational practices can become part of a larger strategy towards accountability or even correction and re-penalisation (Mierendorff 2007). This can be observed in how society reacts to youth offenders. In Belgium as in other European countries, children's rights organisations have been striving for a "justice model" of intervention instead of a "welfare model." In conformity to the principles of the children's rights framework, the former highlights the agency of the child offender (Ellis and France 2010; Muncie 2006). This means recognising the discernment of children and consequently, recognising the responsibility of children for committing criminal acts. At the same time, principles of due process are allocated to children (such as legality, proportionality, subsidiarity, the rights to legal aid, the right to be heard, the right to appeal, etc.). As such, this model is closely linked to the traditional criminal justice model for adults. The fundamental difference between this model and the model for adults lies in the educative character of the sanction, which aims towards socialisation and re-integration into society. Thus, children's rights-based justice interventions for child offenders place increasing attention on the responsibilisation of the child; the criminal act becomes the condition for justice interventions at the expense of the social and personal context of the child offender. Elements in the social context of children, such as the family situation, are neutralised to the advantage of "objective" and more rights-respecting sentencing, by re-introducing the fundamental legal principles of due process. However, when hybridised with "law and order" or "moral panic", children's rights risk becoming an instrument of social control, monitoring the individual behaviour of children. Children's rights may then transform into a repressive instrument, or in the words of Bailleau et al. (2009), a "sword of criminal justice." Such and Walker (2005) observed that children are being held responsible, especially in situations where they have committed an offence. This evolution not only carries with it a tendency towards an increased individual responsibility, but also an agenda of moralisation. Children are expected to behave as "good citizens," as measured by the dominant social norms and values of society. They are expected to know their own needs and wants, as well as their rights and responsibilities and should adequately accommodate these to the expectations and needs of society. As such, children's rights, which emphasise their agency, can appeal to them as "entrepreneurial selves" (Masschelein and Quaghebeur 2005).

Finally, the process of "equalising" the power balances between children and adults (parents in particular) by giving children the same rights as adults allows children to acquire instruments of power to defend their own interest. This can produce conflictual relationships between children and adults (parents) as distinctive individual interests can generate adversarial positions (Pupavac 2001; Roose and De Bie 2008). This is obvious in several cases in Flanders where children playing in public places caused disturbances in the neighbourhood. Residents living in the neighbourhood of kindergartens and playgrounds complained about the intensity of the noise that the children made. They saw this as a violation of their right to rest and privacy. As a counteraction, children and their sympathisers united and claimed their right to play. This case shows that problems related to the condition of "living together" cannot be translated as adversarial interests, certainly not at the individual level. An egalitarian approach of agency is inadequate to deal with these issues, as these matters call for a certain kind of collectiveness and solidarity.

We aim to show with these examples that interpretations of agency based on egalitarian individualism, which have become mainstream in today's discourse of children's rights in Western countries, carry with them a number of risks as children's rights-based social and educational practices are not by definition for the benefit of children.

9.3.2 The Antagonistic Character of the Institutionalised Youth Land

The discussion on children's agency is not limited to the personal or relational dimension of children's rights-based social and educational practices. It also contains a structural dimension that is related to the institutionalisation of childhood in society. While the institutionalised youth land was a product of the child protection movement at the end of the nineteenth and beginning of the twentieth century (Verhellen 2000), the lead-up to the last decades of that century saw this historical socio-cultural structuring of childhood coming under fire. The contestation of the youth land occurred to a large extent by an emerging social movement for children's rights. Against the background of a broader societal contestation, questions were raised in relation to an exaggerated institutional paternalism in dealing with children. With the increasing recognition of the self-determination and participation rights of children, their social and legal position became challenged. As it disapproved of the childhood image of the incompetent child and favoured an alternative image of the autonomous child, the children's rights movement placed the institutionalised youth land under discussion. Breaking through the youth moratorium became a central claim of the children's rights movement under the radical slogan "bring children back into society" (Verhellen 1998: 486). Consequently, the socio-political segregation of children from adults had to be eradicated as much as possible. Children, it was said, are not only the future generation; childhood should likewise be considered as an actual part of current society (James and James 2004).

The merging of the "old" childhood image of the incompetent child that viewed children merely as objects with the "new" image of the autonomous child that considers children primarily as agents has created some confusion. As Honig (2008: 202) noted:

> Thus the pedagogical moratorium provides children and teenagers with a space for self-regulation, although this space is also determined by structural ambivalence. After all, the principle of 'integration through separation' bears within it the contradiction between institutionalized immaturity and independence.

In relation to the historical socio-cultural structuring of childhood, a twin process of antagonistic developments ensued. The first one is a process of "blurring boundaries." Honig (2008: 202), again, stated that institutional moratoria *"(...) face a powerful tension towards erosion; not only young people but children too are acquiring the status of citizens and consumers.*" It seems that, especially in the commercial and cultural sphere, the agency of children is recognised and that childhood in these spheres is increasingly governed by marketing strategies. For instance, Mortier (2002) observed that children from the age of twelve are exposed to consumer retention strategies by financial institutions to become a "client." The second development is a process of "strengthened boundaries." A radical equalisation between children and adults did not occur. What did happen, according to Mortier (2002), was that the particularity of children remained recognised, and children as a group acquired adult instruments of power, i.e. individual entitlements to self-determination and participation, to defend their particular interests. So, instead of the abolition of the institutionalised youth land, a range of new instruments of empowerment-mechanisms were established to support children in advocating for their interests. New institutions such as children's rights commissioners, child legal centres or ministries for children were developed. At the same time, existing sectors of child and youth policy were reformed with the aim of strengthening the legal position of children. In the field of juvenile justice for instance, principles of due process were introduced. However, these new instruments and mechanisms became a part of the wider discursive social policy directed at children, which was historically characterised by its ambiguous and double character, operating in the tension between emancipation and control. Legal guarantees in the case of child offending, guaranteed by article 40 of the Convention on the Rights of the Child, not only protect children in the case of forced government intervention. As we have argued earlier, they can likewise operate as an instrument for increasing control over children by serving as a lever for increasing government intervention (James and James 2001). This dynamic alerts us to an odd paradox in relation to children's rights regarding the agency of children. Guggenheim (2005), among others, remarked that children's rights, with a focus on agency and participation rights, were introduced into child policy to offer a counterweight against the excessive interventionism of social institutions and parents in children's lives.

However, this resulted in a further expansion of social institutions for children and young people, and therefore reinforced the institutionalised youth land.

The last observation reminds us that emphasising agency in the current discourse of children's rights may be associated with some difficulties. When children's rights, understood as individual entitlements that children have to certain resources, are for an important part in the institutionalised youth land, the question arises as to how this institutionalised youth land impacts on children's agency and how a negative impact can be avoided. However, a rights-based approach does not seem to answer this question. Indeed, as proponents of the capability approach have argued, having entitlements and resources is not sufficient since it gives no indication of the opportunities people have to use these resources. Andresen et al. (2006) argued that *"(…) people are unequal in their capabilities of doing and being even with the same rights, social and physical infrastructure, amount of money or the same panel of external assets."* A rights-based approach to agency remains silent on the diversity of contexts within which children make use of these resources. Finally, it remains unclear how resources structured in the institutionalised youth land relate to resources in the broader society, i.e. how child and youth policies relate to the broader social policy. This is an important question relevant to the quest for solidarity in society, especially since the interests of children can come into conflict with the interests of adults, for instance in the case of sharing the public space (cf. the case of playing children causing a disturbance). Complementing a children's rights framework with the capability approach might overcome some of these critiques.

9.4 The Capability Approach and Agency

The works of Amartya Sen (1999) and Martha Nussbaum (2011) on the capability approach (CA) have been extremely important in the development of human and children's rights-based approaches to justice and welfare. The capability approach is concerned with the interplay between entitlements and corresponding social resources (rights) on the one hand, and a person's abilities to use these entitlements and resources on the other. As such, it introduces an agency-based perspective on justice that is concerned with the questions of how and under which conditions a person with entitlements and resources is able to transform these into concrete functionings. The CA recognises that people participate in society in very diverse ways and make use of resources in very distinct manners. There may also be cases in which people do not have access to the minimum amount of resources they need to live with human dignity. "Capability" is defined as the freedom to choose and to act (Nussbaum 2011). As Dean (2009) stated, a capability is more than just what people are effectively able to do and to be. It is about their freedom to lead the kind of life they have reason to value (Comim et al. 2008; Nussbaum 2011; Robeyns 2005). A "functioning," on the other hand, refers to what people are ultimately doing. It is the achievement of something, whereas a capability is the freedom to achieve something. Comim et al. (2011) explained that the difference between capabilities and functionings relates to the difference between an opportunity and an outcome. In order to transform entitlements and commodities or resources into capabilities and subsequently corresponding functionings, people need "conversion factors." These are internal, societal or environmental characteristics that allow individuals to convert commodities and resources into functionings. As Dean (2009: 262) stated:

> Capabilities, therefore, represent the essential fulcrum between material resources and human achievements.

The framework of the CA is valued for a diversity of reasons, not in the least because it advances the theory of social justice that Rawls described in a sense that it "*(...) is better able to accommodate the diversity of human beings and the complexity of their circumstances*" (Dean 2009: 263). Its comprehensiveness is also valuable, as the approach covers all dimensions of human development via paying attention "*(...) to the links between material, mental and social well-being, or to the economic, social, political and cultural dimensions of life*" (Robeyns 2005: 96). Nevertheless, it is not without controversies (for a further discussion, see, among others, Comim et al. 2008; Dean 2009; Otto and Ziegler 2010; Robeyns 2005). In this chapter, bearing in mind the meaning of agency for children as an individual and for childhood as a socio-cultural construct in our society, we will elaborate specifically on what constitutes the child and childhood within the capability approach.

9.4.1 The CA: An Egalitarian Individualistic Approach to Human Agency

Although the capability approach, according to Andresen et al. (2006) and Macleod (2010), has been developed and interpreted in many divergent ways, it nevertheless formulates an "autonomy-based egalitarian position" (Andresen et al. 2006) on human agency with a particular focus on individual freedom (Robeyns 2005). Capabilities are about the power to exercise self-determination and individual liberty with human beings represented as mature agents, capable of taking responsibility. Andresen et al. (2006) explained that the focus on the individuality of human beings is especially emphasised in the context of a social welfare state that is characterised by social investment and activation:

> (...) the position of the 'activating welfare state' is to empower individuals' capability through investments in human capital (...) because this is seen as an important means to increase employability and individual competitiveness and as such a necessary prerequisite for an effective shift towards greater individual responsibility for 'social participation' at the expanse of social responsibility for public welfare and individual well being.

As a consequence of the rhetoric of individual freedom in the development of the current welfare state, a new balance between rights and duties is pursued that makes use of both incentives and sanctions, which would risk a resurfacing of the old discrimination between "deserving" and "undeserving poor" (Andresen et al. 2006).

In the case of children, the autonomy-based egalitarian position seems to be maintained in the capability approach at first sight. Ballet et al. (2011) also argued that children are not passive objects but active agents of freedom and therefore subjects of capabilities. Just like adults, they are able to express their opinions, interpretations and ideals. As such, the CA is in line with the rhetoric of egalitarian individualism that characterises the contemporary children's rights discourse. Nevertheless, Dixon and Nussbaum examined the question of special priority for children. The CA starts from the idea that every person, whether children or adults, comes into the world with basic capacities that need further development; as a result, it is difficult to justify some kind of special priority for children within the framework of the CA: "*The CA provides an account of each person's fundamental entitlements – entitlements that must be secured to everyone as a necessary condition of minimal social justice*" (Dixon and Nussbaum 2012: 567). However, in the case of children and child-rearing, it seems that the capability approach is quite receptive to critique from the angle of a contextual ethics. For instance, Dean (2009) criticised the capability approach because of its liberal-individualistic stance. His critique was inspired by a relational ontology, in particular the feminist ethics of care. Instead of prioritising individual agency and autonomy, Dean highlighted connectedness and solidarity. Human beings, he contended, should be considered as vulnerable and because of that, they aim to attach to others: "*The individual can only exist through and with others within networks of care*" (Dean 2009: 268–269). He argued that individual freedoms might be the central aspiration of human development. However, the way in which these freedoms are defined and realised occurs through our relationships with others. In the case of children and child-rearing, the achievement of children's capabilities can only be realised with the support of parents and other caretakers, including professional institutions, and in their turn, the realisation of the capabilities of parents and caretakers needs to be supported. Therefore, as Ballet et al. (2011: 36) stated: "*A challenge for the CA remains: How can we overcome its individualistic approach when thinking about children?*"

9.4.2 The CA: An Egalitarian Individualistic Approach to Children's Agency?

When evaluating existing scholarly work on children, education, child-rearing and children's rights in relation to the capability approach, it seems that the capability approach has a rather ambiguous position vis-à-vis this topic. As explained above, the capability approach conceptualises human beings from an egalitarian individualism point of view, stressing the individual agency and autonomy of a person. At first sight, this also seems to be the position of the capability approach in relation to children and childhood, as we have shown. However, when taking a more in-depth look at the issue, there is much more evidence for a differentiation of children under the capability approach, with notions of childhood that move towards emphasising protectionism or even paternalism.

Macleod (2010) acknowledged that during the course of a person's lifetime, different phases can be distinguished. Through these phases, capabilities are shaped in distinctive ways. Childhood should be considered as one of those phases. This is consistent with Dixon and Nussbaum's (2012: 593) argument that childhood should be considered as a "fourth frontier of justice" (aside from the rights of people with disabilities, rights across national boundaries and rights of nonhuman animals). The key question is how children and childhood differ from adults and adulthood (or other phases of life), and whether these differences justify a different treatment or even "special priority" under the capabilities approach. In relation to the first issue, most authors who write about the capability approach and children recognise that children are characterised by their vulnerability. Ballet et al. (2011) argued that the focus on self-determination and autonomy might not be applicable to children. Children are not able to have freedom of choice because of their insufficient cognitive development to decide for themselves. This is the reason that, according to the capability approach put forward by Dixon and Nussbaum, children are compared to people with cognitive disabilities. While children and people with disabilities are entitled to all the capabilities of the list, and equally to all rights in international agreements, they also need extra or special attention at the same time:

> (...) theories grounded in the classical social contract cannot adequately incorporate children's unusual vulnerability and their needs for care. Nor, in fact, can they conceive of children's fully equal humanity, since equal humanity is connected to the hypothesized equality of physical and mental powers. (Dixon and Nussbaum 2012: 563)

The "special priority" position is legitimised, inter alia, by the "special vulnerability" principle that defines children in a different way than adults. This is further brought to bear by Saito, whose ideas on children and children's capabilities are considered from a strong utilitarian stance. She argued that in the case of children, freedom of choice has to be considered in relation to the freedom they will have in the future rather than in the present (Saito 2003). This is clearly an "adult-centrist" idea of childhood, especially when it is similarly acknowledged that *"Education makes a child autonomous in terms of creating a new capability set for the child"* (Saito 2003: 27). The focus on future agency and autonomy represents a view of children as "becomings" instead of as "beings," and links with a more protectionist or even paternalist understanding of childhood. In this understanding, the institutionalised youth land is considered as a space in children's lives to prepare them for future participation in society.

Because children are considered as persons different from adults, it has been argued that they need a different treatment under the capability approach. According to Dixon and Nussbaum (2012), getting children above the minimal threshold of the capability list requires special policies. Some groups such as people with cognitive disabilities or children need more support in order to develop and enjoy their capabilities. This is in line with Comim et al.'s (2011: 8) argument that:

> Children may need different resources and policies to be able to enjoy the same basic capabilities and achieved functionings (. . .).

In this sense, age is considered to be a relevant characteristic under the capability approach. This is because children need different policies in order to convert resources and commodities into capabilities and functionings, although they enjoy the same capabilities as adults. Ballet et al. (2011) argued that age shapes capabilities in a qualitatively different way; as a consequence, children ought not to be considered as mini-adults as is the case with egalitarian individualism. Drawing from the notion of the "evolving capacities of the child" within the children's rights framework, Comim et al. (2011) together with Ballet et al. (2011) made a case for applying the capability approach to children. Because the opportunity for self-determination changes over time, different children may need different policies to enjoy their capabilities.

Given that children are arguably different from adults, for instance in their mental, physical and emotional development, two questions remain important to address. The first is whether these differences are relevant, whereas the second, although closely linked to the first, is whether these differences require a specific application of the capabilities approach. On the first issue (the relevance of difference), it seems questionable that the differences between children and adults are as radical as has been assumed. Differences in freedom of choice are often greater between individual children than between children and adults. This has to do with the various issues in society other than age that are important to consider. The impact of socio-economic problems such as poverty or the cultural background, which could result in racial discrimination, might be of more relevance than age. It could be argued that the importance given to age by some proponents of the capability approach might arise from an underlying "adult-centrism" that considers the adult citizen as the standard against which all things are measured. This adult is, according to egalitarian individualism, considered as an autonomous, independent and responsible citizen. The concept of this adult standard underlies certain interpretations of the capability approach; consequently, when a group of people, for instance children, is presumed to share a similar characteristic with adults but does not correspond with the ideal adult, this group becomes defined as "specialised" and "deficient." It is this deficiency that legitimises a special treatment under the capability approach. Again, we do not deny that there can be differences between children and adults, but the focus on age might result in underestimating other parameters.

The question remains regarding the extent to which age justifies special treatment (i.e. the relevance of a specific application of the capability approach). If the main idea of the capability approach is the question of what people are able to do or to be, then the answer to this question does not lie in specialising certain groups in society (in our case, children) but in recognising the singularity of every person. Every person with his or her particular features needs commodities and social resources so they can enjoy their capabilities. As age can be understood as implying a certain degree of vulnerability, it might be more appropriate to argue that every person carries with him/her certain vulnerability:

> A CA starts with notions of human frailty and vulnerability, and it argues that, from a moral standpoint, the state has an obligation to ensure that all persons have access to a life worthy of human dignity – in their frailty and vulnerability. (Dixon and Nussbaum 2012: 572)

While Dixon and Nussbaum acknowledge this position, they nevertheless take a rather ambiguous position towards children when they make a case for a special priority status for children that recognises their special vulnerability.

9.5 Conclusion: "We Are All Children"

If it is the case, as Dixon and Nussbaum (2012) have argued, that every human being is vulnerable – and we think they are – and that agency can only be realised through our relationships with others, as Deneulin and McGregor (2010) have contended, then it might be much more convincing to conclude that "we are all children" (Mortier 2002), rather than assume that we are all adults in the sense of autonomous and free human beings. The idea that is expressed in the statement "we are all children" is twofold. First of all, it suggests that the distinction between children and adults based on the idea of the competent and autonomous human being is less relevant than generally assumed. However, we do not intend to claim that children should be treated as adults by portraying them as autonomous and independent agents. Instead, we argue that the agency of children, just like the agency of adults, is not so much an individual trait. Agency, both for children and adults, is something that is realised within a certain context and in an interrelationship with persons in this context (Stoecklin 2013). Hence, proponents of the framework of children's rights should recognise that the egalitarian individualistic notion of agency does not correspond with reality. As for the capability approach, this means that there is not much ground to grant special priority to children compared to adults. Secondly, since "agency" and "freedom of choice" are contextually shaped, both children and adults need support to be able to realise their agency and freedom of choice. Children's rights offer this support in terms of granting them entitlements to primary resources, while the capability approach pays attention to how people can make use of these recourses and commodities in their concrete contexts. As such, rights and capabilities complement each other in a fundamental way.

Furthermore, if we need a certain degree of belonging to realise agency, the question of solidarity, both at the relational as well as the structural level, then comes into play (Thomas 2012). At the relational level, Deneulin and McGregor (2010) explained that we should not focus on the idea of "living well," but instead "living well together." This expands the issue of freedom from a question of the conditions under which people can "live a life they value to live" to a question of how people "live a life they value in relation to others" in society. The latter requires a learning process where people learn to live together, based on mutual engagement and understanding (Reynaert et al. 2010). As freedom is a principle to value, it should be considered in relation to the freedom of others, including future generations: "*This leads us not to ethical individualism, but to an 'ethic of the social human being', in which individual freedoms are constituted by social arrangements that enable us to live well together*" (Deneulin and McGregor 2010: 510). At the structural level, the relevant question is how people can live a life that *society* has reason to value. From a more negative stance, this interrogates the extent to which "state paternalism" can be allowed. (Legal) norms and public institutions such as courts are necessary to assess whether state paternalism in a certain case is legitimised. From a more positive view, the concept of living well together is about a collective learning process of "public reasoning," where society as a whole learns the valuable freedoms that public policy should promote: "*It is through public reasoning or public discussion that each society is to determine which freedoms it should promote or discourage*" (Deneulin and McGregor 2010: 513). Translated to the issue of the institutionalised youth land, this means that, as members of a society, we must reflect on the significance of the institutionalised youth land today and whether it contributes to a greater respect for the human dignity of children; if it does not, we must determine how to change these institutionalised social arrangements. If the socio-cultural structuring of childhood is progressively expanding, as we have contended, and this expansion results in conflictual relations between children and adults, then the question of intergenerational justice and solidarity cannot be avoided. In terms of children's rights and the capability approach, our attempt should not be focused on how to develop an approach where the CA and children's rights complement each other and vice versa to increase the respect for the human dignity of children, as this would "enclose" the debate *within* the institutionalised youth land. Instead, we should aim to advance a perspective on children's rights and the CA starting from a human rights framework that strives for the respect of human dignity for all people, including both children and adults, and acknowledges the necessary interrelatedness.

References

Alanen, L. (2011). Critical childhood studies? *Childhood, 18*(2), 147–150.

Andresen, S., Otto, H.-U., & Ziegler, H. (2006). Education and welfare: A pedagogical perspective on the capability approach. In *Freedom and social justice*. Documentation of the 2006 International Conference of the Human Development and Capability Association, Groningen.

Archard, D. (2004). *Children. Rights and childhood* (2nd ed.). London/New York: Routledge.

Bailleau, F., Cartuyvels, Y., & De Fraene, D. (2009). La criminalisation des mineurs et le jeu des sanctions. *Déviance et Société, 33*(1), 255–269.

Ballet, J., Biggeri, M., & Comim, F. (2011). Children's agency and the capability approach: A conceptual framework. In M. Biggeri, J. Ballet, & F. Comim (Eds.), *Children and the capability approach* (pp. 22–45). London: Palgrave Macmillan.

Cockburn, T. (2005). Children and the feminist ethic of care. *Childhood, 12*(1), 71–89.

Comim, F., Qizilbash, M., & Alkire, S. (2008). *The capability approach. Concepts, measures and applications*. Cambridge: University Press.

Comim, F., Ballet, J., Biggeri, M., & Iervese, V. (2011). Introduction: Theoretical foundations and the book's roadmap. In M. Biggeri, J. Ballet, & F. Comim (Eds.), *Children and the capability approach* (pp. 3–21). London: Palgrave Macmillan.

Coussée, F. (2008). *A century of youth work policy*. Ghent: Academia Press.

Dean, H. (2009). Critiquing capabilities: The distractions of a beguiling concept. *Critical Social Policy, 29*(2), 261–278.

Deneulin, S. (2008). Beyond individual freedom and agency: Structures of living together in the capability approach. In F. Comim, M. Qizilbash, & S. Alkire (Eds.), *The capability approach. Concepts, measures and applications*. Cambridge: University Press.

Deneulin, S., & McGregor, J. A. (2010). The capability approach and the politics of a social conception of wellbeing. *European Journal of Social Theory, 13*(4), 501–519.

Dixon, R., & Nussbaum, M. C. (2012). Children's rights and a capabilities approach: The question of special priority. *Cornell Law Review, 97*, 549–594.

Ellis, K., & France, A. (2010). Being judged, being assessed: Young people's perspectives of assessment in youth justice and education. *Children & Society, 26*(2), 112–123.

Evans, T. (2005). International human rights law as power/knowledge. *Human Rights Quarterly, 27*(3), 1046–1068.

Fernando, J. L. (2001). Children's rights: Beyond the impasse. *The Annals of the American Academy of Political and Social Science, 575*, 8–24.

Freeman, M. (2007). Why it remains important to take children's rights seriously. *International Journal of Children's Rights, 15*(1), 5–23.

Giddens, A. (1984). *The constitution of society. Outline of the theory of structuration*. Cambridge: Polity Press.

Guggenheim, M. (2005). *What's wrong with children's rights?* Cambridge: Harvard University Press.

Hanson, K. (2012). Schools of thought in children's rights. In M. Liebel (Ed.), *Children's rights from below: Cross-cultural perspectives* (pp. 63–79). Hampshire: Palgrave Macmillan.

Hemrica, J., & Heyting, F. (2004). Tacit notions of childhood: An analysis of discourse about child participation in decision-making regarding arrangements in the case of parental divorce. *Childhood, 11*(4), 449–468.

Honig, M.-S. (2008). Work and care: Reconstructing childhood through childcare policy in Germany. In A. James & A. L. James (Eds.), *European childhoods. Cultures, politics and childhoods in Europe* (pp. 198–215). Hampshire: Palgrave Macmillan.

Huntington, C. (2006). Rights myopia in child welfare. *UCLA Law Review, 53*(3), 637–699.

James, A. (2009). Agency. In J. Qvortrup, W. A. Corsaro, & M.-S. Honig (Eds.), *The Palgrave handbook of childhood studies* (pp. 34–45). Hampshire: Palgrave Macmillan.

James, A. L., & James, A. (2001). Tightening the net: Children, community, and control. *British Journal of Sociology, 52*(2), 211–228.

James, A., & James, A. L. (2004). *Constructing childhood: Theory, policy and social practice*. Hampshire: Palgrave Macmillan.

James, A., & James, A. L. (2012). *Key concepts in childhood studies* (2nd ed.). London: Sage.

King, M. (2007). The sociology of childhood as scientific communication: Observations from a social systems perspective. *Childhood, 14*(2), 193–213.

Macleod, C. M. (2010). Primary goods, capabilities, and children. In H. Brighouse & I. Robeyns (Eds.), *Measuring justice. Primary goods and capabilities* (pp. 174–192). Cambridge: Cambridge University Press.

Masschelein, J., & Quaghebeur, K. (2005). Participation for better or for worse? *Journal of Philosophy of Education, 39*(1), 51–65.
Mierendorff, J. (2007). *Western childhood and the welfare state. Some theoretical reflections about an old interrelationship.* International seminars. European Centre for Social Welfare Policy and Research, Vienna (Austria). Retrieved from http://www.euro.centre.org/detail.php?xml_id=901
Minow, M. (1995). What ever happened to children's rights? *Minnesota Law Review, 80*, 269–297.
Mollenhauer, K. (1993). *Vergeten samenhang. Over cultuur en opvoeding* [Forgotten connections. On culture and education] (2nd ed.). Amsterdam: Boom.
Mortier, F. (2002). We zijn allemaal kinderen: Bruggen tussen rechten voor kinderen en rechten voor volwassenen. *Tijdschrift voor Jeugdrecht en Kinderrechten, 3*(extra editie), 10–17.
Muncie, J. (2006). Governing young people: Coherence and contradiction in contemporary youth justice. *Critical Social Policy, 26*(4), 770–793.
Nibell, L. N., Shook, J. J., & Finn, J. L. (2009). *Childhood, youth, and social work in transformation: Implications for policy.* New York: Columbia University Press.
Nussbaum, M. C. (1997). Capabilities and human rights. *Fordham Law Review, 66*(2), 273–300.
Nussbaum, M. C. (2011). *Creating capabilities. The human development approach.* Cambridge, MA: Harvard University Press.
Otto, H.-U., & Ziegler, H. (Eds.). (2010). *Education, welfare and the capabilities approach. A European perspective.* Leverkusen: Barbara Budrich Publishers.
Pupavac, V. (2001). Misanthropy without borders: The international children's rights regime. *Disasters, 25*(2), 95–112.
Quennerstedt, A. (2010). Children, but not really humans? Critical reflections on the hampering effect of the "3 p's.". *International Journal of Children's Rights, 18*, 619–635.
Reynaert, D., Bouverne-De Bie, M., & Vandevelde, S. (2009). A review of children's rights literature since the adoption of the United Nations Convention on the Rights of the Child. *Childhood, 16*(4), 518–534.
Reynaert, D., Bouverne-De Bie, M., & Vandevelde, S. (2010). Children's rights education and social work: Contrasting models and understandings. *International Social Work, 53*(4), 443–456.
Reynaert, D., Bouverne-De Bie, M., & Vandevelde, S. (2012). Between "believers" and "opponents": Critical discussions on children's rights. *International Journal of Children's Rights, 20* (1), 155–168.
Robeyns, I. (2005). The capability approach: A theoretical survey. *Journal of Human Development, 6*(1), 93–114.
Robeyns, I. (2006). Three models of education: Rights, capabilities and human capital. *Theory and Research in Education, 4*(1), 69–84.
Roose, R., & Bouverne-De Bie, M. (2007). Do children have rights or do their rights have to be realised? The United Nations Convention on the Rights of the Child as a frame of reference for pedagogical action. *Journal of Philosophy of Education, 41*(3), 431–443.
Roose, R., & Bouverne-De Bie, M. (2008). Children's rights: A challenge for social work. *International Social Work, 51*(1), 37–46.
Saito, M. (2003). Amartya Sen's capability approach to education: A critical exploration. *Journal of Philosophy of Education, 37*(3), 17–33.
Sen, A. (1999). *Development as freedom.* Oxford: Oxford University Press.
Sen, A. (2005). Human rights and capabilities. *Journal of Human Development, 6*(2), 151–166.
Stoecklin, D. (2013). Theories of action in the field of child participation. In search of explicit frameworks. *Childhood, 20*(4), 441–455.
Such, E., & Walker, R. (2005). Young citizens or policy objects? Children in the "rights and responsibilities" debate. *Journal of Social Policy, 34*, 39–57.
Thomas, N. (2012). Love, rights and solidarity: Studying children's participation using Honneth's theory of recognition. *Childhood, 19*(4), 453–466.

Valentine, K. (2011). Accounting for agency. *Children & Society, 25*(5), 347–358.
Vandenbroeck, M., & Bouverne-De Bie, M. (2006). Children's agency and educational norms: A tense negotiation. *Childhood, 13*(1), 127–143.
Verhellen, E. (1998). *Jeugdbeschermingsrecht*. Ghent: Mys & Breesch.
Verhellen, E. (2000). *Convention on the rights of the child.´Background, motivation, strategies, main themes*. Leuven/Apeldoorn: Garant Publishers.
Zinnecker, J. (2000). Childhood and adolescence as pedagogic moratoria. *Zeitschrift für Pädagogik, 46*(2), 36–68.

Chapter 10
The Participation of Children in Care in the Assessment Process

Pierrine Robin

10.1 Introduction

In child protection policy, children are regarded more as an object to be protected than as the subject of rights (Wolff et al. 2013). This is tied to the history of child protection. Child protection policy emerged in the nineteenth century with the idea that the State should intervene in the private lives of families to protect the weaker members of the family unit. But as Youf (2002) stressed, child protection policy in France was not built with an approach based on children's rights, but with the intent to preserve the social order and pursue a demographic objective. Child protection law did not intend to promote a philosophy of human rights and children's rights, but aimed to fight the lack of adaptation of children at the fringes of society. In a path-dependent way, the French child protection law of 1945 does not promote the individual rights of the child. This also relates to the familialist social model in France. In a holistic approach, the individual is considered as a part of the family. The family is the proof of the anteriority and supremacy of society over individuals. In this conception, giving individual rights to family members is seen as a step towards the destruction of the social fabric and society (Commaille 2008). Furthermore, in child protection, rights to protection were for a long time seen as antagonistic to civil rights. Children were seen more as vulnerable human beings in need of protection than as possible autonomous actors (Wolff et al. 2013).

Nevertheless, the status of the child in care has evolved considerably with the adoption by the United Nations of the Convention on the Rights of the Child (UNCRC 1989). The States parties to the UNCRC recognize the child as a rights holder, including both socio-economic and civil rights. They must therefore grant him/her protection, provision of services, and effective possibilities for participation. The UN Convention on the rights of child also enhances the rights of children

P. Robin (✉)
Department of Educational Sciences, University of Paris Est Créteil, 61 Avenue du Général de Gaulle, 94010 Créteil, Paris, France
e-mail: pierrine.robin@u-pec.fr

D. Stoecklin and J.-M. Bonvin (eds.), *Children's Rights and the Capability Approach*, Children's Well-Being: Indicators and Research 8, DOI 10.1007/978-94-017-9091-8_10,

in care: for instance, children must be provided the opportunity to be heard in any judicial and administrative proceedings affecting them. Similarly, they have the right to be heard in care during the assessment of their situation. Furthermore, the 2005 Council of Europe recommendation on the rights of children living in institutions sets out a number of specific rights, such as the right to take part in the decision-making process and the individual care plan (Council of Europe 2005). But unlike the UNCRC, these guidelines are not legally binding. In 2009, the European Committee for Social Cohesion evaluated the implementation of the recommendation and showed numerous difficulties (Council of Europe 2009). This is precisely to overcome such obstacles that Sen (2000) pointed out the necessity of paying attention not only to appropriate procedures but also to the availability of adequate opportunities for enhancing participation.

France is beginning to adapt its legislation to these recent international norms. The March 5, 2007 reform incorporated many of these principles: decisions must take into account the best interests of the child, who has the right to take part in the assessment process via the set-up of the individual care plan. In addition, the reform gives administrative services the primary responsibility for conducting the assessment, in line with the principle of double subsidiarity: state intervention is supplementary to the intervention of parents in raising their children, and the intervention of courts does not come until after the intervention of the administration. The main idea is to bolster voluntary help, prior to imposing compulsory help. This reform takes place in the wider context of transforming social work, following a contractual approach where more freedoms but also more responsibilities are given to children and their families (Astier 2007).

But the law doesn't clearly choose between the aforementioned familialist pattern and a new child-centered paradigm. It states, for example, that parents sign the individual care plan, but makes no explicit mention of the child's participation. According to Commaille (2008), although we can see the evolution towards a more child-centered approach, the ambiguity in the law and its implementation shows the lasting weight of the old familialist pattern. It is important in this context to try to understand the difficulties resulting from the gap between formal and real rights of the child during the assessment process. Indeed, it is not because participation with children in care is difficult that implementation of the democratic requirement and research in this area proves any less necessary (Wolff 2007).

Several difficulties immediately arise when designing and implementing a system for children's participation in care. The first lies in the fact that the aid relationship is not equal; it creates dependency by its very nature, especially when it is formed over a long period of time (Chauvière 2002). Furthermore children in this situation do not have a choice as to whether professionals deal with their case, so that help may be constrained. Moreover, this aid relationship is established by adult professionals who face children with lower bargaining power (Robin 2010). Moreover, there are multiple actors with potentially divergent interests in the child protection field. This is why it is vital, according to Wiesner (2006) and Münder et al. (2000), to consider the rights of the child in this context, where s/he finds himself in a vulnerable and unequal position.

But surprisingly, the sociology of weak actors (Payet et al. 2008) has omitted children as a category of vulnerable actors suffering from systematic deprivation of substantive opportunities to participate. However, it would be heuristic to attempt to understand children through the prism of the sociology of weak actors. In this approach, the actors are not seen as weak in themselves, but rather weakened by structural social relations with institutions that make them more vulnerable. This does not preclude their achieving strategies and new rules in the circles of power and within the institutions involved. But very little empirical research has sought to analyze the strategies and possibilities of child participation in care. The latter were mainly developed in the field of childhood studies.

After having been ignored for a long time, the issue of child participation in decision-making processes in care has recently been subjected to extensive research, mainly in the English- and German-speaking literature. Although the epistemological and methodological perspectives are different, the research leads to the same conclusion, pointing out a large gap between the theory and practice of participation (Cashmore 2002). Leading research in this area, notably in Australia, shows the difficulty of conceiving the child as a subject in his/her own right during the assessment process (Mason and Michaux 2005). Professionals show greater ability to communicate with parents than with children during the assessment process; they fear that asking the children direct questions about their situation will make them more vulnerable. And the child's view appears little in the assessment, and is never a key factor in the decision (Mason and Michaux 2005). English studies have led to similar results. Interviewed professionals are convinced of the need for participation, however studies show that children are barely seen or heard during the assessment process. In dangerous situations, professionals are especially unlikely to engage in a process of meaningful child participation. Participation by children is encouraged primarily to get them to accept assistance rather than to give them the possibility of helping to shape it. The words of the child are used to justify the point of view of the professionals (Katz 1995). In this sense, participation is not used to question existing power relations; on the contrary, it strengthens them. This is why Holland (2001) refers to a process of "ongoing silencing of the voices of children".

The issue of child participation in decision-making processes remains unexplored in France. This is why we tried in our PhD thesis to study the participation of children in care assessment processes. We envisage the assessment as a process which "aims to systematically determine the extent to which the well-being of the child is threatened by any element connected to his/her environment, in order to propose appropriate action" (Boutin and Durning 2008: 77). The assessment process can take place as a diagnostic function, before assistance is given, or in the course of action to assess the evolution of the situation. Using biographical interviews with 16 children aged 11–19, in and out of care, we sought to understand how assessments were experienced by the children, and the role they were able to play in the process. We pointed out the enormous gap between the formal rights of the child to be heard in the assessment process and the possibility of exercising those rights. In this chapter, however, we will try to identify the individual and social factors influencing children's participation in the assessment process. After presenting our theoretical and methodological framework, we will disclose some of the results of our empirical study of children's experiences in the care assessment process.

10.2 Theoretical Framework

According to Stoecklin (2013: 454), "The child is considered a 'subject of rights' as soon as the child is born. But the child's ability to obtain respect for personal rights is only progressively elaborated". To understand the discrepancy between formal rights and real rights, it is important to empirically study children's evolving capacities and agency. He argues that "the extent to which individuals develop their agency depends on the interaction between their evolving capacities and dynamic contexts they live in, and this is actually a non-linear lifelong process". Indeed, there is a cumulative interaction between individual factors and social context in the development of agency. In this sense, the capability approach could be of interest in understanding the development of children's agency. This approach insists on the idea of interconnections, interlinkages, and complementarity between individual factors and social opportunities in the improvement of power and agency.

The capability approach was developed by Sen (1999) and Nussbaum (2000) over the past two decades, and focuses on development policies. Central to this approach is the idea that the person is an active participant in change, rather than a passive recipient of dispensed assistance. Participation is a pillar of this approach, which espouses the notion that giving people more opportunities to take part in and make choices reinforces their capabilities to choose the things they have reason to value. The approach aims to capture the ability of people to pursue goals that they value and have reason to value: "The freedoms of persons can be judged through explicit reference to outcomes and processes that they have reason to value and seek" (Sen 1999: 86).

A distinction is made between instrumental freedom and substantive freedom, and capability is defined as a "set of vectors of functionings" reflecting the person's freedom "to lead one type of life or another... to choose from possible livings". According to Sen (1999: 75), "a person's 'capability' refers to the alternative combinations of functionings that are feasible for her to achieve. Capability is thus a kind of freedom: the substantive freedom to achieve alternative functioning combinations".

A key element of this approach lies in the interlinkages between the distinct types of freedom. The central idea of the capability approach is that there are interconnections between individual and social factors in the development of these capabilities. To understand the interlinkages of individual and social factors in the concept of capabilities, Sen developed the concept of "socially determined capabilities" (Sen 2000). In this approach, social arrangements should aim to expand people's capabilities:

> The capabilities that a person does actually have (and not merely theoretically enjoys) depend on the nature of social arrangements, which can be crucial for individual freedoms. And there the state and the society cannot escape responsibility.

The approach attaches particular importance to the role of public discussion and interaction in the emergence of shared values and commitments:

> The politics of social consensus calls not only for acting on the basis of given individual preferences, but also for sensitivity of social decision to the development of individual preferences. (Sen 1999: 253)

To capture preference building through social interaction, Sen develops the concept of "partial accord":

> It's also important to recognize that social arrangements and adequate public policies do not require that there be a unique 'social ordering' that completely ranks all the alternative social possibilities. Practical agreements still separate out acceptable options (and weed out unacceptable ones), and a workable solution can be based on the contingent acceptance of particular provisions, without demanding complete social unanimity. (Sen 1999: 253)

Sen attaches particular importance to the development of capabilities of persons enduring systematic deprivation. Class and sex inequalities were thoroughly pointed out, and poverty was analyzed as a form of capability deprivation. A related concept, stigma, was also seen as a deprivation of the social opportunities to take part in society. The capability "to go without shame" has been given a central position in Sen's (1999) and Nussbaum's (2004) lists of basic capabilities, yet the notion is underdeveloped, philosophically and empirically, in this work (Crabtree 2008: 57). In addition, particular attention was paid to women's agency. Sen stresses that women and men have both congruent and conflicting interests that affect family living. According to him, "the impact of greater empowerment and independent agency of women thus includes the correction of the iniquities that blight the lives and well-being of women vis-à-vis men" in societies with strong "anti-female bias" (Sen 1999: 193).

Children, like women, suffer from inequality, and there is growing interest in integrating the capability approach into the field of children's rights studies (Biggeri et al. 2011) to analyze the development of children's capabilities in vulnerable situations. Nevertheless, its application has yet to be explored. A holistic approach of capabilities could be interesting to better understand the participation of children as a process influenced by individual factors, socio-economic realities of the children's lives, and their relationship with adults and peers in their communities (Feeny and Boyden 2004). The capability approach also points out that participation of children is related to the representations of children, their vulnerabilities, and their capacities. Furthermore, it stresses that participation of children is related to the services at their disposal and the understanding of those services. But according to Biggeri et al. (2011), applying this approach to areas such as health and education is somewhat problematic, though some studies have recently looked into these issues.

However, the development of children's agency has been widely studied in the field of children's rights, principally through the analysis of participatory processes in the context of interdependence and reciprocity (Lansdown 2010). For Smith (2002), participation is not a linear process or one that flows from adult to child, but a reciprocal activity in which children and adults build understanding and common knowledge. For this common understanding, emotion and effective communication are important. Thus, Smith (2002) shows that children are more likely to explain their views to an adult they trust, and with whom they can develop a relationship of reciprocity. Liebel (2010) distinguishes between ascending and descending participation. While descending participation is conducted by adults in a possibly adult-centric way, ascending participation is initiated by children and includes their subjective perspectives. Stoecklin (2013: 453) advocates for more attention to be paid to "children's experience of their rights" and to how children make sense of everyday life. He argues that "assessments of participation remain fragile and possibly ethnocentric as long as we do not have a clearer understanding of the participants' subjective sense of reality" (Stoecklin 2013: 447). He also argues for the development of more child-friendly methodologies to study participation processes.

10.3 Research Methods

In order to develop a child-friendly methodology, we used biographical methods in our work to understand the participation of children in care in the assessment process. The choice of a biographical approach is partly due to its heuristic and ethical attributes. Because it allows the linking of individual dynamics and normative constraints, taking into account the socio-historical contexts in which they occur, the biographical approach has strong heuristic value for sociology and educational science (Bessin 2009). Additionally, from an ethical point of view, the use of narratives can give stigmatized actors a chance to reopen the path to recognition (Butler 2007). Indeed, as Truc (2005) was able to conclude from the work of Ricoeur (1990), narration allows the individual, who is not the author of his or her actions and does not control their consequences, to keep making sense of the situation.

We conducted 16 biographical interviews with children and young people, both in and out of care, on their experiences and perception of participation in their assessment processes in two French sub-regional province[1] (Drôme and Ain). The originality of our methodology lies partly in the fact that each child and adolescent we interviewed nominated a further five people involved in their lives. We got in touch with respondents via children's social services, following a random drawing of a panel and the acceptance of the research process by the respondents.

[1] In French administrative organisation the "departments" are in charge of child protection. The "department" (ie Province) is a local authority between the region and the town council.

Analyzing biographical interviews is not easy. It should be noted that a narrative is always collected at a specific point in time in the history of the subject, and that it is colored by meetings and positive or negative experiences. Therefore, the story and the feelings expressed are marked by reconstruction of the past in the present (Hamman 2002). Taking into account these principles of analysis, we will try in this chapter to understand the experiences of children and young people in assessment processes, and to analyze the factors that facilitate or hinder their involvement. The names of the children we interviewed were changed to protect their identity.

10.4 A Strongly Constrained Context with Little Possibility of Participation

Except in cases where children were involved in the request for assistance, they have few memories of the initial assessment: "I don't remember having met a family assistant. My first memory is the placement." (Adeline, 19 years old) The lack of memories associated with the administrative assessment raises questions; it cannot simply be attributed to a lack of memory in children. In fact, Frechon and Dumaret (2008) emphasize, in a meta-analysis of studies on the fate of placed children, that biographical research showed their capacity to remember such things. Could a weak memory be explained by post-traumatic amnesia, linked to the shock of separation? It is difficult to answer, but we can see that children have very specific memories of other events having taken place during the same period. They can for example give the exact date of court proceedings. This would qualify as partial amnesia, then! But can't we consider the lack of memories about administrative assessments to be related to the low participation of children in the initial process?

Indeed, most of the children interviewed point to their lack of participation in the initial assessment of their own situation. Ten out of the 16 children interviewed mention not being heard in the assessment process: "They spoke while I was not there. I was not in the room. I didn't follow the conversation." (Abdel, 13 years old) Four interviewees said that they were heard alone, while their parents were not present: "I couldn't really talk to my parents, only it was a little better." (Marie, 14 years old) Two emphasized that it was important that parents heard what they had to say, yet they didn't: "Actually, it did not bother me to have the social worker talk to me, but I would have loved my mother to hear it, because afterwards I would not have known how to explain and tell her about it." (Abdel, 13 years old) Although our corpus is not representative, the results reflect the heterogeneity of professional practices in the implementation of child participation, as recognized in Article 12 of the International Convention on the Rights of the Child.

And when they *are* heard, children and young people speak of having difficulty trusting adults during the primary assessment and having had to explain their story to different stakeholders: "We have to re-explain things all the time." (Fred,

19 years old) In addition, children emphasize the difficulty they have speaking in front of adults they do not know: "For a child, it is difficult to talk to an adult because of the age difference." (Marie, 14 years old) This is due to the fact that they feel they will not be believed, if they are not supported by a third person:

> I could not explain my situation; it was mostly her (the province head) who was speaking. She did not see the situation as I did. It looked like she did not believe what I was saying. She contradicted me [...]. At the beginning, I would have wanted to be listened to more. (Elodie, 14 years old)

In this difficult configuration, some of the youth eventually ended up resigned and kept silent about the choice of assistance means.

In defining help, certain children, adolescents and youth remember a meeting with a social worker who helped them choose between different types of assistance: "I saw a social worker. She understood better; she offered me solutions. She told me where I could find them." (Marie, 14 years old) Others emphasize that their participation was limited by the lack of information they were given about the different possibilities for help. Six of the young people interviewed see themselves as actors in the decision made: "I'm the one who decided to come here. I'm the one who wanted to be placed." (Assia, 16 years old). For the ten others, however, the decision was imposed on them: "I didn't want to go. They told me I had to." (Abdel, 13 years old).

In the choice of placement housing, three remember having written a letter to the children's/family supervisor specifying their housing preference in terms of placement facilities. But despite the requests, their preference was not always heeded. The majority of youths interviewed said that the housing facility was imposed on them: "They told me: 'where there's room, you'll be placed'. I would have liked to have been more or less informed." (Elodie, 14 years old).

Regarding their ongoing assessment procedure, only one spoke of having been able to take part in the group review meetings where all the professionals were present. Most only remember the moments they were able to speak one-on-one with their advisor. The group meetings were thus seen by the interviewees as a space reserved for professionals, where children did not belong. One child, however, was allowed to attend a meeting usually reserved for professionals when her case was at an impasse:

> They conducted reviews. They went to the General Council [i.e., province level]. Usually, I wasn't supposed to participate. Children can't go. Usually, I had no business being there. There was a special review. I went because the situation was at an impasse. They couldn't find a solution; that's why I went. (Assia, 16 years old)

In our cases children were given the possibility of attending meetings when adults are essentially unable to find solutions for their situation, whereas they are usually left out of the negotiations. This is what a girl explained to us; the scheduling for weekend family visits was imposed on her:

> They didn't even ask me about the schedule. The General Council came up with the schedule. I got it when it was finished. They opposed... um, I mean, imposed it on me. I told my dad about it. He said that they weren't going to change the schedule for me.

> The schedule itself said that we would rediscuss it together for vacations, but I don't know if I'll be there for that 'together'. Given that it's my situation, I'd like to be able to give my point of view, so that we could look at things together. The social worker does a bunch of stuff I don't know about. I'd like for us to meet and work everything out. (Elodie, 14 years old)

Thus, from the moment they are placed until the preparations are made for them to leave placement, children are not involved in the decisions concerning them, even though they are the ones most affected.

10.5 Inequality, Stigma, and Discrimination

This non-participatory experience can be linked to the asymmetric relationship between professionals and users of social services. But it isn't just the dominant position of professionals that creates difficulties for children, adolescents and youths; it's also the alliances between adults. Indeed, during the assessment process, parents are heard more than their children. As though the child's voice has less value than those of adults, as this young girl explains, trying to show that a child can also be competent enough to make rational choices:

> Children are not heard simply because they are children. It's as if they thought I was lying, and only believed my parents. I cannot understand that. A child also knows what s/he is doing! (Océane, 19 years old)

It took until the 1980s for children's voices to become more credible in the eyes of many, but their voices remain fragile when going up against dominant adult speech. Professionals and parents "go before", children "come second". To make their voices and rationales heard, children, as "minors", have to redouble their efforts in the face of professionals who, caught up in the narrative of the parents, can forget the perception of the child.

Therefore, according to Leeson (2007: 274):

> There needs to be recognition of the power adults have in children's lives. Adults caring for children in these situations wield considerable power vested in them by the authority but are not aware of the power they hold simply by being adults. There is an anxiety to protect the children from making the wrong decisions. This fits with the nature of current social work practice being risk-averse, but leads to serious questions about why children are being denied the right to make mistakes, draw their own conclusions and learn or even to have the right to change their mind.

The over-protectiveness by adults can also be seen as discrimination against children. Liebel (2010: 85) lists as a form of age-based discrimination "the measures justified by the need to protect children but which lead to their being limited and marginalized".

We can see that children in care are marginalized in the decision-making process and that their voice is stamped with the seal of incompetence, the effect of a discriminatory process that can lead to stigma:

> We're not all mean kids, delinquent kids, or battered kids. There are stereotypes in everybody's head. A lot of people think that a placed child has problems, is a disturbed kid, one who has run away or taken drugs. You can't stereotype. Young people are not all the same. Young people are being difficult because they're not being heard, like they want to be. (Océane, 19 years old)

In Goffman's thesis cited by Nussbaum (2004), stigma is seen as an instrument used by a dominant group over a less powerful group to somehow make them appear less competent. Nussbaum (2004: 234) links stigma to primitive shame:

> Often, the reasons why people form such groups and target others is a kind of deeply irrational fear of defect that is part of a more general shrinking from something troubling about human life, a search for an impossible type of hardness, safety and self-sufficiency.

But as the capability approach shows, stigma can deprive people of the basic ability to participate in the community. Indeed, children's capabilities are tied to the representations people have of them and their vulnerability and abilities. Taking into account Sen's analysis of women's agency, we can say that the development of empowerment and independent agency of children in care includes the correction of the iniquity and stigma that blight their lives and well-being.

However, in the context of descending participation with the highly unequal position of children, we observed in our empirical study that the opportunities for children in care to assess their own situation differed and evolved according to individual and social factors.

10.6 Reflexivity and Initiative at the Moment of Entry into Care: Key Individual Factors for Participation

In light of our empirical studies, it appears that two individual factors strongly influence children's possibilities for further participation in the assessment of their situation: reflexivity about their own history and taking initiative when entering the system. Thus, as shown in Germany by Münder and Mutke (2001), we must distinguish between children who take the initiative of entering the arrangement and those who do not.

In our corpus, seven of the 16 children interviewed could say that they were the instigators of their own protection. They are the children who were the most expansive about their family history. They very quickly perceived themselves to be in danger, and said they seized the initiative themselves to reach out to social services. They then had the impression of maintaining control over decisions throughout the process: "I started coming here. (...) In my case, it was me who decided everything from the beginning to the end." (Assia, 16 years old).

On the contrary, children who did not contact social services themselves had the feeling of being subjected to the help of adults. These children, who have a highly fragmented view of their own history, felt unable to take part in the assessment of their own situation. Such was the case of Abdel (13 years old):

> First, I left for a foster family. The foster family was going to look after me. I said nothing; the decision had already been made. (...) They talked about it while I wasn't there. (...) I was little, I couldn't find the right words, and it was done quickly. I did not want to go there. They told me that I had to.

Children in similar circumstances did not feel in control of initial or subsequent placement decisions. Assigned a status akin to an object, they compared themselves to 'bags':

> A social worker told me I was going to change foster families. (...) The decision was imposed on me. I did not want to leave. I felt like a suitcase being transported from one place to another. They did not ask for my opinion. I was introduced to these people. They took me home. I was told 'you will go there'. (Océane, 19 years old)

Nevertheless, some children who perceived themselves to be objects of adult intervention could, through the process of social assistance, consider themselves subjects of the intervention and learn to take part in the decision:

> Before, it happened without me, now it's happening with me. During the first court proceeding, I said nothing, I cried (...). But at the third court proceeding, it was my mother who was crying and it was me who was talking. (Abdel, 13 years old)

In this example, the boy in the first court proceeding was an "infant" who could not speak, only cry. But at the third hearing, he placed himself in the position of an actor capable of speaking and acting, and his mother was the helpless one with only tears to express herself. This illustrates the recursive dimension of participation. Through the process of help and social opportunities, this child was able to develop an individual capacity to take part in the assessment process in care.

This is why the potential involvement of children in assessing their situation is not just linked to individual factors, i.e. reflexivity about their own history and initiating entry into the system; it also evolves through interaction with social factors.

10.7 Crucial Social Factors: The Services Available and Their Design

In our empirical study, the main social factors identified as influences on child participation in the assessment process are related to the services at their disposal as well as their design.

Let us reflect for a moment on the perception of children about social services at their disposal in assessment processes, and the quality of these services, in order to better understand the social factors which influence participation.

First of all, the children interviewed mentioned having had difficulties explaining their story to different stakeholders, due to the turnover of professionals:

> You confide in someone. When that changes, you have to start the file again from the beginning, if it hasn't been transferred during the change in host families, juvenile centers, or psychologists. (Océane, 19 years old)

They want greater importance attached to the transitional period, when they could develop more self-confidence and "be tamed" before undertaking the assessment:

I think they have to try to get to know me a little more. When I saw my psychologist, she immediately asked: 'What's the problem?', even though I don't know her. She needs to know me better, take more time, and talk with the school to see what my behavior is like there. We first have to talk about different things. With the social worker, I take trips; we talked a little about everything. Those were good times". (Elodie, 14 years old)

They also demand to be listened to more carefully: "It's better when you have an adult who will listen. When you explain the situation and they don't believe you, it does not make you want to continue." (Marie, 14 years old) They want to be heard, whatever their age, and not in formal and imposed meetings:

> There should be a little more listening to the wishes of young people, whether they are in their teens, pre-teens, or younger. You can't stereotype. Young people are not all the same. Young people are being difficult because they're not being heard, like they want to be. That listening ear is lacking between the ages of 7 and 12. They should take into account what the young person has to say, give them the opportunity to express themselves when they want and not necessarily impose meetings on them, and act according to the wishes of the young person. Foster families have the right to be heard; why would youth not have the right to be listened to when they want? People only listen when it is required. (Océane, 19 years old)

This narrative echoes the risk pointed out by Pluto (2007), i.e. that professionals only see the formal and procedural side of participation, that they use it when their processes need to be legitimized, while attaching little importance to the results of such participation. She also recommends paying attention to all verbal and non-verbal forms of expression of the children being assessed.

In the narrative of children in care, assessments during placement are in turn presented as a constraint or support, as the approach of assessment was retrospective or prospective.

The ongoing assessment is experienced by young people as a burden they try to avoid when it focuses solely on family history:

> They ask us the same thing all the time: "have you seen your mother? "It ends up being boring. I feel controlled. At the age of 16, I started to shrug it off a little better, almost all the time, but there was always a sense of rehashing things. (Fred, 19 years old)

Conversely, when the assessment served as an opportunity for advice and guidance for the future, it was perceived positively: "Some helped a lot and have been able to support me, understand me, help me, guide me." (Adeline, 19 years old). For Bernoux (2004), returning to the past during the assessment process is only of real interest if it refers to a future perspective. In this sense, we can say that participation is interesting only insofar as it connects to concrete choices for children.

Moreover, for all the children interviewed, the assessment is seen as a time for review, "for an update on what was and what was not", "to share some positive elements, some negative elements, and elements that must be improved" (Albert,

17 years old). It is seen as a time when their behavior is assessed more than their situation: "They wrote a report on my behavior here. It was pretty positive because I'm pretty calm." (Assia, 16 years old). More than just a definition and evaluation of common goals along the lines of a contractual approach, assessment is perceived by children as a time when expectations are set: "Here, the objectives expected of me are recorded." The most reflexive children, and those with the most social capital, are able to negotiate the objectives contained in their assistance plan: "I write the objectives; it gives them more value. The fact that I am writing those objectives means that, unconsciously, I have already accepted them". (Alex, 19 years old). But for the majority of children, the objectives are defined unilaterally. And yet for Pluto (2007), encouraging participation means conducting a bilateral assessment of the child's and the parents' development, but also involving professionals. This would imply, as shown by Wolff (2007), that both parties are on an equal footing, and would help evaluate the actions that have proven implementable and the reasons for failure. Otherwise, the participatory paradigm may be reduced to "a new normative project" in which children are increasingly forced to become personally involved in an individual performance obligation, which can create difficulties for vulnerable persons (Ebersold 2002). This echoes the risk identified by philosopher O'Neil (1998) of participatory approaches masking the child's vulnerability and placing too much responsibility on him/her, while weakening State and parental responsibilities in this sphere.

10.8 Substantive Participation: Do Children Have the Possibility of Pursuing Goals They Have Reason to Value?

In this chapter, we look at participation in its instrumental dimension. But according to Sen (1999), it is necessary to understand participation in both its instrumental and substantive dimensions. Substantive participation refers to the ability of people to pursue goals that they value and have reason to value. This is why we would like, finally, to question the possibility of children pursuing goals they have reason to value through the assessment process.

Three categories of situations can be distinguished in our corpus. In most reconstructed assessment processes, the child had to deal with the judgment of professionals disqualifying his or her family and had to learn to get used to the idea: "In my distant memories, the people who administered care were nasty. (...) Growing up, I realized that it was for my own good. It made me move forward in life. I don't regret it; what I regret is that they did not take the time to explain. (...) After much reflection and several discussions with adults in the province, and those around me, we were able to understand, but later." (Océane, 19 years old). Children have to face the lack of accurate representation in the reasons behind their placement (Abels-Eber 2006). The reluctance of professionals to diagnose a family's situation and communicate to the child the reasons for their placement can be attributed to the fear of intensifying the trauma of separation (Robin 2009). Faced with the difficulty of adults to verbalize their situation, acquiring information about their own case proves to be a long process for young people. But it leads to a difficult acceptance of the placement.

In a second category of situations, children were able to take part in the assessment process and sometimes change other's perceptions of their situation. Children who managed to change professionals' views about their situation were those who built alliances with their siblings or parents to construct a shared view of the situation:

> The head of the province did not believe me. My social worker was silent. Only my mother tried to do something. It was my mother who convinced my father to accept the placement. My father gave in. The province head agreed. (Elodie, 14 years old)

Children could also show, through their actions, their disagreement with the assessment conclusions, leading to a change in the decision-making process:

> I was in a hostel in T., in another province. (. . .) I did not want to come back. They brought me back here by car. I returned to T. by train the next day. They were flexible. They tried again; they tried to keep me. They listened to what I asked. (Ariane, 21 years old)

We could interpret these kinds of situations as "voting with one's feet"[2]: the choices that minors lack in negotiations, they make through movement.

But young people, who are not always able to take ownership over the decisions made or to influence the evaluator's assessment, can express disagreement over the interpretation of their situation, especially when, following the decisions made, their experience is not positive.

The source of gaps in interpretation between children and professionals are to be found in the use by professionals and children of two opposing view on the situations. Any assessment indeed calls for an interpretation of the world. Yet the interpretation by children differs from that of professionals. Children interpretation on their cases is based on a view of an elective family whereas professionals refer to a biological, nuclear family. Indeed children have as their reference point their own subjective experiences of extended, elective families. Young people in our interviews alternately used the words "my real parents" to describe their biological parents ("real" being used here in a legal and genetic sense) and their host family ("real" referring then to subjective and emotional ties). But we can presume that this dual meaning does not reflect confusion about the roles they attribute to each, given that the distinction they make between "biological parents" and "those who teach you how to take all the steps you'll need in life" is very clear: "For me, there's a difference between biological parents and those who teach you how to live and teach all the necessary steps you'll need to take in life. . ." (Fred, 19 years old). Any possible confusion is linked more to the difficulty of explaining and expressing the subjective

[2] The phrase was originally used in the ex-Soviet republics to describe the movement of people faced with a lack of political democracy.

ties formed during placement in the absence of recognized, common terms used in the real world to designate these additional family ties. And one can infer that the absence of such terms signals a "blind spot" in assessments that fail to take into account host parenting. And it's not only "additional parenting" that constitutes a blind spot in professional assessments but the whole of the extended family. The wider belief systems of children rest on diverse and extended families, including biological siblings, host siblings, and biological and host family members. Instead of referring to a *de facto* family, young people speak of elective families:

> At the age of 6, I asked to be baptized. My godmother is the daughter in my host family. The godfather is the brother-in-law of the host family. They're two people I appreciate tremendously. (Fred, 19 years old)

Thus, two belief systems collide, the one of professionals who exclusively refers to biological parents, and the other of users with a vision of diverse and elective families. The two belief systems are in tension and contradiction with each other. The familialist worldview professionals use in assessments stirs disagreement and bewilderment among the minors, who have the impression that their interests and worldview are not being sufficiently taken into account:

> I just so happened to have an educator [specialized social worker] who consistently took my biological father's side, which wasn't the best choice. He did everything according to what my father said. My host family came second, when they were allowed to step in at all. (Antoine, 19 years old)

This situation illustrates the difficulties involved in designing social programs that are open "to the development of individual preferences." (Sen 1999: 253).

10.9 The Development of Capabilities: A Non-linear Process

Children have mostly had a non-participatory experience during assessments of their situations. Our empirical study shows the dominance of adults in this assessment process and the slim possibilities that exist for children to take part in decisions concerning them. But even in a highly constrained, descending participatory context, opportunities for participation of children in assessment evolve through the interaction with individual factors (reflexivity and the initiative taken to enter the system) and social factors (the services available and the design of these services). With the capability approach we can see interconnections and interlinkages between individual factors and social opportunities in the development of children's ability to pursue goals they value and have reason to value.

Indeed, there is a cumulative interaction of individual and social factors in the development of children's agency. Our empirical study shows for example that children who perceived themselves to be in danger, and who say they took the initiative themselves to use social services, have the impression they are in control over decisions throughout the process. They were able to express their views during the assessment process and sometimes change the perceptions of those whom they dealt with. In this situation, a practical agreement and a workable solution were found between the child and professionals. The workable solution is based on "the contingent acceptance of particular provisions, without demanding complete social unanimity." (Sen 199: 253).

Participation is a non-linear process that is cumulative but could also be retroactive (see the diagram in the chapter by Stoecklin & Bonvin in this volume). That's mean that despite inequalities and stigma the individual participation of children evolved during the process of assessment in interaction with social services. Indeed, some children who perceived themselves to be the objects of intervention by adults could, through the process of social assistance, consider themselves subjects of the intervention and learn to take part in the decision. Through the assistance process and the social opportunities offered during placement, the child can develop an individual capacity to take part in the assessment process in care. In this sense, we were able to analyze a recursive dimension of participation insofar as it was possible for some children to move from a position of being an object of the assessment to one in which they were a subject of the assessment and to change the course of action.

Nevertheless, our empirical study demonstrates great difficulties that remain in developing social programs for care that are sensitive to "the development of individual preferences" (Sen 1999: 253), in a context of discrimination and stigmatization. As Astier (2009) stresses:

> The professional is in a dominant position and thus imposes his/her definition of the situation. Even if professional and relationship logics are present, they are dominated by the logic of social control. Even before the relationship begins, the institutional identity of the user is given. These users are, in a certain way, predefined by the work of others. They must remain passive. At best, they accept and adhere to what is imposed on them; at worst, they submit themselves. (Astier 2009: 53, translated by P.R.)

As Leeson (2007) was able to demonstrate in England, this can have serious consequences for the child's future. Leeson stressed that children in care display serious anxieties about their decision skills as a consequence of a lack of opportunity earlier in life. She suggests that ignoring the voices of children in care and their full citizenship, or preventing them from being heard through overzealous notions of protection, is dangerous. Instead of protecting the child, this makes him/her more powerless, dehumanized and marginalized. Thus, there is an urgent need to develop the capabilities of children in care and their resilience to face all types of social and emotional challenges.

How, in this context, can we strengthen the involvement of children in the assessment of their own situation? As shown by Jaffé (2001), the quality of children's participation in the assessment process depends on the adult representations of children's world and, vice-versa, on the children's representations of the adult world. Improving the participation of the children requires both their adaptation to the assessment process—by keeping them informed and giving them the means to understand the process—and that of the assessment process to the children. This requires taking into account the plurality of a children's verbal and non-verbal means of expression, supporting the emergence of their point of view, encouraging participation, not at an imposed time, but at a time chosen by the children, offering them real choices between different means of assistance, but also taking into account the specific view that they have of their situation. More than imposing an external view of children, the assessment should take more into account children's perception of their situation.

References

Abels-Eber, C. (2006). *Pourquoi on nous a séparés? Récits de vie croisés: des children placés, des parents et des professionals* [Why were we separated? Life stories from foster children, parents and professionals]. Erès: Ramonville Saint Agne.

Astier, I. (2007). *Les nouvelles règles du social* [The new social rules]. Paris: PUF.

Astier, I. (2009). Les transformations de la relation d'aide dans l'intervention sociale [Transformations of the aid relationship in social intervention]. *Information Sociales, 152*(2), 52–58.

Bernoux, J.-F. (2004). *L'évaluation participative au service du développement social* [Participatory evaluation in social development]. Paris: Dunod.

Bessin, M. (2009). Parcours de vie et temporalités biographiques: quelques éléments de problématique [Life-course and biographical temporality: Some elements of the problem]. *Information Sociales, 156*(6), 12–21.

Biggeri, M., Ballet, J., & Comim, F. (2011). *Children and the capability approach*. Basingstoke: Palgrave Macmillan.

Boutin, G., & Durning, P. (2008). *Enfants maltraités ou en dangers, L'apport des pratiques socio-éducatives* [Abused or children in danger, the contribution of socio-educational practices]. Paris: L'Harmattan.

Butler, J. (2007). *Le récit de soi* [Telling your own story]. Paris: PUF.

Cashmore, J. (2002). Promoting the participation of children and young people in care. *Child Abuse and Neglect, 26*(8), 837–847.

Chauvière, M. (2002). Les usagers, Ambiguïtés d'un nouveau paradigme pour l'action sociale [Users, Ambiguities of a new paradigm for social action]. In C. Humbert (Ed.), *Les usagers de l'action sociale. Sujets, clients ou bénéficiaires* [Subjects, clients or beneficiaries]. Paris: L'Harmattan.

Commaille, J. (2008). *La politique de la famille* [The politics of the family]. Paris: La découverte.

Council of Europe. (2005). *Recommendation on the rights of children living in residential institutions*.

Council of Europe. (2009). *Rights of children in institutions*. Report on the implementation of the Council of Europe Recommendation Rec(2005)5 on the rights of children living in residential institutions.

Crabtree, A. (2008). The centrality of basic social capabilities: "To go without shame". In J.-L. Dubois, A. S. Brouillet, P. Bakhshi, & C. Duray-Soundron (Eds.), *Repenser l'action collective, Une approche par les capabilities* (pp. 37–60). Paris: l'Harmattan.

Ebersold, S. (2002). Le champ du handicap, ses enjeux et ses mutations: du désavantage social à la participation sociale [Disability, its challenges and changes: Social disadvantage in social participation]. *Analyse Psicologica, 10*(3), 281–290.

Feeny, T., & Boyden, J. (2004). *Acting in adversity- rethinking the causes, experiences and effects of child poverty in contemporary literature* (Working paper series, WP 116). Oxford: QEH.

Frechon, I., & Dumaret, A.-C. (2008). Bilan critique de 50 ans d'études sur le devenir adultes des children places [Critical review of 50 years of studies of children in care becoming adults]. *Neuropsychiatrie de l'Enfance et de l'Adolescence, 56*(3), 135–147.

Hamman, P. (2002). Quand le souvenir fait lien [When memory creates a link]. *Sociologie du Travail, 44*, 175–191.

Holland, S. (2001). Representing children in child protection assessments. *Childhood, 8*, 322–339.

Jaffé. (2001). L'expertise judiciaire des capacités parentales: subjectivité de l'évaluation, utilité du rapport [Forensic parenting skills: Subjectivity in evaluation, utility in the relationship]. In J. L. Viaux (Ed.), *Ecrire au juge* (pp. 119–132). Paris: Dunod.

Katz, L. G. (1995). *Talks with teachers of young children*. Norwood: NJ Ablex.

Lansdown, G. (2010). The realisation of children's participation rights. Critical reflections. In B. Percy-Smith & N. Thomas (Eds.), *A handbook of children and young people's participation. Perspectives from theory and practice* (pp. 11–23). London: Routledge.

Leeson, C. (2007). My life in care: Experiences of non-participation in decision- making processes. *Child and Family Social Work, 12*, 228–277.

Liebel, M., in collaboration with Robin, P., & Saadi, I. (2010). *Children, droits et citoyenneté, Faire émerger la perspective des children sur leur droit* [Children, Rights and Citizenship, Bring out the children's perspective on their right]. Paris: L'Harmattan.

Mason, J., & Michaux, A. (2005). *The starting out with Scarba project: Facilitating children's participation in child protection process*. Paddington: The Benevolent Society.

Münder, J., & Mutke, B. (2001). *Kindeswohl zwischen Jugendhilfe und Justiz- Ergebnisse eines Forschungsprojektes*. München: Sozialpädagogisches Institut im SOS-Kinderdorf.

Münder, J., Mutke, B., & Schone, R. (2000). *Kindeswohl zwischen Jugendhilfe und Justiz. Professionelles Handeln in Kindeswohlverfahren*. Münster: Votum.

Nussbaum, M. (2000). *Women and human development: The capabilities approach*. Cambridge, MA: Cambridge University Press.

Nussbaum, M. (2004). *Hiding from humanity*. Princeton: Princeton University Press.

O'Neill, O. (1998). Children's rights and children's lives. *Ethics, 98*, 705–722.

Payet, J.-P., Giuliani, F., & Laforgue, D. (Eds.). (2008). *La voix des acteurs faibles* [The voice of weak actors]. Rennes: PUR.

Pluto, L. (2007). *Partizipation in den Hilfen zur Erziehung, eine empirische Studie*. München: Verlag Deutsches Jugendinstitut.

Ricoeur, P. (1990). *Soi même comme un autre* [Oneself as another]. Paris: Seuil.

Robin, P. (2009). L'évaluation du point de vue des children [Evaluation from the point of view of children]. *Revista de Cercetare si Interventie Sociala, 25*, 63–81.

Robin, P. (2010). Comment les adolescents appréhendent-ils l'évaluation de leur situation familiale en protection de l'enfance, L'enfant au cœur des politiques sociales. *Revue Informations sociales, 160*, 134–140. Caisse nationale des allocations familiales.

Sen, A. K. (1999). *Development as freedom*. Oxford: OUP.

Sen, A. K. (2000). *Repenser l'inégalité*. Paris: Seuil.

Smith, A.-B. (2002). Interpreting and supporting participation rights: Contributions from sociocultural theory. *The International Journey of Children's Rights, 10*(1), 73–88.

Stoecklin, D. (2013). Theories of action in the field of child participation. In search of explicit frameworks. *Childhood, 20*(4), 443–457.

Truc, G. (2005). Une désillusion narrative? De Bourdieu à Ricœur en sociologie [Disillusionment narrative? from Bourdieu to Ricœur in sociology]. *Tracés, 8*, 47–67.

United Nation as General Assembly. (1989). *United Nations Convention on the Rights of Childrens*.

Wiesner, R. (2006). Was sagt die Verfassung zum Kinderschutz? In H. Kindler, S. Lillig, H. Blüml, T. Meysen, & A. Werner (Eds.), *Handbuch Kindeswohlgefährdung nach § 1666 BGB und Allgemeiner Sozialer Dienst (ASD)* (pp. 1–5). München: DJI. http://db.dji.de/asd/F001_Wiesner_lv.pdf.

Wolff, R. (2007). *Demokratische Kinderschutzarbeit zwischen Risiko und Gefahr, Die KinderschutzZentren*. http://www.kinderschutzzentren.org/pdf/info_wolf_demokratischekinderschutzarbeit.pdf

Wolff, R., Flick, U., Ackermann, T., Biesel, K., Brandhorst, F., Heinitz, S., Patschke, M., & Robin, P. (2013). *Kinder im Kinderschutz – Zur Partizipation von Kindern und Jugendlichen im Hilfeprozess – Eine explorative Studie*. Köln: NZFH.

Youf, D. (2002). *Penser les droits de l'enfant* [Thinking about the rights of the child]. Paris: PUF.

Chapter 11
The UN Children's Rights Convention and the Capabilities Approach – Family Duties and Children's Rights in Tension

Zoë Clark and Holger Ziegler

11.1 Introduction

The UN Convention on the Rights of the Child (UNCRC 1989) – as a part of the human rights movement – has both reflected and enhanced a debate about (individual) justice for children and young people. Following Verhellen (1992: 99) two questions seem to be critical with respect to the current debate on children's rights: "Should the child be seen as a legal subject or as an object of desire and power? Should the child be regarded as a being which should be protected by society or as a partner with full rights of participation?" Even though some point to the fact that the UNCRC is far away from any children's rights "radicalism" (Verhellen 1993), most commentators seem to agree that this convention is a step into the direction of acknowledging children as agentic subjects rather than as immature objects of protection (Sünker 1995).

Amongst the most significant contributions of the UNCRC to the debate is an assertion that children should be seen as subjects with rights. This understanding clearly challenges the relegation of young people's issues into the private domain. Hence, the dependency of young people on the mercy and competencies of their parents (or other legal guardians) is questioned.

However, this is only the case if the status of children as holders of rights is actually taken seriously, i.e. if children are not understood as objects of altruism and charity. In this chapter we argue that the status of children as holders of rights for

Z. Clark (✉)
Department of Educational Sciences, Institut for Social Pedagogy and Adult Education, Goethe University, Grüneburgplatz 1, Frankfurt am Main D-60323, Germany
e-mail: z.clark@em.uni-frankfurt.de

H. Ziegler
Faculty of Pedagogy, Centre for Social Service Studies, Bielefeld University, PO Box 10 01 31, 33501 Bielefeld, Germany
e-mail: holger.ziegler@uni-bielefeld.de

D. Stoecklin and J.-M. Bonvin (eds.), *Children's Rights and the Capability Approach*, Children's Well-Being: Indicators and Research 8, DOI 10.1007/978-94-017-9091-8_11,

which they can make a claim within the public domain is still ambiguous in the UNCRC. Within the UNCRC it is doubtful whether primarily public bodies and agencies are legally obligated to enforce the entitlements of young people. In a number of aspects the UNCRC rather ascribes responsibility to enforce young people's entitlements to their families. At the same time there is a tension within the UNCRC between the status of the family as a private domain to be protected and the scope of the claimed advocatory function of public institutions for the individual interests of children.

Our contribution focuses primarily on those articles of the UNCRC which relate children's rights to parent's (or legal guardian's) rights and duties. In terms of content it is not concerned with the internal coherence of the convention's claims. It is obvious that the UNCRC is a result of international political debates and compromises. The UNCRC is a normatively legitimized contract about what the legal statues of children should be. As such it is both a product and a part of a historically developed controversial political and moral discourse. The categories of the UNCRC reflect what Putnam (2002) calls 'thick ethical concepts' in which fact and value are deeply entangled and which are thus inseparably descriptive and evaluative at the same time. The category of social inequality is an example for such a thick ethical concept. It does not refer to arbitrary variances between persons but to a specific subset of social relevant *normatively* negative valuated difference in respect to *normatively* positive valuated life perspectives. As Andrew Sayer (2009: 777) puts it:

> [I]n any description of any process that is likely to affect people's wellbeing, we are likely to have to use [. . .] 'thick ethical terms', such as 'generous', 'abusive' or 'racist', which are simultaneously and inseparably descriptive and evaluative [. . .]. Thus, when we decide to accept a description of some practice, say, as 'oppressive' or 'racist', we simultaneously accept the implicit valuation.

The UNCRC – for instance when pointing to a "safe, happy and fulfilled childhood" – is obviously full of such thick ethical terms. The same is true for most of the comments, analyses and critics of the UNCRC. The use of thick ethical terms and concepts is not a problem but rather a necessity within social and policy analysis. If we would replace such terms through seemingly non-evaluative descriptions we would not argue scientifically more adequate but on the contrary we would accept a loss of descriptive adequacy and thus a serious threat to the validity of our analyses (Sayer 2009). Problematic is not the fact of normative value judgments, but rather whether these judgments are merely assumed and remain hidden (crypto-normativity) or whether they are reasonably justified. Against this background the purpose of this article is not to suggest that the UNCRC is a normative document. As the UNCRC is a declaration of rights this is obviously and necessarily the case. The purpose of this article is rather to reconstruct the (implicit) normativity of the UNCR (In particular article 3, 5, 12, 14 and 18) towards the institution of the family and towards power relations within families. In a second step we assess whether these normative foundations are convincingly justified. In relation to this purpose our article does not aim to provide a legal interpretation of the UNCRC but to discuss whether and to which extent this convention may be an adequate instrument for progressive or emancipatory policies and for the empowerment of children and young people. We assert that in order to utilize the UNCRC for progressive respectively emancipative political purposes the convention needs to be framed within a broader policy approach and within a specific human rights perspective (which goes beyond formal rights-based entitlements). Therefore, we suggest bringing the capabilities approach and related (liberal) ideas into play. These are considered partially as an alternative to, but preponderantly as complementary to current views on justice for young people. At the same time these perspectives serve as background for a critical analysis of the UNCRC.

In terms of such an analysis this article will in particular

- Introduce some central ideas of the capabilities approach and discuss the potential tension between "welfare oriented" and "participatory" elements of the UNCRC;
- Discuss the question of 'justice for whom' and its meaning and relevance for children and young people. This question is particularly discussed on the fundament of the capabilities approach. In this context different ways of legitimizing children's entitlement to citizenship as holders of rights and capabilities are assessed.
- Reflect critically some aspects of the UNCRC against the background of this philosophical debate. Therefore we propose a view of the nation state as a provider of rights and we draw attention to some aspects of the historical influence of states in the process of developing the convention. The role of the public and the private spheres as areas of justice for young people will be addressed and the unsolved tension between protection, paternalism and the assertion of young people's agency will be debated.

To elaborate the main points of our argument we start with a short introduction of the basic ideas of the capabilities approach.

11.2 The Capabilities Approach: A Rough Overview

The capabilities approach is a philosophically grounded approach, which attempts to reconcile the competing demands associated with fundamental conceptions of equality, recognition and autonomy. While there are different interpretations of this approach – reaching from more or less neo-liberal readings to interpretations which are closely associated with feminist and socialist traditions (Andresen et al. 2008) – the capabilities approach implicitly advocates egalitarian, political conceptions of social justice which are concerned with the cultivation, maximization and just distribution of the (real) freedom of individuals.

A particular feature of the capabilities approach is that it provides a normative framework for the evaluation of the development and well-being of individual persons as well as for the assessment of the quality of social arrangements (cf. Otto et al. 2013 for a broader discussion).

The capabilities perspective is critical about egalitarian approaches which focus exclusively on rights, goods and resources while failing to pose the fundamental question about real freedoms, opportunities and restrictions (young) people face to realize concrete and actual states or/and practices they have reason to value. Thus, inequalities are particularly relevant in terms of restrictions to – or possibilities of – a life that human beings want to realize and in terms of the access to things, relationships and practices which they value (Sayer 2005). The failure to take these issues into account is tantamount to ignoring the fact that variations exist in the extent to which options opened up in principle by the provision of resources, rights and goods can in fact be utilized by concrete people in their actual life circumstances. This however implies that significant inequalities relevant to social justice are neglected. A central idea of the alternative capabilities view is that the rights and resources a person has are undeniably important but still "very imperfect indicators of the freedom that the person really enjoys to do this or be that" (Sen 1980: 37–38). Against this background, the merit of the capabilities perspective is to shift "attention from goods to what goods do to human beings" (Sen 1980: 219). The attention to what rights, goods, institutions or services do to human beings implies the necessity to focus on real, tangible, dependent and vulnerable human beings with their own biographies, specific needs and socially and culturally embedded ways of conducting their lives. Therefore the capabilities perspective commands a high degree of context-sensitivity.

The currency of justice from the perspective of the capabilities approach is what individual – but nevertheless socially and culturally situated and embedded – agents are free to and effectively able to do and to be. In this context the capabilities perspective draws an important analytical distinction between 'functionings' and 'capabilities' (Nussbaum 2000, 2006; Sen 1999). Functionings are actually realized states and actions that are valued for one's life and do not call into question the basis of self-respect. Capabilities, on the other hand, refer to the practical freedom of deciding for or against the realization of different combinations of such functionings. As the metric of justice from a capabilities perspective are 'capabilities' rather than 'functionings', the capabilities approach avoids the paternalistic or at least presumptuous claim to be able to determine, from a supposedly objective perspective, what it is that determines a good or bad life for other people. Nevertheless, the capabilities approach argues that there are objective "prerequisites for living a life that is fully human rather than subhuman, a life worthy of the dignity of the human being [. . .] a life that is flourishing rather than stunted" (Nussbaum 2006: 278) and objective preconditions, opportunities and restrictions for the practical ability of people to recognize and realize different options – i.e. the genuine freedom of people to be able to realize, according to their individual conception of the good life, valuable actions and states. The objective preconditions of flourishing and well-being are conceptualized as

> socially structured: economic resources and institutional preconditions for entitlements together constitute the collective support structures on which depend the choice of the set of chances of realization as well as the choices for the individual's life conduct. (Bartelheimer 2009: 51)

Thus, the capabilities approach demands a relational perspective which combines a focus on the socially structured space in which the life conditions of individuals and the conditions of their capabilities for action are situated, with a view to determine what it is that makes possible or restricts self-determined lives. This view is different from the meanwhile popular but in fact naive and eventually harmful appreciation that all people simply 'have agency'. Based on a sociological understanding of agency as a "situated practical phenomenon" (Moran-Ellis 2013: 333) rather than as a individual attribute, Jo Moran-Ellis convincingly suggests: "The idea of children as agentic needs careful treatment to ensure that allows for the interplay of intergenerational orders, of other power relations, and of the effect of structural conditions" (Moran-Ellis 2013: 336). The capabilities perspective seeming follows this assumption. Rather than ascribing agency to individuals – in terms of an individual or developmental feature – it proposes an evaluating yardstick of public policies. These are to be assessed with respect to their contribution to the qualitative as well as quantitative extension of possibilities and capabilities on the basis of which citizens can decide on various actions and states of affairs for which they find good reason in their life plans.

A decisive problem of this perspective concerns its boundaries. Are all options equally relevant and valuable? Should some options have priority in terms of their public protection and promotion? Is there a limit to the number of potentially relevant opportunities and promotable capabilities?

A highly influential proposal in order to define and justify central areas of capabilities that public institutions are bound to promote (if they want to meet the demands of social justice) is suggested by Martha Nussbaum (2000: 78–80, 2006: 76, 77). Nussbaum (2006: 76f) aims to define universal 'central capabilities' which are currently as follows:

> 1. Life. Being able to live to the end of a human life of normal length; not dying prematurely, or before one's life is so reduced as to be not worth living.
>
> 2. Bodily Health. Being able to have good health, including reproductive health; to be adequately nourished; to have adequate shelter.
>
> 3. Bodily Integrity. Being able to move freely from place to place; to be secure against violent assault, including sexual assault and domestic violence; having opportunities for sexual satisfaction and for choice in matters of reproduction.
>
> 4. Senses, Imagination, and Thought. Being able to use the senses, to imagine, think, and reason – and to do these things in a 'truly human' way: a way informed and cultivated by an adequate education including, but by no means limited to, literacy and basic mathematical and scientific training. Being able to use imagination and thought in connection with experiencing and producing works and events of one's choice: religious, literary, musical, and so forth. Being able to use one's mind in ways which are protected by guarantees of freedom of expression with respect to both political and artistic speech, and freedom of religious exercise. Being able to have pleasurable experiences and to avoid non-beneficial pain.

5. Emotions. Being able to have attachments to things and people outside ourselves; to love those who love and care for us, to grieve at their absence; in general, to love, to grieve, to experience longing, gratitude, and justified anger. Not having one's emotional development blighted by fear and anxiety. (Supporting this capability means supporting forms of human association that can be shown to be crucial in their development.)

6. Practical Reasoning. Being able to form a conception of the good and to engage in critical reflection about planning of one's life. (This entails protection for the liberty of conscience and religious observance.)

7. Affiliation. A.) Being able to live with and toward others, to recognize and show concern for other human beings, to engage in various forms of social interaction; to be able to imagine the situation of another. (Protecting this capability means protecting institutions that constitute and nourish such forms of affiliation, and also protecting the freedom of assembly and political speech.)

B.) Having the social bases of self-respect and non-humiliation; being able to be treated as a dignified being whose worth is equal to that of others. This entails provisions of non-discrimination on the basis of race, sex, sexual orientation, ethnicity, caste, religion, national origin.

8. Other Species. Being able to live with concern for and in relation to animals, plants, and the world of nature.

9. Play. Being able to laugh, to play, to enjoy recreational activities.

10. Control Over One's Environment. A.) Political. Being able to participate effectively in political choices that govern one's life; having the right of political participation, protections of free speech and association.

B.) Material. Being able to hold property (both land and movable goods), and having property rights on an equal basis with others; having the right to seek employment on an equal basis with others; having the freedom from unwarranted search and seizure. In work, being able to work as a human being, exercising practical reason, and entering into meaningful relationships of mutual recognition with other workers.

Nussbaum is concerned in this list with the entitlements of individuals, the guarantee of which she sees as the duty of the state respectively of public institutions. It is important to note that it is explicitly not the aim of her list to give a binding definition of how individuals have to conduct their lives or to impose specific values on individual human beings. Rather, the list is to identify general prerequisites for various versions of leading a good life. These prerequisites need to be concretized, without reverting to cultural relativism, for the societal and cultural contexts in which human beings lead their lives.

From the capabilities perspective it is the task of public institutions to ensure that individuals can, in reasonable and tolerable conditions, decide on their own in favor of the realization of these capabilities, i.e. of the translation of capabilities into functionings. It is, however, by no means a duty of an individual person to make a decision in favor of the actual realization of these possibilities in their own life praxis.

11.3 Welfare and Participation

If one follows the capabilities perspective, it is quite clear that capabilities logically include people's possibility to influence decisions that concern themselves and constitute a framework of self-determination. If this were not the case the whole capabilities perspective would hardly make any sense. Thus, a central aspect of the capabilities approach is to enable people to participate fully in the processes of decision-making. Jean-Michel Bonvin (2009) calls this 'capability for voice'. This capability refers to that process-related aspect of freedom that concerns the real possibility of giving voice and lending proper weight to an individual's opinions, desires and expectations in the public political process, or to ensure that they are taken seriously as relevant perspectives and important concerns. Capability for voice, then, refers not only to making a contribution in accordance with the respective rules of discourse – that is, the rules of what can be said or considered valid – but also to the possibility of exerting influence on these rules themselves as well as on the informational basis of any assessment of issues relating to a theory of justice (Otto et al. 2013). This participatory element is reflected in the UNCRC. In particular Article 12 ("The right to be heard") of the convention recognizes the right of each individual child to freely express her/his opinions with respect to 'all matters affecting the child'. These views should be 'given due weight in accordance with the age and maturity of the child'. A range of commentators seemingly follow the interpretation of Michael Freeman that with this article the UNCRC "recognises the child as a full human being with integrity and personality and the ability to participate freely in society" (Freeman 1994: 319) or, as Daniel Stoecklin (2013: 443) puts it, considers "the child as a social actor, able to reflexively act in an evolving way as a subject of rights".

In particular in the debates in Western countries, as for instance in Germany, the surpassingly high emphasis on children's voice and participation is considered as the central magnitude of the UNCRC. This emphasis on participation at least partly reflects the 'new paradigm' in the evolving academic field of childhood studies, which emphasizes children's agency and the 'competent child' (see Stoecklin 2013 for a broader discussion).

While it remains actually unclear whether the UNCRC ascribes authoritative or merely consultative value to the voice of children, most Western academic commentators and children's rights activists tend to interpret the participatory perspective of the UNCRC as a kind of democratic break-through, which emphasizes children's agency and their extensive right to participate in society. Some argue that the "participatory" article 12 outweighs paternalist welfare approaches in child-related policies. But the UNCRC has also a welfare perspective. Article 3 is often seen as the 'welfare-article' of the UNCRC. This article implicitly acknowledges the fact of young people's dependency and vulnerability and thus explicitly stresses the (potential) need of protective measures in order to secure 'children's best interests'. It is part of the philosophy of the UNCRC that all its articles have equal binding power upon national policies. However, there is an uneasy relation between these two articles. As David Archard and Marit Skivenes (2009: 2) figure out, the

> two commitments seem to pull in different directions: promotion of a child's welfare is essentially paternalist since it asks us to do what we, but not necessarily the child, think is best for the child; whereas, listening to the child's own views asks us to consider doing what the child, but not necessarily we, thinks is best for the child

It remains an open question how the two commitments are to be reconciled. The possibility to reconcile these allegedly contradictory tasks is a major theoretical challenge, in particular because the conceptions of the child behind these two articles seem to be at least partially conflicting. The participating child is considered as an active and fully rational 'agentic' agent whereas the child as a subject of welfare is conceptualized as a dependent and needy individual.

The possibility to reconcile these conceptualizations of the child depends on the notions of agency which is applied in the interpretation of the UNCRC. For any attempt to balance the different directions of article 3 and 12 of the UNCRC, it seems to be inappropriate to formulate an 'athletic' image of young persons which only values that which children actively choose and struggle for and to underestimate the relevance of an unchosen provision of care, welfare and goods (Cohen 1993) or in other words to neglect the importance of what some call the passive empowerment of welfare provisions (Pettit 2001) even if they are not the outcome of active choice and articulated wishes.

We argue that the capabilities approach provides an appropriate perspective to deal with the potential conflict between the articulated wishes and the wellbeing of a person and thus with the problem of paternalism, i.e. the interference "with another person, against their will, and defended or motivated by a claim that the person interfered with will be better off or protected from harm" (Dworkin 2010).

Form a capabilities perspective the safe-guarding of both autonomy and welfare implies complementary provisions. On the basis of this fundamental assumption we argue that a problem with the UNCRC is not so much that an alleged overemphasis on welfare would confine its participators direction of impact. A closer consideration rather implies that the UNCRC is relatively weak with respect to public welfare provisions. With respect to European welfare states it might be the case that the UNCRC gives more emphasis on participatory rights than national legislations, yet whether the UNCRC gives more emphasis on welfare rights than national child welfare legislations of welfare states is at least doubtful. Article 3 of the UNCRC refers to ensuring "the child such protection and care as is necessary for his or her well-being". This is not very specific. There is also relatively little reference to a public duty for the safeguarding of material resources or primary goods. At the same time the article 3 stresses the necessity of "taking into account the rights and duties of his or her parents, legal guardians, or other individuals legally responsible for [the child]". The UNCRC thus puts emphasis not so much on the public responsibility to ensure welfare rights but rather on the responsibility of legal guardians to provide adequate care.

Yet positive welfare rights and welfare provisions might be considered as conditions for a genuine and effective capability of young people to articulate and raise their voice. That welfare rights are a pre-condition in order to make political or participatory rights effective, respectively to ensure the freedoms implicit in civil and political rights, is a common insight within major theoretical approaches in political theory and philosophy. Such welfare rights may go well beyond care of parents or other legal guardians.

In a number of commentaries and interpretations of the UNCRC in the literature, the close relation between passive empowerment and participation, respectively between welfare and political rights, seems to be somehow underestimated or at least partially eclipsed. Thus – independent of the intentions of the UNCRC – there is at least a danger that the participatory rights implied in Article 12 of the UNCRC are interpreted in terms of a naive subjectivism. Article 12 states that state agencies should "assure to the child who is capable of forming his or her own views the right to express those views freely in all matters affecting the child, the views of the child being given due weight in accordance with the age and maturity of the child". There is no doubt that this Article stresses the importance to give voice to children. Yet beyond the right to express their views, only the degree of maturity is taken into account as a context of these participatory rights. At least in some interpretations of this article there is a tendency to celebrate children as active agents without taking the complex social conditions of agency into account. If the idea is that all children have agency, or the "ability to participate freely in society" (Freeman 1994: 319) then agency seems not to be related to social conditions but merely a common feature of individuals. Therefore the celebration of the individual agency of children is often paralleled by a tendency to leave the interpretation of – and the approach to – the neediness of (young) persons to experiences and interpretations of the children themselves. Children are then considered as the experts of themselves. Yet, it is a sociological fact that (young) people's experiences have most typically been formed in accordance with the material and socio-cultural life-worlds they live in. And empirically in most, if not all current societies, these life-worlds tend to be highly unequal and often unjust power-relations. Thus it is not very reasonable to be all too romantic about subjective views and the 'life-worlds', which form them, as such romanticism eventually "affirms the results of societal repression and exploitation" (Brumlik and Keckeisen 1976: 248). Sociologists have pointed to mechanisms of adaptation to the social conditions which imply that prevailing rules, power relations and ideologies or, as the case may be, the given common sense (the world is as it is, and we have to accept this) appear as unquestionable, self-evident and without alternative (Bourdieu 1979).

The problem is not that the UNCRC highlights children's rights to express their voice, but that the UNCRC as well as a number of commentaries and interpretations to the UNCRC remain largely silent about the (pre-)conditions of the capability for voice.

Beyond looking at the actual choices made by children it is much more interesting to consider the fact that they may not have the freedom to choose alternative ways of being and acting, which they may have reason to value. Also, Martha

Nussbaum (2003) sensitively points to the empirical well-known fact of 'adaptive preferences' i.e. preferences that have adapted to their second-class status. Therefore, she convincingly insists on the necessity "to make claims about fundamental entitlements that are to some extent independent of the preferences that people happen to have, preferences shaped, often, by unjust background conditions" (Nussbaum 2003: 33–34).

From a capabilities perspective it is necessary to move "beyond a neoliberal focus on negative rights to a positive endorsement of people's right to the material and social conditions that actually provide them with the freedom to choose" (Stern and Seifert 2013: 182). Thus, it is not unjustifiably 'paternalist' but necessary and conducive to freedom and autonomy if institutions are responsible for insuring that individuals "have access to a particular set of functionings and the freedom to choose a particular set" (Stern and Seifert 2013: 182). A capabilities-friendly welfare provision in the best interests of the child should ensure that young persons have the necessary skills and resources to push their viewpoint and should guarantee 'passive empowerment' which assures that they are also free not to participate without losing rights, entitlements and provisions. In other words, to ensure that participation does not lead into a new form of tyranny which might be used against the worst-off, who have the least amount of effective resources to push through their interests. Again, in the words of Nussbaum:

> A further advantage of the capabilities approach is that, by focusing from the start on what people are actually able to do and to be, it is well placed to foreground and address inequalities that women [and children] suffer inside the family: inequalities in resources and opportunities, educational deprivations, the failure of work to be recognized as work, insults to bodily integrity. Traditional rights talk has neglected these issues, and this is no accident, I would argue: for rights language is strongly linked with the traditional distinction between a public sphere, which the state regulates, and a private sphere, which it must leave alone. (Nussbaum 2003: 39)

This failure of the rights perspective may also hold also true for some interpretations of the UNCRC. We argue that a capabilities perspective is suitable to compensate this failure.

11.4 Capabilities and the UNCRC

Similarly to human rights and children's rights, the capabilities approach as a universal approach to justice includes each person in every context. Hence, children do not have to be treated as an exception within the capabilities approach. With regard to Nussbaum's list of ten central capabilities, the same metric of social inequality is valid for children as for adults. Of particular importance in this context is the question of 'justice for whom'. However, this question is not answered coherently within the capabilities literature. There are different kinds of legitimations of children as holders of rights and capabilities. Subsequently, different perspectives on the recognition of children as citizens have been developed.

For example Biggeri et al. (2011) formulate a legitimation to include children in the normative metric of the capabilities which refers to the broad group of liberal theories. They underline two key classically liberal aspects: "On the one hand, the individual is rational and reasonable; on the other hand, these faculties enable him/her to reappraise her judgment" (Ballet et al. 2011: 26f.)

Subsequently, these authors provide some evidence that children are able to make and revise choices and hence are, to a certain degree, capable agents. Ballet et al. (2011) argue that children are not too different from adults in their abilities of choice-making and revising choices. Thus, their argument is basically a claim for recognition of children based on their abilities. But with this very strong focus on active choice-making and the reflection of choices, rationality and reasonability remain pre-conditions of being addressed by this approach of social justice.

In contrast to this claim, to treat children as active agents, Nussbaum (2006) criticizes the classical liberal contractualism because of the way it characterizes humans as rational beings. Instead of a political contractualism between roughly equals in their ability and will to participate, she argues in favor of an ethical contractualism between each and every human being as an own end, independently of their abilities or their willingness to participate. Instead of a political contractualism between political persons, she argues for an ethical contractualism ensuring dignity for each and every individual. The central point of her critique of classical liberalism is her view on the significance of rationality and her definition of personhood. Her understanding of rationality goes beyond reasonable choices. In her definition, the need for care and the interdependency with others is at least one of the central features of human beings. Thus, instead of trying to include young persons in the notion of the rational and reasonable persons, she argues that vulnerability and interdependency are not characteristics that are unique to children, but are general human features.

This argument can be placed within a feminist tradition, which is critical of the construct of the fully rational, autonomous subject, within the context of care ethics (Kittay 1999, 2011), but also within a liberal, feminist perspective on childhood studies, like those by Cockburn (1998, 2001, 2005) or Lister (1998, 2007a, b), Lister et al. (2003).

One of the main issues in these debates of care ethics and childhood studies is the notion of dependency and interdependency. Core questions relate to which kinds of dependencies are problematized in current discourses and which are not. For example, welfare dependency is characterized as being highly problematic while interpersonal dependency of women on men is not. Another point is the seemingly unidirectional dependency of children on their parents, which ignores interdependency between generations.

We discuss the UNCRC through the lens of these feminist ideas of justice for whom and the capabilities approach as metric for social inequality. This convention represents one major step towards the recognition of children as holders of rights and hence as citizens. Yet, beyond the great importance the UNCRC has for children, there are still some issues that are worth discussing.

In order to discuss children's access to rights as well as the enabling of young people's capabilities, we need to clarify the meaning of citizenship for young people. This is important in order to clarify the issue of the public responsibility of providing these entitlements and enabling. Beyond a discussion about the question which rights and capabilities are possible and necessary to ensure a good life for children; it is also an issue how and by whom rights and capabilities can be provided and to whom they are to be provided. These are the main points of the UNCRC which we will focus on in the following paragraphs:

Citizenship is the basis of a currently dominant political order defining who is entitled to rights as a member of a particular state and who has certain duties at the same time. In the context of states as nation states, citizenship is an exclusive membership on the basis of territorial borders and national power relations. This geopolitical sphere frames the distribution of rights and hence the question of 'Justice for whom?' or in other words "who counts as a subject of justice" (Fraser 2008, 2010). Nancy Fraser (2010) has pointed out that current conceptions of citizenship are typically based on an 'unexamined pre-supposition' of the 'national who'. This turns out to be a highly relevant (and problematic) with respect to the scale and scope of the answers to the 'Justice for whom?' question. In fact, there are many people in this world who are not protected by any nation state or have the right to participate in one. Hart and Boyden (2007) show in their work on child-refugees that about eight million children in this world can be considered as stateless i.e. no state member.

It is an important achievement that the UNCRC – as part of the human rights movement – goes beyond the 'national who of justice'. No criteria of membership like political belonging, shared citizenship or shared nationality does legitimize conditional access to children's rights.

As humanity is the only criteria stated by the Human Rights Convention, being under 18 is the one and only condition necessary to be addressed as subject of children's rights. Opposed to national rights there are no exclusive featured like citizenship or maturity as preconditions for claim-making (Fraser 2008: 61). As such the UNCRC claims universal rights for each and every child independent of culture, ethnicity or national belonging also in protection against potential state violence. However, at the same time, the state as a national institution is named as one provider of children's rights. For political reasons, this represents a dilemma.

A right is by definition ensured by a state. From the perspective of the UNCRC, it is desirable that all states ratify the convention. Therefore, the UNCRC could, for strategic reasons, not be too progressive and hence critical of those who were to be convinced. If the UNCRC had demanded a transformation of fundamental social orders possibly many countries would not have signed it. An overlapping consensus on rights between all of the heterogeneous states requires compromises. Consequently, what the UNCRC can do is to ensure a minimum threshold of rights to participation, protection and provision.

In the sections above we have assessed whether this threshold is adequately conceptualized. Beyond these general considerations, it meaningful an important issue concerns the question how much room is left for a critical consideration of inequalities between classes, genders and citizens and non-citizens or unequal citizens. Using the instrument of the UNCRC there are a number of limitations to addressing these inequalities between young people and also power relations between generations.

As Biggeri et al. (2011) mention, rights are absolute. People either have access to rights or they don't, but rights are not continuous and graded and thus there are no unequal degrees of certain rights.

The capabilities approach could complement the CRC in terms of a metric of social inequality as well as a legitimation of children's entitlements. In contrast to a rights based approach, it delivers a metric which makes the standard of living of young people comparable. Hence, social inequalities and power relations can be put more comprehensively on the agenda than with a binary logic of a rights based approach. As an evaluative framework it is an instrument for a critique of social circumstances and social policies, which does not have to compromise in the same way as the UNCRC (as it is a multinational treaty). While rights are a constitutive part of the state – a fundamental element of the social contract – the capabilities approach can be seen as a critical evaluative framework confronting states and institutions with universal standards of living.

But in the case of children and young people, it becomes more complex than a debate about universal rights in the context of citizenship. Not only the distinction of entitlements between citizens and non-citizens, but also the distinction between the state as public and the parents as private providers of entitlements has to be discussed. The relation between the public and the private spheres and young people's agency within these spheres becomes relevant.

It is one major characteristic of a right that the entitlement is ensured by state agents within the sphere of the public. Yet, in the UNCRC, in many articles, young people are recommitted to the sphere of the private and to their parents (or legal guardians) as providers of access to rights. It is already fixed in the preamble of the children's rights convention that the family is a natural way of growing up and that it is *the* environment for developing well-being as shown in this quote:

> Convinced, that the family as fundamental group of society and the natural environment for the growth and well-being of all of its members and particularly children, should be afforded the necessary protection and assistance so that it can fully assume its responsibilities within the community. (UNCRC: 1)

This sentence has already many implications in terms of family as a natural environment, rather than a political institution; addressing adults as parents and in particular rights of women as rights of mothers and – not least – community orientated policies. That means that the UNCRC is not neutral towards lifestyles of adults, who are parents and is consequently also not neutral towards the lifestyles of their children, but distinguishes between legitimate and illegitimate ways of living. Collectives other than small families are not taken into account within the UNCRC. Considering the family as the natural environment for the growth and well-being of all members of the society does demonstrate ignorance against global patriarchal circumstances. Munos (2010) points to this issue very clearly:

> The character of the relationship between parents and children involves a powerful element of cultural conservatism in which adult males are the main beneficiaries. The male person's authority prevails, and subordination of the wife's and children's interests is deeply rooted in conservative tradition.

This explicit naturalization of the family which is claimed in the preamble is also mirrored in all the articles of the UNCRC which link children's rights, well-being and development to parents rights and duties as discussed in the following section. Children are not first of all addressed as part of a public sphere, but as dependents of their parents in need of protection and guidance within the private sphere. One can hardly argue against a lovely family environment providing young people with care and affiliation. It also cannot be denied that the youngest rely mostly on adult care, but if young people are recommitted by law to an interpersonal dependency it reduces the public responsibility for children at the same time.

Many articles of the UNCRC directly link children's rights to parents' duties. For instance, the children's right to exercise their own rights as well as to develop a conscience, religion and thought is linked to the parent's right and duty to provide appropriate direction and guidance to the children (cf. UNRC, Article 14).

It is summarized in Article 18.1 that "parents or as the case may be, legal guardians, have the primary responsibility for the upbringing and the development of the child. The best interest of the child will be their basic concern." (UNRC, Article 18.1).

If the main responsibility for the development of children is attached to parent's duties, the inequality of development – for instance in terms of achievement – is no political question, but one of the quality of parents. Some commentators argue that the responsibility of states respectively the public is brought back in with Art. 27. Yet it is at least controversial whether the UNCRC is actually a break in the "tradition of allocating power over children to the private realm of family life" (Stahl 2007: 805). Article 27 of the UNCRC states that "the parent(s) or others responsible for the child have the primary responsibility to secure, within their abilities and financial capacities, the conditions of living necessary for the child's development". state parties do have a mediated responsibility. They "shall take appropriate measures to assist parents [...] to implement this right". And they should "provide material assistance and support programmes" for the parents "in the case of need". In other words the responsibility is the responsibility of parents and not (or at least not primarily) a political resp. public issue, even though parents shall receive needs based support to fulfill *their* duties and responsibilities. In that way young people are not equally entitled to social, civil and political rights as adults are, but their provision, participation and protection depend on their parents in many ways. As Quennerstedt (2010) shows, this is also reflected in the language of the so-called triple P's – protection, provision, and participation. While the concept of 'adult' political rights is quite clear, the notion of (child) participation is fuzzy and far away from being clearly defined. Hence it is not by accident that the main articles of the UNCRC were identified as major principles instead of basic rights (Quennerstedt 2010). It is questionable whether those articles of the UNCRC – which are in particular those which link children's well-being to parent's behavior, competencies and resources – can be named as rights at all as there is no way for children to claim these rights. Parental functionings, capabilities and their access to resources (economic, cultural and social capital) are preconditions for the realization of those rights of the UNCRC, which link children's rights to parents' rights and duties. For example in article 5 (responsibilities, rights and duties of parents) as well as in the second paragraph of article 14 (direction and guidance) and in the first paragraph of article 18 (the best interest of the child) the opportunity of state interference into private, family domains are restricted due to the parents' right and duty to provide (age) appropriate guidance to their children. In particular article 18 points to the primacy of responsibility parents (or legal guardians) have for the development of children. Following this article the development of children is a primarily private rather than public concern.

Taking a look at the developing process of the Declaration from 1959 on until the CRC got finally adopted by the UN in 1989, it becomes clear that this relation between parents' rights and duties and children's rights was a major source of conflict and compromise. Two first drafts of the CRC were developed in Poland. The first declaration in 1959 was not signed by most countries (van Bueren 1998; Quennerstedt 2009). After Poland published a second draft for a convention of the rights of the child in 1979, an international consortium was established in order to work out a consensual version which became the UNCRC. As it took as long as 10 years to consent to the final convention, it was obviously a complicated and difficult process.

As in particular Ann Quennerstedt (2009) worked out, there are altogether five articles[1] within the convention which relate children's to parents' rights. One of the most important is the 'best interests of the child', which is identified as one major principle of the convention (Quennerstedt 2010). In her analysis of the reports of the international consortium Quennerstedt (2009) points out that there is a remarkable shift within this article compared to the original Polish draft: The right of the child to be heard was moved from article 3 – which commits parents as well as state institutions to act in the best interests of the child – into article 12. Thus, the right of the child to be heard is rather loosely linked to his/her best interests. Again, given the conflicting notions of safeguarding children's welfare and children's voice, – which is sometimes analyzed as a contradictions orientation towards nurturance and self-determination (Cherney and Perry 1996) – this separation opens up the space for interpretations which may legitimize an unjustified paternalism as it is not balancing the well-being of the child with the free will of the child. In other

[1] "In addition to Article 28, the analysis also considers the drafting of Article 3 (best interest of the child), Article 5 (parental direction and guidance), Article 12 (right to express one's opinion and to be heard), and Article 14 (freedom of thought, conscience, and religion). After an initial reading of the material as a whole these articles were identified as those where conflicts between children's rights and parents' rights surfaced most clearly." (Quennerstedt 2009: 169)

words the ratified version of the UNCRC may allow a unilateral way of defining the best interest of the child which reproduces a binary distinction between seemingly autonomous, independent adults and dependent, non-agential children. Such a binary distinction ignores on the one hand adult's (inter-)dependency as social beings (Nussbaum 2006: 158) and on the other hand children's domain-specific ability to reasonably formulate their own interest (Clark and Eisenhuth 2011).

Such an interpersonal dependency in which children rely on resources, mercy and the knowledge of their parents is in danger of reproducing inter-generational inequalities between children and also blames parents with fewer resources. As Gill Jones (2008) argues, being able to be dependent on parents is a privilege. First of all, the resources between the families are unequal, but also the abilities to mobilize resources differ. In her work, she focuses on young people between 16 and 18 years. She shows that many parents lack knowledge of their legal responsibilities. 74 % of the parents thought that they had no legal responsibility to subsidize their children's low wages. Furthermore, many families with poor relationships evict their children at the age of 16, when they have finished school. Those children often rely on welfare benefits, which have constantly been reduced in Europe during the past decades. This reduction of the welfare state is at least in Germany particularly relevant for young people. Since the welfare reform in 2005, unemployed young people are obliged to stay with their parents until the age of 25. Consequently, they do not receive housing benefits, nor can they receive the full living benefits. It is assumed that each member of a 'community in need' (in this case the family of origin) has fewer needs than single individuals.

In the work of Andresen's et al. (2013) on precarious childhoods, it becomes obvious that dependency on parents is also a privilege for younger children and not only for young people. Her work focuses on young children of working poor parents, who spend long stretches of their days in child day care. What is remarkable about this child day care is that it is not state funded, but realized through charity and voluntary work. The main purpose is to provide the children with basic needs, like lunch and dinner as well as homework support. As the financial resources of this institution are limited and the work of adults is voluntary, the institution only has limited possibilities and is not very well equipped. For large parts of their lives the children who participated in this study do not have the privilege to be dependent on their parents, nor on the state. Zoë Clark's (2014) research about language brokering shows that the dependency of parents on the language skills of their children is structured by social class, gender and migration background. Hence, this kind of responsibility of children to translate for their parents can be discussed as unequally distributed interdependency within families.

These examples can be discussed in the context of unequal wages, and the problematic issue of wages that are neither sufficient for young people to be independent of their family nor for parents to afford professional day care. Regarding the UNCRC, these examples are in particular relevant with respect to the strong family orientation of the convention. As Muñoz (2010: 47) points out the UNCRC's family orientation

> is especially clear in those articles referring to provision rights [. . .]..As a consequence of the implicit agreement between society, family and state, the children's situation depends on their parents' cultural and social position as well as on their capability to earn money in a segmented labour market. The more the parents are well positioned, the more children enjoy a decent standard of living. In contrast, the worse the situation of the parents, the worse is that of the children as well.

At the same times these examples show that there is a lack of public responsibility for those children and young people who do not have any access to the privilege of dependency on their parents or have good reasons why they do not want to be dependent on their family. In the UNCRC the state – or the public – has rather indirect responsibility for the child's welfare. Its responsibility is primarily to establish the completion of the family's obligations and to promote the abilities and capacities of parents. Its space of direct responsibility is reduced in a subsidiary way

> to 'the necessary cases' [. . .] if the *parents* do not tend to their duties properly [. . .] and to resolving problems regarding the most essential questions [. . . . This] addresses one of the characteristics of the residual and assistance model of welfare, in which benefits are not given directly to the children as individual persons, but to the family group as a whole. (Muñoz 2010: 47)

To sum up, even though children's rights are one of the most important steps to justice for children, the UNCRC has to face different, and in particular feminist arguments concerning normative judgments of dependency, about political definitions of being a family; about nation states which cannot be considered as providers of rights only, but also as part of social problems; and it has to face critical voices from childhood studies and their arguments about intra-family interdependency. A general 'bashing' of the UNCRC is neither useful nor appropriate. It might also well be that some interpretations of the UNCRC are able to resolve some of the major tensions, contradictions and shortfalls inherent in the UNCRC. However there is currently little evidence that such interpretations come out on the top of the debate on the UNCRC.

References

Andresen, S., Meiland, S., Milanovic, D., & Blume, J. (2013). Erfahrungen und Erleben von Armut aus der Sicht von Kindern. "Ich würde meiner Familie was schenken und dafür sorgen, dass sie nicht so viel in Schwierigkeiten sind". *Unserer Jugend, 3*, 123–129.

Andresen, S., Otto, H.-U., & Ziegler, H. (2008). Bildung as human development: An educational view on the capabilities approach. In H.-U. Otto & H. Ziegler (Eds.), *Capabilities – Handlungsbefähigung und Verwirklichungschancen in der Erziehungswissenschaft* (pp. 165–197). Wiesbaden: VS.

Archard, D., & Skivenes, M. (2009). Balancing a child's best interest and a child's view. *International Journal of Children's Rights, 17*, 1–21.

Ballet, J., Biggeri, M., & Comim, F. (2011). Children's agency and the capability approach: A conceptual framework. In M. Biggeri, J. Ballet, & F. Comim (Eds.), *Children and the capability approach* (pp. 22–45). Basingstoke: Palgrave Macmillan.

Bartelheimer, P. (2009). Verwirklichungschancen als Maßstab lokaler Sozialpolitik? *Sozialer Fortschritte, 2*(3), 48–55.
Biggeri, M., Ballet, J., & Comim, F. (2011). Children's agency and the capability approach: A conceptual framework. In M. Biggeri, J. Ballet, & F. Comim (Eds.), *Children and the capabilities approach* (pp. 22–45). London: Palgrave.
Bonvin, J.-M. (2009). Der Capability Ansatz und sein Beitrag für die Analyse gegenwärtiger Sozialpolitik. *Soziale Passagen, 1*, 8–22.
Bourdieu, P. (1979). *Distinction: A social critique of the judgement of taste*. London: Routledge.
Brumlik, M., & Keckeisen, W. (1976). Etwas fehlt. Zur Kritik und Bestimmung von Hilfsbedürftigkeit für die Sozialpädagogik. *Kriminologisches Journal, 4*, 241–262.
Cherney, I., & Perry, N. (1996). Children's attitudes toward their rights: An international perspective. In E. Verhellen (Ed.), *Monitoring children's rights* (pp. 241–250). Dordrecht: Martinus Nijhoff.
Clark, Z., & Eisenhuth, F. (2011). Beyond futurority – A capabilities perspective on childhood and youth. In O. Leßmann, H.-U. Otto, & H. Ziegler (Eds.), *Closing the capabilities gap renegotiating social justice for the young* (pp. 277–288). Opladen: Barabara Budrich.
Clark, Z. (2014). Agency, participation and youth inequalities. In C. Hart, M. Biggeri, & B. Babic (Eds.), *Agency and participation in childhood and youth. International applications of the capabilities approach in schools and beyond* (pp. 83–100). London: Bloomsbury.
Cockburn, T. (1998). Children and citizenship in Britain: A case for a socially interdependent model of citizenship. *Childhood, 5*, 99–117.
Cockburn, T. (2001). Youth employment transitions and citizenship: A reflection on a local study of young people's transition to employment in the North of England. *Young, 9*, 2–29.
Cockburn, T. (2005). Children's participation in social policy: Inclusion, chimera or authenticity? *Social Policy and Society, 4*, 109–119.
Cohen, G. A. (1993). Equality of what? On welfare, resources and capabilities. In M. Nussbaum & A. Sen (Eds.), *The quality of life* (pp. 9–29). Oxford: Clarendon.
Dworkin, G. (2010). Paternalism. In E. N. Zalta. (Ed.), *The Stanford encyclopedia of philosophy*. Summer 2010 edition. http://plato.stanford.edu/archives/sum2010/entries/paternalism/.
Fraser, N. (2008). *Scales of justice: Reimagining political space in a globalizing world*. Cambridge: Polity Press.
Fraser, N. (2010). Who counts as a subject of justice? National citizenry, global humanity, or transnational community of risk? In H. G. Soeffner et al. (Eds.), *Unsichere Zeiten. Herausforderungen gesellschaftlicher Transformationen* (pp. 717–733). Wiesbaden: VS Verlag für Sozialwissenschaften.
Freeman, M. (1994). Whither children: Protection, participation, autonomy? *Manitoba Law Journal, 22*, 307–327.
Hart, J., & Boyden, J. (2007). The statelessness of the world's children. *Children & Society, 21*, 237–248.
Jones, G. (2008). Youth, citizenship and the problem of dependence. In A. Invernizzi & J. Williams (Eds.), *Children and citizenship* (pp. 97–107). London: Sage.
Kittay, E. F. (1999). *Love's labor: Essays on women, equality, and dependency*. New York: Routledge.
Kittay, E. F. (2011). The ethics of care, dependence, and disability. *Ratio Juris, 24*, 49–58.
Lister, R. (1998). Citizenship and difference: Towards a differentiated universalism. *European Journal of Social Theory, 1*, 71–90.
Lister, R. (2007a). From object to subject: Including marginalized citizens in policy making. *Politics and Policy, 35*, 437–455.
Lister, R. (2007b). Why citizenship? where, when and how children? *Theoretical Inquiries in Law, 8*, 693–718.
Lister, R., et al. (2003). Young people talk about citizenship: Empirical perspectives on theoretical and political debates. *Citizenship Studies, 7*, 235–255.

Moran-Ellis, J. (2013). Children as social actors, agency, and social competence. *Neue Praxis, 4*, 323–338.

Munos, L. G. (2010). Childhood welfare and rights of children. In S. Andresen, I. Diehm, H.-U. Otto, & H. Ziegler (Eds.), *Children and the good life new challenges for research on children* (pp. 41–52). Dordrecht: Springer.

Nussbaum, M. (2000). *Women and human development. The capabilities approach*. Cambridge: Cambridge University Press.

Nussbaum, M. (2003). Capabilities as fundamental entitlements: Sen and social justice. *Feminist Economics, 2*(3), 33–60.

Nussbaum, M. (2006). *Frontiers of justice: Disability, nationality, species membership*. Cambridge: Harvard University Press.

Otto, H. U., Scherr, A., & Ziegler, H. (2013). On the normative foundation of social welfare – Capabilities as a yardstick for critical social work. In H. U. Otto & H. Ziegler (Eds.), *Enhancing capabilities: The role of social institutions* (pp. 197–230). Farmington Hills: Barbara Budrich.

Pettit, P. (2001). Capability and freedom: A defence of Sen. *Economics and Philosophy, 17*, 1–20.

Putnam, H. (2002). *The collapse of the fact/value dichotomy and other essays*. Cambridge: Harvard University Press.

Sayer, A. (2005). *The moral significance of class*. Cambridge: Cambridge University Press.

Sayer, A. (2009). Who's afraid of critical social science? *Current Sociology, 57*, 767–786.

Sen, A. (1980). Equality of what? In S. McMurrin (Ed.), *Tanner lectures on human values* (Vol. I, pp. 197–220). Cambridge: Cambridge University Press.

Sen, A. (1999). *Development as freedom*. New York: Anchor Books.

Stahl, R. M. (2007). "Don't forget about me": Implementing article 12 of the United Nations convention on the rights of the child. *Arizona Journal of International & Comparative Law, 24*, 803–842.

Stern, M., & Seifert, S. (2013). Creative capabilities and community capacity. In H. U. Otto & H. Ziegler (Eds.), *Enhancing capabilities: The role of social institutions* (pp. 117–134). Farmington Hills: Barbara Budrich.

Stoecklin, D. (2013). Theories of action in the field of child participation in search of explicit frameworks. *Childhood: A Journal of Global Child Research, 4*, 443–457.

Sünker, H. (1995). Gewalt, Kinderrechte und Kinderpolitik. *Widersprüche, 58*, 77–81.

Quennerstedt, A. (2009). Balancing the rights of the child and the rights of parents in the convention on the rights of the child. *Journal of Human Rights, 8*(2), 162–176.

Quennerstedt, A. (2010). Children, but not really humans? Critical reflections on the hampering effect of the "3 p's". *International Journal of Children's Rights, 18*, 619–635.

UN Convention on the Rights of the Child. (1989). Adopted and opened for signature, ratification and accession by General Assembly resolution 44/25 of 20 November 1989, download: http://www.ohchr.org/EN/ProfessionalInterest/Pages/CRC.aspx. 28 May 2014.

Van Bueren, G. (1998). *The International Law on the rights of the child*. Dordrecht: Nijhoff.

Verhellen, E. (1992). Het toezichtsinechanisme in de UNO-Conventie inzake de rechten van het kind. In T. de Boer et al. (Eds.), *De kant van het kind. Liber Amicorum Prof. Miek de Langen* (pp. 93–104). Arnhem: Gouda Quint.

Verhellen, E. (1993). Children and participation rights. In R. Heiliö, E. Lauronen, & M. Bardy (Eds.), *Politics of childhood and children at risk. Provision – Protection – Participation* (pp. 49–65). Vienna: European Centre for Social Welfare Policy and Research.

Chapter 12
Children's Rights Between Normative and Empirical Realms

Karl Hanson, Michele Poretti, and Frédéric Darbellay

12.1 Introduction

We understand the capability approach as a conceptual framework developed from within moral and political philosophy for assessing questions related to poverty, inequality and the design of social institutions (Terzi 2005: 449). Applied to children, the capability approach can be summarized as aiming at the evaluation and assessment of individual children's well-being, social arrangements for children and the design of policies for improving children's place in society (cf. Robeyns 2011). Correspondingly, the children's rights framework which is our own field of expertise, contains a set of closely related normative ambitions, in particular those contained in the 1989 UN Convention on the Rights of the Child (hereafter: CRC). The Preamble of the CRC makes reference to the Charter of the United Nations (1945) and confirms belief in the dignity and worth of the human person directed at promoting social progress and better standards of life in larger freedom. It is via the concept of freedom that human rights have entered development discourse, a movement for which Sen's conception of the capability approach has been highly instrumental (Uvin 2010). The capability approach and international children's rights hence have in common a normative ambition as they both aim to evaluate the degree of respect for a person's dignity and well-being and also prescribe sets of particular social arrangements and policies in order to enhance the said respect.

In our recent work in the field of children's rights studies, we have been intrigued by the way how the normative ambitions expressed in the CRC work out in practice.

K. Hanson (✉)
Children's Rights Unit, University Institute Kurt Bösch, PO Box 4176, 1950 Sion 4, Sion, Switzerland
e-mail: karl.hanson@iukb.ch

M. Poretti • F. Darbellay
University Institute Kurt Bösch, PO Box 4176, 1950 Sion 4, Sion, Switzerland
e-mail: michele.poretti@iukb.ch; frederic.darbellay@iukb.ch

D. Stoecklin and J.-M. Bonvin (eds.), *Children's Rights and the Capability Approach*, Children's Well-Being: Indicators and Research 8, DOI 10.1007/978-94-017-9091-8_12,

We have in particular discussed these issues during an interdisciplinary research project on international children's rights advocacy, entitled "Living rights: An interdisciplinary approach to international translations of children's rights".[1] The aim of this research project was to gain better insights into the processes of prioritisation in children's rights advocacy at the international level. Within these processes, we wanted to explore the extent to which there is also space for taking into account children's own conceptualisations of their rights ('living rights'). Empirical results stemming from this project have been published in a number of journal articles and book chapters (including Hanson 2011; Hanson and Poretti 2012; Poretti et al. 2014), whereas the conceptual framework which revolves around the three key-notions living rights, social justice and translations has been the subject of a separate edited volume entitled *Reconceptualizing Children's Rights in International Development* (Hanson and Nieuwenhuys 2013). For this project we were not in the first place looking at how to improve respect for children's fundamental rights or evaluating children's rights policies, but adopted an empirical perspective with the aim to describe, analyze and understand children's rights discourses, policies and legal arrangements. One of the most salient findings of the research project documents in detail how the iconography of victimhood mobilized by child rights advocates has changed significantly during the past two decades, whereby 'the child victim of violence' has replaced 'the street child' as the dominant icon on the international agenda (Poretti et al. 2014).

The present chapter wishes to present some of our ideas on distinctions and overlaps between normative and empirical concerns in the study of childhood and children's rights which were discussed during this research project (see also Alanen 2010; Reynaert et al. 2009). First, we situate recent developments and critical enquiries on children's rights studies in general (1) and discuss the links between rights, emancipation and interdisciplinarity (2). We then look into discussions on child participation (3). Subsequently, we present two theoretical underpinnings of our approach by explaining further the notions living rights (4) and translations (5). Finally, we give some examples of recent children's rights research (6) which we think are of interest for linking insights obtained from children's rights research to the capability approach.

12.2 Children's Rights Studies

Awareness for children's rights did not come out from a scientific discovery, quite on the contrary: academic recognition that children have rights followed slowly upon what was primarily a social and political process emerging at the beginning of

[1] The project was financed by the Swiss National Science Foundation (SNSF) and was conducted between 2010 and 2012 (Project no. CR11/1_127311). For a description of the project, see: http://p3.snf.ch/project-127311 (Accessed 1 November 2013).

the twentieth century (Veerman 1992). After having gained momentum in 1989 with the adoption and the subsequent almost universal ratification of the CRC,[2] the concern for children's rights continued throughout the 90s and persists until today, where children's rights seem to have gained an established place in society. Research from the 80s to 90s engaged with philosophical and moral arguments about the relevance and importance of children's rights (see for example Archard 1993/2004; Bandman 1999; Freeman 1997). Some scholars have taken an opposite stance, making a case *against* children's rights (see for instance Purdy 1992; Guggenheim 2005). These academic works are little concerned with providing a full picture of the social consequences of children's rights; the empirical material they discuss serves mainly to illustrate previously taken moral or ideological positions. These works form part of what we might call 'early research' on the Convention on the Rights of the Child which explored the context in which the CRC came into being, the vast thematic and geographical areas in which it is to be applied, the newly established national and international monitoring mechanisms and available implementation strategies. Closely related are investigations on how children's rights can be put in practice, addressing technical legal themes surrounding the CRC and its implementation and monitoring procedures (see for instance Detrick 1992, 1999; Van Bueren 1998; Kilkelly 1999; Hodgkin and Newell 2002; Alen et al. 2006; Feria Tinta 2008; Sloth-Nielsen 2008; Lundy et al. 2012). This work focuses on legal scholarship and primarily concentrates on the written law, thereby leaving relatively unaddressed the question of knowing how 'law in the books' relates to 'law in action'.

In parallel with the growing attention for children's rights, since the beginning of the 90s a distinctive field of studies within sociology developed. Initially called the 'new social studies of childhood', this study field is now more commonly phrased as the 'sociology of childhood' or 'childhood studies' and investigates the social reality in which children's rights operate and are enforced (or not). Researchers within this field make use of general social science frameworks applied to childhood and often critically engage with major sociological issues, such as tension between agency and structure, the question of the multiplicity and diversity of childhoods or propose to include 'generation' as a separate distinctive category, besides class, gender and ethnicity (Representative work in this field includes: Corsaro 1997/2005; James and Prout 1990; James et al. 1998; Qvortrup 2005; Qvortrup et al. 1994). Childhood studies have contributed to deconstructing the dominant image of the child as merely 'becoming' a future adult, which has been for a long time children's almost exclusive social position (Archard 1993/2004; Verhellen 2000). For example, children's welfare measures such as the placement of children in an institution or a foster care family, are more often than not justified by referring to their long term effects on children's future well-being, rather than on their immediate benefits for children in the here and now. In such a view, the state of being a child is almost reduced to "an inadequate precursor to the real state of human being, namely being 'grown up'" (James et al. 1998: 18). Conversely,

[2] As of 1 November 2013, only Somalia, the USA and South-Soudan did not ratify the CRC.

scholars writing from a childhood studies perspective have insisted that children have views on their own which have intrinsic value also in the present. Children's social problems should therefore also be investigated from children's own perspectives whereby social welfare measures directed at children cannot be limited to looking at their future life chances but should also, and most importantly, take their present well-being and rights into account. Examples of these include academic writings on child labour (Reynolds 1991; Nieuwenhuys 1994; Liebel 2004); on street children (Ennew 1995; Hecht 1998; Lucchini 1993; Stoecklin 2000); on children and prostitution (O'Connell 2001; Montgomery 2002); or on child soldiers (Boyden and de Berry 2005; Honwana 2005; Rosen 2005). Albeit less prominent than in childhood sociology, the child agency perspective is also receiving growing attention in other disciplines, including developmental psychology (e.g., Flekkøy and Kaufman 1997; John 2003; Burman 2007), history (e.g., Cunningham 2005), geography (e.g., Katz 2004) and legal studies (e.g., Ang et al. 2006). On these views, children are social actors in their own rights and should be treated as 'beings' and not merely as 'becomings' (Lee 2001: 3).

In the past decade a discursive approach to children's rights has emerged, in line with the emerging critical study of human rights (Goodale 2007). This perspective critically engages with the environment in which children's rights are produced and translated into social practice, including their social consequences. Two examples illustrate the nature and scope of the criticism. For Reynaert et al. (2009), the CRC embodies the process of individualization of the Western society and a tendency towards the educationalization and professionalization of childhood (See also the chapter by Reynaert and Roose in this volume). Pupavac situates the human and children's rights project in the context of a 'deep moral, political and social crisis' (2001: 96). She contends that the children's rights discourse embodies a 'misanthropic view of adulthood' (2001: 100) and, ultimately, tends to pathologize Southern families for not complying with the Western views of parenthood. These developments have contributed to a much more critical understanding of children's rights. They emphasise the complex challenges related to child participation, one of the central notions of the children's rights agenda, which will be further addressed below (see Sect. 3 of the present chapter).

12.3 Rights, Emancipation and Interdisciplinarity

Since its adoption in 1989, the CRC has predominantly, and by a vast number of actors and authors, been referred to as an important instrument for improving the position of children in society. Few child rights advocates would indeed disagree with Freeman's wording that "we can and must believe that the state of childhood will be improved if we are prepared to take children's rights more seriously" (1997: 21). However, there is also a certain amount of confusion as to whether the Convention on the Rights of the Child, by itself, has or can have emancipatory features or effects. Already when the CRC was being drafted, a number of authors who defended an emancipatory view on children and adolescents were very critical regarding the possible positive impact of the CRC for advancing children's rights (See for instance De Graaf 1989; Journal du Droit des Jeunes 1989). In particular, they feared that by adopting a specific children's rights instrument, advocates for children's emancipation would no longer be able to rely on general human rights frameworks which they used previously to strengthen children's position in society. In this view, the adoption of a children's rights convention would paradoxically restrict, not expand, children's emancipation. Developments on the national and international levels during more than 20 years since the adoption of the CRC both support and contradict such a scepticism. In matters pertaining to the protection of children against violence, the CRC has for instance contributed to strengthen children's legal position; in other fields, for instance with regard to respect for children's work-related rights, the separate children's rights regime has contributed to confining children to a downgraded set of rights, whereby other submerged interests, such as the protection of the labour force in the North rather than the protection of children have taken pre-eminence (Hanson 2014).

The discussion over the emancipatory features of the Convention on the Rights of the Child is reminiscent to a central debate in legal theory whether the existence and content of law is exclusively grounded in social facts or also in moral facts, known as the 'Hart-Dworkin debate' in legal philosophy (Shapiro 2007). According to Freeman (1997), who refers to Dworkin's *Taking Rights Seriously* (1997), rights are not only entitlements, trumps and valuable commodities, but are also weapons to undermine power. For Freeman a rights strategy is one way in which the hitherto excluded can be included, within the community and within the political structure. H.L.A. Hart (1998) is sceptical about the possible role of law as an instrument for change, for instance to influence the morality of a society. For Hart, the enactment or repeal of laws may well be among the causes of change or decay of some moral standard or some tradition. But he also notes that although the law of some societies has occasionally been in advance of the accepted morality, normally law follows morality. In such a view, emancipation could be reached more effectively by other means than human rights. Raes (1997), who makes a parallel with the mitigated success obtained by the feminist movement in advancing women's claims as human rights, argues that rights claims can be part of a project to make society more egalitarian, democratic, responsible and caring only if prior conditions are fulfilled which these rights as such do not control. The author also warns that in case these conditions are not met, "the implementation of children's rights will not ameliorate their fate but could very well result into an even greater control on children's lives" (Raes 1997: 13).

The expansion of the children's rights field and of its number of supporters also gave rise to a proliferation of views on the meaning and content of children's rights. In academic children's rights literature, various subjects are being discussed not only from a wide range of disciplinary perspectives but also from diverse ideological positions. Simon (2000) for instance substitutes the 'wrongs to the child' for the 'rights of the child' and places the primary focus on children's protection rights. For him, children's rights deal with a universal moral obligation for all individuals to avoid that the gravest harm is inflicted on children. Hunt Federle rejects such a view of children's rights which does not empower children through rights, but "empower[s] ourselves to intervene in their lives" (1994: 365). For her, the value of rights is that they enable children to rely on their rights to challenge existing hierarchies and can contribute to shifting power away from those who have it to children, and can hence equalize relationships. The two authors, who have both published their views in one of the main scientific journals on the subject, *The International Journal of Children's Rights*, refer to children's rights discourses for defending radically different views. Moreover, their contrasting positions illustrate that albeit everybody seems to agree about the importance of children's rights, a true consensus on the meaning and content of the concept is often far away. In order to explore and map different perspectives and stances on children's rights, Hanson (2012) distinguishes four schools of thought in children's rights, namely Paternalism, Liberation, Welfare and Empowerment. Children's rights advocates and researchers are to a great extent influenced by their views on childhood image, children's competence, children's rights and the way how differences between children and adults are valued. The discussion over the emancipatory features of the children's rights paradigm makes clear that claims based on children's rights need careful empirical scrutiny. In other words, it is not enough "to plead for the recognition of rights of children on moral grounds. We should also enquire what people – children, but other persons as well – will (and can) *do* with them." (Raes 1997: 14). Such a view is central to the capability approach, which precisely studies the conditions, or social and personal conversion factors, under which rights can be made operational.

Given the great social interest for children's rights, in its myriad forms and understandings, it is important for children's rights research to find a right balance between 'enlightenment' and 'engineering'. "Is child rights research sufficiently theoretical, and not too practical? (. . .) A consensus on the extent, priorities or even precise content of children's rights is not readily available: children's rights are a moral sensitive domain having to deal with strong and often competing normative and ideological perspectives. (. . .) In addition, children's rights, as is the case with human rights in general, are permeated with high ideals of social justice, making children's rights an arena perfectly fit for social change and advocacy. For researchers, such a contexts poses some particular challenges. Doing scientific research on a subject that has been pushed forward far and foremost from an activist's perspective is not an easy undertaking, as it catches many a human or children's rights researcher between their role of a distant scientific observer, and the role of a human rights advocate wishing to contribute via research findings to make the realisation of children's rights come closer to reality" (Hanson 2007: 635–636).

Confronted with the limitations of 'technical fixes' (see also Fernando 2001) or legal arrangements for children's social problems, a growing part of the scientific literature emphasises the need for various forms of collaboration amongst and across disciplines to start elaborating new theoretical frameworks that can 'give voice' to children. This is also the case for elaborating conceptualizations that take into account how children perceive and live their rights, taking inspiration from gender and feminist theories in law and society and the feminist claim for the ability to produce knowledge 'on women's terms' (Sunder 2007). The challenge to address these complexities is best taken into account by adopting an inter-disciplinary, reflexive perspective to the study of children's rights. The overall objective of interdisciplinary research in children's rights is to foster social enlightenment aimed at describing, understanding and evaluating children's rights (cf. Tamanaha 2001).

12.4 Child Participation

The empirical findings from our research project on 20 years of international children's rights advocacy have highlighted that, in spite of a growing academic commitment towards children's agency and participation rights, the discourse produced by UN entities and international NGOs has paid relatively marginal attention to these themes. On average about 9 % only of the advocacy discourse of the last two decades has been dedicated to children as resourceful agents, including child participation (Hanson et al. 2014). A much more substantial share of child rights activists' attention refers to the image of children as innocent victims in need to be secured rights or to be saved from harm: on the top of the international agenda are themes such as the specific needs and rights of children exposed to emergencies; children's basic needs; the worst forms of child labour; and violence against children.

These findings are consistent with literature that assesses practice and research on child participation, which is an extremely complex principle to implement (David 2002). Participation practices have only very rarely provided children, despite the promise, with real power, and have also failed to include certain groups of children (Thomas 2007). Indeed, the prevailing views about child participation remain deeply embedded in a vertical and binary understanding of implementation, whereby participation is seen as a component of a predominantly top-down process. For instance, children might be invited to give their viewpoints on how to implement a centrally established child labour abolition programme, but are seldom asked what their own policy priorities would be with regards to labour and education. Within the context of globalisation of political decision-making processes, children's participation practice is mostly scaled down to a marginal activity, as children remain excluded from the real centres of power-making (Tisdall et al. 2006). For Thomas, "...there is very little sign of children and young people really participating in the processes that actually produce important political decisions, or in contributing to defining the terms of policy debate" (2007: 207). Butler (2008) argues that we should therefore try to catch a much broader range of activities that constitute, from children and young people's own understandings, forms of the 'political'. Given the relatively weak results of more than a decade of child participation in improving the lives of children in the global South, according to Jason Hart, it may be time for international development practice "to reflect more deeply and thoroughly on the relationship between participatory initiatives and wider societal change" (2008: 416). For Tisdall (2008), the 'honeymoon' of mere advocating children's participation in the public space on the basis of moral and/or rhetorical arguments based on acknowledging children's agency and rights enshrined in the CRC, is over. It is time, she argues, for developing broader theorizations of children's participation that can help not only to better understand, analyse and critique current practices, but that can also assist policy and practice addressing children and young people's participation in public decision-making. Recently, a number of publications have been issued that engage precisely with such broader theorizations of children's participation (see for instance the handbook on children's participation by Percy-Smith and Thomas 2010), and that explore child participation from several perspectives including sociology of action (Stoecklin 2013), the agency of children (Oswell 2012) and children's citizenship (Invernizzi and Williams 2008; Cockburn 2012).

An interesting account of child participation can be found in Gallagher (2008) who emphasises how the Foucauldian conception of power as ambivalent – both a means of control and a means of resistance – can offer a distinctive perspective to gain a better understanding of children's participation. Gallagher thereby usefully summarises Foucault's view on power which circulates through networks and "cannot be viewed as something which flows from the top of a social hierarchy downwards – from the State to the people,... and so on" (2008: 399). Such a perspective on child participation and the circulation of power provides an impetus for overcoming the vertical and binary thinking and giving due weight to local, marginal or 'subaltern' views of children's rights. That is what the concept 'living rights', to which we turn now, aims to do.

12.5 Living Rights

Drawing upon theoretical constructs from critical social anthropology, political science, socio-legal studies and the sociology of childhood, we adopt a non-essentialist approach to the study of children's rights. This perspective looks at human and children's rights as a social construction. This approach has a series of implications to which we now turn, including about how children's rights are defined, the move from a vertical to a horizontal perspective and the relation between human rights and power.

From a non-essentialist perspective, in line with Tamanaha's analysis and definition of the concept of law (2001: 27), rights are here defined as whatever people identify and treat, through their social practices, as 'rights'. In contrast to essentialism that suggests that law possesses certain necessary characteristics, Tamanaha sees conventionalism as an alternative description of a social practice; "law is a human social creation that lacks inherently necessary qualities" (2000: 15). This definition allows taking into account the legal and non-legal meanings of rights and may be transposed to children's rights as follows: a child right is whatever people identify and treat, through their social practices, as a 'child right'. In line with Goodale's discussion of human rights, social practices are understood as "all of the many ways in which social actors across the range talk about, advocate for, criticize, study, legally enact, vernacularize, and so on, the idea of human rights in its different forms" (2007: 24). Social actors include children, institutions, international or non-governmental organisations, and states who practice children's rights within different social contexts. This perspective implies the necessity to study the social practice of the actors involved at both the local (e.g. children, their families, guardians or representatives; and communities) and at the global level (e.g. organizations developing relevant law and intervening on that basis on children's behalf). Tamanaha's reasoning related to the concept of 'law' (2001) can be transposed to the notion of 'children's rights'. However, the above definition of children's rights needs to be qualified, as it raises two key questions:

1. A first question deals with *who* identifies what 'children's rights' are. In our view, we assume that any member of a given group can identify what a child right is, as long as it constitutes a conventional practice. This means that, besides children themselves, self-appointed groups of representatives of children's interests (not necessarily legal, but claiming to represent children's views and acting in the name of their 'rights') may be the source of 'children's rights'. Admittedly, parents/guardians and communities may legitimately speak on younger children's behalf. Admitting the possibility of representation in the identification of children's rights raises the above mentioned problematic of representational power. To what extent do these representatives appropriately represent the interests, views and claims of children? Stammers identifies the existence of functioning and democratically built channels of representation and communication as key to the dynamic of representational power (2009). Applied to small children, this criterion highlights the complex conceptual and practical implications of a non-essentialist approach to children's rights.
2. A second question concerns the number of persons who must see something as 'children's rights' in order to qualify as such. Tamanaha proposes a minimum threshold. A child right can be considered as such if an adequate number of persons with sufficient conviction consider something to be a 'child right', and act pursuant to this belief, in ways that have an influence in the social arena. This criterion requires some degree of continuous social presence of the notion of 'children's rights' and allows screening out the 'lunatic one' who would claim his or her own rights against a sufficiently accepted social practice. It leaves open the question of how many people and how much conviction may be considered as 'sufficient' and hence allows the presence of simultaneous existing accepted social practices, for instance in particular regions or amongst sub-groups in society. The answer to the question how many people are needed for something to qualify as a 'child right' may be sought in conventional social practices and in the relative influence they have on the social arena. It is here that

social research – using, in particular, anthropological forms of knowledge – may play a crucial role in increasing the weight of evidence supporting determinate claims.

From this perspective, international human and children's rights cease to be a metaphysical abstraction of moral norms or the embodiment of universal natural rights. They are seen as an imperfect compromise negotiated at a certain moment in time by individuals representing different national and organizational interests and possessing different knowledge, skills and power that come close to the 'conversion factors' as conceived in the capability approach. International children's rights law becomes thereby one of the many possible understandings of the rights of the child, as legitimate as other more marginal or local conceptions, like those embodied in customs and traditions. A non-essentialist approach transforms the vertical understanding of children's rights embodied in the idea of implementation conceptually into a horizontal relationship between equally legitimate and relevant social practices. Rather than asking whether the CRC is correctly implemented or whether children's rights are compatible with local cultural values, this approach recognizes that children's rights can be made to carry many, even contradictory meanings (Reynolds et al. 2006). According to this line of thought, as Goodale puts it, human rights are a product of 'open source theorizing', i.e. their meaning "will remain contextual and relative [and] all truth claims on behalf of a particular approach to the idea of human rights are reinscribed within the particular intellectual and political histories that produced them" (2007: 26). By recognizing the legitimacy of different understandings of rights, this theoretical framework acknowledges that law and rights are and have always been a social creation (Tamanaha 2001). It also allows analysing international human rights discourse as one among several discourses relating in one way or another with 'rights', thereby elevating social practice to both an analytical and methodological category (Goodale 2007: 8). The recognition of the openness and incompleteness of human and children's rights, as is the case with 'entitlements' within the capability approach, should not be taken as an indication of their failure. In contrast, these characteristics are "essential to the development of what are different – but living and organic – *ideas* of human rights, which can be expressed politically and institutionally precisely *because* their legitimacy does not depend on assumptions or aspirations of universality" (Goodale 2007: 26). Indeed, the legitimacy of rights – and of law in general – highly depends on their relevance to addressing local communities' daily challenges (De Feyter 2007). This approach is close to recent attempts at 'localizing' human rights where localization is defined as "a process whereby local human rights needs inspire the further interpretation and elaboration of human rights norms at levels ranging from the domestic to the global, and serve as a point of departure for human rights action" (Ibid.: 89). Through this perspective, children's rights come to be seen as 'living practice' shaped by children's everyday concerns. Yet, the question of how to understand the other's perspective when the other is a child remains one of the key challenges of research on and with children.

A non-essentialist approach to children's rights also implies looking at the environment in which children's rights practice emerges and at the functions it accomplishes. In this respect, the concept of 'living rights' allows moving away from essentialist views about the function of human rights. Indeed, while the human rights discourse may provide children with a powerful tool for social change in view of their emancipation as social actors deficient in power, human rights are not by definition a tool for social change. The social world is not solely shaped by high ideals of empowerment, but is also taking form as a consequence of pragmatic policies that might make use of human rights discourses not to alter but to sustain extant power relations (Stammers 1999). Extremes on the continuum of conceptions of children's rights, that is those who see them either as entitlements that can empower the powerless or as mere tools in the hands of the powerful, share a naïve instrumentalist view of children's rights that is highly problematic (Summers 1977). The instrumentalist view distorts reality and hides complexity; it fails to take into account variations and commonalities in local contexts. There is for instance a huge difference between powerful trade unions in the North asking that child labour in the South needs to be abolished and grass-root organizations of working children in the South claiming respect, fair wages and decent conditions for children's work. Both groups wish to implement internationally accepted labour standards but from a completely different position with different understandings and interests in the issues at stake (Hertel 2006). Rights are brought into effect through social practices in particular contexts and time frames and do not necessarily always carry the same meaning, nor do the consequences of particular usages of children's rights necessarily coincide with their initial objectives (Foucault 1984; see also Daiute 2008 and Goodale 2007). Social practices emerge from the encounter between everyday experiences and the body of knowledge on which practical decision-making is based. From this non-essentialist perspective, research in children's rights has undertaken empirical investigations of the social consequences of children's rights. In which contexts and on what conditions do they function as an effective tool for change? Well intentioned attempts at addressing the admittedly pressing needs of children in abstracto, may turn into an entirely different affair when put into practice in local contexts (Chowdhry 2006; Khair 2001; Snodgrass Goday 1999). NGO interventions aimed at 'saving' children from sex workers by extracting a handful of them from Kolkata's red light district, as recorded in the documentary film *Born into Brothels* (2004) might support the self-esteem of the saviors but by the same token risks undermining extant solidarity networks amongst the concerned population, including children's organizations, and their existing strategies for improving the living conditions of the whole neighborhood (Sircar and Dutta 2011).

According to the above considerations, all social practices that are conventionally identified as rights may be understood as 'living rights', that is: they are alive – through active and creative interpretations, association and framing of what constitutes in a given context a child right – in people's hearts and minds. In this sense, children's and communities' understanding of rights are equally 'living' than the interpretations of people and organizations who act on children's behalf. This approach has significant implications not only for the analysis of children's rights but maybe also for studying and understanding entitlements within the capability approach. In particular, it may be seen as leaning dangerously towards a certain cultural relativism. Indeed, if all social practices identified as rights by the concerned people are equally legitimate, how to assess what is actually permitted? In order to bypass the dilemmas caused by the horizontality of the living rights concept, we conceive 'living rights' as intertwined with the complementary notions of social justice and translations. It is to the notion of translations that we now turn.

12.6 Translations

International children's rights have primarily been approached and studied as a top-down process whereby principles and rights enshrined in international human rights documents are to be implemented at the national and local levels. In its General Comment No. 5 of 2003 concerning General measures of implementation of the CRC, the Committee on the Rights of the Child defines implementation as "the process whereby States parties take action to ensure the realization of all rights in the Convention for all children in their jurisdiction".[3] Within this view, the ultimate aim of human rights implementation is for international norms to have an impact on the ground, in children's lives. Implementation is thereby considered as the application of given and allegedly universal international norms into practice, from the global to the local, from top to bottom (Hanson and Nieuwenhuys 2013). Such a standard view on implementation of children's rights has however also been challenged, both on normative as well as on empirical grounds. From a normative standpoint, the binary and vertical vision underpinning the dominant focus on implementation of international norms fails to appropriately recognize the legitimacy of concurring or at times dissenting local interpretations of human rights (De Feyter et al. 2011; Goodale 2007). Empirically, anthropological research into the effects of the application of international children's rights for the lives of children has shown that in the top-down implementation process also unintended consequences occur – children's rights may be refracted in a variety of ways and not necessarily always in the child's best interests (Reynolds et al. 2006).

There are a number of different understandings of the notion of translations. In his framework 'Localizing human rights', De Feyter (2007) refers to the translation concept in international human rights in a vertical fashion. He thereby refers to Merry, for whom "various actors in the localisation process contribute to 'translating' international human rights 'down' into local systems and 'translating' actors' local stories 'up' by telling these stories 'using global rights language' to achieve their objectives" (Merry 2006: 211).

[3] CRC/GC/2003/5, para. 1.

Fig. 12.1 Top down and bottom up translations

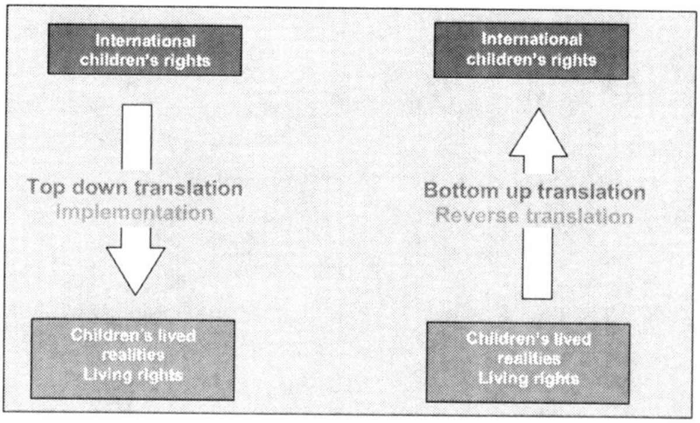

Figure 12.1 applies these top down and bottom up translations to the children's rights field:

Goodale's (2007) concept of translation contributes to bypassing the binary spatial metaphor of the global and the local by focusing on a third space, the 'betweenness' in which the dialogue between individual and groups on values and norms takes place. It is here, in the exchange between equally legitimate sets of values and norms that new social practices may emerge.

We understand translation, in line with this horizontal approach, as a dynamic, circular and continuous practice. Coming from an interdisciplinary approach as explained above, the concept 'translation' thereby relies on interdisciplinary notions of complexity, circularity and interrelations. It is our contention that 'translations' has a strong potential to serve as a rallying concept for encouraging an interdisciplinary dialogue amongst socio-legal studies, communication sciences, human geography, social anthropology, sociology, psychology and political science. Overall, it is expected that this emphasis on an interdisciplinary approach will lead to better insights into children's rights translation processes, and in particular to developing a theory that can fully take into account the growing attention to children's living rights. A dynamic, circular translation concept can graphically be represented as follows in Fig. 12.2:

Translation is not a one-way but a two-way process, whereby both sides of the exchange get transformed. Young phrases such a dynamic translation concept as 'Carribean creolization', which "comes close to a foundational idea of postcolonialism: that the one-way process by which translation is customarily conceived can be rethought in terms of cultural interaction, and as a space of re-empowerment" (2003:142). Within the children's rights field, strategic configurations in the game between different social groups can equally be detected. In the dynamic two-way translations, children, human rights institutions and transnational advocacy networks all contribute to the 'creoalization' of children's human rights. Competing or complementary strategies are generally deployed together, so that no person or group can claim ownership. Large development agencies, grass-root children's rights groups and local governments make use of children's rights to support their claims. For instance, according to Raoul Kienge-Kienge Intudi, the

Fig. 12.2 Translation processes

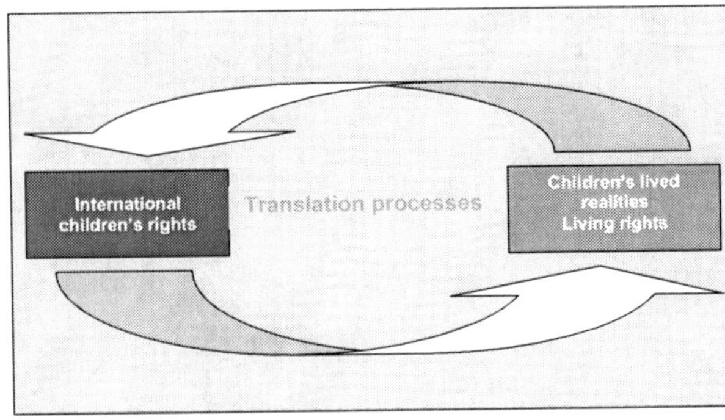

CRC is instrumentalised by both African governments and local NGOs for gaining access to scarce and much needed resources (2007). Gallagher supports that it may be "unhelpful to imagine children's participation as a process by which adults, who 'have' power, empower children by 'giving' them some of this power. It might be more interesting to look at precisely how power is exercised, through a whole range of different techniques, in the interactions between the individuals involved" (2008: 402–403).

12.7 Children's Rights Research in Practice

Children have the capacity not only to submit but also to act upon the world in which they live, including in problematic social contexts such as those experienced by many children around the world. Empirical childhood and children's rights studies have made clear that in order to understand their realities, children cannot be reduced to the mere image of passive victims of dire circumstances but that if we want to understand and engage with their lived realities and rights, the complex situations they face and the agency they exercise need to be taken into account (Hanson and Nieuwenhuys 2013).

Anthropological enquiries into the phenomenon of children accused of witchcraft, have for instance not only found that witch children suffer violence and ill treatment perpetrated by adults, but also that these children are at the same time active subjects who make use of their agency in their relation with their elders (de Boeck 2009). Witch children are of course victims who require help due to the many forms of violence they face (Hanson and Ruggiero 2013). However, as de Boeck explains, "children, especially in the often extreme living conditions in which they grow up in the African context, are not only vulnerable and passive victims, subjected to (. . .) the context in which they live, but they are also active subjects (. . .) of that reality" (2009: 140). Being a victim is only part of the whole picture which reveals that children and young people in fact do play an active role and need to be regarded "as social actors in the present, with a marked role and presence in the very heart of the societal context, and fully responsible for their own actions" (Ibid.: 141). Another example concerns children's experiences and understandings of war. Also in this field, anthropological literature has provided a complex and nuanced picture of how many current and former child soldiers exercise agency in circumstances of armed conflict (Hanson 2011). The empirical findings not only point at the frequency of forced recruitment but also highlight the political and economic motivations why young people might voluntary join armed forces (Lee 2009). When confronting international human rights norms pertaining to children in the context of armed conflict with these empirical insights on the diversity and complexity of local realities of war and violent political struggles, the absence of an agency perspective on child soldiering is remarkable. It were mostly humanitarian groups that have contributed to shaping the international legal treaties that seek to ban the use of child soldiers on moral grounds. Prevailing interpretations of these treaties assume that persons younger than 18 are unable, per definition, to exercise agency and stand in contrast with results from empirical studies in anthropology that draw attention to the agency of young people during armed conflict. The contrast between the legal and social realities highlights the continuing tensions between normative and empirical perspectives. However, dominant interpretations of international human rights law, by ignoring children's agency that lies at the very core of the human rights framework, risk overlooking the lived realities of young people participating in and affected by armed conflict (Hanson 2011).

Our conceptual framework opens up space for considering children as active translators of international human rights. Based on a non-essentialist perspective, it conceptually transforms the vertical understanding of children's rights, which is embodied in the idea of implementation, into a horizontal relationship between different social practices. It provides, in particular, legitimacy to those 'subaltern' claims that – due to their marginality in relation to the dominant human rights practice – are not being heard or are easily discarded because they cross the boundaries of moral acceptability. To paraphrase Merry, the examination of "areas where paternalism prohibits agency" (2009: 386) suggests that children's competences and ability to make choices tends to be denied when local social practices contradict the dominant moral standards. However, issues like child labour, child soldiering or child witchcraft, which we have discussed in this chapter as examples of controversial practices, cannot simply be dismissed on moral grounds. They gain new salience and complexity and require in-depth assessment in each context. This statement should however not be misunderstood. By providing the space for giving due consideration to marginal or 'subaltern' social practices, our approach does not intend to justify them, nor it contends that they are necessarily beneficial to children. It simply argues that competing social practices and the social contexts in which they arise should be given equal consideration. It also contends that the effectiveness of the two-way translation processes – whose outcomes are uncertain precisely because they provide equal access to all to the production of universality – plays a key role in grounding the legitimacy of human and children's rights in the daily reality of individuals and communities. By investigating and comparing these tensions between normative and empirical realms in their respective fields, children's rights studies and the capability approach might have a lot to learn from each other.

References

Alanen, L. (2010). Taking children's rights seriously. *Childhood, 17*(1), 5–8.

Alen, A., Vande Lanotte, J., Verhellen, E., Ang, F., Berghmans, E., & Verheyde, M. (Eds.). (2006). *A Commentary on the United Nations Convention on the Rights of the Child*. The Hague: Martinus Nijhoff Publishers.

Ang, F., Berghmans, E., Cattrijsse, L., Delplace, M., Delens-Ravier, I., Vandresse, C., & Verheyde, M. (2006). *Participation rights of children*. Antwerpen: Intersentia.

Archard, D. (1993/2004). *Children, rights and childhood*. London: Routledge.

Bandman, B. (1999). *Children's right to freedom, care, and enlightenment*. New York: Garland.

Boyden, J., & de Berry, J. (Eds.). (2005). *Children and youth on the frontline. Ethnography, armed conflict and displacement*. New York: Berghahn Books.

Burman, E. (2007). *Developments, child, image, nation*. London: Routledge.

Butler, U. M. (2008). Children's participation in Brazil – a brief genealogy and recent innovations. *The International Journal of Children's Rights, 16*(3), 301–312.

Chowdhry, G. (2006). Post-colonial readings of child labour in a globalized economy. In R. Stubbs & G. R. D. Underhill (Eds.), *Political economy and the changing global order* (pp. 233–245). Toronto: Oxford University Press.

Cockburn, T. (2012). *Rethinking children's citizenship*. Basingstoke: Palgrave Macmillan.

Corsaro, W. A. (1997/2005). *The sociology of childhood*. London: Sage

Cunningham, H. (2005). *Children and childhood in Western society since 1500* (2nd ed.). Harlow: Pearson Education.

Daiute, C. (2008). The rights of children, the rights of nations: Developmental theory and the politics of children's rights. *Journal of Social Issues, 64*(4), 701–723.

David, P. (2002). Implementing the rights of the child. Six reasons why the human rights of children remain a constant challenge. *International Review of Education, 48*(3–4), 259–263.

de Boeck, F. (2009). At risk, as risk: Abandonment and care in a world of spiritual insecurity. In J. La Fontaine (Ed.), *The devil's children: From spirit possession to witchcraft: New allegations that affect children* (pp. 129–150). Aldershot: Ashgate.

De Feyter, K. (2007). Localising human rights. In W. Benedek, K. De Feyter, & F. Marella (Eds.), *Economic globalisation and human rights* (pp. 67–92). Cambridge: University Press.

De Feyter, K., Parmentier, S., Timmerman, C., & Ulrich, G. (Eds.). (2011). *The local relevance of human rights*. Cambridge: University Press.

De Graaf, J. H. (1989). De betekenis van de Ontwerp–Conventie inzake de Rechten van het Kind. In M. De Langen, J. H. De Graaf, & F. B. M. Kunneman (Eds.), *Kinderen en recht* (pp. 14–24). Arnhem: Gouda Quint.

Detrick, S. (Ed.). (1992). *The United Nations Convention on the Rights of the Child, a guide to the "travaux préparatoires"*. Dordrecht: Martinus Nijhoff Publishers.

Detrick, S. (1999). *A commentary on the United Nations Convention on the Rights of the Child*. The Hague: Martinus Nijhoff Publishers.

Dworkin, R. (1997). *Taking rights seriously*. Cambridge: Harvard University Press.

Ennew, J. (1995). Outside childhood: Street children's rights. In B. Franklin (Ed.), *The handbook of children's rights, comparative policy and practice* (pp. 201–214). London: Routledge.

Feria Tinta, M. (2008). *The landmark rulings of the Inter-American Court of Human Rights on the rights of the child. Protecting the most vulnerable at the edge*. Leiden: Martinus Nijhoff.

Fernando, J. L. (2001). Children's rights: Beyond the impasse. *Annals of the American Academy of Political and Social Science, 575*, 8–24.

Flekkøy, M. G., & en Kaufman, N. H. (1997). *The participation rights of the child: Rights and responsibilities in family and society*. London: Jessica Kingsley.
Foucault, M. (1984). Qu'appelle-t-on punir?. In F. Ringelheim (Ed.), *Punir mon beau souci. Pour un raison pénale 1–3* (pp. 35–46). Revue de l'Université de Bruxelles.
Freeman, M. (1997). *The moral status of children: Essays on the rights of the child*. Dordrecht: Martinus Nijhoff.
Gallagher, M. (2008). Foucault, power and participation. *The International Journal of Children's Rights, 16*(3), 395–406.
Goodale, M. (2007). Locating rights, envisioning law between the global and the local. In M. Goodale & S. E. Merry (Eds.), *The practice of human rights: Tracking law between the global and the local* (pp. 1–38). New York: Cambridge University Press.
Guggenheim, M. (2005). *What's wrong with children's rights?* Cambridge: Harvard University Press.
Hanson, K. (2007). Does practice also work in theory? In A. Alen, H. Bosly, M. De Bie, J. Vande Lanotte, et al. (Eds.), *The UN children's rights convention: Theory meets practice* (pp. 633–646). Antwerpen: Intersentia.
Hanson, K. (2011). International children's rights and armed conflict. *Human Rights and International Legal Discourse, 5*(1), 40–62.
Hanson, K. (2012). Schools of thought in children's rights. In M. Liebel (Ed.), *Children's rights from below. Cross-cultural perspectives* (pp. 63–79). Basingstoke: Palgrave Macmillan.
Hanson, K. (2014). Separate childhood laws and the future of society. *Law, Culture and the Humanities, 11* (in press).
Hanson, K., & Nieuwenhuys, O. (Eds.). (2013). *Reconceptualizing children's rights in International Development. Living rights, social justice, translations*. Cambridge: University Press.
Hanson, K., & Poretti, M. (2012). Living Rights' ou l'enfant sujet de droits: la traduction de la compréhension de leurs droits par les enfants eux-mêmes à l'attention de la communauté internationale. In P. Meyer-Bisch (Ed.), *L'enfant témoin et sujet: les droits culturels de l'enfant* (pp. 81–101). Genève: Schulthess.
Hanson, K., & Ruggiero, R. (2013). *Child witchcraft allegations and human rights. Briefing paper for the European Parliament's Subcommittee on Human Rights*. Brussels: European Parliament.
Hanson, K., Poretti, M., & Darbellay, F. (2014). *Whose rights? What claims? A quantitative analysis of the priorities of two decades of international children's rights advocacy*, Manuscript in preparation.
Hart, H. L. A. (1998). *The concept of law*. Oxford: Clarendon Press.
Hart, J. (2008). 'Children's participation and international development: Attending to the political. *The International Journal of Children's Rights, 16*(3), 407–418.
Hecht, T. (1998). *At home in the street: Street children of Northeast Brazil*. Cambridge: Cambridge University Press.
Hertel, S. (2006). *Unexpected power. Conflict and change among transnational activists*. Ithaca: Cornell University Press.
Hodgkin, R., & Newell, P. (2002). *The implementation handbook for the Convention on the Rights of the Child* (2nd ed.). New York: Unicef.
Honwana, A. (2005). *Child soldiers in Africa*. Philadelphia: University of Pennsylvania Press.
Hunt Federle, K. (1994). Rights flow downhill. *The International Journal of Children's Rights, 2*(4), 343–368.
Invernizzi, A., & Williams, J. (Eds.). (2008). *Children and citizenship*. London: Sage.
James, A., & Prout, A. (Eds.). (1990). *Constructing and reconstructing childhood: Contemporary issues in the sociological study of childhood*. London: Falmer Press.
James, A., Jenks, C., & Prout, A. (1998). *Theorizing childhood*. Cambridge: Polity.
John, M. (2003). *Children's rights and power*. London: Jessica Kingsley.
Journal du Droit des Jeunes. (1989). Le projet de Convention internationale sur les droits de l'enfant. *Journal du Droit des Jeunes, 1989*(7), 5.

Katz, C. (2004). *Growing up global: Economic restructuring and children's everyday lives*. Minneapolis: University of Minnesota Press.
Khair, S. (2001). Street children in conflict with the law: The Bangladesh experience. *Asia-Pacific Journal on Human Rights and the Law, 2*(1), 55–76.
Kienge-Kienge Intudi, R. (2007). The application of the international Convention on the Rights of the Child in Africa: When the law is tested by the reality. In: A. Alen, H. Bosly, M. De Bie, & J. Vande Lanotte et al. (Eds.), *The UN Children's Rights Convention Theory meets practice* (pp. 23–31). Proceedings of the International Interdisciplinary Conference on Children's Rights, 18–19 May 2006. Ghent/Antwerpen/Oxford: Intersentia
Kilkelly, U. (1999). *The child and the European Convention on Human Rights*. Dartmouth: Ashgate.
Lee, N. (2001). *Childhood and society. Growing up in an age of uncertainty*. Buckingham: Open University Press.
Lee, A.-J. (2009). *Understanding and addressing the phenomenon of 'child soldiers': The gap between the global humanitarian discourse and the local understandings and experiences of young people's military recruitment*, 52 Working Paper Series Refugee Studies Centre, University of Oxford. Oxford: Department of International Development, 2009. http://www.rsc.ox.ac.uk/publications/working-papers-folder_contents/RSCworkingpaper52.pdf. Accessed 1 Nov 2013
Liebel, M. (2004). *A will of their own: Cross-cultural perspectives on working children*. London: Zed books.
Lucchini, R. (1993). *Enfant de la rue. Identité, sociabilité, drogue*. Droz: Genève/Paris.
Lundy, L., Kilkelly, U., Byrne, B., & Kang, J. (2012). *The UN Convention on the Rights of the Child: A study of legal implementation in 12 countries*. Belfast: Queen's University Centre for Children's Rights.
Merry, S. E. (2006). *Human rights and gender violence: Translating international law into local justice*. Chicago: University of Chicago Press.
Merry, S. E. (2009). Relating to the subjects of human rights: The culture of agency in human rights discourse. In M. Freeman & D. Napier (Eds.), *Law and anthropology. Current legal issues 2008* (Vol. 12). Oxford: Oxford University Press.
Montgomery, H. (2002). *Modern Babylon? Prostituting children in Thailand*. New York: Berghahn Books.
Nieuwenhuys, O. (1994). *Children's lifeworlds, gender, welfare and labour in the developing world*. New York: Routledge.
O'Connell, J. D. (2001). *Children in the global sex trade*. Cambridge: Polity Press.
Oswell, D. (2012). *The agency of children: From family to global human rights*. Cambridge: University Press.
Percy-Smith, B., & Thomas, N. (Eds.). (2010). *A handbook of children and young people's participation: Perspectives from theory and practice*. London: Routledge.
Poretti, M., Hanson, K., Darbellay, F., & Berchtold, A. (2014). The rise and fall of icons of 'stolen childhood' since the adoption of the UN Convention on the Rights of the Child. *Childhood, 21*(1), 22–38.
Pupavac, V. (2001). Misanthropy without borders: The international children's rights regime. *Disasters, 25*(2), 95–112.
Purdy, L. M. (1992). *In their best interest? The case against equal rights for children*. Ithaca: Cornell University Press.
Qvortrup, J. (Ed.). (2005). *Studies in modern childhood: Society, agency, culture*. Houndmills: Palgrave Macmillan.
Qvortrup, J., Bardy, M., Sgritta, G., & Wintersberger, H. (Eds.). (1994). *Childhood matters: Social theory, practice and politics*. Avebury: Ashgate.
Raes, K. (1997). Children's rights and modern culture. The politics of juridification and its limits. In E. Verhellen (Ed.), *Understanding children's rights* (pp. 9–26). Ghent: Ghent University, Children's Rights Centre.

Reynaert, D., Bouverne-De Bie, M., & Vandevelde, S. (2009). A review of children's rights literature since the adoption of the United Nations Convention on the Rights of the Child. *Childhood, 16*(4), 518–534.

Reynolds, P. (1991). *Dance civet cat: Child labour in the Zambezi Valley*. London: Zed books.

Reynolds, P., Nieuwenhuys, O., & Hanson, K. (2006). Refractions of children's rights in development practice. *Childhood, 13*(3), 291–302.

Robeyns, I. (2011). The capability approach. In E. N. Zalta (Ed.), *The Stanford encyclopedia of philosophy* (Summer 2011 Edition). http://plato.stanford.edu/archives/sum2011/entries/capability-approach/. Accessed 1 Nov 2013.

Rosen, D. (2005). *Armies of the young: Child soldiers in war and terrorism*. Camden: Rutgers University Press.

Shapiro, S. J. (2007). *The "Hart-Dworkin" debate: A short guide for the perplexed*. University of Michigan Law School, Public Law And Legal Theory Working Paper Series, Working Paper No. 77. http://ssrn.com/abstract=968657. Accessed 1 Nov 2013.

Simon, T. W. (2000). United Nations Convention on wrongs to the child. *The International Journal of Children's Rights, 8*(1), 1–13.

Sircar, O., & Dutta, D. (2011). Beyond compassion: Children of sex workers in Kolkata's Sonagachi. *Childhood, 18*(3), 333–349.

Sloth-Nielsen, J. (2008). *Children's rights in Africa. A legal perspective*. Aldershot: Ashgate.

Snodgrass Goday, A. (1999). "Our right is the right to be killed", making rights real on the streets of Guatemala City. *Childhood, 6*(4), 423–442.

Stammers, N. (1999). Social movements and the construction of human rights. *Human Rights Quarterly, 21*, 980–1008.

Stammers, N. (2009). *'Keynote address', Living rights: Theorizing children's rights in international development Research Seminar*. Sion: IUKB.

Stoecklin, D. (2000). *Enfants des rues en Chine. Une exploration sociologique*. Paris: Karthala.

Stoecklin, D. (2013). Theories of action in the field of child participation: In search of explicit frameworks. *Childhood, 20*(4), 443–457.

Summers, R. S. (1977). Naïve instrumentalism and the law. In P. M. S. Hacker & J. Raz (Eds.), *Law, morality and society. Essays in Honour of H.L.A. Hart* (pp. 119–131). Oxford: Clarendon.

Sunder, M. (Ed.). (2007). *Gender and feminist theory in law and society*. Aldershot: Ashgate.

Tamanaha, B. Z. (2000). A non-essentialist version of legal pluralism'. *Journal of Law and Society, 27*(2), 296–321.

Tamanaha, B. Z. (2001). Socio-legal positivism and a general jurisprudence. *Oxford Journal of Legal Studies, 21*(1), 1–32.

Terzi, L. (2005). Beyond the dilemma of difference: The capability approach to disability and special education needs. *Journal of Philosophy of Education, 39*(3), 443–459.

Thomas, N. (2007). Towards a theory of children's participation. *The International Journal of Children's Rights, 15*, 199–218.

Tisdall, K. M. (2008). Is the honeymoon over? Children and young peoples' participation in public decision-making. *The International Journal of Children's Rights, 16*(3), 419–429.

Tisdall, K. M., Davis, J. M., Hill, M., & Prout, A. (2006). *Children, young people and social inclusion. Participation for what?* Bristol: The Policy Press.

Uvin, P. (2010). From the right to development to the rights-based approach: How human rights entered development. In A. Cornwall & D. Eade (Eds.), *Deconstructing development discourse. Buzzwords and fuzzwords* (pp. 163–174). Warwickshire: Practical Action Publishing.

Van Bueren, G. (1998). *The International Law on the Rights of the Child*. The Hague: Martinus Nijhoff Publishers.

Veerman, P. E. (1992). Towards a more integrated basis for the children's rights movement: The aims and outcome of the first International Interdisciplinary Study-Group on Ideologies of Children's Rights. In M. Freeman & P. E. Veerman (Eds.), *The ideologies of children's rights* (pp. 357–363). The Hague: Martinus Nijhoff.

Verhellen, E. (2000). *Convention on the rights of the child. Background, motivation, strategies, main themes*. Leuven: Garant.

Young, R. J. C. (2003). *Postcolonialism. A very short introduction*. Oxford: Oxford University Press.

Chapter 13
Growing Up in Contexts of Vulnerability: The Challenges in Changing Paradigms and Practices for Children's and Adolescents' Rights in Brazil and Mexico

Irene Rizzini and Danielle Strickland

13.1 Introduction

The observations of the UN Committee on the Rights of the Child for monitoring progress towards the principles of the UN Convention on the Rights of the Child (hereafter UNCRC) have led to significant advances in the realm of children's and adolescents' rights. In both Brazil and Mexico, the recommendations have influenced new laws and amendments of existing legislation (UNCRC 2004, 2006). More importantly, however, the Committee offers concrete recommendations to address shortcomings in the specific case of each nation. The reports show wide variation among countries in progress towards achieving the recommended goals set by the Committee to understand, respect and enforce the principles of the UNCRC. Mexico, for example, is considered to have made very few advances in joint efforts between civil society and government, while in the case of Brazil the Committee is more concerned with "dramatic inequalities based on race, social class, gender and geographic location which significantly hamper progress towards the full realization of the children's rights enshrined in the Convention" (UNCRC 2004, 2006:par. 12).

In Brazil and Mexico, as elsewhere, achievements have been made, but notable challenges remain. Brazil is a country with exceptionally strong constitutional and legal protections for children and youth and an increasing number of policies and

I. Rizzini (✉)
Pontifical Catholic University of Rio de Janeiro, PUC-Rio, Department of Social Work, International Center for Research and Policy on Childhood, Rua, Marquês de São Vicente, 225. CEP 22453-900. Gávea. Rio de Janeiro, RJ, Brazil
e-mail: ireneri26@gmail.com

D. Strickland
Doctorado en Desarrollo Educativo, Universidad Pedagógica Nacional, Unidad Guadalajara, Plan de San Luis 1696, Colonia Chapultepec Country, Guadalajara, Jalisco, Mexico
C.P. 44420
e-mail: danielle@upngdl.mx

D. Stoecklin and J.-M. Bonvin (eds.), *Children's Rights and the Capability Approach*, Children's Well-Being: Indicators and Research 8, DOI 10.1007/978-94-017-9091-8_13,

programs to put rights into practice. These guarantees are enshrined in the 1988 Constitution and the 1990 Statute on the Rights of the Child and the Adolescent, which itself was inspired by the UNCRC. Since the turn of the century, Mexico has been following Brazil's lead with the implementation of children's rights laws on a federal level and in almost all Mexican states, as well as several constitutional amendments to promote the best interest of the child. The notion and the language of "rights" are responsible for a key discourse that expresses the need for social change in both nations. Brazil and Mexico both show significant efforts regarding the promotion of children's rights as they seek to be considered nations with balanced development in social, political and environmental issues, along with the renowned economic growth which has kept both countries in the international spotlight for the past decade.

Despite the clear progress in the discourse of young people's rights in Brazil and Mexico, there is still a considerable gap between the rights guaranteed by law and the harsh realities children face. There have been advances in healthcare and school attendance, for example, but the low quality of public education, the persistence of large scale poverty and violence against children and youth remain major issues (REDIM 2012; Rizzini et al. 2010).

In this chapter, the authors focus on children who live in contexts of vulnerability, with low income families, in poor and often violent neighborhoods. They are particularly interested in children who have left their family and community contexts to live on the streets. Though these children do not lack a sense of agency – for they have to act with great autonomy to survive on the streets – they are seen as a threat to society and agents of violence.

In research conducted by the authors portraying their life trajectories, young people in street situations[1] often said that they would like to be seen simply as human beings and treated like anyone else. They are faced with enormous barriers for social inclusion, as their participation in society is rarely valued or even recognized. This chapter explores how their formal liberties, or the rights children and adolescents are entitled to by law, are far from their real freedoms, or the opportunities and capabilities found on the streets and in the impoverished neighborhoods of Brazil and Mexico.

The capabilities approach, developed by Amartya Sen and Martha Nussbaum, "is focused on choice or freedom, holding that the crucial good societies should be

[1] The term "children and youth in street situations" has come to replace "street children", children 'on' and 'of' the streets", and "homeless youth" in the language of academics and activists with a rights-based approach, as it allows for analysis in a broader context and considers their position in the streets as a condition that can be overcome (Rizzini et al. 2007). The term covers both categories of children 'on' and 'of' the streets, but is not a category in itself; it is rather a way to stress the importance of describing and understanding the "situations" in which young people can be found on the streets. The other term that has become accepted in reference to these children is "street-connectedness", again reflecting a potentially temporary condition, rather than labeling them as belonging to the streets, trying to categorize them as never or always sleeping on the streets, or having or not having a home (Thomas de Benítez 2011).

promoting for their people is a set of opportunities, or substantial freedoms, which people then may or may not exercise in action: the choice is theirs" (Nussbaum 2011:19). The poverty and rights violations, resulting from the discrimination and marginalization described in this chapter, are further magnified by the lack of real freedoms for most young people in Brazil and Mexico. As Nussbaum explains, this approach "ascribes an urgent task to government and public policy – namely, to improve the quality of life for all people, as defined by their capabilities" (ibid.).

In the first part of the chapter the authors focus on the context for implementing children's rights in Brazil and Mexico. The second half of the chapter examines the efforts of each nation to promote, defend and restitute children's and adolescents' rights. This analysis shows the need to transform discourses and policy into practices that will truly increase capabilities for youth. The historical tension between civil society organizations and the government in both nations is a clear obstacle for increasing real freedoms for vulnerable young people, as neither nation reports successful joint efforts between these sectors. Furthermore, the absence of opportunities for young people to participate in their homes, communities, schools and other spaces to promote and protect their rights, especially in Mexico, also slows the progress for changing paradigms of children's and adolescents' rights. Finally, while there is a clear interest in this topic by certain public officials and members of both countries' civil society, discrimination, racism and obvious gaps in opportunities available to wealthy and poor children, continue to hinder progress towards becoming nations that truly respect the rights of all children and adolescents.

13.2 The Context for Implementing Children's Rights in Brazil and Mexico

Half of Brazil's population is under 24 years of age (IBGE 2010).[2] After centuries of massive income disparities, inequality in Brazil is slowly beginning to lessen due to a variety of factors including an expanding economy, steady increases in the minimum wage, and a family income supplement called *Bolsa Família* (Family Allowance). From 1990 to 2010, the number of Brazilians in extreme poverty measured by a per-capita household income of less than 25 % of minimum wage decreased significantly.[3]

Bolsa Familia was started by the Brazilian federal government in 2004 and includes the project *Fome Zero* (Zero Hunger), a public policy aimed at ensuring the human right to adequate nutrition. It combined and extended several existing

[2] In Brazil, the term "youth" often includes young people up to the age of 24. Some of the statistics in this text use this age limit for youth.

[3] Note that the most common measure of poverty in Brazil is the monthly per capita income, a figure controlled by family size.

welfare support programs for low income families in Brazil. *Bolsa Família* and other major conditional cash transfer programs in Latin America, such as those in Chile and Mexico, have had an impressive targeting performance, even though they have adopted different methods (Soares et al. 2007; Mourão and Macedo de Jesus 2011). The program has three major aspects: the immediate alleviation of poverty by direct financial support, conditions to receive the allowance that promote social development, and complementary programs in health and education. Currently, the program serves 13 million families with an average allowance of R$100 or roughly US$50 per family per month. While that amount can significantly help a family in a low-income rural area, it is less assistance to an urban family. However, there is a fear that creating a two tier system would merely accelerate urbanization. The conditions for receiving the allowance include that all the children in a household have their vaccinations up-to-date, that children under the age of 15 have at least an 85 % attendance record at school, that pregnant women attend pre-natal visits and that nursing women between the ages of 14 and 44 schedule health exams. The World Bank considers *Bolsa Famila* to be one of the factors that has reduced the very large level of income inequality in Brazil, along with the gradual increase in minimum wage and economic expansion in Brazil.[4]

Still there is an estimate by the Ministry of Social Development of almost nine million people living in extreme poverty and surviving off an income of less than R $127 or US$63 a month, while the official poverty line in Brazil is a per diem, per capita income of R$6.80 or about US$3.40 (approximately R$204 or US$102 per month).[5] Between 1997 and 2008, the percentage of Brazilian children under the age of 18 living below the poverty line declined from 43 to 36 %, but that decline still leaves over a third of the nation's children and youth living in poverty[6] (Bush and Rizzini 2011).

The context for implementing children's rights in Mexico is equally complex. Mexico has approximately 40 million children and adolescents, representing 37 % of the nation's population, over half of whom live in poverty. One out of every 50 children between the ages of 0 and 4 suffers from extreme malnourishment, and an estimated 36.8 % of the population under the age of 18 lacks running water in their homes (REDIM 2012). Healthcare for children is also far from universal in Mexico. Despite recent initiatives to offer free public healthcare in the nation with the program *Seguro Popular*, one out of every five Mexican children still lacks coverage.

Mexico's poverty continues to drive thousands to immigrate to the United States each year with dreams of earning a decent salary. The minimum wage in Mexico is

---

[4] See http://bolsafamilia.net/bolsa-familia-2012-reajuste-valor-bolsa-familia/html (unofficial blog of Bolsa Família) and http://www.mds.gov.br/bolsafamilia (official government reports on *Bolsa Familia*) [Accessed 27 May 2013].

[5] Based on exchange rate of April 1, 2013.

[6] The time periods and age groups used in this section reflect the ranges used by different sources of data.

set regionally and ranges from 61.38 to 64.76 pesos (approx. US$5) a day.[7] Furthermore, 30 % of the working age population in the country is self-employed and another 4.85 % is unemployed. As a result, in 2010, 10 % of all Mexicans lived in the US, half of whom resided there illegally (Terrazas 2010).

Many of those who do not migrate require the entire family to work in order to cover their basic needs. The most recent survey by the National Institute of Statistics and Geography (INEGI) reports three million child laborers in Mexico, primarily active in the informal economy (INEGI 2010). In 2012 an estimated 2,145 Mexicans joined the informal economy every day (Rodríguez 2012). This statistic includes people cleaning windshields, performing in intersections or selling chewing gum in streets across the nation.

While all young people who live in low-income communities face difficulties in mainstream society, challenges are much greater for children in street situations.[8] A recent national census in Brazil of such children and youth showed that while the majority still lived at home, almost 40 % of them had no stability of residence (Secretaria de Direitos Humanos e Instituto de Desenvolvimento Sustentável 2010). Twenty-four percent of those who had abandoned their homes had been on the streets for between 2 and 5 years. Nearly all the children and youth in the study begged for spare change, and 16 % of the girls admitting to prostitution. Despite this constant hustling, almost 30 % of the national sample said they did not eat every day. Their future prospects are also grim. Only 24 % of the 16 and 17 year olds had completed elementary school and only 2 % had graduated from secondary school (ibid.).

Another set of questions particularly relevant to children in street situations concerns the high rates of abuse and violence in their daily lives. In Rio de Janeiro, an unfortunately named city initiative, *choque de ordem* (shock of order), has police adopting a so-called zero-tolerance approach to a variety of "urban nuisances". Many of the visible signs of *choque de ordem* involve cracking down on the ubiquitous illegal street vendors. However, their action also includes picking up poor children on the streets in middle class neighborhoods and taking them elsewhere. In the course of this exercise, street educators report that young people in street situations suffer high degrees of harassment and abuse. They tend to be "expelled" to the periphery of the city and hence are even more hidden and out of reach of the civil society organizations dedicated to helping youth in street situations in more central parts of the city (Rizzini et al. 2012).

As in Brazil, a significant part of Mexican child laborers are found in urban street situations. While Mexico City is the only urban center in the country where one can still find large groups of young people living together on the streets, children selling candy, begging for change and cleaning windshields are a regular part of the scenery in all Mexican cities. In 2011, nearly 900,000 adolescents between the

[7] Based on exchange rate from April 1, 2013.

[8] This term refers to children who spend a significant amount of time on the streets out of need, regardless of whether or not they sleep on the streets.

ages of 12 and 17 reportedly worked in Mexico without pay and 1,089,665 adolescents in the same age group worked more than 48 h a week (REDIM 2012).

Also similar to the scenario in Brazil are the high levels of discrimination and exclusion suffered by children and youth in street situations in Mexico. *Tolerancia Cero* (Zero Tolerance) and other programs similar to *Choque de Ordem* in Rio have made them less visible, and they are generally ignored by policy makers. This is illustrated by the fact that 18 years have passed since an official census of children and adolescents living on the streets was carried out in Mexico (Strickland 2009).

The government programs directed towards street populations in Mexico are either welfare-based and lack basic pedagogical guidelines to help beneficiaries overcome their dependence on the streets, or focus on social cleansing, with the basic philosophy of "out of sight, out of mind" (Pérez 2009). These programs seek to put children and youth found on the streets into state-run institutions or orphanages, or bribe parents with food baskets and scholarships to keep their children off the streets, even though this usually means leaving them without supervision. They lack a long-term vision based on the capabilities approach that would increase opportunities with training for skilled labor, critical thinking or other initiatives to empower marginalized youth, for example. As in Brazil, the Mexican police's interactions with these youth are plagued with violence in arbitrary detentions, interrogations and incarcerations (Guillén 2012). Examples of abuse against children and youth in street situations in Mexico include:

- In April 1998, manhole covers were sealed shut in the Alameda Park in downtown Mexico City, trapping 17 children inside.
- In July 2002, approximately 250 children, youth and adults in street situations were removed from the streets in preparation for a visit from Pope John Paul II. They were locked in a warehouse for 2 weeks.
- In November 2009 a group of youth living on the streets in downtown Mexico City was drenched by city water trucks while their belongings were taken by city trash collectors.

The UN Committee's recommendations to Mexico state that, "In particular, the Committee regrets the violence to which [children in street situations] are subjected by the police and others" (Committee on the Rights of the Child 2006: par. 68).

It is true that there are fewer children visible on the streets in both Brazil and Mexico than there were a couple of years ago, at least in the areas where the police have been more active. However, until new policy measures are taken, it is unlikely that these children's needs will be fulfilled in their own communities, nor should we expect an increase in opportunities for young people in these nations or a decrease in reported levels of violence towards them.

In fact, since 2006 there has been a dramatic surge in violence throughout Mexico, largely related to ex-president Felipe Calderon's war against the drug trade. During his 6 years in office, Human Rights Watch estimates 70,000 murders related to the Mexican drug war, a death toll rivaling Syria's civil war (Vivanco 2013). The annual number of homicide victims between the ages of 15 and 17 reached 964, an increase of 250 % from 2005 (REDIM 2012).

In general, violence against children in Mexico is socially acceptable and considered a necessary part of their education. In 2006, the UN Committee on the Rights of the Child noted with great concern the fact that "corporal punishment is still lawful in the home, and is not explicitly prohibited in the schools, in penal institutions and in alternative care settings. . .consequently corporal punishment is widely used" (Committee on the Rights of the Child 2006: par. 35). The National Survey on Discrimination in Mexico in 2010 reported that 95.5 % of Mexicans consider that children are hit with the intention of being "educated or corrected." Interestingly, 80 % of the same surveyed population believes that children's rights are respected in Mexico (Consejo Nacional para Prevenir la Discriminación 2011). That said, the number of cases of child abuse reported each year steadily decreased from 34,023 in 2008 to 14,289 in 2011 (REDIM 2012).

The normalization of violence in low-income communities or *favelas* is also a notable obstacle for guaranteeing real freedoms in Brazil. International comparisons in youth homicides show a vast difference between northern and southern hemisphere countries. The publication, *Mapa da Violência, Os Jovens da América Latina*, (Map of Violence, the Young People of Latin America) showed 2008 homicide rates for youth (ages 10–29) of 51.6 per 100,000 in Brazil, 73.4 in Colombia, 1.7 in Portugal and 12.9 in the United States (Ritla 2008). In Brazil, the appalling rates of death by homicide among young black men and the lack of appropriate measures to prevent this tragedy as well as high levels of violence in society in general have caused some commentators to refer to the phenomenon as *banalização* (trivialization) of violence (Secretaria de Direitos Humanos 2010:11).

As in Mexico, however, some statistics reflect recent drops in the levels of violence in Rio de Janeiro. One of the reforms introduced in 2007 was a new policing program with the unfortunate name of *Unidades de Polícia Pacificadora* (Police Pacifying Units, hereafter UPP) which constituted the first ever attempt at regular policing of the low-income communities. Given the decades of trafficker and militia violence in the *favelas* of Rio, with the police responding only when the violence reached surrounding middle class communities, and then shooting and killing indiscriminately, it is not surprising that there are mixed feelings about this initiative. Notwithstanding, some of the results have been striking. UPP has been installed in one *favela* at a time because of the enormous person power needed to enter the communities in force, secure them, and then establish a permanent police force. The major Brazilian news conglomerate *O Globo* regularly reports that most of the residents in these communities are pleased with the result, many of whom say they feel safer.

However, critics accuse the program of being a façade for the 2014 World Cup and the 2016 Olympic Games, both of which will be held in Rio. It is still unclear whether the UPPs will be systematically extended to all *favelas*, especially those outside the middle class southern zone of the city, and whether more attention will be paid to the militias since most of the initial focus has been on the traffickers. Critics also note an increase in casual crime in pacified *favelas*, previously forbidden by the traffickers, and there are many doubts as to whether or not infrastructure renovation or "urbanization", as well as educational and social programs in *favelas* will be extensive.

Low-income communities in urban Brazil vary significantly, in geographical dimensions, population density and poverty levels, but youth in many of them suffer from high absentee and failure rates in low quality schools, and in turn, pressure to drop out of school to earn small amounts of money to contribute to household expenses. Most youth who are behind grade level blame their learning difficulties on themselves rather than on the schools; yet they report classrooms constantly disturbed by talking, fighting, and playing. Low-income youth with the highest risk for poor academic achievement are those with parents who have limited education, black males and those from large families (Bush 2007). While certain key indicators of education in Brazil, most notably formal enrollment, show great improvements, the reality in low-income neighborhoods is that fundamental problems remain. Children only go to school for half a day because of the shortage of classroom space and teachers. Drop-out rates and the number of children scoring below grade level are very high. For example, in 2009, 51 % of children and youth from 8 to 14 years of age who lived in urban areas were behind grade level.[9]

Similarly, Mexico shows many incomplete efforts in its war on poverty since the turn of the century. Vicente Fox, president of Mexico from 2000 to 2006, was successful in bringing the nation to be labeled as a "developing country" by international standards with strategic actions to reduce extreme poverty indicators, such as replacing dirt floors with concrete. According to INEGI, during Fox's administration, the number of homes with dirt floors dropped from 2,900,000 to 2,400,000 (Alcántara 2012). However, the results were far from achieving his promise to eliminate dirt floors in homes across the nation, and concrete floors did little more to improve the beneficiaries' quality of life.

Other government efforts in Mexico to fight poverty since the turn of the century include the internationally praised program *Oportunidades* (Opportunities) that offers stipends to cover living expenses in exchange for sending children in school and attending medical appointments. These handouts have had little impact on really combating poverty, however. From 2010 to 2012, the number of poor Mexicans increased by half a million people, stressing the need for new strategies in their programs (CONEVAL 2012).

For 2013, the program has a budget of over 66 billion pesos or US$5.4 billion for 5.6 million Mexican families. When President Enrique Peña Nieto presented the 2013 budget he emphasized the importance of ensuring that the program includes more than basic welfare assistance and is really generating significant improvements in the quality of life for these families (Valdez 2012).

Similar to the positive results of *Bolsa Familia* in Brazil, *Oportunidades* has generated a steady increase in primary school enrollments and attendance in Mexico since the turn of the century. The national average of children between the ages of 5 and 11 who do not attend school has dropped from 7.3 % in 2000 to

[9] See the CIESPI data resource at www.ciespi.org.br, Table 14.

2.2 % in 2010. The percentage of 16 year olds who have completed middle school increased from 57.3 % in 2000 to 74 % in 2005, but dropped to 70.2 % in 2010.

Nevertheless, the public education system continues to be plagued by corruption, resulting in costly fees for uniforms and enrollment, overpopulated classrooms and high dropout rates. Only two-thirds of adolescents between the ages of 15 and 17 attend school, and 90 % of mothers in this age group have abandoned their formal education or never attended school. National test scores reflect the poor quality of the education system for those who remain. In 2011, 96.6 % of students in the ninth grade tested at an "insufficient" or "basic" level for Spanish on the primary national standardized test (ENLACE). The same low results were obtained by 88.4 % of this grade level in math. Corruption and the poor allocation of funds are part of the problem, as less than 50 % of elementary schools in Mexico have a computer. The number is even more shocking in indigenous primary schools where less than 22 % have a computer.

The quality of schools in indigenous communities is just one factor reflecting the serious problem of racism and discrimination in Mexico. While the black population is limited mostly to the Caribbean coast, there are 62 different indigenous groups in the country that can be seen as victims of this national problem (INEGI 2010). The discrimination suffered by Mexico's indigenous citizens is wide-ranged: only 57 % have access to public healthcare, 22.6 % live in homes with dirt floors, and more than a quarter of the population (27.3 %) is illiterate (ibid.).

While the indigenous population is not nearly as prevalent in Brazilian cities as in Mexico, part of the current challenges facing young people in Brazil is directly related to issues of race and geography. According to the 2010 census, 38.5 % of the population identified themselves as brown or mixed race, 6.2 % as black and 53.7 % as white (IBGE 2010).

In general, the arid northeastern states of the country are much poorer than the prosperous southeast. There are also large differences in living conditions and access to the mainstream economy among low-income communities in the same city. In Rio de Janeiro, for example, the *favelas* close to middle-class neighborhoods offer many more economic opportunities than the low-income communities on the periphery of the city. Whatever the color, many youth who live in low-income communities feel discriminated against when they enter middle class sections of their cities.

Racial discrimination along with a lack of opportunities and capabilities has driven a large percentage of the nations' rural populations into the cities where racism plays a significant role in urban poverty. TV, billboards and magazines are dominated by European-looking white faces. In Mexico, poor *mestizos* (mixed raced citizens) generally consider themselves at least one rung higher on the class ladder than their indigenous country people. Marrying a lighter-skinned person is often considered a way to "improve" the family bloodline.

The Committee on the Rights of the Child (2006) highlights this problem in Mexico in the 23rd paragraph of its last recommendations for the nation in stating:

> The Committee is deeply concerned about the significant disparities in [Mexico] in the implementation of the rights enshrined in the Convention, reflected in a range of social indicators such as enrolment in and completion of education, infant mortality rates and access to health care, indicating persistent discrimination against indigenous children, girls children with disabilities, children living in rural and remote areas and children from economically disadvantaged families.

While many civil society organizations, legislators and other government officials have jumped on the Latin American bandwagon of Human and Children's Rights, much of the general public remains in the dark. The National Survey on Discrimination in Mexico in 2010 reported that only 60 % of those interviewed believed that children should be guaranteed the rights given to them by law (Consejo Nacional para Prevenir la Discriminación 2011). Children's rights are often associated with or conditioned to responsibilities and are further seen as a "social imaginary" controlled by the government, far out of reach for the average citizen. In nations driven by immediate necessity, where so much of the population lives hand to mouth, promoting a public consciousness to protect and promote children's rights is undeniably challenging.

13.3 Formal Rights in Brazil and Mexico and the Remaining Challenge of Converting Them into Real Freedoms

Despite the challenges described in the last section, Brazil has accomplished some major advances in policy for children and youth over the last decade. The rate of infant mortality, for example dropped from 53.7 per 1,000 live births in 1990 to 22.8 in 2008 (Rizzini et al. 2010). Most recent indicators show a rate of 16.1 per 1,000 live births (IBGE 2010). Between 1982 and 2008, the rate of illiteracy among 15–17 year-olds dropped from 13.1 to 1.7 %. In 1992, 60 % of adolescents between the ages of 15 and 17 were attending school, a figure which increased to 83.7 % in 2011 (ibid).

Recent initiatives for young people which mark important advances include the National Policy for Youth and the creation of the National Secretariat for Youth (SNJ), the National Council of Youth (CONJUVE), and the National Program for the Inclusion of Youth: Education, Training, and Community Action (ProJovem). The problem, as we have identified in previous research, is related to the difficulty of implementing laws and policies in Brazil. Some of the challenges for implementing policies for children in street situations are: the lack of sustainable discussions about these children in Brazil, excessive responsibilities for children rights Councilors[10] and consequently the lack of time and resources to address all demands, and the difficulty of funding approved policies. Regardless of how well

[10] This honorary position is described on the following page.

policies are written, "centuries of imperial and oligarchic rule and the comparatively recent end of the military dictatorship left little tradition of citizen action to advocate for the passage and implementation of reform programs" (Bush and Rizzini 2011:66).

In Brazil, as in Mexico, there continues to be an acceptance of passing laws that are not really enforced. While these initiatives are clearly a step in the right direction, there is no evidence of them actually increasing real freedoms for marginalized Brazilian young people. National programs that promote the participation of youth have given them a voice in public policy, but the influence of this voice remains to be seen.

There are a variety of Brazilian organizations that provide opportunities for young advocates to sharpen their leadership skills and exercise their citizenship. In a study of activist youth in Rio de Janeiro, Mexico City and Chicago, the authors discovered the way in which different organizations including churches, cultural associations, political parties and advocacy groups gave the next generation of leaders opportunities to express and develop their proclivity for civic engagement (Rizzini et al. 2009; Torres et al. 2013). Both in Brazil and Mexico, youth became involved in advocacy projects through family, friends, the presence of the institution in their regular lives, such as school and church, and through what several described as "internal restlessness", meaning a sense of indignation that made them feel compelled to do something about the injustice they perceived. The Brazilian young people who participated in the study explained that their involvement was stimulated by recognition of the deep disparities in Brazilian society and the physical danger that threatened young people in the cities, but also by a sense of optimism that key aspects of Brazilian society were improving or were capable of improvement. The importance of social solidarity as a facet of social existence and as a vehicle for change seems to be a lot stronger in Brazil than for example in the United States or Mexico. The young people were quite aware of the risks of participation including getting labeled as an activist and having to sacrifice time with family and friends for their commitment to a cause. The critical conditions for this type of participation were found to be support from family members, especially parents, and access to organizations that encourage youth participation and are clearly an asset in achieving real freedoms for Brazilian children and youth; in other words ensuring the rights guaranteed in the 1988 Constitution and the 1990 Children's Rights Act in Brazil.

Part of the return to democracy in Brazil was a serious effort to include citizens in the ongoing task of government decision making. One vehicle was the establishment at the federal, state and municipal levels of Councils with federally mandated powers to debate public policy. Fifty percent of each Council is composed of public officials and the other half by civil society members. The members not serving in a public office are elected from civil society organizations that are registered by the Councils as organizations that provide services to children and youth.

The Children's Rights Councils are one of two Oversight Councils that have the power to formulate as well as review policy.[11] This power is described in Article 88 of the Statute on the Child and the Adolescent which states that the Children's Rights Councils are decision making and monitoring organs.[12] The guidelines of the enforcement policy for the provisions of the Statute are detailed in the same Article and include the following (with original paragraph numbers):

I – Municipalization of enforcement;
II – Creation of municipal, state and national councils of child and adolescent rights, which will be deliberative and controlling entities of actions at all levels, in which equal popular participation is ensured through representative organizations, according to the terms of federal, state and municipal legislation;
IV – Administration of national, state and municipal funds connected to the respective councils of child and adolescent rights;
VI – Mobilization of public opinion so as to achieve the essential participation of the different segments of society.

Thus the Children's Rights Councils are a key democratic tool for monitoring enforcement of rights. While the Councils exist at the three levels of government, it is the municipal councils that have the day to day responsibility for local implementation.

The Children's Rights Council in the municipality of Rio de Janeiro worked between 2008 and 2009 in the formulation of a policy specifically for children in street situations. The process of the Rio Council formulating and adopting this policy demonstrated both the possibilities and challenges of Children's Rights Councils. With pressure from Rio's Children's Network (Rede Rio Criança), and critical technical support from the International Center for Research and Policy on Childhood at PUC-Rio University (CIESPI), the project was successful in adopting a policy to assist children in street situations (Conselho Municipal dos Diretos da Criança e do Adolescente 2009). The policy contains concrete, feasible instructions for eight municipal departments regarding children in street situations. This process reinforced the principle of civil society-public sector parity by maintaining equal membership of both sectors in the working group that was charged with developing a draft policy. The working group and the Council used all available data in this process.[13] Once the Council had adopted the policy it established an implementation committee which in turn developed an agenda that continues to be monitored. The policy adopted by the Council represented a dramatic step from seeing children in street situations mainly as threats to public order to respecting them as active citizens with rights.

Despite the difficulties mentioned above in implementing policies in Brazil and the challenges the newly established Children's Rights Councils face to enforce

[11] The following material on the current Children's Rights Councils comes from Rizzini (coord.) 2010: pp. 166–174 and from Secretaria de Direitos Humanos and CONANDA 2005.

[12] Available in Portuguese at http://www.planalto.gov.br/ccivil_03/Leis/L8069.htm

[13] The national census on children in street situations was only completed after the Council had adopted the policy.

rights, these Councils exist in almost 6,000 municipalities in Brazil, have the federal legal mandate for adopting policies for children, and must include key public and civil society actors. They have an established institutional structure and attract key actors. They also have the opportunity, enforced by mandate, to examine the condition of children excluded from current programs and political agendas, thus allowing them to raise issues often overlooked by the executive and administrative branches of government. The challenges they face are serious, however "they should not obscure the set of advantages which no other group of independent or semi-independent actors possess" (Bush and Rizzini 2011:72).

The Rio experience also underlined some of the national challenges in making and implementing policy changes through Councils. While the Brazilian system of Councils is an adventurous step in participatory democracy, actions fall short of the promise on paper. The civil society members of Councils are unpaid and, therefore, have little time for their Council duties. In the particular example of Children's Rights Councils, most of the Councils' time is spent on their federally mandated duty to register all nonprofit groups that work with children. During CIESPI's work with the Children's Rights Council in Rio, many of the public sector councilors were junior employees without the authority to act on behalf of their departments, and councilors from both government and civil society lacked experience in policy making. While Brazil has a complex, centralized system for monitoring public budgets at all levels of government, it lacks transparency. In Rio de Janeiro, a combination of disinterest and opposition by the current city administration to the policy for street children has essentially halted its implementation.

This is just one example of how bureaucracy impedes the conversion of formal rights into capabilities. Without a clear budget and consensus on spending priorities, it is virtually impossible to develop projects that will increase the real freedoms of children in street situations, or any other group of marginalized youth. Furthermore, the use of impact indicators in program designs is far from universal, resulting in careless, inefficient expenditures of public funds. If Councils were to use the capabilities approach as a basis for their policy making, the impact of their efforts would greatly increase the real freedoms for project beneficiaries.

Apart from the Councils, Brazil has other avenues to enforce and implement existing laws, policies and plans. The Councils are but one part of a theoretically comprehensive system for implementing rights known as the *Sistema de Garantia de Direitos* (System to Guarantee Rights). This System encompasses all public and civil society actors responsible for guaranteeing the rights of citizens (Associação Brasileira de Magistrados, Promotores de Justiça e Defensores Públicos da Infância e da Juventude 2010).

There is no doubt that Brazil has accomplished great advances over the past two decades in legislation and policy in favor of children and youth. Young Brazilians have come to be considered as citizens with rights and now occupy a very different place in society than what was previously designated and permitted. Brazil has a new generation of active youth and Rights Councils, leading the way to a nation where children's rights are a reality, not just a discourse. Now the idea of passive children and the image of a child who will "someday become" an active member of society are refuted. The remaining challenge to truly achieve this paradigm shift is to convert policy into actions that will increase opportunities for young people. More real freedoms for marginalized youth will naturally decrease the number of children and youth who turn to the streets for survival as well as the violence and poverty found in *favelas*.

Mexico also has an impressive track record regarding legislation in favor of children's and adolescents' rights; however, when we consider actual actions that promote rights and give youth a voice in public policy, Mexico falls far behind Brazil. Several international treaties and agreements in favor of children's rights have been adopted, including the International Covenant on Civil and Political Rights; the Hague Conventions on the Civil Aspects of International Child Abduction and on the Protection of Children and Cooperation in Respect of Intercountry Adoption; the Worst Forms of Child Labor Convention; the Protocol to Prevent, Suppress and Punish Trafficking in Persons, especially Women and Children; and the UNCRC (Guerra 2007). By virtue of Article 133 of the Mexican Constitution, all international treaties are automatically incorporated into national legislation.

Mexico ratified the UNCRC on September 21, 1990 and adopted the first two Optional Protocols (OPs) to the Convention, proposed by the UN General Assembly in 2000.[14] In addition to having adopted these international treaties, Mexico passed a Federal Act on the Protection of the Rights of Children and Adolescents in 2000. Throughout the following decade, 30 of the 31 national entities further passed state laws to protect children's rights.[15] Mexico also amended articles 4 and 18 of its Constitution to strengthen the protection of children's rights in 2000 and 2006.

Despite these advances in national legislation, Mexico received a lengthy report of observations and recommendations from UN's Committee on the Rights of the Child in 2006. One of the most notable hindrances to children's rights is the "complexity of implementation due to the federal structure of [Mexico], which may result in new legislation not being fully implemented in practice at the state level. In particular, a number of laws, such as the Act on the Protection of the Rights of Children of 2000, have yet to be fully integrated into state laws" (Committee on the Rights of the Child 2006, par. 6).

In 2011, Mexico amended Articles 1, 4 and 73 of its Constitution, making notable improvements in the area of human and children's rights. The reform of the first article specifies that international treaties ratified by Mexico, along with the Constitution, share the highest level of normative hierarchy throughout the nation. Prior to this reform, the Mexican Constitution limited children's rights specifically to the basic necessities of "nutrition, healthcare, education and recreation for their

[14] The OP on the Sale of Children, Child Prostitution and Child Pornography was passed on January 18, 2002 and the OP on the Involvement of Children in Armed Conflict followed on February 12, 2002. The most recent Protocol regarding Communications Procedures has been open since February 28, 2012, but has yet to be passed in Mexico.

[15] Currently, Chihuahua is the only state that does not have its own law for the protection of children's rights. This is also the state with the highest teen homicide rate; in 2010 over 26 % of homicide deaths of adolescents between the ages of 15 and 17 occurred in Chihuahua.

healthy development" (Art. 4, par. 6); however, the reform now implicitly includes all the rights of the international treaties signed by Mexico. While it would be better to explicitly mention the four guiding principles of the CRC: non-discrimination; adherence to the best interests of the child; the right to life, survival and development; and the right to participate, this reform represents a significant step for rights-based legislation in Mexico. The constitution thus has moved from covering basic needs to recognizing that all children shall be guaranteed the economic, social and cultural rights, as well as the civil and political rights stipulated in the UNCRC.

Reforms to Article 4 of the Constitution make a clearer reference to the "obligations" of the State to guarantee children's rights. They also explicitly mention the importance of ensuring the "best interest of children" and that this principle should guide the design, implementation and evaluation of all public policy related to children. However, as the Committee notes, there is a general lack of congruency in the different levels of legislation, and federal and state laws have not been reformed to fully reflect the CRC, despite recommendations by the Network for Children's Rights in Mexico (*REDIM*). Proposed reforms to Article 73 of the Constitution attempts to address this problem. The reform would adapt the legal frameworks of the various federal agencies with the UNCRC and other relevant instruments through the proclamation of a general law. This law would be obligatory for all Mexican states and would override poor local legislation that lacks congruency with the UNCRC. It would also allow for "a clear attribution of obligations and faculties of each level of government, as well as the designation of coordination mechanisms for the implementation of children's rights in the country, that are currently missing" (REDIM 2012:27).[16]

Unlike the Councils in Brazil that are made up of an equal number of government officials and representatives from civil society, there are very few joint efforts between these bodies in Mexico. The Committee criticized the exclusion of civil society organizations in the coordinating mechanisms implemented thus far in Mexico to promote children's rights. "The Committee recommends that [Mexico] ensures that relevant NGOs be actively involved in the drafting, planning and implementation of policies, legislation and programs" (Committee on the Rights of the Child 2006:par. 20). The tension and resistance between government and civil society, especially in Mexico City, is a major barrier for changing paradigms and practices in favor of children's rights in Mexico. Unfortunately the Committee recommendations do not include specific guidelines for the coordination between government and civil society, and there is currently very little initiative from either part to work together.[17]

While it is apparent that the somewhat forced relationship between civil society and government in Brazilian councils has not yet accomplished the conversion of formal rights into real freedoms, collaboration between these groups is essential to

[16] Translation by author.

[17] One exception is the 2013 agenda of the REDIM to collaborate in the design of a general law for children's rights.

achieve the expected paradigm shift. Multiple elements, including legislation, public resources, civil society's experience, public funds and the influence of policy makers, are all necessary to increase the capabilities of marginalized youth in these nations. While it is challenging to mix some of these ingredients, they are all necessary parts of the recipe for increased capabilities in the field of children's and adolescents' rights.

Another major challenge for Mexico is the lack of opportunities for children and adolescents to actively participate in policy making. While it is one of the UNCRC's four guiding principles, it is not included in the seven guiding principles of the national Act of the Protection of the Rights of Children. The law does not establish obligations for institutions to guarantee children the right to participate in public policy, and actions to promote children's participation, such as annual Children's Parliament sessions and a Children's and Young People's Survey during national elections, have been isolated. Marking a clear difference from Brazil, the Committee "remains concerned at the persistence of traditional attitudes in [Mexico] which, among other things, limit children's right to participate and to express their views. . .in decision-making procedures affecting them, particularly in courts, schools and communities" (Committee on the Rights of the Child 2006:par. 27).

There are great barriers on Mexico's path to becoming a nation that truly respects and promotes children's and adolescents' rights and actively seeks to increase opportunities and capabilities for young people. The rough relationships between government and civil society, limited opportunities and initiatives to promote children and adolescent participation, specifically in issues affecting their rights, along with corruption at all levels of government and in the public education system are largely responsible for the 20 pages of "great concern" expressed in the recommendations by the Committee on the Rights of the Child regarding the situation of Mexican children's and adolescents' rights. Fortunately the REDIM, UNICEF Mexico and various civil society groups are not giving up. Their campaign *10 por la infancia* (10 points for childhood) is guiding political agendas of children's and adolescents' rights for Mexico's new president, Enrique Peña Nieto, as well as governors and mayors across the nation.[18]

13.4 Conclusion

In Brazil and Mexico there have been important achievements as well as notable remaining challenges in the field of children's and adolescents' rights. Both countries continue to pass laws that improve the legal framework for young people's rights, but there are serious deficiencies in their implementation and enforcement. While these initiatives are clearly a step in the right direction, there is little evidence of them actually increasing real freedoms for vulnerable young people. As

[18] See http://10xinfancia.mx/.

inequality persists in both nations, opportunities in impoverished communities continue to be limited, forcing many young people to turn to the informal economy and the streets for survival.

The needs and challenges have been detected. Opportunities for Mexican youth to participate in public policy are scarce, as are initiatives to give civil society a voice in law-making and government programs. While Brazil has more structured spaces to include youth and civil society in efforts to guarantee children's and adolescents' rights, their Councils are clearly not going to overcome all of the remaining obstacles noted in this chapter. Due to Brazil and Mexico's similar histories of inequality, centralization of power, corruption, lack of transparency and political participation, the challenges for achieving a rights-based society in either nation are considerable. However, despite the remaining challenges, Mexico's legislation and Brazil's Councils and various efforts to promote youth participation represent important steps towards achieving crucial changes that will benefit children and families.

Twenty years ago, children were basically invisible. Their opinions were rarely considered when it came to making choices, and little attention was given to the ways children could express themselves. The days when children were meant to be seen and not heard are history. Recent policy and legislation proves that children's and adolescents' rights are now valued by both countries. The challenge now is to implement these rights in all cultural, economic, social, civil and political aspects of society and thus increase the real freedoms for all young people.

From youth activists to civil society leaders, to academics and politicians there are many engaged actors committed to changing paradigms and practices in favor of children's and adolescents' rights in Brazil and Mexico. Combining efforts between these distinct groups would strengthen each initiative and ensure a smoother, faster path to becoming more equal and just nations.

References

Alcántara, L. (2012, April 10). ¿Qué es el programa 'Piso Firme'? *El Universal*, México D.F.

Associação Brasileira de Magistrados, Promotores de Justiça e Defensores Públicos da Infância e da Juventude ABMP. (2010). *Organização de Eduardo Rezende Melo: Cadernos de fluxos operacionais sistêmicos. Proteção integral e atuação em rede na garantia dos direitos de crianças e adolescentes*. São Paulo: ABMP.

Bush, M. (2007). *Barriers to youth connections to work: The case of young people in the low-Income neighborhood of Caju in Rio de Janeiro*. Chicago: Woodstock Institute.

Bush, M., & Rizzini, I. (2011). *Closing the gap between rights and realities for children and youth in Urban Brazil: Reflections on a Brazilian project to improve policies for street children*. Rio de Janeiro: CIESPI-PUC-Rio.

Committee on the Rights of the Child. (2006). Consideration of reports submitted by States Parties under Article 44 of the Convention, Concluding observations: Mexico.

Consejo Nacional de Evaluación de la Política de Desarrollo Social (CONEVAL). (2012) Resultados de pobreza a nivel nacional y por entidades federativas 2010–2012. http://www.coneval.gob.mx/. Accessed 2 Nov 2013.

Consejo Nacional para Prevenir la Discriminación. (2011). Encuesta Nacional Sobre Discriminación en México, Enadis 2010, Resultados Generales, México, D.F.: CONAPRED.

CONANDA. Conselho Municipal dos Direitos da Criança e do Adolescente da cidade do Rio de Janeiro. (2009). Delibera a Política Municipal de Atendimento a Crianças e Adolescentes em Situação de Rua no Rio de Janeiro. Aprovada em junho de 2009 – Deliberação 763/09.

Guerra, G. (2007). Children's rights: International and national laws and practices. Law Library of Congress. http://www.loc.gov/law/help/child-rights/mexico.php. Accessed 27 Mar 2013.

Guillén, P. (2012). Niños de la calle: víctimas de explotación, violencia y crimen. http://www.animalpolitico.com/2012/05/ninos-de-la-calle-victimas-de-explotacion-violencia-y-crimen/#axzz2UE2HbrWs. Accessed 24 May 2013.

IBGE. (2010). Brazilian population census. http://www.ibge.gov.br/english/estatistica/populacao/censo2010/default.shtm. Accessed 27 Mar 2013.

INEGI. (2010). Censo General de Población y Vivienda. www.inegi.gob.mx Accessed 27 Mar 2013.

Mourão, L., & Macedo de Jesús, A. (2011). Bolsa Família (Family Grant) Programme: an analysis of Brazilian income transfer programme. *The Journal of Field Actions*, Special issue 3, 2011. http://factsreports.revues.org/1314. Accessed 20 May 2013.

Nussbaum, M. C. (2011). *Creating capabilities. The human development approach*. Cambridge, MA: The Belknap Press of Harvard University Press.

Pérez, R. (2009). *Vivre et survivre à Mexico. Enfants et jeunes de la rue*. París: Karthala.

REDIM. (2012). La Infancia Cuenta en México 2012: Desafíos actuales para la garantía de los derechos de la infancia. Análisis del marco legal mexicana. México, D.F.: Red por los Derechos de la Infancia en México.

RITLA. (2008). *Mapa da violência. Os jovens da América Latina*. Brasília: Rede de Informação Tecnológica Latino Americana.

Rizzini, I. (coord.). (2010). *Direitos humanos de crianças e adolescentes: 20 anos do Estatuto*. Brasília: Secretaria de Direitos Humanos.

Rizzini, I., Butler, U. M., & Stoecklin, D. (Eds.). (2007). *Life on the streets: Children and adolescents on the streets: Inevitable trajectories?* Sion: Institut International des Droits de L'enfant.

Rizzini, I., de los Ángeles Torres, M., & del Rio, N. (2009). *Youth and civic engagement in the Americas. Preliminary findings from three city study: Rio de Janeiro, Chicago and Mexico City*. South Bend: Helen Kellogg Center for International Studies, Notre Dame University.

Rizzini, I., Caldeira, P., Ribeiro, R., & Carvano, L. M. (2010). *Crianças e adolescentes com direitos violados: situação de rua e indicadores de vulnerabilidade no Brasil urbano* (2nd ed.). Rio de Janeiro: CIESPI/PUC-Rio.

Rizzini, I., Princeswal, M., Caldeira, P., & Bush, M. (2012). *A efetivação de políticas públicas no Brasil. O caso das políticas para crianças e adolescentes em situação de rua*. Rio de Janeiro: CIESPI-PUC-Rio.

Rodríguez, I. (2012). Se incorporan a la economía informal 2,145 mexicanos al día en un año: Inegi, en La Jornada.

Secretaria de Direitos Humanos e Instituto de Desenvolvimento Sustentável (IDEST). (2010) *Primeira pesquisa censitária nacional sobre crianças e adolescentes em situação de rua*. Available at: http://www.teleios.com.br/wp-content/uploads/2011/03/Pesquisa-Censitaria-Nacional-sobre-Criancas-e-Adolescentes-em-Situacao-de-Rua-Mar-2011.pdf. Accessed 30 May 2013.

Soares, F. V., Ribas, R. P., Osorio, R. G. (2007). *Evaluating the impact of Brazil's Bolsa Familia: Cash transfer programmes in comparative perspective*. Brasilia: International Poverty Centre, United Nations Development Programme.

Strickland, D. (2009). La calle de los jóvenes en la Ciudad de México: territorios y redes de las poblaciones callejeras, en Revista Rayuela No. 1, Nov. 2009. http://ednica.org.mx/revistarayuela/numeros/textos/mexico/rebecca.pdf. Accessed 27 Mar 2013.

Terrazas, A. (2010). Mexican immigrants in the United States. Online article by the Migration Policy Institute. http://www.migrationinformation.org/usfocus/display.cfm?ID=767. Accessed 27 Mar 2013.

Thomas de Benítez, S. (2011). *State of the world's street children: Research. Part 2*. London: Consortium for Street Children.

Torres, M. d. l. Á., Rizzini, I., & del Río, N. (2013). *Citizens in the present. Youth civic engagement in the Americas*. Chicago: University of Illinois Press.

UN Committee on the Rights of the Child (CRC), UN Committee on the Rights of the Child: Concluding observations: Brazil, 3 November 2004, CRC/C/15/Add.241, http://www.refworld.org/docid/42d288d54.html. Accessed 24 May 2013.

UN Committee on the Rights of the Child (CRC), UN Committee on the Rights of the Child: Concluding observations, Mexico, 8 June 2006, CRC/C/MEX/CO/3. http://www.refworld.org/docid/45377ee60.html. Accessed 24 May 2013.

Valdez, B. (2012). Oportunidades ya no será un programa asistencial, en El Milenio. 12 Sep 2012. http://www.milenio.com/cdb/doc/noticias2011/ec5bb93ae3ed8dc80f748d6f86e5e96d Accessed 27 Mar 2013.

Vivanco, J. M. (2013). Obama: evitar abusos en la estrategia contra el narcotráfico en México. New York: Human Rights Watch. http://www.hrw.org/es/americas/mexico. Accessed 11 May 2013.

Conclusion

Daniel Stoecklin and Jean-Michel Bonvin

The wealth of topics that can be found in the contributions to this volume makes it difficult to pinpoint some and not others. Therefore, we have selected several issues that lead us, so we think, to follow important tracks. Our conclusion will therefore highlight some of what seems to us the most important prospects in the continuing task of building bridges between children's rights and the capability approach. We identify three major topics that can be seen as the most relevant prospects. These are the question of individual and social conversion factors, the issue of the child as a social actor (which relates to both participation and agency), and the debate over the vulnerable and competent child.

Individual and Social Conversion Factors

Biggeri and Karkara underline that in the last two decades the dialogue between the human rights approach (HRA) and the capability approach (CA) increased substantially. A synthesis of this debate was found in the Millennium Development Goals (MDGs), most of which are indirectly connected to children issues. Apart from this very important process aiming at settling a 'common vision of future goals and targets', much is still to be done from the theoretical, practical and empirical perspectives. Biggeri and Karkara explore the relationships and synergies between the CA and the HRA in the case of children. A key issue in this respect lies in the

D. Stoecklin (✉)
Children's Rights Unit, University Institute Kurt Bösch, P. O. Box 4176, CH 1950 Sion 4, Switzerland
e-mail: daniel.stoecklin@iukb.ch

J.-M. Bonvin
Ecole d'études sociales et pédagogiques (EESP), University of Applied Sciences Western Switzerland, Chemin des Abeilles 14, CH 1010 Lausanne, Switzerland
e-mail: jmbonvin@eesp.ch

D. Stoecklin and J.-M. Bonvin (eds.), *Children's Rights and the Capability Approach*, Children's Well-Being: Indicators and Research 8, DOI 10.1007/978-94-017-9091-8,

combination of individual and social conversion factors that facilitate, or conversely impede, the development of capabilities and the effective implementation of children's rights. The book provides insightful reflections into the complex interaction between social and individual conversion factors.

Liebel points to a crucial question when stating that rights become effective only when their holders (here children) are put in a position where they can actively use and transform them. This holds particularly for so-called "agency rights", where agency designates the "capacity of individuals to act independently" (James and James 2012: 3). Indeed, while protective rights call mainly for an external action (be it the State, third sector institutions or the family in the case of children), i.e. for appropriate social conversion factors, the enhancement of "agency rights" is more complex and requires to consider the individual as a co-author in the implementation of these rights: s/he is not only a passive recipient, but also a doer; however, s/he is not the only doer, but needs adequate support from the State and other external actors. Indeed, the subject is not considered in isolation from his/her context, as James (2009) clearly emphasizes when she relates agency to the subject's capacities for action as well as to the opportunities to make use of them. In this later definition of agency, we are clearly closer to the capability approach, taking into consideration the individual skills and the social opportunities to use them. In the same vein, many contributors to this volume speak of interdependencies. For instance, Baraldi and Iervese point to the fact that agency has also a collective dimension. Thus, the concept of agency does not only indicate an individual competence, but also the social relationships in which individuals are involved (Alanen 2009; James 2009). Relying on James' (2009) definition of agency, Liebel highlights that the social opportunities are especially crucial, and many others also support this point when considering children in socially disadvantaged situations. Thus, the relational aspect of agency is underlined: it is not something that individuals possess; it is rather inscribed in the interdependencies (Oswell 2013). So we must rather see agency as a certain degree of autonomy that is favoured or obstructed by particular interdependencies or combinations between individual and social conversion factors. We therefore insist that agency cannot be "something" (be it in the form of a protection, a service, or participation) that States can guarantee. If agency is inscribed in the relationships among individuals, including children, then what the State must guarantee is the democratic and participative nature of these relationships, which boils down to guaranteeing the participation rights enshrined in the UNCRC. Hence, agency lies in the relationship between individual and social factors and what must be provided when implementing agency rights lies not in a specific form of social support, but in the conditions for the setting-up of capability-friendly or agentic relationships. Procedural rights are required here, more than substantial rights focusing on benefits, services or specific protections. Therefore a relational perspective on rights is needed.

Stoecklin and Bonvin's contribution emphasize the necessary complementarity between individual skills and social opportunities in the field of participative rights and their effective implementation. The child's "own views" are pragmatically formed when the child is able to actively participate in social life. Indeed, individual agency is enhanced when adequate social structures and opportunities actively promote the participation of children, which in turn calls for the setting up of new structures and opportunities, adjusted to the increased level of agency, and so on. This development of individual agency is captured by the concept of "evolving capabilities" presented in great detail by Biggeri and Karkara. Their Fig. 5.1 is a synthesis of the existing knowledge in this respect, it also points to further developments and prospects that, in the view presented by Stoecklin & Bonvin and Robin, go along the complex notion of "recursive and non-linear agency".

These authors insist that the participative capability is narrowly linked to individual entitlements, like participation rights, and the responsibility of any social system is to expand the choices (or freedoms) that people enjoy. In such a perspective, the exercise of participative rights is much more important than the knowledge of these rights. As the analysis of organized leisure along the framework of the "system of action" shows, actual social relations (and the extent to which they are participative) play a greater role than formal children's rights in their subjective evaluation of participatory projects. Conversely, experience shapes children's knowledge of their rights which they roughly know, without needing to quote the articles contained in the UNCRC. This means that the actor doesn't need to be clearly informed about his/her rights before acting in a rightful way. Eventually, participation rights become real only through the exercise of participation, which may contribute to gradual capacities gained by children as social actors having voice and agency. Hence, the factors transforming children's rights into effective capabilities are derived from direct experience of participation stimulating reflexivity about one's own rights. The recursive aspect of participation, as a "system of action" is therefore underlined. Another key finding is the non-linearity of the development of individual agency: if appropriate social structures and opportunities are not given at a specific stage, this may result in reduced individual agency at the later stages.

The recursive and non-linear dynamics of agency, which make it "evolve" (not necessarily upward), is something that may be helpful to specify the notion of "evolving capabilities". We hence put emphasis on the subjective reconstruction and reinterpretation of a world that changes along people's capabilities. In other words, the social structures are crucial in shaping capabilities, of both individuals and groups, but their reconstructions of what these structures mean to them offer an ever evolving margin of manoeuvre. The example of children in street situations offers insight into this question. The most resilient distanciate themselves from the structures that are trying to control, educate, "save", or "empower" them. It seems that one's margin of manoeuvre grows when one is distanciating her-/himself from the dominant discourse and is able to give another meaning to a life that, to outsiders, can only appear as horrendous (Aptekar and Stoecklin 2014). The individual's own reconstruction of reality (or "system of action") seems to be therefore crucial when analyzing the combination between individual and social conversion factors.

The importance of "recursive agency" is also underlined in other contributions that show that transformation processes themselves involve children's own reflexivity. This is for instance reflected in Baraldi and Iervese's use of Conversation Analysis to explore children's expression and their capacity for social change through the projected orientation of their interlocutors' subsequent actions. This is coherent with the definition of interaction itself as a process of reciprocal adjustment. Baraldi and Iervese show that an important conversion factor lies in adult-children interactions when they break the common hierarchical "generational order" (Alanen 2009). They highlight the interactional facilitation of active participation as a powerful social conversion factor. Following Baraldi and Iervese, we could indeed say that capabilities exist only in interaction. This clearly shows that it is not because the CA observes the individual, as a unit, and not the social, that capabilities are not the outcome of social processes. Rather the contrary, even if what is measured relates to individual capabilities, how these capabilities evolve calls for an analytical approach embedded in social processes. It is true that children, as any social actor, are able to interact in ways that enable them to change somewhat the structuring of social relations. But to what extent this is done is another question.

This calls for investigating the type of social support that is required to promote individual agency, i.e. the effective implementation of the participative and agentic rights contained in the UNCRC. Key issues relate to the degree of incompleteness of the institutional framework and that of the adaptability expected from children. If the institutional framework is precisely defined, i.e. if it prescribes clear normative expectations as to what agency should mean and how children should be prepared for this, then a top-down version of participation is privileged that goes very much in the direction of so-called 'adaptive preferences'. Beyond the institutional framework, there are also informal social or cultural norms by which children and other individuals may be called to abide. Again, the more complete or exhaustive these norms, the more constrained the agency of individuals. By contrast, if these social norms or the institutional prescriptions leave more margin for interpretation, this will also translate into more spaces for effective participation and more influence left for children and other stakeholders. Dahmen's contribution illustrates this point: he focuses on life course transitions from school to work conceptualised as temporally (and socially) embedded processes of engagement with one's future, in which young persons strive to make meaningful choices and try to achieve governance over their life. Results show that their autonomy and scope of opportunities are strongly influenced by culturally mediated self-interpretations. Thus the degree of individual agency enjoyed by young people depends on the dominant culture and social norms. A gap is identified between accounts of agency grounded in the lived experiences of youth as social actors and hypothetical models of agency that are influential in policy design and in conceptions of youth and children as welfare subjects. In the same line, Robin aims to analyse the possibility for children and young people in alternative care to be agents and to participate to their own protection. With a qualitative research made in France, she shows that the right to be heard in the assessment process is a formal resource which does not lead to real rights for all children in care. Therefore she identifies individual and social factors which influence children's participative capability and discusses how to devise an ascending participation, which considers subjective perspectives of children and young people in care. Both contributions emphasize the necessity for an "open" and "incomplete" social support, in order to leave enough space for the deployment of individual agency.

Another pitfall to be avoided with respect to the type of social support is an exaggerated focus (conveyed by social norms and/or the institutional framework) on individual responsibility. In this respect, Liebel's concept of ascending participation makes a particularly important contribution, stating that both the CA and the CRC are ambivalent in that they may be considered to emphasize individual responsibility while actually looking at the conditions that transform rights into real freedoms. This ambivalence is illustrated in the CRC notion of "evolving capacities". For Liebel, as long as adults possess the definition power on what are these capacities, this principle risks being used in the sense of limiting children's rights. Liebel wonders whether the concept of 'evolving capabilities' (Biggeri et al. 2011: 23) could be an alternative, insofar that the CA doesn't look simply at the attributes or abilities of the subjects, but also at the available opportunities (their concrete living conditions). This is a very complex issue that will need further developments.

Malatesta and Golay also highlight the importance of the institutional goals and the roles and motives of all involved actors when it comes to participation processes and procedures in children's councils. They critically concentrate on children's councils implementation in Lausanne, Switzerland, to see whether these can act as devices enabling an experience of recognition. The authors consider the role the institution plays in defining the frame and the goals of the participation processes, as well as the opportunities and the barriers of councils' implementation. They adopt Liebel's perspective on "living rights" (Liebel 2008), to show how children's experiences of the group, the institutional context and the inequalities in terms of class and gender are influenced and reinforced by these devices. This contribution provides insightful clues into the conditions to be fulfilled for the design of social and individual conversion factors that could enhance the recognition of children.

Andresen and Gerarts emphasize the importance of temporality. They convincingly argue that children see themselves in the here and now and, at the same time, as being in a condition of development and becoming. This juxtaposition of statuses in the here and now and in the future seems to be a matter of life course for them. This shows the necessity to envisage the combination of individual and social factors not only in relation to the present, but also to the future. All in all, it looks like the quarrelling couple formed by individual skills and social opportunities cannot divorce... They stay together for better and for worse! It is difficult to speak of the one without mentioning the other. Throughout the book, there is a wide-ranging consensus on the necessary complementarity of individual and social conversion factors in the development of capabilities: children do not develop independently of the social context, and they are not determined by this context. Rather, there is a kind of mutual interdependency between individual agency and social environment. This is a rather commonsense conclusion, but this book allows making steps forward by shedding light on some significant features of the interaction between individual and social conversion factors: hence a relational perspective on agency or participation rights is advocated, as well as a focus on evolving capabilities and recursive and non-linear agency, an emphasis on an incomplete and open social support (especially not insisting unilaterally on individual responsibility) in order to foster adequate recognition of children, and last but not least the integration of a dynamic element via the taking account of temporality (child as being and becoming). We contend that the further development of synergies between the children's rights perspective and the capability approach will allow addressing these issues in more refined ways and bridging the gap between sociological theories of action and the prescriptive claim to treat children as subjects of rights.

The Child as a Social Actor: Issues of Participation and Agency

A very important issue is the processual nature of participation. Many authors have highlighted participation rights both as an end and a means: they have a constitutive dimension because they enrich children's lives (which is an end in itself), whereas they are instrumental as they are used for the realisation of other rights (Hanson and Vandaele 2003: 82). We can notice the complementarity with the "constitutive" and the "instrumental" role of freedom for development (Sen 1999: 189). Both an end (constitutive dimension) and a means (instrumental dimension), participation is a process in which children acquire the capacity to build one's views "freely". The distinction between the instrumental and constitutive dimensions of participation must therefore be seen only as an analytical one. In daily life, people learn about the intrinsic value of participation by the very fact that they participate, which comes back to Dewey's pragmatism: learning by doing. Hence, participation is a process. Stoecklin's (2013a) attempt to identify explicit theories of action to assess the dynamic, processual, recursive, and cumulative features of participation, finds some more food for thought with the capability approach. The latter can help overcome the sociological blind spot in the notion of the "actor child", which is the processual interplay between individual competences and social opportunities. Participation can be seen in terms of the freedom people have to lead the life they have reasons to value (Sen 1999). Transformation of children's lives by their rights is thus a complex outcome involving many processes that have both constitutive and instrumental dimensions. While the law is constitutive of the formal status of a child, the social status relies on instrumental strategies and social dynamics. Not only in the commonsense discourse but also to some extent in the children's rights industry, the taken-for-granted "actor child" ignores this difference.

The existence of rights is not sufficient to guarantee capabilities, because the individual capacities do not solely depend on rights. Reversely, rights may favour the development of some level of command on social processes. Participation rights give the possibility to have some say on the definition of reality, which cannot be reduced to a single point of view but rather is the outcome of a social construction (Berger and Luckmann 1966). Recognition of this specific interplay between right and capability is the basis on which participative rights can be better granted to children. The instrumental dimension of participation is being constructed by social actors interacting in specific configurations. As a rights-holder, or a subject of rights, the child may have "participation rights", but in reality he/she has a certain capability regarding real participation according to the different power structures in the places where he lives. The actor's access to hearing procedures is both given by these structures and gained through the actor's competencies.

Baraldi and Ieverse's chapter offers a valuable insight for the processual dynamics of participation. They deal with the issue of adult-child interactions in classrooms and, using the discourse analysis, they identify the concept of "next positioning" to understand the ways in which any current action may project one among a range of possible future actions. They are also aware that analyzing structures of interactions is not sufficient to explain agency, because these interactions are embedded in wider social systems. Baraldi and Iervese thus show several indicators that are necessary to take into account if one wants to "measure" children's agency. These are linked to the turn design, the structure of sequence organisation, and structural presuppositions. Their material shows various ways in which the sequential dynamics of participation allow children to expand (or not) their capabilities.

These empirical findings question whether one's own views are actually "freely" built. Hence, they contribute to critical considerations on the hidden assumptions contained in the UNCRC. The social process of building one's views "freely" is not addressed in the formulation of participation rights. The assumption behind them is that this process must be accessible to any child under any circumstance. In the UNCRC, the instrumental dimension of participation is put at the forefront, and the conditions conducive to the constitutive dimension of participation are addressed only indirectly by the fact that the UNCRC holds that it is through protection and provision rights that participation may eventually occur. The UNCRC "recognizes that children only gradually gain the necessary competencies to exercise these rights as adults do. The CRC recognizes, as well, that children do not always have the physical, personal, and social power to protect their rights. Hence, children are accorded need-based, or protective, rights, such as the rights to be nurtured, sheltered, educated, and protected from exploitation" (Pufall and Unsworth 2004: 13).

It is the combination of rights that allows the children's well-being in the present and their development in the future. As underlined in Asher Ben-Arieh's foreword, as well as in Stoecklin and Bonvin's chapter, the child's being and becoming are the two sides of the same coin. They cannot be opposed, they are bound together. We can thus see that the distinctions between *being* and *becoming*, between the *instrumental* and *constitutive* dimensions, or Woodhouse's (2004) distinction between "need-based rights" (protection) and "dignity-based rights" (life, identity, expression), and even that between the individual and social factors, are merely analytical. Social actors experience things not in an analytical way but rather as a continuous flow of events that they reflexively reconstruct in order to give meaning to their actions and those of others. Hence, the gradual competencies gained by children, like agency and voice, are granted by the UNCRC through diverse combinations of "need-based" rights and "dignity-based" rights that are not necessarily thought of by the actor in the same terms.

It is therefore mistaken to interpret the UNCRC as ending with an image of the child making use of participative rights as a rational social actor. Rational-choice theories have pervaded the analytical thinking in such ways that they have become naturalized. This makes it appear as a logical and natural fact that the right to be heard (art. 12 UNCRC) is not granted to "any child" but only to "the child who is capable of forming his or her own views" and also that consideration for the child's opinion should be "given due weight in accordance with the age and maturity of the child". The analytical distinctions we make as scientists may therefore have the side effect of underscoring children's lived experiences. Our conceptual apparatus relies on notions that theoretically separate what is experienced in direct interactions where emotions impact on how people behave, and this certainly holds true for children. Therefore, considering that children's views can be taken into consideration only under specific circumstances (views freely formed and expressed) is quite limitative. And it is our own analytical apparatus, which contributes to the alienation of children's opinions, as the latter would have to enter the hidden analytical framework in order to become intelligible and legitimate.

How can we say that children who do not yet form their own views are not assured to express their views freely? How do we assess that the views expressed are theirs? In the way their answers and opinions are structured? Does it mean that children who do not yet have a well structured opinion are not entitled to Art. 12? This would be an infringement of the cornerstone human rights principle that the holder of rights is subject of rights independently of his/her actual talents. Indeed, the "due weight" given according to the child's age and maturity is another restrictive element in this article. The "due weight clause" in Article 12 and the circumstances under which children's views shall be taken into account actually pose some problems for the very constitution of one's own views. How can children constitute their own views if attention to what they say is restricted to what appears to adults as rational thinking (maturity)?

The "Aristotelian conception" (Matthews 2008) of childhood, which is widespread, sees "the Formal Cause of the organism as the form or structure it normally has in maturity (. . .). According to this picture, a human child is to be understood as an immature specimen of the organism type human, which, by nature, has the potential to develop into a mature specimen with the structure, form, and function of a normal and standard adult" (Matthews 2008: 40). Therefore, if discourses have to be recognizable by adults who evaluate the degree of maturity of the child, then the constitutive dimension may well be shaped by instrumental goals of other actors. Matthews shows for instance how classical utilitarianism is used to deny children's different ways of looking at things (Matthews 2003). This might lead to manipulation through adult-induced child participation, where so called "rational" discourses are in fact outcomes of imposed ideologies. This kind of "child participation" has been for instance prevalent during the Chinese Cultural Revolution when children were encouraged to assume an active role in the construction of a new society.

Actually, we might argue that participation rights (art. 12, 13, 14, 15, 16, 17 and 31 UNCRC) have a constitutive and an instrumental dimension exactly because it is the very nature of social interaction to be constitutive and instrumental. As a social actor, to have one's own views is necessary in order to act reflexively and hence behave in socially acceptable ways. The theory of structuration (Giddens 1984), where things are at the same time structured and structuring, helps understand that the constitutive dimension of participation has to do with socially defined ends (participation is an end itself, as it is said to "enrich one's life"). Whereas the instrumental dimension of participation is bound to the individual capacity of structuring or shaping his/her environment. Actually, social actors learn to become instrumental in the ways admitted by their culture and in the room for interplay given in specific social configurations (Elias 1991). Therefore, the instrumental dimension may be embedded in the constitutive dimension in such a way that it is not a "freely" built view that the child is expressing. What then about the notion of "living rights" (see Liebel and Hanson et al., in this volume). Can they really express the children's freely built views, or are they already embedded in power relationships and to some extent reproducing them, which poses to observers an impossible question: who is exactly saying what? To study "living rights" requires therefore that we clarify our understanding of the "social actor" in order to consider how the child can make use of the instrumental dimension of participation rights.

As an agent acting on things, the social actor is himself constructing the instrumental dimension of participation. The child has a "right to participation" and a capability regarding participation. The specific grasp on the way he/she wants to be heard is a social competence, a "command" that is constructed and that can neither be given nor guaranteed by the judicial tool itself. This distinction between potential and real agency is, so we argue, conducive to better respect for overall children's rights. The instrumental dimension of participation rights is really understandable only once we have a clearer idea of how social actors act.

These considerations allow us to deal in new ways with the important challenge of refining the notion of agency. As we have seen, some contributors use the notion of "agency rights" (Liebel) or "children's right to agency" (Baraldi and Iervese). So a first question is: What difference does it make to speak of "participation rights" or "agency rights"? Liebel discusses whether the notion of capabilities contributes to re-conceptualize children rights in the direction of "agency rights". He uses the term 'agency rights' with a reference to Brighouse (2002). For him, 'agency rights' do not refer only to participation rights but to all subjective rights in the juridical sense (Alanen 2009; James 2009).

If all children's rights can be agency rights once they are "used" by children, the question remains about what processes are needed to help children, who have evolving capacities, to actively use their rights. Isn't it that participation rights have first to be guaranteed as entitlements to truly become instruments in the hands of children who can use and influence all rights thereafter? But isn't it also true that participation rights can mean something to individuals only after they have first practiced participation in some ways, and not before they can have any consciousness of what a right may be?

The problem is then contained in the following question: how can we link individual outcomes with social processes? Baraldi and Iervese indicate that participation is located not just in decision making but in communication, more precisely in the interaction seen as a specific system of communication. Therefore, participation is seen as a social process more than a freedom to achieve, which means that the authors focus on the instrumental nature of participation. Is it really a paradox that children's agency depends on adults' promotion of their agency? Baraldi and Iervese hold that children's agency is directly linked to adults' agency. This comes back to the question raised notably by Clark and Ziegler, Liebel, and Reynaert and Roose regarding the dependency of children towards adults considered as parents and not equals.

Stoecklin and Bonvin also underline the necessity to have a clearer definition of agency, as there are many underlying assumptions with this notion that, most of the time, remain implicit. They consider agency as the capacity of an individual or a group to decide, act and interact in a socially competent way (Nibell et al. 2009). This means that children's actions and agency are not only recognized when they contribute to a social order defined by others, mostly adults, but also in their challenging, opposing, and conflicting dimensions. Because, as Simmel pointed, the forms of socialization also include conflict as a socially recognized form of interaction. Therefore the fact that children's agency is linked to adult promotion is not so much a paradox. It is a form of socialization that is normal. The question is then: how much can children oppose adult views if they want to be recognized?

Some answers may be found in Malatesta and Golay's chapter. Agency can be observed as a specific kind of rights of participation, that is as a right of choosing and making decisions. Agency means that a course of action is only one among various possibilities (Giddens 1984; Harré and van Langhenove 1999). It implies availability of a range of possible choices, opening different courses of action. In other words, the idea of agency emphasizes that children can condition the actions of the interlocutors communicating with them, above all in interactions, and can, in this way, transform the existing social structures. By choosing among different courses of action, children can enhance social change, therefore agency can be defined as active participation which enhances social change. Agency does not mean only building consensus or searching for an agreement, but also opening and managing conflicts. Here, our main questions are: To what extent can children's agency enhance social change? What kind of social change? How is such social change achieved?

Scientists face therefore a big challenge and we want to highlight that the UNCRC itself may help them in having children acting as participatory inquirers in this matter. This is especially true as article 12 has a unique feature that makes it special in comparison to the subjective rights and the other general principles (Art. 2, 3, 6) contained in the CRC. As rights are themselves "matters affecting the child", we may consider that the right to be heard is a right to express freely one's views on all rights, including the right to be heard itself. This makes of article 12 simultaneously a subjective right – the right to be heard – and a procedural right (like art. 2, 3 and 6), but with the uniqueness of having the procedure being defined with the participation of the subject of rights. To use the UNCRC as an asset for participatory research is a recommendation that we would like to make. This might also contribute to push forward another debate around whether children have a right to agency. Baraldi and Iervese speak of "children's rights to agency", which in this phrasing considers agency as a "substance". What if we replace the substantive by an adjective? In other words, shouldn't we speak of participation rights as being "agentic" (we can also use the qualificative for rights: namely agentic rights) instead of "agency rights"?

Therefore, we have to make things clear between three alternatives:

1. Either we equate participation rights (art. 12–17 and art. 31 UNCRC) to rights that are "agentic", as their respect confers higher levels of agency to children.
2. Or we consider that every right is an "agency right" in the sense that the active exercise of any right gives some more agency to the actor.
3. Or we say that we have to invent new "agency rights" in order to guarantee children's access to agency.

The third option is hardly possible. Baraldi and Iervese speak of the changes required in the education system to favour an "effective promotion of children's rights to agency". The challenge according to them is to stabilize children's agency in the education system. They recognize that "the right to agency" and the process that would be needed to guarantee such a right are out of the State's reach or control. As already stated, the State can only guarantee democratic and participative processes and not agency in itself. An additional right, called "a right to agency", cannot be guaranteed.

Liebel's use of the notion of "agency rights" is slightly different and it falls into the second option. He claims that agency rights stands for all rights contained in the UNCRC as long as these entitlements become real instruments for children, which implies a reflexive movement: Formal rights first have to be "re-conceptualized" by children before they transform into real freedoms. The capability approach might of course help situate the factors that contribute to transform the rights contained in the UNCRC into "agency rights". But neither this approach nor any other can ever empower very small children to make sense of notions like rights that are not within their cognitive reach. The child's competence in making sense of what a right may be is not only a social construct. It also has a biological base, as the new sociology of childhood acknowledged already from the start.

The first option considers that participation rights of the UNCRC are sufficient to strengthen children's agency. What is needed is not an additional right but processes that make the existing rights come true. But even if participation rights are especially agentic by nature, this is not enough to make children's agency flourish. So we should have a fourth option, which would be more cautious and less ambitious. It would be to speak of "children's potentially agentic rights" which would attract attention on the real levels of agency. The potential level of agency and the real level of agency depend on factors (rights, contexts, people) that are interdependent, and none of which is decisive by itself. It is not sufficient for agency to develop to have either a right, or a social context in which rights can be experienced, nor is it sufficient to have people able to give meaning to rights in relation to social contexts. It looks like agency only occurs after the three elements (rights, contexts, people) are sufficiently bound together. With children, this can be observed from the moment that any right contained in the UNCRC is directly exercised. In other words, the challenge is to help children transform the formal rights contained in the UNCRC into real freedoms that can be experienced to the maximum extent. But this can be rather diverse according to the context (social opportunities) and to children (individual skills). All children's rights are potentially agentic, but the levels of agentivity will always depend on the possible understanding of rights, in social contexts, and in individual children's minds.

We leave this debate open, as it entails a major prospect: the necessity to assess to what extent (participation) rights are really agentic, or, to be more precise, how the implementation of these rights, according to the conceptions of the responsible institutions, leads to more or less agency. This is what Stoecklin and Bonvin tried to address when observing how much participation processes in leisure activities are bottom-up or top-down. Taking this perspective, we can highlight that participation processes can "open" or "close" children's agency, and more precisely see what elements are enabling or constraining: by using the "actor's system" (Stoecklin 2013a), we can identify specific children's activities, relations, values, images of self and motivations as enabling or constraining their agency. This approach is sensitive to the recursive and cumulative nature of action, and allows to see shifting logics (sometimes bottom-up, sometimes top-down) that make up children's participation. This recursive approach to agency developed by Stoecklin and Bonvin also responds to an overarching challenge which is to approach agency in terms that can be understood by children and therefore assure more cross-cultural validity to the observed trends. The actor's agency, or command over the social process, can be reflected by children when using an explicit tool stimulating their reflexivity over their own experiences (Stoecklin and Bonvin in this volume). The concept of 'evolving agency' (Stoecklin 2013b) might be a way to specify the notion of 'evolving capabilities' (Biggeri et al. 2011: 81; and Liebel in this volume). It refers to the recursive dynamics of agency, which make it 'evolve' (not necessarily upward) or fluctuate. This puts emphasis on the subjective reconstruction and reinterpretation of a world that changes along people's capabilities.

The Vulnerable and Competent Child

Last but not least, the topic that the contributions to this book help underline is the opposition between the vulnerable and the competent child. The activist discourse using the rhetoric of the "actor child" puts forward the competent child. It therefore often has the paradoxical side effect of putting responsibility on children just because they have been labelled as "actors"... The case of children's capability is particularly interesting as it shows that the capability of the youngest individuals may heavily depend on the capabilities of others, i.e. their parents or caregivers. Children's provision, participation and protection rights depend on their parents in many ways, as Clark and Ziegler argue. Besides, as the main responsibility for the development of children is attached to parents' duties, the inequality of development is not pointed to as a political question, but as an issue related to the quality of parents. This is also due to the fact the UNCRC constructs the family as a natural entity and not as a political institution. Therefore the public responsibility towards children is mediated by the private familial sphere. According to Clark and Ziegler, this leaves little room to address inequalities between classes, genders, citizens and non-citizens.

The divide between adult rights and what Reynaert and Roose call a "youth land" raises questions regarding its justification, its impact on relationships with adults and issues linked to a fair redistribution of social resources. They show how this "youth land" is still based on a childhood image of the vulnerable and incompetent child, limiting the development of their capabilities. Dahmen also shows how the CA itself is dealing with children mainly as becomings, while Baraldi and Iervese suggest that the CA has already shifted from a focus on the future realization of children's capabilities to an interest in the developing of capabilities during childhood (Biggeri et al. 2010; Biggeri et al. 2011). Baraldi and Iervese underline that according to Sen's approach (1999) participation consists of the possibility for the individual to freely make decisions about his life, which is simultaneously both a capability and a way to reach other goals for individual development.

The papers in this volume suggest that there is a need to go past the dichotomy between children seen as "beings" or "becomings". The child is both being and becoming and therefore the question of the evolving capacities, as contained in the UNCRC, becomes a central issue. Liebel questions the conditions that have to be in place to enable children to make use of their rights and points to the "evolving capacities" as an ambivalent concept. It can be understood in contrary ways: as a precondition for the use of rights or as a result of a learning process that (also) arises from the knowledge about and the use of rights. For Liebel, the UNCRC evolving capacities principle is up to now understood as a question of "subjective" competences without taking into account the "objective" living conditions as relevant for gaining and using them. Furthermore, there is only little discussion on the criteria of what may count as capacity (or the opposite) and who may decide about it. Liebel pays attention to theoretical aspects of justice and particularly to the sense of justice of children living in socially disadvantaged situations. He asks if the CA and particularly its concept of "capabilities" can contribute to re-conceptualize the CR in such a way that they might become an entitlement or instrument in the hands of the children, or become relevant as "agency rights" of the children. This makes sense only if we understand the CR not exclusively as "welfare rights". The question is how strong the CA is oriented towards the new status of the child as rights bearers, and what are the schools of thought in the CR that are actually the most coherent with a CA. Hanson (2012) suggests that there are different schools of thoughts, ranging from paternalistic to liberationist, with a majority of scholars and practitioners located within the protectionist or emancipatory approaches.

Starting with the concept of the "social actor" in the context of the right to education, Dahmen shows the heuristic potential of the CA from an educational perspective. He makes the case of youth access to secondary education, highlighting transitions of "vulnerable" school leavers from school to secondary education. The arguments are exemplified through showing how the gap between the "right to education" (UNCRC art. 28) and the "effective" participation in education can be conceptualised through the capability approach. The article concludes that conceptualising youth as "social selves", whose capacity to act on the basis of own value commitments depends on social preconditions not included in the informational basis of actual welfare policies, can shed new light on the academic and political discourse on youth's agency.

What is then the possible contribution of the CA for understanding and re-conceptualizing the evolving capacity principle? The CA doesn't look simply at the attributes or abilities of the subjects, but also at the available opportunities (the concrete living conditions). While emphasizing the centrality of autonomy and of value-orientated own decisions seems crucial, the capability approach sees human rights as 'entitlements to capabilities' (Sen 2005) and looks both at the individual and social factors that help convert these formal freedoms into real freedoms. But even with the best arsenal of legal provisions, children' lives are very much embedded in power relationships that are hard to change. The gap between the legal framework of children's rights and their concrete implementation in the case of street children in Brazil and Mexico (Rizzini and Strickland) attracts attention on the structural limits of children's agency. While this case is probably the most obvious, the other contributions in this book also underline the importance of collective action and the problems of seeing the child only in individual terms. The individual responsibility in the actor's "own" choices and the discourse regarding children as competent social actors both contain problematic dangers. It is therefore by contextualizing children's rights that the capability approach can help overcome the paradoxes and risks of instrumentalizing children either as frail or as powerful "actors" in processes that they have entered just because they were born.

These are important questions that the contributions to this volume help tackle. New avenues for reflection about children's rights and capabilities are thus opened, which might make a significant contribution both in theoretical and practical terms. However, the chapters of the present publication are meant as a starting point to this quite challenging and hopefully fruitful dialogue between specialists of children's rights and of the capability approach.

References

Alanen, L. (2009). Generational order. In J. Qvortrup, G. Valentine, W. Corsaro, & M. S. Honig (Eds.), *The Palgrave handbook of childhood studies* (pp. 159–174). Basingstoke: Palgrave.

Aptekar, L., & Stoecklin, D. (2014). *Street children and homeless youth: A cross-cultural perspective*. Dordrecht: Springer.

Berger, P. L., & Luckmann, T. (1966). *The social construction of reality: A treatise in the sociology of knowledge*. New-York: Anchor Books.

Biggeri, M., Ballet, J., & Comim, F. (2010). The capability approach and research on children: Capability approach and children' issues. In S. Andresen et al. (Eds.), *Children and the good life: New challenges for research on children* (pp. 75–89). Dordrecht/Heidelberg/London/New York: Springer.

Biggeri, M., Ballet, J., & Comim, F. (2011). *Children and the capability approach*. Basingstoke/New York: Palgrave Macmillan.

Brighouse, H. (2002). What rights (if any) do children have? In D. Archard & C. M. Macleod (Eds.), *The moral and political status of children* (pp. 31–52). Oxford: Oxford University Press.

Elias, N. (1991). *The society of individuals*. London/New York: Continuum.

Giddens, A. (1984). *The constitution of society: Outline of the theory of structuration*. Cambridge: Polity.

Hanson, K., & Vandaele, A. (2003). Working children and international labour law: A critical analysis. *The International Journal of Children's Rights, 11*(1), 73–146.

Hanson, K. (2012). Schools of thought in children's rights. In M. Liebel (Ed.), *Children's rights from below. Cross-cultural perspectives* (pp. 63–79). Basingstoke: Palgrave Macmillan.

Harré, R., & Van Langenhove, L. (1999). *Positioning theory*. Oxford: Blackwell.

James, A. (2009). Agency. In J. Qvortrup, W. A. Corsaro, & M.-S. Honig (Eds.), *The Palgrave handbook of childhood studies* (pp. 34–45). Hampshire: Palgrave Macmillan.

James, A., & James, A. L. (2012). *Key concepts in childhood studies* (2nd ed.). London: Sage.

Liebel, M. (2008). Citizenship from below: Children's rights and social movements. In A. Invernizzi & J. Williams (Eds.), *Children and citizenship* (pp. 32–43). London: Sage.

Matthews, H. (2003). Children and regeneration: Setting an agenda for community participation 810 and integration. *Children and Society, 17*(4), 264–276.

Matthews, G. (2008). Getting beyond the deficit conception of childhood: Thinking philosophically with children. In M. Hand & C. Win Stanley (Eds.), *Philosophy in schools* (pp. 27–40). London: Continuum.

Nibell, L. N., Shook, J. J., & Finn, J. L. (2009). *Childhood, youth, and social work in transformation: Implications for policy*. New York: Columbia University Press.

Oswell, D. (2013). *The agency of children. From family to global human rights*. Cambridge: Cambridge University Press.

Pufall, P., & Unsworth, R. (2004). *Rethinking childhood*. London: Rutgers University Press.

Sen, A. (1999). *Development as freedom*. New York: Alfred Knopf.

Sen, A. (2005). Human rights and capabilities. *Journal of Human Development, 6*(2), 151–166.

Stoecklin, D. (2013a). Theories of action in the field of child participation. In search of explicit frameworks. *Childhood, 20*(4), 443–457.

Stoecklin, D. (2013b). Children's participation in organized leisure. Evolving capacities or evolving agency? Paper presented at the European Sociological Association in Torino (ESA 2013).

Woodhouse, B. (2004). Re-visioning rights for children. In P. B. Pufall & R. P. Unsworth (Eds.), *Rethinking childhood*. London: Rutgers University Press.

Index

D. Stoecklin and J.-M. Bonvin (eds.), *Children's Rights and the Capability Approach*, Children's Well-Being: Indicators and Research 8, DOI 10.1007/978-94-017-9091-8,

CPSIA information can be obtained at www.ICGtesting.com
Printed in the USA
LVOW11*1216280615
444166LV00010B/216/P

9 789401 790901